I tem 614

THE UNITY
OF EUROPEAN HISTORY

BOOKS BY JOHN BOWLE

Western Political Thought
Hobbes and His Critics
Politics and Opinion in the Nineteenth Century
Vicount Samuel, A Biography
Man through the Ages
Henry VIII: a Study of Power in Action
England, a Portrait

JOHN BOWLE

THE UNITY
OF EUROPEAN HISTORY

A POLITICAL AND CULTURAL SURVEY

Revised and Expanded Edition

OXFORD UNIVERSITY PRESS

LONDON OXFORD NEW YORK

OXFORD UNIVERSITY PRESS

Oxford   London   New York
Glasgow   Toronto   Melbourne   Wellington
Cape Town   Salisbury   Ibadan   Nairobi   Lusaka   Addis Ababa
Bombay   Calcutta   Madras   Karachi   Lahore   Dacca
Kuala Lumpur   Hong Kong   Tokyo

CONTENTS

WE SHALL only save ourselves from the perils which draw near by forgetting the hatreds of the past, by letting national rancours and revenges die, by progressively effacing frontiers and barriers which aggravate and congeal our divisions, and by rejoicing together in that glorious treasure of literature, of romance, of ethics, of thought, and toleration belonging to all, which is the true inheritance of Europe.

THE RIGHT HONOURABLE WINSTON CHURCHILL,
at the Hague Congress of Europe, May 7th, 1948.

PREFACE

To sketch the outlines of the rise of civilization in Europe in so small a compass has been a difficult enterprise, and the limitations of the present work are implicit in its design. There are available several short accounts of the evolution of England, but very few contemporary surveys of the history of Europe by English writers on a similar scale. In view of the crying need for popular understanding of European as well as of English history, it has been my object, within strict limits of space, to provide such a book.

On so large a canvas I have had to employ an impressionist method; the problem has been not what to include, but often, as in painting, what to leave out. It has been necessary to block in the bare essentials of political history, stressing the highlights and the shadows, and indicating intellectual and artistic progress with a broad brush. As usual, the foreground has presented major difficulties, and I have been compelled in the interests of proportion to deal rather shortly with the history of our own time. My overriding object has been to present for the ordinary reader the unity and the development of the great cosmopolitan traditions of Europe, to relate economic and cultural achievement to the political background, and to set the mythologies of current nationalism in their proper place. If this object has been partially achieved, I hope that so ruthless a treatment of so great a subject may appear justified.

In preparing this survey, I have received valuable help from Sir Maurice Bowra, Warden of Wadham, who has read most of the original draft and whose suggestions have enriched the classical and literary aspect of the work: to him my principal thanks are due. The late Mr. A. B. Rodger, of Balliol, was good enough to advise me on certain aspects of modern economic history; Sir Isaiah Berlin on cultural developments of the nineteenth century; Professor Hawkes and Mr. J. S. P. Bradford on the chapter dealing with the dawn of civilization; to all these critics I owe a notable debt. I would also like to acknowledge my debt to the late Professor R. M. Dawkins, and to the Rev. Gervase Mathew, who has kindly gone through the Byzantine chapter of the book, and to the late Mr. R. W. Ketton-Cremer for his help in suggesting improvements in design and style. Finally I wish to express my gratitude to my mother, without whose perseverance and clear judgment the book would never have come to a completion in the war-time difficulties under which much of the original version was written.

JOHN BOWLE
OXFORD
October 1969

INTRODUCTION

Of the political problems which confront mankind the reorganization of Europe is one of the most urgent. Two world wars and their sequel have masked with a fog of conflict and confusion the fundamental unity of the European tradition; and the memory of recent danger and the uncertainties that lie ahead demand the reassertion of the common interests of Europe. It would be intolerable if the Continent which has created the dominant culture of the world should continue one of the plague-spots of political tension, likely to involve the planet in a conflict which would destroy the fabric of ordered society.

To the generation which has grown up under the shadow of war, the unity and success of our civilization has become obscure; yet still the historian may discern, as through a clearing mist, the permanent structure of the European tradition. The period of competing national states, of the naked power of unbridled sovereignty, has extended only over five centuries, and during that time the cultural, if not the political, life of Europe has continued in an expanding tide. The cosmopolitan culture of Antiquity and of the Middle Ages extended for a greater duration, and probably the stabilized order of the future will dwarf the phase of confusion which has come to its tragic climax in the twentieth century. It is for the peoples and statesmen to determine whether this prospect can be realized; in particular, for the European peoples to see to it that the forces of national, economic, and class conflict are brought under control.

There can be no better equipment for this task than an understanding of the evolution of European society. During the last quarter of a century the outlook of historians has changed; the foundations of this outlook are the affair of specialists, but its broad conclusions concern all responsible men and women. Contemporary scholarship transcends the strident provincialism of racial, nationalist, and class propaganda; it takes account of the contribution of all the European peoples to a common historical evolution against a favourable geographical background, reflected in remarkable enterprise and variety. The moral of the story is plain: the vitality and the success of European civilization.

The scientific outlook and scientific power increasingly dominate our age; but unless the humaner values can be adapted and preserved, the progress of science will be empty and catastrophic. The study of the European past demonstrates the unity of Western culture, the contributions of the Christian and the Humanist tradition, and the pernicious limitations of nationalism and class war. In the light of such knowledge, science might yet build a society which combines the power of modern technique with the depth of old experience.

This book is an attempt to bring home to ordinary men and women, sickened and bewildered by the tragedies of our time, the solid achievements of the past; to take a short view of the perspective of European history, and to give some account of our civilization's success. For the forces of evil and disruption have not prevented the evolution of a brilliant European culture. With this fact in mind, we may face the future with greater confidence.

PART I

THE HERITAGE OF EUROPE

CHAPTER I

THE DAWN OF CIVILIZATION

EUROPEAN civilization derives from the village community and the city state. Both originated in the Near East. While the former began the conquest of the land—the undercurrent of political history—the latter, in its Greek interpretation, achieved political and intellectual liberty.

The background of these developments reaches back into remotest antiquity. In the first place, the spread of an agricultural peasantry, in uninterrupted sequence from Neolithic times, laid the racial foundations of the Continent, later diversified by migration and conquest, and stabilized by the first millennium before Christ. The rise of the city state, revolutionary in spirit and the focus of subsequent advance, owed its material foundations indirectly to the River Valley cultures of Mesopotamia and Egypt. The underlying unity of European culture is, indeed, emphasized in its origins, in the racial fusion imposed by the structure of the continent from the earliest times, and by the debt to the Near East, a conclusion which puts modern national rivalries and 'racial' prejudice in a proper perspective.

The millennia of the Palaeolithic Age form a solemn background to the emergence of mankind. Very slowly, after the fluctuations and recession of the ice, came the spread of a settled economy. It came late in Europe, and the earliest Neolithic or Stone Age cultures are found wholly in Western Asia and North-

Eastern Africa: the origins of urban life in Persia and Iraq, the Syrian region and Egypt. It will be well, then, to examine these fundamental developments in turn, for they are the foundations of later economic, political, and intellectual progress. But before turning to the agricultural economies of the New Stone Age, one must glance at the Palaeolithic and Mesolithic hunting cultures, which form a prelude to the Neolithic Revolution and to the establishment of settled agriculture, to the rise of metal-working and the foundation of cities.

In the closing millennia of the Palaeolithic Age, Northern Europe lay under a mantle of ice; the south was mountain and tundra; the Sahara still prairie, with a temperate climate. This environment saw the effective appearance of modern man—'homo sapiens'—anatomically· distinct from 'trial men,' hominids of several species.

He was a rare animal, accustomed to prey on the migratory herds of reindeer, mammoth, horse, and bison then numerous in Europe. The sparse Aurignacian hunting cultures are found well developed throughout most of the southern half of the Continent, while another appears in South Russia, spreading westward at least as far as Central Europe. All these peoples possessed a considerable range of hunting tackle; they were good artificers in flint and bone. In time the throwing spear was supplemented by the bow, perhaps brought from North Africa into Spain; in the last Palaeolithic phase Europe contained a variety of hunting cultures right up to north Britain and the margins of the Baltic ice. The best known is the Magdalenian. Skilled in tracking and observation, these people hunted and trapped the big game and preyed on the salmon runs with spears. Severe cold demanded a heavy meat diet, garments of hide and fur; in a stable climate theirs was a well-adjusted economy, in some aspects not unlike that of the primitive North American Indian and the Eskimo.

In the darkness of deep cave interiors are found the brilliant remnants of Palaeolithic art. Drawn with a vivid naturalism which catches the pose of the animal with a skill unsurpassed in the history of painting, these pictures reinforced the incantations of the medicine men, themselves sometimes portrayed, masked and prancing, on the cave walls. Here, in the fading Ice Age, is the prelude to magic and religion. Slung between poles, or hauled on a crude drag, the dead beast, steaming at the cave mouth, was cut to pieces in the frost, while the man-pack crowded about its fire. One can imagine them, sturdy squat figures in the bleak spaces of an unpeopled world, huddled in their cave dwellings or stamping out their ritual inside the hills.

They were not all cave dwellers. On the Don in South Russia hunters built winter 'houses,' shacks of skin and turf, half hollowed into the ground; others, camped on the seasonal migration routes through the Hungarian and Moravian passes, or the Polish and North German plains, took yearly toll of the moving beasts. The economy of all these savage peoples was based on the use of fire and implements skillfully cut from a flint core, from bone, antler, and wood. They buried their dead with goods and gear; they were tough, courageous, and very few.

With the gradual, fluctuating, retreat of the ice and the encroachment of forest, these highly specialized hunting cultures disappeared, but others took their place—Mesolithic peoples, in part newcomers, in part descendants of the old hunters, adapting themselves to the changed conditions. Some hunted the red deer and the wild ox; some still lived in caves; but settlements were often by the sea or by inland watersides. They became scavengers of shell fish and snarers of wild fowl; in Northern Europe they devised crude axes and so made boats. Their fishing tackle included nets, but comparatively little has survived of Mesolithic equipment. For all their seeming poverty, these Mesolithic Europeans have a great significance; they lived on into Neolithic times, especially on the northern plains, and by interbreeding with the Neolithic peoples, made lasting contributions to our racial stock.

For, meanwhile, in Hither Asia, Eastern Europe, and North Africa, the Neolithic revolution had begun. Gradually the temperate climatic belt had been moving north; coniferous forest gave way to beech and oak, as the European climate gradually approximated to its modern form. Slowly the Sahara changed from grassland to desert, while oases and alluvial valleys became the refuge for human and animal life. Man and beast were driven together by this climatic change; but it was not completed without an intermediate phase, moist enough to encourage the beginnings of stock-breeding and of agriculture.

Following on these long-drawn climatic changes, came the development of settled agricultural life, of a mixed hunting and farming economy. Parts of Hither Asia, especially, favoured the growth of wild wheat and barley, and here also were found the ancestors of the sheep, the goat, and the pig. Neolithic settlements were established in the Syrian region, in Anatolia, and the Balkans by the eighth millennium, and in Egypt—for example round the Fayum Lake.

With settled habits of life came further advance; pottery, weaving, the creation and handing down of an accumulated tradition. By the end of the fourth millennium B.C. over wide areas of Hither Asia, the Balkans, and along the Nile, a peasant economy came into being; the stage was set for the Early Bronze Age with its great inventions, leading up to the origin and growth of urban civilization.

While these achievements were being consolidated, Western Europe remained relatively backward. The early Bronze Age culture antedates the spread of a Neolithic economy in the North; but since Europe is here our primary concern, we will turn first to this gradual and fundamental European agricultural development, which later formed the basis of the spread of the use of metals and, later, of a civilized tradition.

It must be remembered that Neolithic culture was scattered and elementary, and knowledge of this dim period is built on relatively slender evidence. Neolithic agriculture was based on hoe cultivation and the settlements seldom exceeded thirty households. None the less, they had made the first step out of savagery; they were self-sufficient except for unexpected climatic catastrophes. They had made a beginning.

The Neolithic settlement of Europe came from Anatolia, the Balkans, and from the South. A peasant culture spread up the Danube and beyond into the Ukraine and Galicia; stock-breeding peoples, possibly from North Africa, moved into North-Western Europe out of the Iberian Peninsula. The 'Danubian' peasantry were peaceful farmers, raising cereal crops on the loess soil of the inland plains; their settlements are widespread along the Danube, the Dnieper, the Oder, and the Rhine. When the soil was exhausted the settlement would be moved, but the population was increasing steadily. They built defences and stored their produce in barns; their communal villages were planned in order; here are the earliest ancestors of the later villages of Europe, and the foundation of a solid peasant tradition.

The Danubians were beginning the great task of colonizing and populating the Continent: over most of Europe the tradition spread. South of the Alps, where land was limited, the settlements became relatively static, with a fuller exploitation of the soil. North of the mountains, where land was easier come by, agriculture shifted and spread. Meanwhile, in the West the other group of Neolithic peoples, herdsmen and cultivators, established their settlements and built their ditch-enclosed camps among the hills; while the pottery of the Danubian peasant agriculturalists tends to imitate a gourd, the pottery of the Western peoples is often copied from a leather original.

These tribes seem to have spread across Western Europe from the south-west, and the search for fresh pasture may have kept them on the move. Further, Megalithic funeral customs and fertility cults, the reflection of Oriental, Aegean, and possibly Egyptian influence, had long been spreading to Malta, Sicily, and Sardinia. They found fullest expression in the Iberian Peninsula. As early as 2700 B.C. this curious culture was spreading across the Toulouse Gap and along the Atlantic coasts to Northern France, the British Isles, and parts of Scandinavia, as witness their ritual stone monuments at Carnac, Avebury, and the earliest part of Stonehenge.

Such in outline was the background of pastoral farming and peasant agriculture which in time enabled Europeans to assimilate the inventions of the Early Bronze Age and, later, the urban culture of the Middle East. But it was a peripheral development; Western Europe remained a backward and sparsely populated area when Oriental civilizations had long been established.

II

We must now turn from the dawn of Neolithic Europe into the sunrise of the Early Bronze Age in the Near East and the Balkans and into the high noon of the great river valley cultures which made the Urban Revolution. To these Oriental peoples, whose civilization was already old when Western written records begin, Europe owes a great debt; Anatolians, Sumerians, Babylonians, Egyptians, all played an indirect but fundamental part in the creation of our culture. Hence the stupidity and ingratitude of those 'racial' heresies, which depict Eastern peoples as inferior and assign them no credit for their immense achievement, the building of civilization itself.

The culture of cities was first fully established in Mesopotamia and Egypt, arising naturally from riverine villages linked by a common irrigation, yet behind the rise of cities there is an important phase of invention and enterprise. The climatic changes already described left a belt of warmth and fertility which included Mesopotamia, Anatolia, the foothills of Iran and the Syrian steppe, as well as Palestine and Egypt. Here, over a period extending roughly from 5000 to 3500 B.C., the use of copper and inventions of cardinal importance had been discovered. The settlement of the great valleys, originally overgrown with brushwood swamps and reed beds, required a systematic clearing and irrigation only a comparatively advanced people could achieve; the technique was first developed in the oases and on the upland settlements of the Middle East and North Africa. During these millennia outstanding advances were made: the use of the plough, the yoking of oxen, the construction of wheeled carts, the invention of sail. Here was a revolution in transport, and with it went a notable advance in agricultural methods: the cultivation of the date palm and the exploitation of a limited water supply demanded careful irrigation which in turn gave rise to a variety of plants and fruit trees. A vital element in all this progress was the mastering of the art of metal working: first copper was used, as a more durable stone; later, the art of smelting and the use of alloys were discovered and bronze was made.

The situation of the all-important copper, and, later, of the tin mines—generally far from alluvial areas—and the traffic in amber and gold, obsidian and lapis lazuli, created extensive trade routes and forwarded the expansion of knowledge. For the use of pack animals there is a very early evidence; the ass had apparently been widely domesticated by the close of the fourth millennium, though the horse was not generally employed until a much later date. Thus, behind the development of cities, lies a period of invention unparalleled in history until the sixteenth century of our own era.

The next landmark in human progress, the Urban Revolution, the foundation of the cities, occurred most fully in the specialized environment of Mesopotamia and Egypt, though there were less elaborate centers contemporaneously established in Anatolia and the Balkans. Here, once the task of clearance and irrigation had been accomplished, the alluvial soil, renewed annually in Egypt by the river flood, systematically irrigated in Mesopotamia by a network of canals, produced an unprecedented surplus of wealth, the basis of a rich urban culture.

By 3500 B.C., in the lower delta of Mesopotamia, appear considerable cities based on a complex economy of cereal crops, orchards, and date palms, disposing of great wealth in cattle and sheep. The Sumerians, exploiting the original population, probably colonized the delta from the Iranian plateau; they were masters of methodical organization. The careful poses of their sculpture, the solidity of their buildings, the accuracy of their writing and accounts, belong to a world far removed from the village and the clan. By about 2700 B.C. writing had developed from seals and pictographs; numerals and measurements had been invented; a systematic bureaucracy was in being, centred on the temple of the city's god. The Sumerian officials were priests who administered the surplus of the divine household; specialized classes of scribes, craftsmen, artisans appeared. The wheat and barley, hides and wool which made up the temple's wealth demanded literate administration. The urban revolution was the logical development both of the patriarchal household and the priestly brotherhood serving a shrine, both characteristic of more primitive societies; it was based on the great inventions of the early Bronze Age, applied to a particular environment and theoretically developed.

These cities, Lagash and Erech, Ur and Akkad, with a population running often to 40,000, could only be sustained by a wide network of trade in metals and timber, in luxury goods, in silver and gold. They could only be protected by disciplined armies, by the phalanx and the co-ordinated missile fire of sling and bow; the large-scale merchant and the professional soldier first appear. Further, this complex social organization demanded the discipline of written law. The earliest laws, and, later, the code of Hammurabi, are concerned not only with the regulation of business, with wages, with disputes over water rights, with strayed animals, but assert by implication the principles of a wider justice. Defence and administration demanded strong leadership, and war leaders and governors appear; but they remain largely under priestly influence and regard themselves not as divinities but as the 'tenants' or representatives of the civic god. They are 'Shepherds of the People'; they boast of the foundation of cities, the conquest of the river, the creation of plenty. The urban revolution was due to combined enterprise, wise administration, careful planning.

If we turn to Egypt, we shall observe a parallel development. The Egyptian environment was less exacting than the Mesopotamian, the area smaller, the climate less extreme. Though the Egyptian state was more centralized and much larger, the structure of civilization was the same; intensive irrigation, the development of a ruling class of priests, scribes, and professional fighting men, with the whole community based on a highly productive agriculture and bound together by religion. Egypt was easier to defend, more self-contained; its architectural and artistic achievement has unique and curious characteristics.

The pre-Dynastic Egyptians lived in villages strung out along the Nile valley, mainly practising a Neolithic economy and united in clans generally following an animal totem. These villages developed rudimentary commerce and rudimentary war; their territories, termed 'nomes,' persisted as units of administration after the unification of Egypt, and their totems had a peculiar influence on Egyptian religion. In part Egyptian culture derives from the Delta, but our knowledge of this phase is limited, since the Nile silt has long submerged the area: Mesopotamian influences seem to have contributed much to this early development. Evidence from Upper Egypt is relatively ample; from early times these people showed the characteristic Egyptian obsession with an after-life and constructed tombs adorned with representations of a next world and a judgement, as well as river battles and hunting scenes. They combined an agricultural with a fishing and hunting economy; they pastured their livestock and raised their crops on the banks whose fertility the yearly inundation punctually renewed; in boats of papyrus bundles they nosed their way through the high reed beds of the Nile.

Egypt was first united by Menes (c. 3000 B.C.), a chieftain of the Falcon clan, who established what is termed the Old Kingdom: during this period the domination of the Pharaoh was extended over the whole land, and the massive, conservative, tradition of Egypt established. Here is no federation of cities, but an absolute state centring on the royal household. Already the energies of the country were focused on the construction of monstrous pyramids, on the cult of the Divine Pharaoh and the upkeep of the temples. It is a temple state which has been built, already employing great numbers of objects and officials, based on the tribute and labour service of a subject peasantry.

Like Mesopotamia, the Nile Valley was devoid of resources of metal and timber. The prototype of Egyptian architecture is the reed hut; later this primitive original was translated into the massive structure of palace and temple by the use of sun-dried brick. Egyptian religion was intensely practical, aiming at a repetition in an after-life of the solid satisfactions of the present; their art, devised to this end, early attained distinction within a rigid convention; Egyptian sculpture and architecture shows a sense of mass and proportion surpassed only by the best achievement of the Greeks. Hieroglyphic writing, a relatively clumsy medium of expression, was early developed. Methods of calculating the Nile flood gave rise to a calendar, and in elementary medicine the Egyptians were notable pioneers. All this progress was due in the first place to the priests and officials of the Pharaoh's 'Great House,' who created what was in effect a totalitarian society, harnessing the combined effort of the land and the people. Egyptian society was early stratified, and some of the earliest documents refer to the oppression suffered by the peasantry, who remained in a semi-Neolithic stage of culture. The vast pyramid of Cheops, for example, can only have been built at the price of ruthless exploitation of serf labour. None the less, the Old Kingdom created conditions of stability which enabled the population to multiply, and a habit of routine administration, of craftsmanship, and order, which remained through millennia the basis of a solid civilization. The wealth of Egypt was proverbial throughout Antiquity.

By the early Bronze Age, then, in Egypt and Mesopotamia, the archaic civilizations of the Old Kingdom and the Sumerian cities had laid the foundations of urban life. The Mesopotamians and Egyptians had exploited and developed the inventions of the Copper Age; never before had societies so lasting or so numerous been established. So indestructible were these great Oriental communities, so rich and so highly organized, that the successive waves of war and pillage which broke over them served only to alter the personnel of their ruling classes without disrupting the fabric of society itself.

This great achievement was brought about by a concerted effort to master a favourable though initially exacting environment, inspired by a materialistic religion conceived in terms of the prosperity and propitiation of the civic gods. Leadership, throughout, comes from the priesthood and the divine king; magic, like propaganda in our own time, is an essential ingredient in the art of government. At the same time, the complexity of writing and the esoteric quality of knowledge put a gulf between the literate and the illiterate classes. In Mesopotamia, a conservative culture developed, based on the Sumerian language which persisted as the classical tongue of successive empires. The prestige of the scribes at once strengthened their position and gave their outlook a conventional and, in time, an unpractical bias; though originally experimental, their science ossified into a series of mnemonic spells and never achieved speculative theory in the Greek sense of the term; an elaboration of ancient maxims, a weight of tradition, made for stability but paralysed initiative.

Not only had the rulers the monopoly of knowledge, they had also the monopoly of metal. Bronze weapons were confined to a minority, who by their military skill reinforced the influence of the priestly caste. With the development of the art of war, an able Priest King tended to emancipate himself from priestly control, to assert his personality and military prestige. As the centuries passed, the power of the priesthood diminished, though the rulers were always careful to propitiate the gods and even to claim divine attributes. In consequence, the next phase of Near Eastern civilization, in the full Bronze and early Iron Ages, saw the rise of great military empires. The constant theme of Oriental history is the conquest of the rich static civilization of the river valleys by invaders from the desert and the steppe, who, at a price, brought new qualities and new vigour into the older societies. Along with this enterprise, the conquerors brought habits of pillage and extortion which came to dominate Near Eastern history. The patiently accumulated surplus of the Archaic civilizations was dispersed in the clash of great military empires, or hoarded in the treasuries of rival states: The relatively peaceful and constructive atmosphere of the Archaic civilizations, of the Sumerian cities and of the Old Kingdom in Egypt, gives place in the full Bronze Age (c. 2000–1150 B.C.) to spreading military conflicts; in the Iron Age (c. 1150 B.C. ff.) to tyranny, plunder and deportation on a monstrous scale. Already, in Mesopotamia, the Sumerian Sargon of Akkad, about the twenty-seventh century B.C., had established the prototype of all Eastern Empires; he ruled from Lebanon to the foothills of Asia Minor and the Persian Gulf. By 1900 B.C. the first Babylonian dynasty had been founded; Hammurabi later extended his rule over a wide area.

In Egypt, after the decline of the Old Kingdom, an age of confusion was followed by the revival of centralized government under the rulers of Thebes, but in the eighteenth century B.C. Egypt was overrun by the Hyksos, Semitic 'Princes of the Desert.' Coming from the East and using chariots and war-horses, hitherto unknown in Egypt, they established their domination in the delta. In the middle of the second millennium they were expelled by Ahmose I (1580–1557), who re-established a native dynasty, which in the climax of the Bronze Age raised Egypt to a level of unprecedented opulence and splendour. Under Thutmose I Egypt extended her power over Syria, and the brief reign of the Queen Hatshepsut, marked by monumental building enterprise, was followed by the sanguinary triumphs of Thutmose III, the victor of Megiddo. This age saw the building of the great temples of Karnak and Luxor, of the sphinx avenues and metalled obelisks, of the painted colonnades and sculptured gateways of the greatest period of Egyptian architecture.

Meanwhile in Mesopotamia, by the eighteenth century, the pace of warfare and imperialism had been stepped up. The Kassites, Indo-European invaders, were also using trained war-horses, and improved chariots; the fire power of archers and slingers was greatly increased. The Hittites, whose power rose to its height in the fourteenth and thirteenth centuries, were the first people to exploit the secret of the use of iron; finally, in the later decades of the second millennium, Bronze Age civilization, after reaching its climax, went down before the onslaughts of Indo-European and Semitic invaders. Later, the military efforts of the Kassites, Hittites and Egyptians of the New Kingdom were surpassed by the Assyrians of the full Iron Age, who evolved a war machine of revolting complexity.

So, at the height of the Bronze Age and in the Age of Iron, the Oriental tradition of kingship becomes increasingly imperialistic; rulers are represented as terrible war leaders, armed to the teeth, trampling on subject kings, and consigning hecatombs of captives to the sword. When not engaged in war, the Assyrian rulers, in particular, are depicted hunting lions of peculiar ferocity or transfixing bulls of formidable calibre. The symbols of their power are massive and muscular animals, half-man, half-beast; they themselves, with jutting beards and conical helmets, present a striking contrast to the relatively mild servants of the Archaic gods. The blood and dust of millennia of Near Eastern history can already be smelt through the boastful and ferocious records of Hittite and Assyrian power, and even the Persian rulers, though highly civilized, were irresponsible and capricious tyrants, for all the magnificence of their entourage and their architecture.

The clash of these rival imperialisms was not without benefit. The static limitations of Archaic civilization gave place to an expansion of trade and the extension of a money economy. Loot and destruction meant chances for middle-class initiative outside the great temple households; the demand for armaments meant more prospecting for metals and the spread of civilized influence into Europe. The administration of great empires living by tribute meant expansion of bureaucratic method, better communications, a postal service; the whole technique of Near Eastern empire. Of this inheritance Alexander, and afterwards Rome, were the beneficiaries; the latter imported great-scale government into Europe.

So the peoples of the Near East achieved the basis of civilization; first, the inventions on which human society is built, including especially the use of metals; second, the foundation of cities and the tradition of urban life. They had multiplied exceedingly and established societies rich and strong enough to survive barbarian onslaughts and the conflicts of later imperialism. These massive civilizations invented writing, systematic accounts, the beginnings of empirical science; they produced remarkable art and architecture, a mature though materialistic way of life, and they never developed the abstract speculation of European thought.

III

Meanwhile, the situation in Europe, and indeed on the periphery of Bronze Age society in general, reflected the Oriental advance. Egypt extended its commercial and military influence not only south to Nubia, whence came slaves, ivory, and gold, but north-west into Palestine, Lebanon, and Syria, and over the sea to Cyprus, Crete, and mainland Greece. In the Levant, a piratical and commercial civilization grew up along the coasts of Asia Minor and more particularly in Crete. This European development, the background of Hellenic civilization, will later be described.

The Mesopotamian cultures were now spreading their influence over Asia Minor, the Iranian plateau and over the Caucasus as far as the steppes of South Russia, where the *Kurgans* or barrows of Bronze Age chieftains reflect Sumerian contacts.

The warrior cultures of these Bronze Age European 'Battle Axe' peoples, radiating from the Baltic-Black Sea corridor, are a landmark in the history of the Continent. They foreshadowed a widespread development, at once a bulwark against Asiatic invasion and a unifying influence over the diverse local traditions of the Neolithic peasantry, for the Mediterranean culture had taken root mainly in the periphery of the South, and the evidence of archaeology may well over-emphasize a material unity of culture, not probably expressed in language or tradition. The culture of Northern Europe, for all its debt to the South, owes much of its homogeneity to the Steppe.

These presumably Indo-European speaking peoples, descendants perhaps of the Mesolithic hunters of the eastern plains, who had absorbed Neolithic techniques into a pastoral-nomadic way of life, adapting, it may be, chieftainship and its trappings as a reflection of Sumerian-Akkadian influence, contributed an original strain to the evolution of Europe. From their diffusion westward as a ruling element was to spring a long ethnic, social and spiritual development, beginning with the 'Battle Axe' people, and culminating eventually, sophisticated but recognizable, in mediaeval chivalry. Here, as will later be apparent, is the background against which later barbarian development must be set.

In the middle of the second millennium, Bronze Age cultures developed in Italy and Central Europe, particularly in Bohemia and Hungary, in Transylvania and the foothills of the Austrian Alps. From Troy, commanding the Dardanelles, Bronze Age influence spread up the Danube northward even to the Baltic, while a trade route over the Brenner through the Moravian gate linked Denmark and the amber coast with the South. According to their means, the Barbarian Bronze Age rulers imitated the southern way of life. They had learnt the use of certain luxury goods and eastern armaments, of spear and rapier; thus equipped, they imposed their domination on the Neolithic peasantry, but made no contribution to agricultural progress. Theirs was a warlike and hunting society, superimposed on subject peoples. In the final decadence of the Bronze Age, barbarian war bands, descending from the Balkans, looted the civilization of the Levant. It was only after a dark age of confusion that in the seventh century Greek civilization began to emerge. Although, therefore, the population of Europe was increasing and nomadic peoples were successively penetrating out of the Steppe, outer Europe reflected only faintly the achievements of the East. The foundation of Neolithic agriculture and stock farming was there, but, except in the Levant and along the western fringes of the Great Sea, there was as yet no widespread establishment of cities.

Greek civilization of the Iron Age, the result of the first independent European initiative, must be seen against an overwhelming Oriental background. And how much these Near Eastern peoples had achieved! First, the Neolithic Revolution itself; next, the use of metals and the great inventions; then the smelting of bronze, and, in Mesopotamia and Egypt, the building of cities, writing, calculation, the measurement of time. Here, in the hot sunshine, and under the great stars, in lands of teeming fertility and predictable climate, where population multiplied and life and skill were cheap, man first settled deeply into a civilized tradition. Here, the unique endowment of our species, the use of speech, was made permanent in cuneiform inscriptions and in hieroglyphs on the rolled papyri. Priests, scribes, and administrators, sustained by the surplus wealth of great societies, could pause from the close preoccupation of the struggle for life to take stock of the surrounding world. Artists provided passports to immortality, or glorified their city or their Pharaoh; craftsmen and artisans, supplying the needs of city and court, devised an accumulating tradition of custom and technique, and over the far-flung trade routes there grew up a network of exploration and commerce feeding the markets of the valleys. Civilization had been achieved, but with it came war. First, defensive against the attacks of outer barbarians; later, as predatory invaders established their successive dominations, war for territory and plunder. Great empires, greedy for tribute, imposed themselves on the patient masses, on a subservient trading class; the range of administration was extended, but civilization staggered under successive blows—staggered but survived, so strong were the foundations, so unbreakable the millennial routine.

Thus in Europe the conquest of the land had been begun, and in the Near East the urban revolution consolidated. The first achievement, jointly undertaken in Neolithic settlements up and down Europe and the Middle East, in a thousand nameless villages of the Copper Age in Asia Minor and North Africa, laid the foundation for the second. This steady and unrecorded effort, the result of limited but widespread enterprise, forms the common background to the history of all the European peoples; it is far more important than the conquests and revolutions celebrated in political history. It was made by a multitude of nameless, ordinary men and women, by the basic Neolithic populations with whom subsequent invaders intermarried, and from whom the majority of Europeans descend. Here, indeed, is a solid fact of material progress common to the history of all peoples.

The next stage, the urban revolution, is specifically to the credit of the Near East. Men of many races and many languages contributed to it; from their efforts and their foresight the modern world takes its beginning, and it is to their attainments rather than to the records of competing empires that history directs attention today.

A well-known authority writes, '. . . in the long run the vitality of Europe is what it is, precisely because its history is so mixed and moving, and of this vitality no race has ever had the monopoly. And so it is only by a falsified account of the past that the concept of race can be used today for the inflaming of nationalism. . . . Prehistory can help here by promoting a truer valuation of European culture, emphasizing that its progress has come not through racial exclusion, but through the continual mingling and interaction of its diversity of component groups and peoples.'[1]

Such, in bare outline is the historical significance for Europe of the Neolithic revolution and of the Near Eastern civilization of the Bronze and Iron Ages, which the Levantine peoples were learning to exploit, to which the European warrior aristocracies were turning envious eyes, and of which the barbarians of the West were dimly aware.

---

[1] Prof. C. F. S. Hawkes, 'Race Prehistory and European Civilization,' *Man,* published by the Royal Anthropological Institute, Nov.—Dec. 1942.

CHAPTER II

THE GENIUS OF HELLAS

'This also said Phocylides,
A tiny rock-built citadel,
Is finer far, if ordered well,
Than all your frantic Ninevehs.'

PHOCYLIDES (*fl. c.* 544 B.C.) (trans. C. M. BOWRA)

THE immense practical achievements of the Near Eastern peoples, the creation of fully organized urban life, of far-flung trade and administration, formed the first and indispensable phase of civilization. It remained for the genius of Hellas to invent speculative theory, objectivity, and a new freedom of discussion. Oriental societies, with their teeming populations, large-scale government and priestly domination, with their cult of Divine Rulers and archaic conventions, had little room for the assertion of the value and dignity of the speculative mind. Their knowledge consisted in the main of recipes for particular occasions, bound up with religious ceremonial, intensely conservative. The wisdom of the East, like tribal tradition, appealed to an ancestral past, the weight of precedent and authority crushed enterprise; Eastern civilizations, though stable and indestructible, were probably, in this phase, incapable of further advance.

The brilliance, originality and power of Greek genius can only be realized when set against the relatively primitive background in which it developed. Greek thought, art, and poetry, the language itself, together equal, and in some respects surpass, any subsequent European achievement. The minds of Plato and Aristotle, of Aeschylus, Thucydides and the great lyric poets, both in power and maturity of thought are of a calibre unsurpassed in the history of the world. The debt of Europe to Greece is immeasurable; yet all this came about in a relatively small area and in a short span of time.

The civilization of Mediterranean Antiquity, though organized by Rome, was inspired by the genius of Hellas. The framework, political and economic, of the Mediterranean world remained in terms of the 'polis' or city state, as did later civilization in Europe until the rise of great national states in the sixteenth century, the Roman and Mediaeval Empires being cosmopolitan, superimposed on a structure of cities. This brilliant Greek culture resulted from a blending of the Minoan-Mycenaean Bronze Age tradition with the influence of new Indo-European invaders of the Iron Age, moving down from the Balkans, Central Europe, and the steppes of Southern Russia; this background explains many Greek characteristics.

The geography of Greece made it the natural scene of a fusion of races and ideas. With the spread of civilization westward, the peninsular characteristics of Europe assert themselves: the Mediterranean was profoundly different from the great river valleys or the plateaux of Asia Minor and Iran. Uniformity of relief and climate gave place to self-contained valleys and to relatively narrow maritime plains; the mountainous structure of Greece and Italy made for variety of culture and government. Within the tiny area of southern Greece the contrasting city states of Athens and Sparta could develop; in Italy, Etruscan and Roman communities, with a fruitful variety of tradition, could flourish and ultimately blend. Limited resources meant specialized and tenacious agriculture; olive and vine cultivation implied production for export, while the presence in the European peninsulas and islands of metals and marble, timber and obsidian, meant the development of overseas trade. Fishing, the school of maritime lore, was from the beginning a staple means of livelihood. The epic literature of both Greeks and Romans, *Iliad, Odyssey* and *Aeneid,* are pervaded by the glitter of the Mediterranean, by the adventure and the danger of the sea.

In Greece, as later in Scandinavia, emigration was constant. Independent colonies were founded, and Greek influence spread to North Africa and Sicily, to Italy, Provence, Spain, and the Black Sea. Such particularism meant war as well as commerce; piracy and exile, as well as enterprise; but on balance the Mediterranean environment was more favourable to initiative, once the initial foundations had been secured, than the relatively uniform geography of the Near East. The far-flung tyrannies of Darius and Xerxes could not live in this dynamic and alien world.

The background of the great age of Greek culture extends into Neolithic times, to the Helladic settlements on the mainland and the Islands. The Minoan pre-Indo-European civilization of the Levant originated in the third millennium, and reached its climax in the first half of the second; with the decline of Bronze Age culture the Minoan world was overrun by Mycenean warbands who, by the fourteenth century, had established a widespread domination. The Mycenean rulers were typical of the barbarian aristocracies developing on the fringes of Bronze Age civilization; they were the prototypes of the heroes of the *Iliad* and the *Odyssey*, but they developed principalities that owed much to the massive civilizations of the Near East.

The basis of Minoan wealth was sea-borne commerce; the shipment of oil and wine, of metals and timber to Egypt and the Middle East. Further, the surplus population practised piracy and served as mercenaries in the war fleets of the great continental powers. Minoan art and architecture are at once Oriental and European, their huddled palaces serving as warehouses and factories as well as strongholds. The Palace of Knossos, with its squat pillars, complex stairways, and cellars crammed with merchandise, recalls palaces in Syria or the Great House of the early Pharaohs; but the brilliant frescoes which adorned its walls, the lines of a Minoan vase, the economy and freshness of Minoan art, seem already in part European. Their wall paintings, with patterns of waves and fishes, reflect the influence of the sea; in the close, low-built throne room, the back of Minos' chair itself is edged by an undulating design. Minoan sport and religion were peculiar; the athletes, with close-girt hips, leapt headlong at the charging bulls, gripped the beasts' horns and swung clear; the painted priestesses, with flounced skirts and tiered head-dresses, practised a curious cult of serpent and double axe. By the sixteenth century the Minoan princes used chariots and imported Nubian slaves in imitation of the Pharaoh, but their power depended on their fleets. Once Minoan sea power was broken, their hegemony collapsed; by the close of the fourteenth century, Knossos had been sacked. No wonder this strange and picturesque civilization caught the imagination of the Greeks, that the

legend was handed down of the tribute of girls and boys to the
Minotaur, the Bull Man; that the word labyrinth, coined to describe the sinister corridors of the House of the Axe, persisted in
their language and descended to our own.

Mycenean culture retained the essentials of the Minoan background: the late Minoan script is now known to be primitive
Greek; the wealth of the Mycenean princes and the beauty of
Mycenean art show that the world they exploited was highly
civilized, if politically decadent. By the fifteenth century B.C., the
lords of Tiryns and Mycenae and their dependent cities had imposed their domination on mainland Greece; in the fourteenth
they extended their power over Crete and the Islands. These
centuries coincided, as we have seen, with a brilliant phase of
Egyptian civilization, the climax of the Bronze Age. The citadel
of Mycenae, dominating the road from Corinth to the plain of
Argos, is strategically well placed; Tiryns, even more heavily
fortified, lies a few miles distant, commanding the coast. Both
fortresses show a greater power of structural engineering than the
Cretans possessed. The famous Lion Gate and the treasury of
Atreus are built out of Cyclopean blocks of composite masonry.
The royal tombs, discovered by Schliemann, contained a hoard
of treasure of superb craftsmanship which indicates contact with
Asia as well as Egypt. Minoan designs of dolphins and hunting
scenes persist, and the engraved daggers, horns, and drinking
cups are masterpieces of art. Yet these treasures were created by
native artists; the Mycenean rulers were barbaric, living for war,
hunting, and plunder; their hard features are preserved by masks
of beaten gold upon the faces of their dead. The Mycenean aristocracy was complete with sacred king, dukes, counts, and feudal
barons holding land by service, and the Mycenean princes realized the ambitions of other and poorer Bronze Age aristocracies
in Europe: they had come into the wealth of a decadent civilization, and, with spears and rapiers, chariots and hunting dogs, exploited the treasures and the luxuries of the Minoan world. To
the courts of these prototypes of the Homeric heroes flocked artists, bards, and metal workers, and the accumulated surplus of
the old world sufficed for a period of barbaric splendour.

But by the twelfth century B.C. the social disorder in which the
Bronze Age foundered was overwhelming the Levant. Migration,

piracy, and pillage diminished sea-borne trade; exports dwindled, art was barbarized, agriculture reverted to subsistence farming; in the end there remained of Mycenae only the memories enshrined in Greek legend. Yet, in spite of the darkness which covers this period, there was no break with the essential of the ancient culture. Old agricultural methods, traditions of metal working and pottery, persisted; though there was a decline in wealth, population did not seriously diminish. Besides the legends and memories of the past, the magic and ritual of the indigenous population, there was handed down a solid foundation of craftsmanship and agriculture, of olive and wine cultivation. Copper mines and marble quarries were still worked on a lower output; a substantial legacy of the Bronze Age remained for further exploitation by the new techniques of the Age of Iron.

The background of the invasion of the post-Mycenean, Indo-European Greek tribes into the Levant was the economic and military development following on the use of the new material. We have seen that the Hittites, as early as the twelfth century, possessed the secret; slowly this revolutionary discovery had been spreading through the Near East, and by 1000 B.C. iron was widely employed, not only for weapons and war chariots but for agricultural implements. The results of this revolution were manifold, and of cardinal importance. In the first place, since iron was common and relatively cheap, the days of the Bronze Age aristocracies were numbered. Henceforward, military operations were on a greater scale, and the single combat of the *Iliad* gave way to the coordinated Assyrian chariot charge and to the disciplined organization of infantry. Hence the political importance of the heavy-armed foot soldier, reflected in the early history of Athens and Rome: the small farmer became the backbone of citizen armies. Of even greater importance was the widespread use of iron agricultural implements, which greatly increased productivity, causing an increase in population which spread gradually but steadily across Europe.

Outside the Levant by 700 B.C. the Hallstatt Iron Age economy was in being among the Celts of Central Europe and extending northward through Bohemia. By the middle of the first millennium, this influence was beginning to penetrate the British Isles, though the Irish long continued to enjoy an Heroic Bronze Age.

By the fourth century the Celts of La Tène period were swarming into North Italy and the Balkans, for the use of iron not
only increased the wealth and armaments of the civilized world,
but armed the barbarian war-bands with cheap and formidable
weapons.

Such was the external background of Hellenic civilization. The
age of confusion which witnessed the collapse of Bronze Age
culture extended over the Levant and into Asia Minor and
Egypt, but the situation was beginning to stabilize by the beginning of the eighth century. This period, besides widespread war
and migration, saw a revival of trade and colonization.

The natural middlemen of the Levant had long been the
Phoenicians. Based on Tyre and Sidon, on the fringe of the Asiatic continent, they had early challenged the monopoly of Minoan commerce; they had carried on through the dark centuries,
and by the Early Iron Age had pushed westward to Malta and
Sicily, Sardinia and Spain. They founded Carthage in North Africa, a commercial republic destined to flourish exceedingly, to
challenge and be broken by the power of Rome. These enterprising Semitic traders had a simplified alphabetic script, assimilated
by the Iron Age Greeks; with modifications it is the basis of our
own writing. Another innovation of this period was the widespread use of coined money of small denominations: Bronze Age
transactions had been conducted primarily in bars and slabs of
metal; the creation of a guaranteed currency began in Asia Minor
in the eighth century B.C. and was to extend to the Greek cities
by the sixth century. The result was an extension both of production for the market by the small farmer and a widening purchasing power. Colonization was not confined to the Phoenicians;
the Etruscans, too, settlers out of Asia Minor, moved westward to
Tuscany and enforced their domination on the native Italians;
the Philistines on the flat Palestinian shore traded with Greece
and Egypt and harried the Jews in their strongholds in the
interior.

II

Against this shifting scene of enterprise and migration must
be set the development of the Hellenic peoples. The Greek tribes-

men from the North had found a world in ruins but full of opportunity; the cities had dwindled to a village economy and revival was comparatively slow; but in the islands prosperity revived sooner and here the first brilliant beginnings of Greek civilization occur. At the courts of the local 'Tyrants' (the word is pre-Indo-European), who owed their wealth to piracy and commerce, the early philosophers and poets found their patrons; Ionian Greece witnessed the foundation of European philosophy, poetry, and science. On the mainland, the background was more elementary, and it was not until Athens and Corinth developed their export trade that the intellectual initiative of the islands was reflected, developed and surpassed. Where the island cities flourished on maritime trade, the foundation of the mainland cities was small-scale farming.

The originality of Greek intellectual development reflects the adaptability and vigour of the invaders and the strength of the old Levantine tradition. The Greek ruling classes were originally warlike invaders imposed on the native population; hence the aristocratic outlook of earlier Greek philosophy, the assumption that slavery is natural and inevitable, the contempt felt by the Greeks in general for barbarians and artisans. The most highly sophisticated Greek philosophers were the recent descendants of tribesmen, emerged suddenly out of barbarism into the full sunlight of Iron Age civilization; hence, in part, the vigour and ruthlessness of the Greek outlook. The Spartans, in particular, were of a ruling minority which retained a primitive social pattern; their organization in age groups, communal living and deliberately brutal education paralleled similar customs among the Zulu impis and the war-bands of the Masai. Even the thought of Plato is tinged with this primitive inheritance.

Democratic Athens, through its maritime situation and widespread commerce, broke the political power of the land-owning oligarchy, but the city contained a large slave population and excluded the numerous resident aliens from citizenship. Many Greek customs, moreover, were thoroughly Oriental. The relative poverty, the lack of amenities of dress and furniture, and simplicity of household arrangements should also not be forgotten. On this limited basis, the Greeks displayed a power, an originality, and range of thought which are the foundation of the European intellectual achievement. Not only did they display impartial curiosity and accurate observation, the basis of all scientific thought, but they were capable of profound criticism of life. Aristotle, their greatest all-round genius, is not only the outstanding scientist and political philosopher of Antiquity; he is a shrewd and ironical man of the world. The Greek poets not only command the majestic rhythms of Epic narrative and a tragic Drama depicting the contest of man with Fate, but their lyric poetry expresses subtle and controlled emotion.

This Greek achievement, the first independent expression of the genius of Europe, was paralleled, though not surpassed, in contemporary civilizations in Northern India and China; and indeed, from the eighth century onwards there appears to have been a widening of consciousness throughout the world of Antiquity, a new level of moral and intellectual awareness. In India the Buddha in the seventh century reached the heights of religious experience; in China Lao-tse and Confucius created the ancient code of Chinese morality; in Palestine the Prophets of the Old Testament achieved a new moral insight. Humanity was entering on new fields of morality and thought. The Greek initiative was not, therefore, unique, but it combined scientific with religious and moral progress to an unparalleled degree. Apart from their humanistic achievement, here is the beginning of Europe's original contribution to the world, the creation of scientific method itself.

Greek philosophy appropriately began with practical speculation. The Ionian philosophers were concerned with the observation and control of nature, with the discovery of a 'kosmos' or natural order. Such speculation may have been originally designed to discover the magical properties in number, and to devise spells for the control of evil spirits; but the Greek intellect soon shook off the trammels of Eastern influence and opened up a world of exact observation and abstract analysis. Pythagoras and Democritus in the second half of the sixth century were, respectively, the founders of geometry and physics, the latter anticipating the atomic theory of matter. Thales was a founder of astronomical science, and Hippocrates of Chios was the greatest medical man of Antiquity. His systematic clinical method and the ideal of the medical calling expressed in his famous oath defining the duty of a doctor, have won him enduring fame. The aims of all these early scientists were practical and immediate; in the process they discovered the most powerful instrument of European thought—the power of abstraction and impartial observation.

This original achievement was balanced in the fifth century by the development of ethical and philosophical speculation. The circumstances of Greek society made such a transition natural. Both in the islands and on the mainland there was a leisured ruling class, whose hard vigour of mind seized with avidity on ethical and political problems. Here, and in other Greek cities, the life of the Agora, of the Piazza, characteristic of Mediterranean society, was fully developed. Hence was a clash of wits, an urban quickness and versatility, an interest in politics and an intense civic patriotism paralleled in the cities of Renaissance Italy. In democratic Athens, as in Florence, the intellectual interests of the minority were increasingly shared by the mass of the citizens; and they were bred in a common literature.

Before examining their political, philosophical, and artistic achievement, it will be well to glance at this inheritance, which has come down both directly and through Roman writers, and forms a common background to the main European literary tradition. The extent to which the Greek outlook was coloured and pervaded by the Homeric poems is paralleled by the influence of the translated Bible on the Protestants of North-Western Europe and America. The Homeric outlook and mythology dominated Greek literature, and with such a beginning, it is not remarkable how great was the Hellenic achievement. The *Iliad* and *Odyssey* surpass other Epic literature in delineation of character, in the economy and realism in which situations are presented and designed, and in the subordination of descriptive background to the main theme. The rush and thunder of the Homeric hexameters, the rapidity and sustained interest of the narrative, the far darting similes, and the singing quality of the words are unequalled in later Epic; the *Iliad* and *Odyssey* have remained treasures of all Europe.

Besides the Homeric poems and hymns, dating from the ninth century, the more homely writings of Hesiod formed the background to later Greek literature. Hesiod's *Theogony,* a history of gods and men, sets out the doctrine of cycles of history, of the four ages of Gold, Silver, Bronze, and Iron; his *Works and Days* describe life on a Boeotian farm with convincing observation; he is the first of the great European nature poets.

In the sixth century a more personal poetry appears. At the courts of the island tyrants of Ionia there came to be written an eligiac poetry of unsurpassed beauty. Though few of their writings are extant, the love poetry of Theognis (*c.* 550 B.C.) and particularly of Sappho (*c.* 590), had a wide reputation in Antiquity; the fragments extant achieve intensity of emotion in a small compass, the mark of highly civilized minds. At the Court of Polycrates of Samos, Anacreon and Ibycus continued this poignant and restrained tradition; their short love poems, written to be sung, are paralleled by the sterner epigrams of Alcaeus and Simonides which lament the vicissitudes of fortune and exile; the terse dignity of the latter's epigram on the Spartan dead at Thermopylae is famous. All these writers show an intense individuality, accurately expressed.

Besides love poetry, drinking songs and epigrams, the Greek poets developed the lyric choral Ode. These ceremonial poems, paeans in praise of the gods, odes to the victors in the pan-Hellenic games, hymns for processional singing and dirges for the dead, constitute an elaborate and original literary form. The Theban poet, Pindar, was the greatest master of this genre.

By the sixth century B.C., the Greeks had thus created a superb and varied poetry, an integral part of their social life. They were united by this common literary tradition; they were also, in the late sixth and early fifth centuries, united by the menace of Persian expansion.

The full brilliance of Greek culture appears after the defeat of Persia by the Hellenes, combined under the leadership of Athens and Sparta. The Persian menace had been growing since the subjugation of the Ionian islands by Cyrus in the middle sixth century and the conquest by Cambyses of Egypt and Tyre, which put Phoenician sea-power at his disposal. His successor, Darius (521–485 B.C.) turned to the conquest of Europe. It would seem the Persians understood there would be nothing between them and the Atlantic, once the Hellenic resistance was overcome; according to Herodotus, Xerxes declared, 'Once let us subdue these people . . . we shall extend the Persian territory as far as God's Heaven reaches. The sun will then shine on no land beyond our borders; for I will pass through Europe from one end to the other.' The Greeks were defending not only their own territory but the future of the Continent.

Although the Persian Empire was tolerant and often enlightened, at the turn of the century the Ionian Greeks revolted against Darius, who had already moved across the Danube to subdue the Scythians. He resolved to deal once and for all with the Hellenes. He therefore prepared a great army, and after an initial failure through breakdown of supply services, he invaded Attica by sea, only to be flung back from the beaches of Marathon (490 B.C.). After this disaster, the Persians drew off for a decade; but ten years later, Darius' successor, Xerxes, launched a great combined operation against Greece, while by a concerted strategy the Carthaginians attacked the Greeks in Sicily. The crossing of the Hellespont by this monstrous army, the cutting of a canal through the Isthmus, the carnage and heroism of Thermopylae, have been described by Herodotus in a masterpiece of narrative. The Persian host overran the Spartan resistance and poured into Boeotia; they advanced into Attica and occupied Athens; but when all seemed lost, the brilliant naval victory at Salamis, a turning point if ever there was one in the history of the world, broke and scattered the Persian fleet under the eyes of the Great King. In the same year the Carthaginians were defeated at Himera, and Xerxes led the bulk of his armies out of Greece; in the next, the Spartan Pausanias crushed the Persian Army of occupation at Plataea and the victorious Hellenes launched a counter offensive into Asia Minor. They later liberated the islands, captured Cyprus and took Byzantium, regaining command of the Dardanelles. The prospect of Persian domination had been deferred and, in the event, abolished.

Against this background the achievements of fifth-century B.C. Athens must be set. The political sequel was to be less fortunate; under the threat of Persian domination the Hellenes had sunk their differences; with the waning of the danger, old rivalries reappeared. The great king, moreover, remained a potential menace in the offing, and Persian diplomacy and Persian gold continued to foster dissension between the cities. None the less a phase of brilliance set in; the centre of power had shifted to the mainland, and Athens became the economic, political, and intellectual capital of Greece. The full glory of Periclean Athens, which saw the building of the Parthenon and the climax of Athenian power, occurred between the defeat of Persia and the opening of the Peloponnesian War. Yet, in spite of her high qualities, Athens never imposed unity on Hellas, and the second half of the fifth century is one of deepening tragedy, with Athens and Sparta, at the head of their respective confederations, fighting for the political and economic domination of Greece.

The contrast between the two states and all they stood for is dramatic and famous; on the one hand, the sea-power of the Delian confederacy, led and exploited by democratic Athens; on the other, the land-power of the Peloponnesian League, led by the conservative oligarchy of Sparta. Thucydides has described in immortal pages the vicissitudes of the struggle during the last three decades of the fifth century, his theme the failure of Periclean Athens to combine democracy and empire. The final Athenian gamble, designed to bring the resources of Magna Graecia to bear on the war in the Peloponnese, culminated in the disastrous expedition to Syracuse, the revolt of the Allies, and the destruction, in 405 B.C., of the Athenian fleet.

The political power of Athens was broken, but the city was not destroyed, her intellectual leadership not lost. Yet, in spite of the lessons of the war, the inter-state rivalries continued and increased; Spartan ascendancy was challenged by Epaminondas; finally, Philip of Macedon brought the cycle to a temporary conclusion at Chaeronea (338 B.C.) where he defeated the combined armies of Athens and Thebes. At last the Hellenes were united by a superior power. The sequel was to be the conquest of the Near East.

It will be seen that for all their genius, the Hellenes were not able to transcend the political limitations of the city state; the nationalistic wars which were later to tear Europe to pieces are paralleled in miniature in the history of Greece. The sequel was the imposition of peace by a relatively alien power; first by Macedon, later by Rome. The moral of this story is plain.

It must, indeed, be remembered that, though Athens created democratic institutions, and Plato and Aristotle the framework and terms of political thought, the civilization of fifth- and early fourth-century Greece must be seen against a background of almost incessant conflict, later, in the Hellenistic period, complicated by class war. It may be said, however, that these tragic aspects of Greek life strengthen the realism and heighten the tension of Greek political thought. Without this experience, the profound judgements of Thucydides' *History,* of Plato's *Republic,* and of Aristotle's *Politics* might not have been achieved. Their writings reflect a disillusioned world.

III

Against this political background we must now glance at the theoretical, literary, and artistic achievements of classical Greece. We have seen that the Hellenic cities had developed a brilliant culture and an inheritance of intellectual freedom, toleration, and accuracy, which was to inspire the greatest thought of Europe. Political problems, in particular, were subjected to a new analysis: as a geometrical proposition had its correct answer, so, it was believed, the best form of government could be defined in terms of the 'good life.' This subordination of politics to ethics marked an immense advance. It implied, at least in theory, that power is only justified if it furthers the development of human faculties and the participation of free citizens in policy, since without political responsibility no man can come to his full moral stature. It is incompatible with any doctrine of state idolatry or unbridled power.

Greek political thought combined civic solidarity with critical intelligence. The Athenian ideal of all-round ability, self-reliance and patriotism is expressed by Thucydides in Pericles' famous oration over the Athenian dead. 'We are lovers of beauty without extravagance and lovers of wisdom without unmanliness. Wealth to us is not mere material for vainglory but opportunity for achievement. . . . Other men are bold in ignorance while reflection will stop their onset, but the bravest are surely those who have the clearest vision of what lies before them, glory and danger alike, and yet go out to meet it. . . . In a word I claim that her members yield to none, man by man, for independence of spirit, many-sidedness of attainment and complete self-reliance of brain and limb.'[1] Such an ideal implies a new intellectual freedom and self-confidence; it expresses the most original qualities of the European outlook, to be reflected, in the phase of European expansion, in an intellectual and practical enterprise which was to dominate much of the world.

The greatest moral genius of Greek civilization was Socrates, whose thought has come down to us through Plato and indirectly through Aristotle. He was put to death for his convictions, but his method of ruthless analysis exerted an incalculable influence. His disciples, Plato (427–347) and at one remove the famous Aristotle (384–322), are the two greatest masters of philosophy and political science in Antiquity. The former believed that a rigid pattern of political orders should be imposed by experts, whom he designated 'Guardians.' The *Republic,* his most famous treatise, depicts an ideal state in which the social order is so arranged that each free man holds the position he deserves, and the whole polity is designed to ensure an austere good life for a ruling minority. It is the first example of a planned pattern for a state. In the *Laws* a more rigid system is designed, an intelligent version of the Spartan society. It serves as a warning of the disadvantages of ruthless planning. But, great as was Plato's contribution to political science, it was in the philosophical field that his influence was most fundamental.

Where Plato's thought reflects an abstract ideal, Aristotle is an empirical scientist. The volume of his scientific, philosophical, and political writings is immense; of all the great writers his influence has been the most salutary, the most pervasive and the most profound. The aim of the state, he insists, is to promote the 'good life' of the citizens, and the good life can only be realized in a well-balanced community. Since man is a 'political animal,' the 'solitary man is either a beast or a god,' and man 'when perfected . . . the best of animals, but when separated from Law and Justice, the worst of all.'[2] Both Plato and Aristotle concur in the belief that a right education is the foundation of a healthy, if oligarchic and slave-owning, society.

In the realm of metaphysical, ethical, and political theory, Plato and Aristotle thus formulated a most essential and charac-

---

[1] Thucydides II, 38–9.
[2] *Politics* I, 2.

teristic Western ideal. A synthesis of Greek and Christian tradition was to be a great achievement of Europe, and remains today, backed by the new range of scientific knowledge, an inspiration of much modern thought. The lucidity, the dispassionate appraisal of facts, the toleration of new ideas and the constructive force of Greek thought are fundamental to the West. It has consistently fought, and generally overcome, the murky and violent influences of undisciplined emotion, the cult of Will and Force, the rationalization of a barbaric urge for destruction.

The Athenians of the fifth century further created the European Drama. Attic tragedy and comedy arose out of the ritual mumming of primitive religion; the forms of tragedy were dictated by the masks and robes of early ritual, the forms of comedy by the peasant buffoonery of games and fertility rites. The subjects of drama were first taken from Homeric stories well known all over Greece; they were written in public competition for civic performance, and formed the vehicle of a profound criticism of life, for meditations on Destiny and Justice. Their abiding theme is the limitation of human personality before the dictates of Fate.

Aeschylus and Sophocles are the two great masters of the earlier tragic school, Euripides of its later and more contemporaneous interpretation. In the field of comedy, Aristophanes mocked at the follies of gods and men, and such was the Athenian love for wit that this critic of the dominant democracy was allowed free rein.

The Athenians, like the Romans after them, set great store by oratory; the eloquence of Pericles and, later, of Demosthenes laid the foundations of a millennial tradition, classical and modern; while in history, Herodotus and Thucydides are masters of the first order—Herodotus, entertaining, discursive, full of tall stories, is the father of the general run of historical narrative; Thucydides, the greatest of ancient historians, the creator of a fine tradition of impartial judgement and cool analysis. His packed sentences, summing up the complexity of political action and circumstance, his sense of proportion and of the dignity of events, reflect a profound insight and pity—the conclusions to which, like Plato, he had been led by hard experience.

Meanwhile Greek sculpture and architecture had attained an extraordinary brilliance. The earliest statues resemble the ritual figures of other peoples, but, with the development of the full

Greek genius, there appears a poise and distinction unsurpassed
even by the sculptors of the Italian Renaissance. Already Minoan
art had displayed a freshness which even Egyptian artists had not
attained; to this Levantine tradition the Greeks added a new
hardness and power. Following on the superb distinction of the
earlier work, the later periods produced a finished portrait-sculp-
ture and detail within a well-proportioned design, both of the
first order; and, indeed, a comparison of the grace and individuality of the frieze of the Parthenon with Persian or Assyrian representations of captives bearing tribute to the great kings of the
East, sums up the contrast of this side of the spirit of Hellas with
that of most Oriental societies.

In architecture the Greeks adapted the original painted
wooden structure of their temples to the medium of marble and
stone. Nowhere in the world have buildings of such finish and
precision been designed; the style and economy of the best
Greek work reflects the lucidity of their philosophical speculation. This architecture has been the inspiration of the most widespread and vigorous European tradition. Though the Roman
and Byzantine achievements were more massive, and Gothic inspiration more imaginative and bizarre, the sanity and proportion of Greek design have persisted through the centuries as the
standard to which the European peoples, whatever the originality
and variety of their architectural genius, have consistently
returned.

There is no space here to dwell on the excellence of Greek vase
painting, on the lost splendours of Greek pictorial art, on the
details of Greek ornament silver and jewellery; in these fields
also the genius of Hellas set standards for the Classical, Renaissance, and Modern worlds.

Such are the outstanding and lasting achievements of the civilization of mainland Greece, the sequel to the original culture of
the Greek islands. In the fourth century Hellenic influence was
to expand over a much wider area.

I V

As has been indicated, after a succession of fratricidal wars,
the ancient centres of Greek culture had been overwhelmed by

the relatively barbarous power of Macedon. The Macedonian phalanx, perfected by Philip, not only won supremacy in mainland Greece, but proved the instrument of the enormous conquests of Alexander. The Persian Empire, long dependent on foreign mercenaries and penetrated by Hellenic influence, fell before this well-organized assault, and with its fall Europe first established superiority over the ancient centres of civilization. The scale of Greek influence and action was thus transformed and the Middle East subjected to deliberate Hellenization. Alexander planned to stabilize his conquests by the foundation of cities; from Northern India, across the Iranian plateau and the Tigris-Euphrates Valley, over the Syrian Steppe to Asia Minor, to Egypt and North Africa, replicas of the polis were established. By taking over the Persian administration, and by the conquest of Egypt, he disposed of power and wealth greater than that of any previous European. He was highly intelligent, with the force of the Macedonian tribesman crossed with the predatory enterprise of his mother's Albanian forebears; he had been educated by Aristotle, the greatest intellect of Classical Greece; he displayed an advanced self-consciousness, chivalry, and curiosity. He despatched his fleets on voyages of deliberate exploration, and though early beginning to show ruthlessness and instability, he retained and imposed many of the values of Greek civilization. His meteoric career, cut short at thirty-two, profoundly altered the history of the Levant and the Middle East; it is interesting to speculate on the subsequent history of Europe, had Alexander lived out a normal span, turned westward and mopped up Carthage, Syracuse, and Rome.

Antioch and Pergamon, Seleucia and Priene, many flourishing cities which bear Alexander's name, were spread about the Middle East. Alexandria in Egypt, the largest and richest of these foundations, remained the intellectual and economic capital of the Hellenistic world for centuries: it was only the greatest among many cities. The successor states of Alexander's empire were organized on a scale and with an efficiency unknown to classical Greece; economically they were comparable to the European states of the mercantile era of the seventeenth century. But this wealth was concentrated in the hands of great landowners and merchants and implied the existence of a large and dependent proletariat.

The curse of this civilization was internecine warfare; but when Rome, after playing one state off against another, was strong enough to impose peace over the whole area, a phase of prosperity for the ruling classes set in. Here, indeed, were the richest and most civilized parts of the Roman empire. Meanwhile, though political unity was still distant, cultural unity had always been achieved; the pattern of civic society was the same over Hellenistic Asia, Egypt, North Africa, and the Levant. It was a cosmopolitan culture imposed on the native peoples, including the native aristocracies and the urban upper classes within its pale. The result was curious and interesting. In many ways it was incongruous in the East; for example, the Greek cult of baths and athletics was uncongenial to the traditions of the Jews; their prophets denounced the fashionable tendencies of a renegade minority and nationalism expressed itself in the fanatical revolts of the Maccabees chronicled by Josephus.

The material essentials of the original 'polis' were realized in Asia, often on a more splendid and exotic scale. Colonnades and aqueducts, temples and piazzas, statues and gardens, were laid out with a lavish hand; local plutocrats vied with one another in the embellishment of civic amenities. In Egypt, Babylonia, and Cyrenaica native luxury was transformed by Hellenistic architects into a new elegance; in Greece itself, in Asia Minor, and North Africa, great universities became centres of systematic classification, literary criticism and a conservative research; the immense library at Alexandria housed the accumulated learning of Antiquity. The Hellenistic epoch, indeed, stands in relation to Classical Greece as our own eighteenth century to the culture of the Renaissance; this highly sophisticated world later formed the background to the formulation of Christian theology. The culture both of Byzantium and of the Abbasid Caliphate of Baghdad in the tenth century derived from Hellenistic sources, and it was largely through Muslim Spain and Sicily that Mediaeval Europe inherited the more advanced aspects of the learning of Antiquity. Far from being a decadent sequel to the achievements of the fourth and fifth centuries, Hellenistic culture expanded, elaborated, and developed the thought of that creative age.

In the sphere of philosophy, in particular, a new universality appears; Stoic and Epicurean ideas transcended the boundaries of the city state; the Orphic and Eleusinian mystery cults, Mithraism and, later, Christianity, were cosmopolitan. It was a natural development; with the swamping of the polis by great scale power, in the confusion of class and inter-state war, men were torn out of the close community of the city state and set adrift in a cosmopolitan world. Loyalty to the family's and to the city's gods no longer sufficed; men sought 'self-sufficiency' or individual 'salvation.' The Stoic philosophy, the inspiration of many of the noblest characters among the ruling classes of Antiquity, derived from the teaching of Zeno, who taught in the 'Stoa' or porch of the Academy at Athens. The Epicurean philosophy, on the other hand, inculcated an avoidance of pain, and tended to a withdrawal from public life. Both these doctrines were the result of a new self-consciousness, a mature criticism of life; both were the concern only of an élite minority.

For the masses, salvation was more interesting—the escape out of the misfortunes and fluctuations of the present life. Deep in the racial memories of the native populations were the traditional fertility rites, the cult of local agricultural deities, of the spirits of the corn and wine, of the god who dies for the people. To these ancient rites was added the new cult of individual salvation: the initiates of the mystery religions, like the ancient Egyptians, secured a passport to the next world, redemption from the pains of Hell. Doubtless, also, tired or satiated members of the ruling class sampled the consolations of these curious superstitions, the Orphic and Eleusinian mysteries and, later, the religion of Mithras, the slayer of the Sacred Bull.

In the field of literature the Hellenistic age established the texts of the old authors and devised the apparatus of critical scholarship as well as making new departures in pastoral and romantic poetry, drama, and prose. Theocritus, the father of pastoral poetry (*floruit* 295–270 B.C.), was born in Sicily, where he spent his youth. After living for a while in Alexandria, he settled in Kos; his poetry reflects the beauty of Sicilian and Aegean scenery and his *Idylls* have formed the model for many poets from Virgil to Milton and Tennyson. Menander, the Athenian dramatist, wrote with a verve and sophistication which made him the most popular of all the playwrights of Antiquity, and the model for Roman writers of the same school. Plutarch (A.D. 46–120), though he dates from the full maturity of the Roman empire, was Hellenistic, born in Boeotia and educated at Athens. He was an intimate of Hadrian and held high office as Procurator of Greece; his famous biographies, the *Parallel Lives,* compare the great figures of Greek and Roman history. They show a power of judgement and a fine Stoic outlook which long rendered them models for subsequent writers in this form of literature. These authors are only the best known of a great number of writers, critics, and scholars who elaborated, extended and often vulgarized the inheritance of ancient Greece.

Meanwhile commerce and agriculture flourished. The Hellenistic rulers were rich and enterprising; in the West, Carthage and its colonies developed into wealthy commercial republics, though the Phoenician plutocrats never sloughed off the cruel and barbarous ritual of their Asiatic origins, the cult of 'Baal' and Moloch and the Fire. At Syracuse a succession of able tyrants exploited the resources of Sicily and extended their influence to Italy; while in the North the peasant state of Rome was beginning to be formidable.

During the fourth century B.C. mathematical and astronomical progress continued. Euclid (*fl. c.* 323–285 B.C.) systematized the study of geometry. Archimedes laid the theoretical foundations of mechanical science; he devised an ingenious machine for hoisting water, and military engines which hurled missiles for considerable distances. According to tradition, further useful discoveries were prevented by a soldier who put an end to the philosopher, found wandering by the seashore at the time of the sack of Syracuse. Notable discoveries were made in the measurement of distance by astronomical observations; sun-dials and water clocks were improved; agricultural methods classified and defined; medical knowledge augmented, but not extended to anaesthetics, aseptic surgery or preventative sanitation. Though inferior in method to Hippocrates, the Hellenistic authority Galen exercised a dominant influence on medical science up to the Renaissance; but the causes of disease remained mysterious, and it was not until the seventeenth century that doctors discovered the circulation of the blood and not until the nineteenth that the major discoveries of modern medicine were made.

Economic processes expanded but were not transformed; there

was factory production on a considerable scale for a wide market but little development of machinery or harnessing of power comparable to that achieved by the Industrial Revolution. This relative backwardness in the exploitation of nature was due in part to the cheapness of slave labour, which also degraded the status of the craftsman and the mechanic. The ruling classes of Antiquity were uninterested in the elaboration of mechanical gadgets and despised the drudgery of systematic research. Further, instruments of precision remained elementary, efficient telescopes and microscopes were unknown; in consequence, precise investigation was impossible, and sources of power which would have transformed the social economy remained undeveloped.

None the less, by the fourth century B.C., a brilliant and far-flung civilization had come into being. It was, indeed, based on slavery and its culture confined to a minority; the rural proletariat and the native populations were in the main excluded, ultimately with disastrous effects. But, until the middle of the second century, the population increased; the courts of the Hellenistic rulers and the civic universities were centres of intelligent life; a formidable capital of knowledge had been built up and the range of civilization greatly extended. It was a dynamic and cosmopolitan world; travel was easier, trade had widely increased. Regular voyages were made to India; caravan routes were extended into Central Asia as far as China and the interior of Africa; the lands of the Western Mediterranean and Central Europe were brought into the network of Hellenistic commerce.

An unprecedented mixture of races and languages was included in this expanding world; slaves from the Celtic and northern countries, from Germany and Russia, from the Balkans, India, and Africa—many of them skilled in their respective trades—converged upon the markets of the Levant, for in return for wine and luxuries, the chiefs of the outer barbarians were ready to supply the needs of civilization. The variety, enterprise, and scale of Hellenistic culture makes it a new phenomenon. Great as had been their material achievements, eastern peoples, apart from the Chinese, whose technological skill was already great, and whose literature, as in Manrya and Gupta India, was highly sophisticated, had not displayed the same constructive intellect, moral insight, artistic ability, or power of literary expression.

V

Such were the broad results of the first great European initiative. In the cities of Ionian and mainland Greece men of genius had formulated the terms and categories of subsequent Western thought; they had discovered and charted fresh fields of knowledge, philosophical, ethical, political, and scientific. This service to humanity had been achieved by the fourth century B.C. Further, in the realm of literature, Greek Epic and Lyric poetry had opened up a new range of expression; Greek drama, oratory, and history had already determined the standard of subsequent European development; Greek sculpture and architecture had given models to the West. Thus the capital of knowledge, on which the culture of Antiquity was based and without which mediaeval and modern civilization would have been impossible, was formulated and secured, a common heritage of Europe. The second great achievement of European initiative was the diffusion of classical Greek culture over the Hellenistic world. For the first time Europeans dominated the ancient civilizations of the East; in return, the culture of Antiquity was enriched and diversified by Oriental influence. The Near Eastern conception of empire, of great-scale organization, was later taken over by the Romans, who imposed, at a price, peace and order on the Hellenistic world which they inherited, exploited, and sustained.

CHAPTER III

THE ROMAN PEACE

WHILE the genius of Hellas inspired the culture of Antiquity, the legal and political genius of Rome created the framework of European order. Rome was to expand Hellenistic culture to the west and north, to impose on Western and Southern Europe a long and widespread peace. The Roman empire in extent and scale was a colossal achievement; apart from its vast expanse in Europe, it included North Africa, Egypt, and extensive territories of the Middle East. Throughout European history the memory of Rome has never been lost; it haunted and overshadowed the Mediaeval world, and the culture of the Renaissance; and the seventeenth and eighteenth centuries, for all their originality and scientific advance, was dominated by Classical learning. The culture which Rome broadcast and preserved has remained the paramount intellectual influence in the West, and, in its Byzantine interpretation, in the Slavonic world. Without the legal and administrative genius of Rome, Hellenistic civilization would not have survived so many centuries; it would not have spread so widely and so deeply over the European continent; and the structure of Byzantium and the organization of the Catholic Church, which together preserved the traditions of civilization through the Dark Ages, would have been impossible. Not only the existence of the empire itself, but the overwhelming prestige of the imperial legend among its successor states are the dominant political facts in European history until the era of sovereign national governments.

It will be well, then, first to examine the origins of the Roman state, to trace the gradual rise of the Roman people to political and economic control of the Mediterranean, and the expansion, under Roman protection, of civic and agricultural progress to the west and north. Next, to trace the painful adaptation of the institutions of the Roman republic to the responsibilities of empire; to appreciate the phase of achievement after the settlement stabilized by Augustus; to follow in broad outline the economic and political fluctuations of the third and fourth centuries; finally, to examine the causes of the decline of the ancient world, a study which has its bearing on the problems of our own age.

The geographical situation of Italy has many advantages. The Peninsula is the natural centre of the Mediterranean; the soil and climate of central Italy west of the Apennines, the nucleus of Roman power, form a favourable environment. From earliest times the limited area of fertile land had put a premium on intensive and specialized agriculture, and the backbone of the Roman republic was the smallholding peasant farmer; the peasant armies of Rome broke Carthage and Macedon and subdued the East. The Roman republic, with its senate and magistrates, the solid structure of Roman law and language, reflect the traditions of this sturdy and tenacious stock. The leaders of the early republic formed an agrarian aristocracy, closely rooted in estates conserved for generations. Convention forbade them to take part in trade, and within their own class they were social equals; the Roman matrons commanded influence and respect, and women played an important part in social life; for in this aspect Roman society differed from that of Classical Greece.

Their religion was similar to that prevalent in the Mediterranean; the cult of civic patriotism, of the gods of family and farm. Sacrificial superstitions, auspices, omens, and astrology haunted the Roman mind and sometimes interfered with Roman strategy. But, generally speaking, Roman official religion was a bracing and austere influence, reflecting a strain of puritanism in the old Roman stock.

Besides the basic racial qualities, the institutions of the republic were the secret of her immense vitality. The Romans, like the

Greeks, were an Indo-European people; they entered Italy before the Iron Age and brought with them the vigour and freedom of a Steppe background. Their earliest traditions reflect a hatred of tyranny, and like the Greeks they had developed the practice of voting and election. An intense civic patriotism reflected their original tribal solidarity, and decisions were made by an hereditary senate which submitted laws to the ratification of a popular assembly. Consuls, appointed for short terms of office, summoned and presided over the meetings of the senate which controlled financial business and foreign policy. The interests of the body of citizens were represented by the tribunes of the people, and the Romans devised the appointment of commissions for particular tasks; in theory, though the senate determined policy, the sovereign power was in the hands of the Roman people.

The Romans had a greater capacity than the Greeks for politics and a stronger sense of public obligation; their law was at once practical, flexible, and comprehensive. It was the great achievement of Rome to devise adaptable laws capable of universal application. Greek individualism too often disregarded the laws, and Oriental conservatism tended to petrify them; Rome combined the Greek capacity for abstract thought with a sense of the changing realities of government. Further, the Romans of the republic held the statesman's office in high respect and regarded their military leaders as the servants of the state. In spite of gross cruelty and corruption and civil war, this tradition of responsibility and service was one of the finest of their legacies to Europe.

The origins of Rome are obscure. The traditional foundation of the city dates from the early eighth century; its position on a ford of the Tiber and at the meeting of road communications gave it an economic and military importance; but Roman power was long overshadowed by the Etruscan state in the north and by the cities of Magna Graecia in the south, while her Sabine and Samnite neighbours did their best to stifle the rise of a new rival. According to legend, the Romans expelled their kings by the close of the sixth century B.C., and in the opening decades of the fifth the Etruscans were crippled in a war with Syracuse. Meanwhile, the plains of Northern Italy were still inhabited by Gallic tribes, who overran Tuscany and sacked Rome (390 B.C.). This disaster was followed by a period of expansion; during the fourth century the weakened Etruscan cities were subdued and Roman power extended southward to include Naples. By the time of Alexander Rome dominated Central Italy.

The defeat of Pyrrhus, one of Alexander's imitators, who, based on the Balkans, invaded Italy and for four years threatened Rome (279–275 B.C.), was the first notable triumph of Roman arms. The next challenge was more formidable. The organization and qualities of the rising state were severely tested by the first and second Punic wars; their course had been chronicled by the contemporary Hellenistic writer, Polybius, who lived as a hostage in Rome. Schooled in this bitter contest, the senate were able to hold their own in war and diplomacy with the states of the East and ultimately to dominate them all. The tradition of the struggle with Carthage left a lasting mark on the Roman mind; it was won through predominant sea-power and the tenacity of military and political leadership. The crisis of the struggle, the Second Punic War, resulted from the calculated aggression of Roman policy, from their seizure of Sardinia, and their interference in Spain. The Roman command of the sea forced Hannibal to the gamble of invading Italy from Spanish bases vulnerable to Roman counter-attack. The crossing of the Alps (218 B.C.), probably over the St. Bernard, has been dramatized as a great feat, but apart from the difficulty presented by the elephants, Hannibal, by making his venture in the early autumn, risked no worse dangers than those faced by the migratory hordes of barbarians who with their women, children, and ox-wagons, have entered Italy through the centuries.

After Cannae, it looked as though the Carthaginian gamble would succeed; it was then, while the populace resorted to human sacrifice in the Forum, that the senate displayed the calm and resolution of the high Roman tradition. Meanwhile Scipio reduced the Carthaginian bases in Spain, and Roman delaying tactics wore down Carthaginian man-power in Italy; this, and the policy of scorched earth, was the ruin of Hannibal; and the sequel of Zama, where the avenging Roman armies destroyed the Carthaginian power (202 B.C.), gave Rome the mastery of the Western Mediterranean. Carthage itself was spared, but in 146 B.C. the Third Punic War ended with her utter destruction, after a siege and a massacre later paralleled by the destruction of Jerusalem, the other focus of Semitic power.

By the middle of the second century, Rome was easily able to take this final revenge, for the sequel to the conquest of the Western Mediterranean had been the extension of Roman power to the east. The Hellenistic states had long involved themselves in a succession of state and class wars, which form in miniature a parallel to the recent wars of the great national states of the West. The wealth of these kingdoms was spent in armaments; intolerable taxation destroyed the civic classes and forced labour spread discontent among the masses: Roman diplomacy took advantage of this situation to prevent any one state dominating the rest, and by preventive wars, the establishment of protectorates and forced alliances, Rome brought first mainland Greece and, later, Asia Minor into subjection. The Macedonian wars, the defeat of Mithridates, the establishment of a protectorate over Egypt and Pergamon, gave Rome a mastery of the Eastern as well as of the Western Mediterranean. The discipline, the bravery, and the tenacity of the old Roman stock had thus enabled Rome to survive her early vicissitudes and to become a world power. Further, the Roman tradition of public duty, efficiency, and realism had been consolidated. In the third and second centuries the most characteristic Roman qualities had already appeared, qualities shown by men racially of Roman stock. Later, with the building and administration of the empire, Rome also created a wider rule; but it was a more cosmopolitan achievement, a sequel to Hellenistic civilization, not simply a native affair, and some of its greatest figures were not even of Italian origin, let alone Roman.

The sequel to this political and economic expansion in the second century was a widening but feverish prosperity and a social revolution. Republican Rome, with its civic vitality and free institutions, had broken the power of Carthage and subdued the East; the finest Roman traditions date from the republican period. But the old order was unable to cope with the conditions its success had brought about. The senatorial class, descendants of the leading citizens of the republic, developed into an oligarchy which grew rich on the spoils of the new conquests. The revolt of the Gracchi was an unsuccessful attempt to restore the old peasant state; and, although the finest expression of Roman political ideals is to be found in the writings of Cicero, he was the prophet of a dying order.

The monopoly of social and economic power by the magnates

of the later republic was challenged both by the rise of generals commanding the loyalty of professional armies and of bankers and business men enriched by the republican conquests. The tide of social development was with these new men, who had learnt the commercial methods of the Hellenistic East. The ancient structure of senate and popular assembly, already disrupted by social and economic change, was unequal to the growing responsibilities of empire and unable to control the armies. The civil wars of Marius and Sulla showed the weakness of the old order and its incapacity for reform; they formed the prelude to the wider struggles between Julius Caesar and Pompey. It is not likely that Caesar wished to establish a monarchy, but he was driven towards dictatorship to break the power of the senatorial plutocracy, who were disrupting the life of the empire by their competition for power and their control of what were virtually private armies. Brutus, the traditional champion of republican liberty, was immensely rich; when he and his confederates murdered Caesar they were not striking a blow for anything but the privileges of an oligarchy and the memory of a tradition.

It was essential that the political life of the empire should be stabilized if the fruits of expansion were to be enjoyed. With the wealth of the conquered territories pouring into Italy, the background to the civil wars, in the main fought out in the provinces, was one of growing prosperity. Immense estates grew up in Italy financed by the capital accumulated from the plunder and tribute of the empire and worked by slave labour; Rome became a huge and expanding metropolis; magnificent villas and luxurious cities equalled the splendours of the Hellenistic East, while Northern Italy was now more fully exploited and agricultural and technical methods improved.

Unfortunately the development of great estates worked by slaves and client cultivators, often retired soldiers, was offset by the ruin of the indigenous small farmers and by a steady stream of emigration which drained Italy of some of her best agriculturists. Further, during the first century B.C., many free peasant farmers had changed their status to that of tenants to escape the obligations of military service abroad. Emigration was particularly heavy towards the newly won territories in the West, notably, after the conquest of Gaul, into Provence, where flourishing

Roman cities were established, destined to remain relatively prosperous after the ruin of Italy. Moreover, the native Roman traditions became swamped by the influx of foreign slaves, particularly from the East. Meanwhile, the sporadic flames of civil war, carried on by relatively small armies, licked round the comfortable life of the richer classes, making inroads now in one area, now in another; but the stream of loot and tribute continued to pour in, opportunities for speculation to increase, and the standard of living to expand. Architecture became more splendid and Greek artists embellished the temples and palaces of the capital; the period of the late republic and of the early empire marks the cultural climax of Roman civilization.

II

This prosperity was the sequel to the establishment of the Principate. Following on eighty years of intermittent civil war, it created the conditions of peace and stability essential for the new capitalistic economy. The full realization of this prosperity followed the victory of Octavian, afterwards the Imperator Caesar Augustus (68 B.C.–A.D. 14), who was the nephew and heir of Julius Caesar and grandson of a provincial banker. He concluded the sequel to the civil wars between Caesar and Pompey by defeating Antony at Actium. An alliance of middle-class and military power, representing the substantial elements in the Roman state, backed by plebeian support and determined on peace, had broken the senatorial magnates, while the threat of orientalized kingship, symbolized by Antony, had been staved off.

With the establishment of the Principate, the institutions of the Roman city-state were adapted to the responsibilities of world power. This solution of the problem which had baffled the republic was due in part to the ruthless political genius of Octavian; in part to the widespread disgust at the civil wars; and to the pressure of interests determined to exploit the Roman conquests. This compromise solution commanded general support, not only among the civic and professional classes of Italy and the provinces, but among the armies. The lines then laid down determined the development of a viable empire for nearly two centuries; the return of a 'golden age' was celebrated in the magnificent if artificial epic of Virgil's *Aeneid*. Europe owes much to the creators of the Roman peace; for all its vicissitudes, the extent and duration of Roman rule laid the foundations of that sense of European unity and order which survived, intermittently, into the Middle Ages, so that the Pax Romana is the outstanding political fact of the civilization of Antiquity.

The Princeps was at once the first citizen and first magistrate of the old Roman state, and the Imperator of the Legions. In theory he derived authority from the senate and people of Rome; in practice this authority predominantly devolved from the long-service professional armies without which the empire could not be maintained. This dual rôle enabled the head of the state to control the armed forces where the republican senate had failed, but his success was dependent on his personal influence. The principate was too often at the mercy of the soldiers and after the time of the Antonines it lapsed into a military dictatorship.

The political history of the Roman empire may be divided into three parts. The first comprises the sequel to the work of Augustus, the apparently constitutional principate; it survived, with many vicissitudes, for two centuries through the reigns of the Julio-Claudian and Flavian emperors to the end of the Antonine period, which concludes with the tyranny of Commodus in the last decade of the second century. Following a ruinous struggle between the armies, the empire emerged as a military autocracy under Septimius Severus (193–211), which survived the terrorist regime of Caracalla and the excesses of Heliogabalus and ended with the death of Alexander Severus (235). After a time of chaos, pestilence, and destruction, lasting through the middle years of the third century, the empire was rebuilt as a socially debased semi-Oriental despotism by Diocletian (248–305) and Constantine (306–37).

Before turning to the major features of Roman civilization and to the barbarian world beyond the borders, it is worth examining the political evolution of the empire. Here is a society which went through a series of crises and revolutions and ended in a tragic paralysis, but which long sustained a high civilization and twice recovered itself out of a desperate situation.

The Julio-Claudian house, as relatives of Augustus, enjoyed a family prestige, but they were dependent on the armies and their position was not hereditary. Their strength lay in the personal wealth which enabled them to outbid the senatorial plutocracy and conciliate the Roman mob, in the support of the civic bourgeoisie whose development the wiser emperors encouraged; in the growing bureaucracy; and in the cult of personal divinity they devised to secure the loyalty of the more backward provinces. Their power was still based in the main on Italy; their weakness that their interests became increasingly confined to Rome. Tiberius was an able if sombre character; Caligula, a degenerate; Claudius, an intelligent neurotic; and Nero, a murderous third-rate artist of deplorable tastes. His misuse of the armies and their distrust of his un-Roman habits were the end of him. The position of all but the strongest personalities was unenviable; the absolutism of precarious power produced suspicion, debauchery, and even madness. The examples of the evil of arbitrary rule provided by the worst Roman emperors have rung down the European centuries.

After a crisis (69–70) following the death of Nero, in which Galba, Otho, Vitellius, and Vespasian contested the empire, the latter established a new peace, based on a reorganized army, drawn in the main from the provincial cities. Vespasian (69–79) came of tough Italian farming stock, but he based his power originally on the armies of the East and the Danube, eventually on the empire outside Italy. His son Titus was a remarkable soldier, but Domitian proved a tyrant who was got rid of by the army and the civic classes on which the Flavian power was based. There followed a period of enlightened despotism lasting from the reigns of Trajan (98–117) and Hadrian (117–138) to that of Marcus Aurelius (161–180), which saw some realization of the stoic ideals of disinterested and intelligent administration, the golden age of the cosmopolitan empire, equal in distinction to the Augustan Age, which was primarily Roman. Hadrian came from Spain; Marcus Aurelius from Gaul; both were minds of high cultivation and sensibility, both successful and able rulers. The Hellenized upper classes of the empire worked in harmony with the imperial bureaucracy, and the army, which was recruited and paid from responsible civic elements, was still under control. But the expansion of the empire rendered the volunteer army insufficient; a degree of conscription had to be introduced, and by the second half of the second century the legions were increasingly drawn from the less-civilized country districts. Ironically, Commodus, the son of the great philosopher emperor, reverted to the worst imperial traditions. He proved a crazy and irresponsible tyrant; with his murder the Antonine period ends, and with it the constitutional principate.

The dictatorship of Septimius Severus (193–211) depended upon a semi-barbarized army. The bane of Roman civilization, unbridled military power, was becoming parasitic on the empire it had to defend. Further, the loss of educational and administrative ability following the ruin of the civic class by taxation, the gradual whittling down of standards, mark the beginning of the decline of ancient civilization. Caracalla systematically plundered the upper classes to conciliate the soldiers, and Heliogabalus was obsessed with Eastern religious cults and dreams of Oriental conquest; after a rally under Alexander Severus (222–235) the empire lapsed into military anarchy.

The work of rehabilitation achieved by Diocletian won peace at a heavy price. The upper class which had ruled the empire in the second century had now been eliminated; the principate had become an hereditary despotism, the ruling class a proletarian army. Debased, standardized, but vigorous, this crude organization gave the empire a final lease of life.

The causes of the decline of the empire must later be examined; in spite of vicissitudes, it had been highly successful. The whole duration of the Roman world-state covers roughly half a millennium, a great span of time, and though ancient civilization declined after the second century, the empire secured peace for long periods over wide areas, whose inhabitants came to regard the imperial government as a fact of nature and to assume the unity even of a debased civilization.

By the close of the first century A.D., the empire included Transylvania and Roumania, Armenia and Iraq, while, in the West, Britain had been annexed, the hold on Gaul consolidated, and the Rhine frontier secured. Over the western seaboard and the Iberian Peninsula, over Switzerland and France, over Provence and North Italy, over most of Bohemia and the Danubian lands, over the borders of the Southern Ukraine and over all the

Balkans, the Roman rule held sway; while outside Europe were the rich North African provinces, Egypt, and great territories of the Near East.

The Augustan principate laid the foundations of a bureaucracy which reached its highest efficiency under Hadrian and the Antonines; it was developed steadily through the vicissitudes of imperial politics, staffed by freedmen of the imperial household and from the *curiales*. Under the later empire it became militarized and debased; but in the earlier period administrators were carefully chosen, corruption notably decreased, and taxation was organized according to Hellenistic method.

Roman law developed steadily from the time of Cicero to that of the great jurists Ulpian and Papinian. The Romans translated Greek ideas into their own monumental language, where they gained wider currency and a rigid definition suited for survival through the Dark Ages. They also built up a body of law reflecting the experience of wide administration and applicable to a world state. The most important aspect of Roman law was its universality and relative humaneness: the idea of a universal law which particular laws reflect is already defined by Cicero in the *De Republica* and the *De Legibus* in the middle first century B.C.

Though equality of wealth and ability is impracticable, all citizens, he argues, should be equal before the law . . . 'unalterable and eternal . . . one law for all people and at all times.' Such a law transcends the personal fiat of a dictator; if a tyrant should 'put to death with impunity anyone he wishes . . . without trial,' he violates an eternal justice. These principles, the distinction between the prince who rules according to law and the tyrant who declares that the laws are 'in his own breast,' are of cardinal importance, the basis of civilized society, reinforcing the Platonic and Aristotelian idea of the moral purpose of the state. They survived into the Middle Ages to be a powerful influence in Modern times.

Under the empire Roman law became further extended and universalized; the great jurists elaborated and defined the inheritance, and Justinian's Byzantine lawyers in the sixth century codified it in its final form. Together with the Latin language, it formed a binding link between the diverse populations of the imperial cities.

The empire, and very often the stability of the government, depended on a relatively small standing army of not more than half a million men, based on supply services and communications of unprecedented efficiency. The legionaries were trained in the methodical conduct of war; unlike the armies of the republic, they were soldiers by career, drawn from all over the empire. Illyrians and Spaniards formed part of the garrison of Britain; German and Gallic soldiers policed Judea; the later emperors themselves, as we have seen, were often of diverse racial origins.

The legions were equipped for siege warfare and trained in disciplined battle tactics. Their equipment was comprehensive and efficient: besides the short stabbing sword and throwing spear, they carried entrenching tools and defensive armour; their leggings and heavy boots were designed for campaigning in all weathers and rough country, and they could cover twenty or thirty miles a day. Some of their marching songs have come down to us; their subjects are generally unprintable, and their rhythms catching.

Against the disciplined attack of these professional armies, the Belgic chariot charge and light armed Gallic cavalry were ineffective, and since the use of stirrups was unknown to Antiquity and the evolution of the heavy armed knight impossible, only in desert and steppe warfare had mounted troops a good chance against infantry. The standard of Roman generalship could be very high: the campaigns of Scipio Africanus, of Julius Caesar, and of Vespasian are notable examples. The organized might of Rome conquered the outlying empire with comparative ease; it was only through the barbarization of the armies and internal social collapse that the outer barbarians got their opportunity in the fourth and fifth centuries.

Roman sea power, on the other hand, seems to have developed, not by natural aptitude, but by necessity, though the Carthaginian wars had been won by naval supremacy and the empire was always dependent on sea-power and communications. The Romans conducted a naval action on the principles of a land battle; their war galleys were propelled, in the ancient tradition of Mediterranean warfare from the days of Salamis to Lepanto, by the beat of banked oars. They manœuvred either to ram their opponents, or, shearing sideways through splintering timber, to close, grapple, and board. Conditions on the benches were generally hideous; the chant of the overseer was punctuated by the crack of the lash over the sweating galley slaves. The navies of Roman Antiquity, unlike the fleets of the western seaboard, were no school of ingenuity and self-reliance; brutal and elementary as may have been life in the great days of sail, it marked an improvement in morale and living conditions over the days of rowers chained to the oar. Outside the Mediterranean, Roman sea power never notably developed; during the first invasion of Britain, confronted with the Channel tides, even Caesar miscalculated. In general the shipping of Antiquity, though it attained a considerable tonnage, never came near the power of sail and manoeuvre achieved in the Channel and the Atlantic by the sixteenth and seventeenth centuries. Though climatic conditions explain much, it is likely also that enterprise in this field, as in others, was limited by the cheapness of slave labour.

The Roman empire was thus sustained by standing armies formidably equipped and highly organized, but too small to meet the widespread external threats liable to develop on many fronts if internal war diverted the armed forces from their proper function. The policing of the seas, vital to the continuance of Mediterranean civilization, was long maintained; but in the middle third century piracy revived; then the barbarians took to the sea, and communications deteriorated. When in the fifth century the Vandals conquered North Africa and thence invaded Italy, the relative order of the Mediterranean world was broken.

III

Within the framework of the empire, sustained by the structure of a world state, and protected from external aggression until the collapse in the third century, a great cosmopolitan culture developed; its most enduring monument is the Latin language. Latin literature may be considered in four periods; the first covering the third and second centuries B.C.; the second, the late Republic; the third, the Augustan Age; the fourth, the Silver Age of the second century.

The beginnings of Latin are extremely crude; it was the dialect of the farmers of Latium, clumsy and uncouth but already direct, compendious, memorable. It included Etruscan and Celtic elements, and with its curious reduplications and ugly genitive and ablative endings, would have appeared a tongue with little future to a Greek of the third century; yet it was destined to prove one of the strongest influences in imposing and maintaining the common culture of Europe. Apart from folk chants, gnomic verses, harvest homes and the like, the earliest Roman writings are Laws, Annals, and Fasti recording public events; the Twelve Tables of Roman Law date from the middle fifth century.

During the third century Greek influence transformed Latin into the lucid instrument of Roman power. It is with the playwright and poet Ennius, a Hellenized Calabrian in the first half of the second century B.C., that the first sustained Latin verse appears; he introduced the hexameter, and though his lines are often halting and clumsy, he could already coin the massive and memorable phrase commemorating Q. Fabius Maximus Cunctator—*Unus homo nobis cunctando restituit rem.*[1]

Through the expansion to the east in the third and second centuries, the parvenu conquerors of the Hellenistic world were confronted with the full brilliance of Greek civilization. It was through the Drama that Greek influence was most widely brought to bear on the Roman mind; the plays of Plautus and Terence imitate the technique and outlook of the Greek dramatist Menander; their popular plays gave the provincial Roman audience a glimpse of the sophisticated life of Athens. A more native outlook is apparent in the writings of Cato the Censor, who wrote an encyclopaedic treatise on law and agriculture in the first half of the second century, a characteristic prologue to later Latin literature.

Under the late republic, Latin attained its full maturity. The writings of Cicero and the great philosophical poem of Lucretius, the lyric poetry of Catullus and the terse narratives of Julius Caesar, show Latin writers masters of their own medium. The brilliant prose of Cicero, the flexible complex cadence of his oratory, show a complete assimilation of Greek originals; his influence both on the early Christian Fathers and on mediaeval writers was to surpass that of any other classical author. The

[1] 'One man restored our fortunes by delay.'

English poet Hoccleve, writing a lament for Chaucer in the opening years of the fifteenth century, could still think the highest
praise to give his master was to compare him to 'Tully.'[1]

During this period Rome produced two remarkable poets:
Lucretius (99–54 B.C.) whose *De Rerum Natura* is the forceful and
profound Roman expression of Hellenistic epicureanism; and
Catullus who, like Virgil, was born in Cis-Alpine Gaul, of a family
of small landowners settled near Verona. His love poetry, modelled
on the Greek, is individual, introspective, and elegant; he was a
master of intricate rhythm and turns the phrases of colloquial
speech into musical and moving poetry.

Seldom has a soldier of genius recorded his campaigns with a
more deceptive impartiality than Caesar. This inflexible careerist,
brilliant, versatile, and hard, was the master of a detached and
lucid prose. The *Commentaries* or 'Notes on the Gallic Wars,'
with their modest title and studied understatement, were designed to demonstrate that personal ambition was not their author's motive in adding Gaul to the Roman Empire. Though
with the writings of Livy, the *Commentaries* have been a scholastic plague to generations, when studied in relation to the geography of France and to modern knowledge of the Iron Age Celtic
peoples, they are revealing and interesting.

The Augustan Age saw the climax of Latin poetry in the writings of Virgil and in the mellow urbanity of Horace, the Latin
poet most congenial to the eighteenth century, who expresses
with finished technique the disillusionment of a mature society.
Virgil, the greatest Latin poet, was born near Mantua in Northern Italy; the *Aeneid* is a studied and deliberate glorification of
the Roman state; the serenity and power of Augustan Rome is
commemorated in majestic and splendid language touched with
a sense of the sadness of mortal fate, and Virgil's bucolic and
pastoral poetry, following on the tradition of Theocritus, shows a
sense of landscape unusual in ancient writers.

Livy is the most famous prose writer of the Augustan Age; he
was born near Padua and he is in theme, if not in style, the Ma-
caulay of Roman literature. His immense history, of which three-
quarters has been lost, formed a deliberate writing up of the

---

[1] '. . . for unto Tullius
    Was never so lyke amonges us.'

heroic period of Roman tradition, the Carthaginian Wars. His conception of history is rhetorical and his idea of a battle academic, but his prose is flexible and compact and his influence on historical writing has been considerable.

One of the most technically proficient and best known of the Augustan Roman poets is Ovid; his narrative skill rendered his verse popular among his contemporaries and made an unfailing appeal to the mediaeval mind. The *Metamorphoses* in particular, with their neat and obvious metre, their assembly of popular stories in compendious form, and their easily memorable turn of phrase, have endeared this knowing writer to many hearts.

Ovid marks the beginning of the Silver Age in Latin literature, which is characterized by incisive satirical verse, one of the few original Roman literary inventions. Of the poets, Juvenal and Martial castigated the manners of the age; both wrote a hard-hitting epigrammatic style, similar to that of Dryden and Pope in the English classical period. Juvenal's satire is singularly brutal and Martial's meaning is all too plain.

The writers of metropolitan Rome produced not only epigrams and invective but also a more urbane observation of the social comedy. The *Satyricon* of Petronius, a fragmentary picaresque novel, depicts the contemporary Roman underworld. Petronius, who lived in the reign of Nero, was a man of the world whom nothing could disconcert: he employs the argot of common speech to depict the adventures of runaway slaves and the solecisms of the *nouveau riche* Trimalchio. His narratives live, and his book has affinities with Voltaire's *Candide*, the characters being helpless before a social situation of which the horror is redeemed only by the farce. He also left fragmentary poems of merit.

In contrast to the observant Petronius, Seneca in the first half of the first century, who came of Spanish extraction, carried on the portentous tradition of Roman moralizing; he popularized a solid tradition and his essays were widely imitated in classical and modern times. A greater artist in prose was Tacitus, an historian of outstanding calibre and a stylist of the first order: his *Annales, Agricola,* and *Historiæ* are in the tradition of Thucydides. Like his master's, his theme was one of disillusionment: in attacking by contrast the corruptions of his age, he gives a tendentious description of the Teutonic tribes on the Rhine, taken too often *au pied de la lettre*. Suetonius, who wrote *The Lives of the Caesars*, was private secretary to the Emperor Hadrian; he had access to the imperial archives, and made full use of it. The result was a straightforward and lurid history, written in a fluent style, which has long enjoyed wide popularity. Two other well-known writers of the early Imperial Age are the Elder and Younger Pliny. The first wrote an encyclopaedic *Natural History*, a storehouse of inaccurate information, taken for gospel truth throughout the Middle Ages; the second has left correspondence which much illuminates his age.

Under the later empire, from the age of the Antonines to the days of Eusebius and Lactantius and the panegyrists of Constantine in the fourth century, there was a literary decline. Though the Christian Fathers evolved a prose of alarming eloquence and immense vocabulary, of which St. Augustine's *De Civitate Dei* is the greatest example, serving as a model for mediaeval Latin, the general tendency was towards a degradation of style reflecting social circumstance. And, indeed, looking back over the development of the major Latin writers, it is remarkable how the changing tone and quality of the literature reflects the qualities of its age. The sturdy limitations of early Latin develop into the eloquence of Cicero and the terse narrative of Caesar; the maturity of the Augustan Age is reflected in the *Aeneid;* the beginnings of decadence in the versification of Ovid and the bitterness of Juvenal; Petronius mocks a situation that might otherwise call for tears, and with Tacitus the old order analyses a world heading for disaster. In the fourth century too, the writings of Ausonius, a native of Bordeaux, who was tutor to Gratian and rose to be consul, though redeemed by a Celtic appreciation of the beauty of the Moselle vineyards, in general show a mechanical and perverse ingenuity. The same close reflection of social circumstance is to be found in other literatures; like art, literature is, in general, a telling indication of the health or decadence of a society.

The surviving Latin literature became, in variously garbled forms, the inheritance of mediaeval Christendom. With the Renaissance it was more fully explored, and in the eighteenth century became an overwhelming influence; this legacy, like that of

Roman Law, has united Europeans for generations in a common literary background. It will be seen how various interpretations were made in different countries of this ancient tradition; in conjunction with Greek literature and the Bible it was destined to form the common basis of the national literatures of Western Europe.

To the material advance of civilization Rome made notable contributions, particularly in architecture and engineering. The scale of Roman buildings was remarkable and the impression they made on barbarian peoples overwhelming. The ruins of Roman aqueducts overshadowed the huddled mediaeval towns of Italy and Southern France, and the architects of such monumental works were regarded as magicians.

The building of early Rome were uninspiring, but Rome, like Athens, was fortunate in her access to good marble. The quarries of Carrara, like the quarries of Pentelicus for fifth-century Athens, provided superb material for the buildings of the Augustan Age. Sun-dried brick had been the basic material for republican Rome; the extensive use of burnt brick and of cement encouraged the construction of vaults and arches on a large scale. Problems of drainage and water supply were systematically tackled by Roman architects, who developed Hellenistic ideas. Roman towns in the conquered provinces were laid out on the plan of a camp; after the Legions came engineers and architects. Pilate's attempt to bring an aqueduct to Jerusalem to give the Jews a clean water supply was one of the reasons for his unpopularity.

The principles of Roman architecture and town planning were formulated by Vitruvius, who dedicated his famous work, *De Architectura,* to Octavian; it was to exercise an immense influence over the architects of the Renaissance and eighteenth century. The author was Controller of Artillery of the Roman armies and had organized the plumbing of Rome: his work is very full and comprehensive; he quotes extensively from Greek treatises, and lays down not only the principles of building but of the selection of sites, of town planning in relation to the prevalent winds, and of the orientation of roads. The architectural inheritance of Rome is one of her greatest legacies to Europe; though the scale and weight of Roman public buildings can seem gross, and to lack the fine lines and economy of the best Greek work, the good sense of Roman town planning, the vision and force which could drive Roman roads over immense distances, and the skill reflected in the construction of great fortifications and aqueducts, set a standard which was revived in Early Modern times.

In artistic creation Rome was less successful. The standard of wall painting and decoration was pleasing but derivative; only the sculptors inherited the finished Hellenistic skill, though the force of the colossal statues of the emperors and the subtlety of many private busts of the first and second centuries for long showed a healthy tradition, but, save in mosaic, after the Antonines there is a gradual debasement of art, reflecting the tastes of a new ruling class.

And indeed generally, apart from the fine taste of a Hellenized minority at the top, Roman society was elementary in its tastes. The amphitheatre played a central part in the life both of Rome and the provincial cities. The games bulked particularly large in the life of the capital. Gladiators, blinking through visored helmets and swathed and padded to the eyes, stabbed at one another with practised virtuosity. Unarmed combat had to be made more deadly by binding lead inside the clenched fists of the competitors, and the climax of the day was the beast fight. Numidian lions, elephants and tigers from India, wild bulls from Spain, were imported over great distances for the benefit of the Roman mob. It was also a widespread custom to use the arena as a scene of executions, and the disposal of criminals or religious minorities during a phase of persecution was methodically unpleasant. There were mass crucifixions, a form of torment characteristically popularized by the Carthaginians, while criminals were driven in droves to the animals. Alternatively, the victims would be bound to stakes fixed on small hand-carts and trundled into the ring by slaves; the beasts could then easily settle on their prey, while the crowd roared under the silk awnings, and rose petals and perfumes, scattered by an ingenious device, descended on to the hot sand of the arena. This kind of entertainment, taken for granted in Roman Antiquity, gives the measure of the callousness and brutality of the pre-Christian world and can still be sensed by anyone who visits the Colosseum at Rome.

Such bestial public spectacles show how thin was the veneer of

Classical culture over the masses in Antiquity, and here we have perhaps the main clue to the decline of this great civilization. But before turning to the causes of this decline, it will be well to glance at the situation outside the empire; first to sketch the characteristics of the Germanic barbarians who were to be the most formidable and the most baneful influence on the empire, next to trace the contrasting development of the Celtic peoples, finally to note the characteristics of the Dacian and Sarmatian barbarians of Eastern Europe.

IV

From the ninth century B.C. the dominant fact of Central European history had been the expansion of the Germans. The centre of Germanic disturbance appears to have been Southern Scandinavia and the Baltic Plain: the bulk of these tribes had probably settled there out of the Eastern Steppe or swarmed out of Scandinavia. It is certain that the Vandals, Burgundians, and Goths, who were to push southwards with devastating results in the closing years of the empire, were in the Baltic plain by the third century B.C. It is thought the Vandals came originally from Jutland, the Burgundians from Pomerania and Southern Denmark, and the Goths from Sweden; the Lombards, too, emerged from this climatically unfavorable area.

Now, although the migrations of these peoples are most conspicuous in the Dark Ages, Teutonic tribes had long been pushing down into Central Germany; by the middle of the first millennium before Christ, they were displacing the Celts in North-West Germany and the Rhineland. Their incursions, together with a deterioration of climate, account in part for the Celtic migrations. These had already affected Italy in the fourth century, and were paralleled by the movements of Iron Age Celtic peoples into the Balkans, Spain, Gaul, and the British Islands. Thus the trend of the barbarian world was migration, radiating south and west from the focal pivot of the South Baltic area. By the time of Caesar there were Germanic tribes west of the Rhine, and when Tacitus described them in the second century, they had also consolidated their position in Central Germany—the Chatti in Hesse, the Cimbri on the Weser, the Suebi in Saxony and Thuringia. In the course of centuries they had intermarried with the old Neolithic population in the North-East, with the aboriginal populations of the Baltic lands, and as they approached the plateaux and mountains of the South, with the Alpine roundheads who had long been settled in the area. The original northern strain was thus modified.

The Germanic tribes early displayed common characteristics. Their basic economy of mixed peasant farming and stock breeding was adapted from the Neolithic and Bronze Age peoples. They possessed small hornless cattle, in which they reckoned wealth, and practised the ordinary agriculture of the Early Iron Age, carried on mainly by women and slaves. The tribal warriors regarded such work as degrading and during the summer employed themselves in war; during the winter they passed the time in drinking, hunting, and gambling. They were a rapacious and bellicose people and by the second century their aggression was not the result of land hunger but of temperament. They loved crude ornament and in course of time drained the increasingly subservient empire of a high proportion of its gold.

Their social organization was tough and healthy. Tribal and family feeling was strong, the sentiment of personal honour and loyalty well developed; moreover, the results of their violent temper were modified by the substitution of agreed fines for blood feud, and without such arrangements their numbers might have gravely diminished. The Germans, like other barbarian peoples, worshipped deities of fertility and war and personified the forces of nature in the cult of various gods. Like other Indo-European peoples, they had folk-moots and tribal assemblies and their kings possessed no absolute authority. This talent for rudimentary self-government was more fully developed among the kindred Franks, and particularly among the Scandinavians and the Anglo-Saxons; it was destined to contribute a most valuable element to the political development of Europe and it will be more fully described in an ensuing chapter. Here, then, by the second century A.D., was a formidable fact for Southern Europe. Scattered throughout the forests and clearings of Central Germany, superimposed on the aboriginal Neolithic and Bronze Age stocks, were a variety of predatory and vigorous peoples who constituted an increasing threat to the peaceful way of life on which the empire was based. As the man-power of Italy and the provinces diminished, the legions were recruited more and more from the Germans, who were also invited to settle inside the borders as clients and allies. In consequence, the empire became increasingly Germanized from within, while the external threat remained a steady menace. The sequel will be apparent in the history of the Dark Ages.

The other dominant peoples in the outer barbarian world of Antiquity showed marked contrast in temperament and manner of living with the German tribes. From the eighth century onwards the Celts emerge into history, spreading outwards from settlements in Central Europe, in Bohemia, on the upper Danube, in the Rhineland, and the northern foothills of the Alps. Although their origin is obscure—like other Indo-European tribes they probably came into Europe out of the Steppe—they first appear east of the Rhine, and the so-called Celtic lands on the Atlantic seaboard were among the last they settled. It seems partly they were pushed outwards from their original Central European settlements by Germanic pressure from the North-East. Around the middle of the first millennium B.C. Celtic migrations spread to France and Spain, to Italy and the British Islands, finally to the Balkans and Asia Minor. No more than the Germans were they ethnographically a separate race, but intermarried with the peoples on whom they imposed their domination. The Celts had marked common characteristics; they early assimilated a veneer of civilization, and in contrast to the often crude and destructive Germans, possessed artistic and poetic imagination. The Celtic aristocracies of the Iron Age show the turbulence, the love of display, the recklessness, and the political instability which were to persist among their descendants in those areas where Celtic influence was predominant. They fought on horseback or from chariots drawn by small shaggy ponies; they buried their dead in barrows or in big cemeteries, and built massive hill forts with complex fortifications: they had a passion for ornament; for bizarre and brightly coloured clothes, for rich shields and helmets, for necklaces and amulets of bronze and beaten gold; they imported quantities of wine from the South and set store by elaborate drinking horns and jewellery. The

Romans were impressed by their stature, by their white skins and reddish hair, which they wore long and arranged in striking fashions. They would rush yelling into battle, naked, and brandishing great swords so badly tempered that after a blow they might need straightening under foot. According to contemporary accounts, the Celts were quick, truculent, and boastful, given to flattery and full of charm; hospitable and honourable according to their code, but unreliable for any sustained effort, individualists impatient of discipline. They could seldom combine against a common enemy and were much given to internecine feuds. Yet they were a forceful and talented people, patrons of minstrels and artists. By the fourth century they were beginning to absorb a veneer of Greek influence; their Druid priests combined barbarian cults with ideas assimilated from the Hellenistic world. While Augustus and his successors were ruling in Rome, the Celtic peoples even on the outer fringes of civilization had, indeed, attained a considerable prosperity. They imposed a barbaric culture on their subject peoples. The Celts would seem to have blended most fully with the dark longheads of the Atlantic seaboard; 'Half civilized, half savage, they lived masterful, passionate lives in an atmosphere utterly remote from what literary men today term the Celtic twilight.'[1] The romantic legends which have clustered about these people, particularly in the West, derived probably from the subject peoples on whom they made a vivid and alarming impression.

Other picturesque barbarians made their appearance on the fringes of the Roman world. We have already observed how Darius attempted in vain to subdue the Scythians of the lower Danubian steppe; in the second century the Dacians and the Getae had penetrated into the Hungarian plain, and the former were raiding south into the Balkans. Like the Celts, the Dacians imposed a predatory domination on the descendants of Neolithic agriculturalists: they built Cyclopean fortresses in the foothills of the Carpathians. Like all these steppe peoples, they were skilled horsemen and archers; they worshipped a Holy Bear from whom they imagined themselves descended, and they rode into battle under a dragon ensign.

Eastward of the Danubian lands the Sarmatians and the Alans,

[1] *C.A.H.* Vol. VII, p. 74.

Indo-European peoples of Iranian origin and speech, had established themselves north of the Sea of Azov and were moving westward by the time of Augustus. These people were culturally Asiatic and little influenced by Hellenistic ideas; their art, like the Scythian, with its angular animal motifs, is paralleled in Central and Eastern Asia. They were horsemen who moved in close formation over the steppe; heavily armed cavalry with pointed helmets and scale armour of metal or horn, flanked and preceded by a cloud of trousered archers, slung about with scarlet quivers and using the small twisted Tatar bow. These steppe barons grew rich on the plunder of the lands of the black earth and the coastal plain, and their craftsmen wrought bizarre and brilliant enamel plaques and brooches, cloaks and saddle cloths. The Byzantine heavy cavalry modelled their tactics and equipment on these redoubtable enemies. The designs brought by these Eastern peoples into Europe, like the curves and spirals of Celtic decoration, were destined to contribute a new element to European art.

On the scale of this canvas one cannot give more than this summary sketch of the mysterious, picturesque and fluctuating barbarian world beyond the borders of the empire. In outer Europe, superimposed on the basic aboriginal populations, were peoples with already recognizable characteristics, destined to affect profoundly the development of civilization. And of these peoples the most influential were the Germans and the Celts.

The threat of the German barbarians was the most formidable, the more so as Roman power was never extended into the interior of Germany. The ferocity of the tribes and the extent and nature of the wooded country daunted the Roman generals; after the defeat of Varus, the Romans, having consolidated the Rhineland, the most fertile and accessible part of Germany, reverted to a defensive policy. Though conquest was probably impracticable, the failure to include Germany in the empire had important results both in the short and the long view. The country remained a reservoir of barbarism which threatened the empire near its weakest link of the Danube, where the land communications from the East passed into Italy, and the failure of the Germans to assimilate Latin ideas of order and legality, the temperamental antagonism they showed to the tradition of European order and to the ways of Classical thought, were later to be apparent.

V

The causes of the decline of ancient civilization are manifold and interesting. As already noted, politically the Roman world state stifled the vitality of the Hellenistic cities, while foreign influences undermined the ancient republican order. With the deification of the emperors, the empire became increasingly orientalized, while the barbarian elements in the armies were a source of violence and unrest. Yet the Roman world was not destroyed by barbarians, though by infiltration as mercenaries and allies, and by direct attack they contributed to its decline. Nor was the growing poverty of the later empire due mainly to the exhaustion of the land—there was depopulation in Greece and Italy, but Greece had always been a poor country; deforestation diminished fertility in the South, but Egypt and Gaul retained a good level of prosperity. There was indeed a steady decline in the birth rate among the upper and official classes, but this alone could not account for the collapse. It is true also that the economic system of Antiquity never disposed of the markets which would have made further expansion possible, since purchasing power was never extended to the mass of the people; in the geographical and social circumstances of Mediterranean Antiquity, modern industry and modern advertising never developed. The expensive and clumsy imperial bureaucracy, the heavy taxation, the cycle of civil wars, and the widespread imposition of an economic caste system in an attempt to retain industrial skill, all these things contributed to a gradual but steady decline. But the fundamental cause was the failure of the upper class to extend their culture to the rural and the urban proletariat. The Russian historian Rostovtzeff, still the best authority on the age, after analysing various explanations of the decline, comes to the following considered and significant conclusion. 'We may say, then, there is one permanent feature of the development of the ancient world during the Imperial Age, alike in the political, social and economic, and in the intellectual field. It is a gradual absorption of the higher classes by the lower, accompanied by a gradual levelling down of standards. . . . The evolution of the Ancient World,' he concludes, 'has a lesson and a warning for us.'[1]

By the middle third century the failure of civic vitality and the deteriorating economic position were producing serious results. As already remarked, the period of the Antonines saw the last revival of a distinguished but derivative culture. The political weakness of the empire had always been the failure of the civil power to control the armies, and the discontent of the masses was exploited in a series of conflicts between rival adventurers. Power fell to military leaders, often of proletarian origin, who could command the widest following among the legions. Those who fought their way to power established a precarious and orientalized despotism; the threat of military tyranny which had haunted the empire since the days of Caesar had materialised in a crude and brutal form. Since power was now in the hands of uncouth military despots, dependent on supporters who claimed their reward, the remnants of the urban upper class on whom the whole civic structure of the empire depended were ruined by taxation and the imperial bureaucracy terrorized by their new masters. In consequence corruption and incompetence increased, while the economic position went from bad to worse. Markets within the empire were contracting, the standard of living was going down, and there were no new fields for exploitation. And all along the demands of administration and defence were insistent, while the more able rulers tried to stabilize the situation according to their lights. But the loss of intellectual standards was reflected in the growing stupidity of an administration which at its best had bungled the economic problem. Policy became more fumbling and ineffective: by the fourth century there is a growing note of timidity, even of despair, and a coarsening of artistic and literary expression.

The scapegoats for the catastrophes which befell the empire had long been the Christians, whose organization, none the less, had been spreading during the second and third centuries. The nature, background, and effects of the new religion will be examined in the following chapter. By the time of Diocletian the movement was extremely powerful and the emperor made an

[1] *Social and Economic History of the Roman Empire.*

ineffective attempt at its final destruction. Following on this failure, Constantine, in the early fourth century, allowed toleration to Christianity and made it virtually the established religion of the empire, though he was cautious enough to postpone baptism until his deathbed. After a phase of renewed persecution under the Emperor Julian, the Christian Church was established by Theodosius (A.D. 379–95) as the sole religious authority within the empire.

The decision of Constantine, together with the transference of the capital to Constantinople, marked the completion of a process whereby the Augustan Principate was transformed into a totalitarian state organized on Oriental lines. The emperor assumed the leadership of the Church and appointed the Patriarch; the new Imperial Government thus developed affinities with the Persian despotism and with the Mohammedan Kalifate in Mesopotamia of the early Middle Ages. By placing the new capital in a strategically defensible position, and tying down the imperial household to one locality, Constantine's foresight prevented his successors from becoming the puppets of the legions. The imperial capital was a great and splendid city; no longer, as it had tended to be, a movable camp. At the price of losing some of the most valuable and original aspects of the Roman inheritance, the Byzantine theocracy preserved the security of the East, and so consolidated the position that Justinian, in the sixth century, was able to reassert a short-lived domination over most of Italy. But the outlook of Constantine's empire was already profoundly different from that of Classical Greece and Republican or Augustan Rome. Orthodox and bureaucratic, this civilization was more akin to the ancient states of the Near East; like them, its government was autocratic, and like them, it was intensely conservative. Indeed, the barbarized West was to prove more inventive than the Graeco-Roman world. Already, in the so-called Dark Ages, the stirrup, the horse-collar and the heavy plough would provide the dynamic technological basis for the twelfth century revival in the West in all its originality and vision.

Yet for all its depressing conclusion, the Roman achievement had been immense. The initiative of a small peasant state, strategically well placed in the centre of the Italian peninsula, itself the natural pivot of the Mediterranean world, had built up an organization which included most of Western and much of Eastern Europe, Asia Minor, and North Africa. The Romans had broadcast and secured the cultural inheritance of the Hellenistic peoples, of which the material basis had been created in the Near East in far-distant times, and of which the intellectual inspiration was Greek. Though this culture was confined to a generally callous minority, disfigured by slavery, economically inefficient and periodically convulsed by civil war, yet a habit of peace set in over great areas and over many years. Further, the compact, lucid, and memorable Latin speech, the vehicle of imperial edicts and civic administration, and the medium whereby Hellenistic ideas became widely known in the West, superseded the native languages in the countries subsequently termed Latin. In its mediaeval form it became the language of the Roman Church and of European learning until modern times. The legacy of Roman Law and architecture has been stressed; the discipline and order behind the Roman name. For all their limitations, their lack of originality, their lack of scientific flair, the legacy of Rome to Europe is comparable in importance to that of Hellas, for, in spite of brutality and exploitation, it set a standard of statesmanship, administration, and justice which, in its own sphere, can compare with the intellectual brilliance of Greece. The credit for the building of the Roman republic, from which all else followed, must go to the limited, forceful, and tenacious peasant farmers of the original Roman stock. To them, as to the free citizens of Hellas, Europe owes a great debt.

CHAPTER IV

THE CHRISTIAN REVOLUTION

WITH the decline of Classical culture, the loss of standards and of political power by the educated minority, a profound revolution had set in. There were many reasons, as we have observed, for the catastrophe, but the failure suggests the spiritual limitations of Graeco-Roman civilization. In these circumstances, in a world given over to proletarian and barbarous influences, ruled by military dictators and displaying an increasing degradation of intellectual and artistic skill, only a highly emotional religion was strong enough to inspire constructive action. By a fortunate event this religion was Christianity. From obscure beginnings the new religion had long been permeating all ranks of society; it was destined to transform the civilization of Europe. Yet Christianity was more than a means whereby the remnants of Classical culture were preserved and the social order reinvigorated; it brought a new and deeper spiritual insight. Though defined in terms of Jewish theology and bringing with it a mythology and an intolerance inferior to the intellectual freedom of the Classical world, it contained within this medium a 'Gospel,' a 'Good News,' of salvation and charity which endowed it with daemonic power. The spiritual force and compassion of the Lord's Prayer and Beatitudes were the inspiration of Christianity; it is, therefore, just to speak of a Christian revolution, so new an element was brought into human affairs, so new a turn given to the development of the European tradition. Christianity brought a radical change of outlook; its influence profoundly differentiates Mediaeval and Modern civilization from that of Antiquity.

It will thus be necessary first to follow in outline the development of the Jewish tradition, the medium through which the new religion was brought into Europe, and to trace the two strains, one of charity, love, and faith in the Fatherhood of God, the other of asceticism and intolerance which disfigured Jewish thought and in its Gentile interpretation conflicted with the original spirit of Christianity. Having examined the nature of the new movement, we will observe its rise to political power, and give some account of the influence of the early Christian Fathers, who elaborated the theological doctrines which determined mediaeval thought. Next one must take account of the social structure of New Rome, the city of Constantine, deliberately founded to preserve the declining society of the Ancient World. It was a retreat of civilization nearer to the lands of its origin and it succeeded in retaining the traditions of Antiquity under the altered forms of orthodox Christianity and a theocratic state. Though the unity of the Empire was broken, the transference of the Imperial capital to Constantinople allowed a free and original development in the West, the result of the combined initiative of the converted Northern peoples and of the Papacy.

The Semitic race has produced three world religions, Judaism, Christianity and Mohammedanism, all monotheistic, all proclaiming the omnipotence of a Universal God. The conquest of Europe by the second and of great tracts of Asia and Africa by the third are outstanding facts of history. What were the qualities which enabled the Prophets of these great religions to spread their gospels to the ends of the earth? The history of the Jews may give some answers, and since Western Europeans for centuries were mentally dominated by the Jewish scriptures, it will be well to set Jewish history in a short perspective and relate it to our main theme.

We have seen already how the Phoenicians had swarmed over the seas of the Levant and had captured the carrying trade of the decadent Minoan and Mycenean world. By the Early Iron Age they had founded Carthage (*c.* 800 B.C.) and were achieving a gross prosperity. Meanwhile, during the Middle Bronze Age, another branch of the Semitic race had settled in Egypt. With the expulsion of the Hyksos in the sixteenth century, the Jewish tribes were driven out of Egypt and took to the desert. Here under the leadership of Moses, they developed a fierce solidarity and Puritanism. Their tribal God, Yahweh, waged ruthless war upon other Gods and detested the sacrifices, image worship, and fertility rites universal in the Near East. He was a desert God who thundered out of Sinai, an incalculable God whose name was unspoken and whose appearance remained mysterious, since it was blasphemy to portray him. This uncanny quality shocked and alarmed the Greeks and Egyptians and later the Romans, who, like the Sumerians and Babylonians, were accustomed to the material representation of their Gods.

The Jews came to regard themselves as a race apart, and when in the fourteenth century B.C. they settled in Palestine, they retained the desert austerity of their religion against the more usual cults of the native inhabitants. The area in which they settled was fertile in the north but relatively barren in the hill country of Judaea, which became the centre of Jewish nationalism.

The challenge of the Philistines, a sea people, settled as we have seen on the Palestinian coast, forced the Jews to abandon the rule of elected Judges and adopt the expedient of kingship. Their ruler David, in the early twelfth century, probably about the time of the Trojan War, saved his countrymen from the Philistines, founded a royal line and established a kingdom of which the glories became an undying legend. His son, Solomon, imitated on a smaller scale the magnificence of Egyptian and Babylonian rulers; the splendour of his court and the size of his harem are famous in Eastern and Western fable.

In the tenth century B.C. the Northern tribes of Israel seceded from the House of David, who retained the kingship of Judah and continued to reign in Jerusalem. Meanwhile, with the decline of Bronze Age civilization and the rise of the predatory empires of the Early Iron Age, the Jewish states were caught in a rising tide of conflict. Their geographical position in the main highways of the Near East invited attack. In the eighth century the northern kingdom fell before the chariots and archers of the Assyrian armies, and though Jerusalem survived the Assyrian siege, its rulers were forced to pay a heavy tribute. In 612 B.C., with the destruction of the Assyrian Empire by the Medes and Babylonians, the Jews became subject to new masters. In the early sixth century Judah rebelled against Babylon, in concert with the waning Egyptian power; the rebellion was crushed, Jerusalem and the Temple sacked, Zedekiah, the last reigning King of the House of David, deported to Babylon along with the leading elements of the nation.

It was now that the Jews became a people of a Book. Before the Exile the priests had committed to writing the ordinances and ritual of the Mosaic Law; in their new circumstances the Jews clung to the Law with added tenacity. Further, their thought was altered and enriched by foreign contacts. The book of Genesis, which dates from this period, and which was destined to dominate the historical outlook of Europe until the nineteenth century, reflects plainly Babylonian and Iranian influences.

During this chequered history, extending over the early centuries of the Iron Age, not only had the Jewish Law and ritual been developed and a priestly class established, but the ancient inspiration of the desert had been kept alive by a series of prophets, many of them of peasant origin, who continued the Puritan tradition of the Mosaic period, denounced foreign influences and fanned a flame of fierce nationalism. The writings of the greatest of these men, of Isaiah and Jeremiah, reach a high level of spiritual insight and attain a universality which transcends the limitations of Jewish exclusiveness; all of them show a poetic genius and power which rendered their writings a mine of quotation and eloquence, not only to their own people but later to Europe. The prophet Elijah lived at the close of the ninth century; Amos and the first Isaiah in the eighth; Jeremiah and Ezekiel, the prophet of the Exile, saw the sack of Jerusalem; they were contemporaries of Sappho and Thales, the Ionian founder of astronomical theory, in so small a geographical compass were contrasting civilizations developing.

The vicissitudes of war and exile embittered the Jewish outlook not only against foreigners but against opposing factions within their own camp. They hankered for the traditional splendours of Solomon's kingdom and looked forward to a Day of Judgement in which a scion of the House of David would establish a temporal kingdom over the whole earth. The remnant of the Elect, reinforced by the resurrected and righteous dead, would then come to their glory, while the wicked would perish in deserved catastrophe. Materialistic and vengeful though this conception may appear, in the writings of the greater Prophets it contains two major contributions to thought; first the idea that according to his righteousness so shall the individual be judged, secondly that of a universal Kingdom of God. Shorn of some of the intolerance of Jewish nationalism, these ideas were to be inherited by the Christian Church.

With the conquest of Babylon (539 B.C.) by the Persians, the fortunes of the Jews took a better turn. Cyrus, the Persian King, and his successor Cambyses, showed them a new tolerance; those who elected were allowed to return to Jerusalem and the Temple was rebuilt by the middle of the fifth century, the new Temple being contemporary with the Athenian Parthenon.

During the fourth century the re-established Jewish State retained its autonomy. Alexander showed himself well disposed to the Jews, treated their religion with respect, and established a large Jewish colony in Alexandria. Jewish communities multiplied in the Levant and the prosperity of Carthage increased Semitic influence in the western Mediterranean and in the Near East. But the cosmopolitan prosperity of the Hellenistic epoch, though it brought profit to the Jewish colonies overseas, was uncongenial to the nationalists of Judaea, and when in 175 B.C., Antiochus Epiphanes, the Seleucid ruler of Antioch, attempted to impose Hellenistic customs on Jerusalem, including the establishment of gymnasia and the wearing of hats of Greek fashion, he provoked a formidable explosion, which resulted in the setting up of the autonomous kingdom of the Maccabees. The ferocity of this rebellion, the short-lived glories of the Maccabean Priest Kings, the wealth which accrued to the Temple from the contribution of the extra-Palestinian Jews, and the growing pilgrim traffic to Jerusalem, set the minds of Jewish fanatics on Messianic fantasies of world rule. The unhealthy prosperity of the priesthood was increased by the final destruction of Carthage (146 B.C.) which made Jerusalem the rallying point of the western Semites and increased the number of proselytes, for as the Carthaginian political power disappeared from history many of the Carthaginian communities were assimilated by the Jews.

When the Romans extended their power into the East, they

treated the Jewish State with fairness and toleration, establishing a native monarchy under Roman patronage and allowing a wide measure of self-government. None the less, the first fifty years of the Christian era saw the Jews increasingly obsessed with dreams of world domination. The Zealots, desperadoes who practised direct action, fomented revolt against all foreign influence, and by the middle of the first century this strategically important country was seething with unrest. Lost to all sense of reality, the Jewish leaders were preparing to fling themselves and their countrymen against the might of Rome. The revolt came to a climax in the reign of Nero, when in A.D. 66 the Jews massacred the Roman garrison at Jerusalem. After Nero's suicide, Vespasian determined to deal once and for all with this situation, and in A.D. 70 his son Titus besieged Jerusalem. After a seige of un-exampled horror, in which the starving defenders fought the Romans and one another, the citadel was taken by storm, the Temple razed to the ground and the Jewish state destroyed. Such was the sequel to the tragedy which had long been accumulating, which demonstrated the fanatical courage and political irresponsibility of the Jews, and which, in its earlier stages, formed the background to the teaching of Jesus.

Meanwhile the political folly of the Jewish leaders had not prevented the growth and development of the religious genius of the people. The Hellenistic period saw the production of some of the greatest of the Hebrew scriptures, of Ecclesiasticus, of the Proverbs, of many of the Psalms, the Book of Daniel, and the later Isaiah; the Book of Job dates from the beginning of the second century B.C. Along with an obsession for a revived earthly Kingdom went a widening and deepening of religious consciousness which was to culminate in the teaching of Jesus: the sense of the omnipotence and inscrutability of a universal God, of dependence and faith, makes the Book of Job in particular one of the greatest of the Old Testament. This sense of life's mystery and of the universality of God goes beyond the traditional wisdom of the East and rises to the level of the most penetrating Greek thought; Isaiah regards the Kingdom of God as a reign of universal peace; his teaching relates directly to the Gospels.

The background of the Gospel teaching differed from that of Judaea: Galilee was not only a more genial country than the hard-bitten upland of the south, but it had only been incorporated in the Jewish state towards the close of the second century and it contained a number of flourishing Greek cities; here Semitic traditions were mellowed by Hellenistic influence. In this setting there appeared one of the greatest religious geniuses in history, Jesus of Nazareth, whose teachings were to colour the main tradition of Europe.

The teachings of Jesus turn on his interpretation of the Kingdom of Heaven, an idea much canvassed by his contemporaries, who were mainly concerned with the establishment of a Messianic Kingdom, in which the Chosen People should rule the world of the *goyim,* the foreigners. In the Gospels this concept is given a radically new interpretation; the Kingdom of Heaven is the Kingdom of Eternal Life, realized in the light of the universal and loving Fatherhood of God. Since all men, not merely the elect or the citizens of a 'polis,' are the children of God, men should love their neighbours as themselves; God is the Father of Mankind and all Creation. In stories which parallel the simplicity and beauty of much Greek poetry, the Prophet brought home his teaching to the unlettered audience over whom he exercised an evidently magnetic power. Here is not the traditional asceticism of the East, but a conviction of the goodness of the order of life and of the value of personality; 'I am come,' he said, 'that ye might have life and have it more abundantly.' An acceptance of life is combined in the Gospels with intense mystical experience. In the light of it the prospects of humanity and the values of life are transformed; there are new possibilities of spiritual awareness, of expanding power, unknown to the more static religions of Antiquity. This dynamic quality in the Christian Gospel has made an immense contribution to European civilization. Political problems are now interpreted in terms of character; before the force of love, patience, and faith, the conflicts and corruptions of political and economic life resolve. The power of the teaching of Jesus is the power of character which compels not through authority but by a serene humility which has long seen through the clumsy manœuvres of imposed power. Hence the perennial influence and power of the Gospel, which profoundly altered the whole course of civilization.

Such an outlook was anathema to the hierarchy which ruled

the Temple at Jerusalem, often obsessed with the lust of money and power, and steeped in the 'realism' of short-sighted expediency. When, therefore, the new Prophet rode into Jerusalem in triumph, at the time of the Passover when the city was packed with an inflammable concourse of pilgrims, when he invaded the precincts of the Temple and launched a direct attack on the moneylenders and traders who supplied beasts for sacrifice, the priesthood resolved his ruin. The Roman governor, who preferred the pacific doctrines of this reformer to the familiar chicanery of the priests, and who was perhaps attracted by the personal charm of Jesus, manœuvred to save him, but the Jewish leaders were implacable. Pilate's primary function was to keep the peace; he gave way, and a supreme artist in life, like many of the greatest exponents of moral, musical, and poetic genius, was hounded to death by the cruelty and stupidity of inferior men. This ancient theme of tragedy, which has been worked out in other times and places and in many books, is immortalized in the New Testament. The tragic and triumphant story was to be the heart of the Christian tradition, forming the background to the Gospel of Jesus. The teachings and the story account for its novelty, its universality, and its power.

When the apparently despairing cry, *'Eloi, Eloi, lama Sabacthani,'* rang out over the Judean hill-side, the Jewish rulers must have congratulated themselves on their victory. Never were men more profoundly deceived; for the Crucifixion proved the means of the triumph of Christianity. Gradually, among the scattered and despairing followers, the conviction spread; the Messiah had risen and would return in glory. He was not merely a prophet, He was the Incarnate God, the Redeemer of the world. The tiny Christian communities, still a Jewish sect, spread and multiplied. They began to assimilate Hellenistic ideas of sacrifice and salvation, and among their enemies none was more active than a Rabbi of dynamic genius named Saul. Hastening to Damascus, Saul underwent a fateful mystical experience. Suddenly he believed, and with all the force of a convert, set himself to spread the Christian Gospel, as he conceived it, to the ends of the earth. The incessant activity of St. Paul and of other missionaries whose names have been lost, changed the prospects of Christianity. Paul, with his short stature and frail physique, journeyed up and down the Levant, to Crete and Athens, Antioch, and Ephesus, and westward to Rome where he was destined to die in the persecutions. He believed that since the Jews had rejected the Messiah, though with a temporary blindness, Salvation and Election were transferred to the Christian community, irrespective of race. The Jewish idea of an elect people was thus expanded to include all Christian men. Through St. Paul Christianity became a world religion, but it retained the idiom and background of Jewish thought and began as a heresy of Judaism. The earliest Christians were Jews, and St. Paul though proud of his Roman citizenship, a 'Hebrew of the Hebrews.'

It has been observed that the Babylonian story of the Creation had been incorporated into the Jewish scriptures and with it the story of the Fall of Adam. Paul was convinced of the fundamental wickedness of the natural man; through Christ's death men had been redeemed, and through His Resurrection the Elect had triumphed over death. 'As in Adam all die, even so in Christ shall all be made alive.'[1] Salvation, in the mind of Paul, could not come by the Jewish Law, but 'We are justified by faith; Christ died for us and we are justified by his blood.' This conviction of Salvation, immortality, and brotherhood in Christ, was bound up with the view that the history of the world had been designed to fulfil a Divine purpose. History was a working out of a progressive revelation in time, not the cyclic recurrence it was generally held to be by the Hellenistic and Roman philosophers, and there can be no doubt that Paul and his contemporaries lived in expectation of an Apocalypse.

Christianity thus developed in a form capable of assimilation by contemporary minds. Through the cities of the Empire it spread like fire, for it gave hope to the oppressed, a prospect of salvation to the guilty, solace for those weary of the world, and wherever the Christian teaching spread went the words of Jesus, the Gospel teaching, lambent, serene, indestructible. Thus it came about that the religion of the declining Empire and of Christian Europe had at its heart the teaching of a supreme religious genius, words of universal brotherhood and forgiveness, of acceptance and glorification of life. At the same time, Pauline Christianity brought with it the idea of human guilt; of asceti-

---

[1] I Corinthians xv. *v.* 21, 22.

cism, of punishment, election, and redemption, which played a
dominant part in the doctrines of the established Churches and
which were to be the cause of savage religious conflicts, persecution, and intellectual intolerance. The Jewish hatred of alien
government and particularly of the Roman power deeply influenced the early Christian communities and was emphasized by
the persecutions, which at once purged the movement of luke-
warm adherents and deepened the Jewish hatred of the world.
During the centuries in which Christian doctrines were formulated by the highly sophisticated and complex minds of the Christian Fathers, steeped in the desire to escape from a demon-
haunted and pessimistic outlook, the chasm between the Elect
and the reprobate world was widened. With the expansion of
Christianity, organization developed, wealth accumulated, the
primitive community of the original sect was abandoned. By
the early fourth century the social responsibilities and the property of the Church were already enormous. St. Augustine's *City
of God* (413–26), written after the official establishment of the
Church, makes a new division between Church and State; a
highly complex theology has been defined; theocracy and authority are setting themselves to impose the Kingdom of God.

Now the writings of the Fathers, together with the Christian
scriptures, were to form the mind of mediaeval Christendom.
While the Fathers were elaborating a theology which was to
change the intellectual climate of Europe, the Roman Empire
was heading towards a cultural and economic collapse. We have
noted that the cause of this disaster was fundamentally a loss of
intellectual standards, owing to the failure of the *élite* of the
Graeco-Roman world to civilize the masses or to raise their standards of living. The new religion appealed profoundly to the
common people; in a proletarian and barbarized world the clear-
cut theology of Salvation and Judgement, of Heaven and Hell,
was intelligible and dynamic where the old culture was ineffective. Christianity was only one of the religions of the Graeco-
Roman world; we have already observed the influence of the
Stoic and Epicurean philosophers on the upper classes; among
the masses the cults of Isis and Osiris, of Serapis and Mithras
were winning increasing popularity. The ancient ties of civic
patriotism had worn thin, and the official cult of the Emperor

was a merely formal observance: the austere distinction of a Marcus Aurelius was alien in an increasingly proletarian world. The legionaries and the vast slave populations followed a variety of crude and barbarous religions; the mercenaries from beyond the borders followed their native beliefs, and the 'pagani,' the country people, continued their ancient fertility and agricultural rites which had come down through the Bronze Age from Neolithic times. To quote again from Rostovtzeff, 'Another aspect' (of the decline of ancient civilization) . . . 'is the development of a new mentality among the masses . . . it was the mentality of the lower classes based exclusively on religion, and not only indifferent but hostile to the achievements of the higher classes.' As in the face of the ineffectiveness of liberal ideas in twentieth-century Europe, the hysteria of popular nationalism developed, so in the later centuries of the Empire, many of the intellectuals and the majority of the common people took refuge in mass emotion. Apart from the new hope of salvation brought by Christianity, anyone who reflects on the barbarism and cruelty of many of these popular cults, who realizes from the bitter experience of our own day the possibilities for evil in such movements of hysteria, may well be thankful that the Christian religion succeeded. Though Christianity was destined at many times and in many places to bring not peace but a sword, and though its mediaeval interpretation certainly handicapped intellectual progress and twisted the bent of the Western mind away from many of its natural interests, the alternative possibilities were indeed appalling. The debt of Europe to Christianity on this score alone is immeasurable.

The victory was bought at a price of worldly commitments and assimilated superstitions. Hellenistic society was still highly civilized; the Egyptian priests of Serapis and Isis had inherited and elaborated a complex and impressive ritual; the Greek philosophers, notably Plotinus, had developed a sophisticated system of metaphysics; the early Fathers were in the main highly educated rhetoricians, the heirs to a great though degenerating tradition: St. Augustine is the master of a superb and flexible prose. All these influences were brought to bear on Christianity.

The rulers of the declining Empire were aware of the problem confronting them—how to maintain the grip of government on the masses. Christianity was the most powerful of the popular religions, but it was also the most hostile to government: the Emperors, therefore, had either to destroy or exploit it. They attempted both. Diocletian tried the first alternative: he set himself to destroy the Christian Church. Ruthless methods were employed, but the movement was too widespread. Then Constantine, as already remarked, by the Edict of Milan reversed Diocletian's policy. Having decided to consolidate his government with the aid of the Church, he was determined that doctrine should be defined and with this object he convoked the Council of Nicaea which produced the Nicene Creed. Here was an instrument which could compel the allegiance of the people by reward and fear, and Theodosius confirmed the work of Constantine.

During the centuries of struggle, the Christians had held their own. Christianity, like Judaism, had become a religion of a Book, the sacred canon of Scripture preserved the teachings of the Founder, and gave Christianity an advantage over less defined religions. Much that was new had also been absorbed; many converts from other religions joined the Christian communities; the practices of other cults found their way into the Christian ritual. Celibacy and asceticism were already old in Egypt, where monastic communities following other Gods had long been established. Hermits and anchorites, in the ancient tradition in the East, had long sought escape in the desert from the metropolitan life of Alexandria. The Christians took over and developed this way of life; during the third and fourth centuries the famous legends of the desert saints found their way into the Christian tradition, legends which, together with the stories of the martyrs, were to be the theme of European art for generations. Here was a new element in Western civilization, akin to the religions of India, and indeed the tonsure and the telling of beads are originally Indian customs. Curiously enough, this side of Christianity appealed strongly to the Celtic and Anglo-Saxon peoples of the far West and North.

By the fifth century, then, the Church was the most powerful religion in the Empire. The alliance between spiritual and secular power had been made none too soon, for it was a time of grave crisis. We have already remarked how the Empire was crumbling without and within, and how the barbarians were pressing in from beyond the borders, how it was no longer possible to assimilate them. By the end of the fourth century the Vandals had already settled in Pannonia, the modern Hungary, threatening the strategic heart of the Empire. In Roumania were the Visigoths, and behind them in South Russia were Ostrogoths and Alans. Moving down through Bulgaria, the Visigoths had already defeated the Emperor Valens at Adrianople; Theodosius thrust them back from Byzantium but the Balkans were dominated by Alaric the Goth, and Italy by Stilicho. The lure of the Mediterranean drew the barbarians to the South; by the close of the century there were Visigothic rulers in Spain, and a Vandal migration had followed them. By the thirties the Vandals were in North Africa, and after the turn of the century their armies crossed to Italy and sacked Rome (455), already devastated by the Goths in 410. Unlike the Philistines, a maligned people, the Vandals appear to have deserved much of their traditional odium; they established a widespread domination over the western Mediterranean.

But behind these numerically small barbarian hordes, and in part the cause of their migration, came a more outlandish threat. Out of Central Asia came a new peril to give the unity of the Empire its *coup de grâce;* Attila the Hun, with his Mongolian horsemen, swept into Europe. These nomads poured into Hungary, they overran the Rhineland, they devastated North Germany and thrust deep into Gaul. They were held at the Battle of Troyes (A.D. 451), but from his camp near the Danube Attila threatened much of Europe. Constantinople remained inviolate behind its walls, but Italy seemed at his mercy. According to tradition it was then that the Bishop of Rome showed his power. Attila was in North Italy; he had captured Aquileia and advanced south: Pope Leo I proceeded to the banks of the Mincio and by skilful diplomacy is said to have stopped the barbarians' further advance. In the following year Attila burst a blood vessel during an orgy, and the Mongol hordes withdrew.

Having faced the Mongolian, the Pope had to deal with the Vandal King Genseric. Already it was clear that the leadership of Italy was falling to the Bishop of Rome. For the Empire was disrupted; the Byzantine power, indeed, defied the barbarians and Constantinople was destined to remain the eastern bulwark of Christendom throughout the Middle Ages, the dominant architectural and artistic influence in Europe until the twelfth century, but in the West the pulse of civilization was running low. In 476 the last Western Emperor, a Pannonian boy, Romulus Augustulus, reigning in Ravenna, was deposed by Odovacer, commander of the barbarian troops in Italy, and the Western Empire came to an end. By the close of the century, a Gothic kingdom had been established by Theodoric, with its capital at Rome; the writings of his unhappy minister Cassiodorus have left a picture of the intellectual and political degradation of the age.

As previously noted, in the sixth century the Byzantine Emperor, Justinian (527–65), made a brilliant but short-lived attempt to restore the command of the Mediterranean world; he sent Belisarius, a soldier of genius, to win back North Africa and Sicily, and to free Italy from the barbarians. In a series of famous campaigns Belisarius took the peninsula and for a few decades Byzantine power again ruled from Ravenna. But this success was ephemeral, and new invaders, originally from the lower Elbe, the Lombards, carved out a fresh barbarian kingdom. The Byzantine grip gradually relaxed, and the leadership of the West passed finally to the Papacy.

So by the changes of time and fate, the guardian of the remnant of the civilization of Antiquity was a Christian priest, backed by the formidable power of an Oriental religion, which combined a ritual and a theology inherited from the ancient priesthoods of the great river valleys and from the Mystery Religions of the Hellenistic Age, with the clear-cut design, monotheism and universality of the Jewish tradition, now inspired by the teaching of Jesus.

Mediaeval Christendom was to be the heir to the remnants of a culture already transformed before its final collapse, and to a dogmatic and emotional religion which gave the Middle Ages a tone which contrasts strangely and fruitfully with that of Hellenic culture, or of the subsequent post-Renaissance civilization in the north-west. In the alternation of steppe and maritime influence which is a constant theme of European history, in the interaction of North and South, we enter a phase in which the Mediterranean Southern influence is dominant. As the peoples of the North came within the pale of Christian civilization, their hard and practical characteristics were mellowed by this influence, though their aggressive qualities were also encouraged by theological prejudice. Yet the caritic and humanitarian side of Christianity outweighed its less fortunate effects, and Europe gained a new faith and optimism, a new belief in human nature and a new respect for personality. The dynamic and constructive qualities characteristic of the West had already expressed themselves in the adventurous thought of Greece and in the administrative genius of Rome; here at the heart of Christianity, was a new outlook, intolerant, indeed, but with a hope and confidence strong enough to convert the barbarians, to burn its way through the accumulation of dogma and superstition, and destined to prove a third great element in the old European inheritance.

CHAPTER V

THE NORTHERN PEOPLES AND THE LATIN CHURCH

THE decline of ancient civilization left Europe on the defensive both in the East and West; from the fifth century until the First Crusade Christendom underwent a time of severe danger and fundamental readjustment. Out of these desperate but creative centuries mediaeval culture emerged, reflecting a strange compound of barbarian and civilized qualities, combining the influence of the Northern peoples with the Christianized inheritance of the South. From Christendom the national states of modern Europe in turn developed and the mediaeval period contributed original and vital elements to the modern world.

The present chapter will attempt to outline the circumstances which led to this development, and to indicate the foundations of Western mediaeval society; the ensuing chapter will give some account of the settlement and conversion of the Slavs.

We have already observed the defeatist and superstitious mentality widespread in Antiquity by the fourth century, the growing political and economic degradation, the disruption of the Empire. The Middle Ages, indeed, preserved the Roman tradition of a common culture, but the far-flung unity of East and West achieved by Rome was lost. Not only was most of Asia Minor, Egypt, and North Africa overrun by the Muslims, but the writ of Byzantium, the direct inheritor of the Empire, ceased to run in the West. A new Western Empire, with a Latin speech and a new outlook, grew up in Central and Western Europe, though the Eastern Empire held as a bulwark against Arab and Turk, and maintained a high, though static, culture through the worst centuries of Western barbarism, setting a standard which, particularly in art and architecture, deeply influenced the West.

The disruption of Graeco-Roman civilization into the Eastern and Western Empires had a vital effect on the development of Europe, for the Slavs of the Balkans, the Danubian plains, and of Russia took their religion from Orthodox Byzantium, while the western and northern peoples looked to Rome. Hence a divergence of cultural development, though Eastern Orthodox civilization was as much the heir to Greece and Rome as that of the West, and the Slavs are the direct inheritors through Byzantium of the traditions of Antiquity.

During the Dark Ages, the memory of civilization itself was hard put to it to survive. We have seen that the internal collapse of the Empire laid it open to the incursions of successive invaders: the Franks pushed westwards into Gaul from the Rhineland, the Visigoths and Vandals into Spain and North Africa, the Lombards into Italy, the Goths into Italy and the Balkans; by the close of the sixth century the West had been barbarized and Byzantium was hard pressed. Of course the process was very gradual; the Germanic warlords were not aiming at the liquidation of the Empire itself—its structure and continuance were taken for granted—but rather at carving out careers for themselves within its borders. The theoretical authority of the Byzantine Basileus was not specifically challenged, though in practice the rulers of the West were independent; the barbarian Odovacer, when he deposed Romulus Augustulus, acted on a mandate from the Emperor Zeno, and the Frankish ruler, Clovis, was proud to receive the incongruous title of Consul. The social prestige of the ancient titles of nobility and office was still maintained; it was the ambition of the petty barbarian rulers to trick themselves out with the pomp and insignia of Rome, and they married into Roman official families. The barbarian invaders were comparatively few and the huge Frankish, Visigothic and Gothic Kingdoms misrepresent the depth of barbarian influence.

The new rulers were dependent, too, on administrators trained in the old routine of affairs and capable of sedentary labour, a thing irksome to the invaders, whose interests lay in other directions.

None the less, the disruption entailed proved a steady and cumulative cause of the decline of the Empire, particularly when combined with a new external danger. For now there came another and even more serious threat; in the seventh century the tribes of Arabia, united by a fanatical religion, swarmed out of the desert in the greatest expansion of their history and flung themselves first on the Byzantine defences. They were held in Asia Minor, but Syria was lost and Egypt, and the wave of invasion swept through North Africa. The great library at Alexandria was gutted, the prosperous countryside of Cyrenaica, with its high cultivation and Hellenistic cities, overrun; the Vandal Kingdom of Carthage was smashed and the Mohammedan cavalry swept westward to the Atlantic. Nor were they held in Africa; the Arab and Berber armies crossed the straits of Gibraltar into Spain, and by 732 they were deep into South-Western France. But they were broken near Poitiers by the Franks under Charles the Hammer, in the battle known to history as the Battle of Tours. The Western way of life and the inheritance of Rome had been saved by Barbarian converts, by the Frankish warriors who had beaten the Visigoths in the early sixth century. For their ruler Clovis, at the head of a confederation of Frankish tribes, had adopted Christianity at the close of the fifth century, and extended his power over most of Gaul; his descendants had defeated the Burgundians, subdued the Bavarians and the Alamanni, and brought Thuringia and Franconia under their sway. Here is the clue to the whole run of Western historical development during the Dark Ages. For the northern peoples had never destroyed the tradition of Rome; by the eighth century they had begun to assimilate the old culture in its Christian form and become its protectors. The son of Charles the Hammer was Pepin, who made a close alliance with the Papacy, and his grandson, Charlemagne, was the first of the Holy Roman Emperors.

So the Frankish barbarians, partially tamed by conversion to Christianity, broke the threat of Arab domination to the West, as Byzantine military science was able to defy it in the East.

Thus political initiative passed to the Franks and Germans, and the centre of the Western world was no longer Italy, for the focus of Frankish power was the Rhineland and North-eastern France. Further, the loss of Spain and North Africa destroyed the conditions of the continuance of the Western Empire in its old form. With North Africa and Spain, went the command of the western Mediterranean; the 'Great Sea' was no longer a highway, but a barrier. Henceforward, until the nineteenth century, Europe was to look south towards a North African shore dominated by an alien, and in the early Middle Ages, in some respects, a higher culture; only at the close of the Middle Ages was Spain completely regained. The economic and social results of this development were to be profound.

None the less, by the eighth century the tide was on the turn; the tradition of the Empire in the West had been saved. We have already seen that only an emotional religion could revive a society so far gone into decadence as the later Empire; it was the Papacy and the Christian missionaries that were to preserve ancient culture and convert the Northern peoples, bringing a new vitality into the service of Western Christendom, and laying the foundations of the revival of the twelfth century. The mantle of Rome had fallen on Pope Leo when he successfully negotiated with the Huns; the work had been carried on by Gregory the Great (590–604) who not only continued the administrative tradition of Imperial Rome, but inspired a new missionary movement to the north. His pontificate marks the consolidation of the Papal power in Italy, and the beginnings of the extensive domination of his mediaeval successors.

Gregory the Great was a commanding personality born of Roman stock; he reorganized the Papal administration and asserted the claim of the Bishop of Rome to the headship of the Church. With untiring energy he supervised the missionary drive to the north which converted the Anglo-Saxons; he was one of the greatest statesmen of the Roman Church. During the seventh and eighth centuries the Popes continued to assert their authority in Italy and to emancipate themselves from Lombard control; by the middle eighth century Pope Stephen approached the Carolingian Mayor of the Palace, Pepin, son of Charles Martel, and induced him to invade Italy, where he defeated the Lombard king who was claiming jurisdiction over Rome itself. The sequel to the coronation of Pepin by Stephen's successor in 753 was another Italian expedition and the formation of the Papal States, the basis of the temporal power. By this judicious alliance the Pope's position was greatly improved, though dependence on help from the North was afterwards to prove a mixed blessing.

Meanwhile the Church continued the tremendous task of preserving the rudiments of learning and converting the barbarians; and indeed it was only through the Church that knowledge was to some extent preserved.

As previously emphasized, the civilization of Antiquity was already Christian before its full decadence, and the learning of the Dark Ages survived within a dogmatic framework; Biblical chronology and, in particular, the salient episodes of the Old Testament, dominated the minds of the monkish transmitters of the remnant of Classical knowledge. This learning was closely bound up with legends of saints and miracles and slavishly submissive to the authority of its garbled traditions. Intellectual, though not technological, initiative all but disappeared; argument consisted of a series of ungainly and breathless bounds from one generally inept quotation to the next; knowledge and, indeed, literacy, became increasingly a clerical monopoly. For such were the conditions of life in the fifth and sixth centuries that the main refuge for learning had become the monasteries. It was during the worst phase of the Dark Ages that St. Benedict (480–540) had acclimatized these Eastern institutions in Europe: the foundation of the Benedictine monastery at Monte Cassino and the devising of the Benedictine rule, were the first of a number of movements of organized asceticism, destined to preserve the rudiments of learning. The breakdown of civilized routine left no better alternative to temperaments unfitted to the rough and tumble of Lombard, Merovingian, or Visigothic life than secession into self-contained communities, shielded by the prestige of religion; further, the state of affairs in contemporary lay society made it natural to seek compensation in an after-life, for which the taking of monastic vows was a preparation and an insurance. None the less, the widespread popularity of monasticism is strange, seeing how alien such a way of life must have been to the West; it deprived society of many of its ablest leaders, and moulded many of the best minds to a narrow pattern; but it was mainly through the monasteries that manuscripts were copied and preserved, the tradition of education kept alive, stability and routine maintained. Habited in coarse but practical garments, tonsured, disciplined, and celibate, the monks were taught to regard their essential task as worship, but they were bound to assume other responsibilities, and the monastic movement in its varying forms played an important part not only in the conservation but in the diffusion of Mediaeval culture.

The intellectual limitations of the fifth and sixth centuries can best be understood from contemporary records and the documents through which the Classical inheritance was transmitted through the Middle Ages; compared with their Byzantine contemporaries these writers are barbarians. For example, one of the most influential books through which the tradition survived, the extraordinary *Etymologia* of Isidore of Seville (*c.* 560–635), is staggering in its limitations, based as it is on mainly erroneous verbal analogies. The enterprise of Greek speculation was long abandoned and the confident sweep of Roman thought gave place to a timid learning by rote; knowledge became a clerical monopoly, esoteric and despised by the fighting aristocracy. Lay society became illiterate, and only in the Eastern Empire were the old habits of lay education preserved. Technologically, however, these centuries were more inventive than Antiquity.

The economic background to monasticism, and to the barbarization of the empire in general, determined the social structure not only of the Dark Ages but of Mediaeval Europe. We shall later see how it was reflected in feudal society; we are here concerned with its ecclesiastical aspects. The structure of Antiquity had developed in terms of city states on the one hand and of village communities on the other; with the decline of the towns a rural economy reasserted itself, the great estates of the nobility became increasingly self-sufficient, dwindling centres of a sub-Roman life in a setting of peasant communities. As trade diminished and communications became insecure, the whole economy subsided into poverty and subsistence agriculture; the cities became dilapidated, aqueducts and drainage fell into decay, population declined. Though the ruin was never fundamental, the major towns were never deserted and the peasantry carried on, the resources of secular society dwindled to a low level. Here again, as in the cultural field, was the opportunity for the Church. Just as in Rome the bishop took the lead, so in the other cities of the empire men turned to the ecclesiastical authority. The episcopal diocese often coincided with the boundaries of the ancient city, while the extension of the parochial system spread the influence of the clergy into the rural areas. Here were the rudiments of a system, episcopal diocese and parish priest, destined to include most of Europe and to remain the foundation of clerical influence until the industrial revolution of the eighteenth century. The parochial organization provided just the link between the civic and rural communities which the urban culture of Classical Antiquity had conspicuously lacked. The peasantry shared the religion of the educated classes; in this important respect, Christendom was healthier than Hellenistic society.

The other major achievement of the Church during these dark centuries was the conversion of the outer Barbarians. In the West, in particular, the Papacy won powerful allies among the Anglo-Saxons. Celtic Christianity, moreover, had survived the invasions; when the civilization of the South was in jeopardy, the Celtic and Anglo-Saxon Churches maintained a relatively high level of learning and played an important part in converting the Germans and Scandinavians.

Ireland had been subjected to Christian influences in the fourth century; but widespread conversion had been the work of St. Patrick, who arrived in the country from Gaul in 432 and died in 461; his ministry coinciding with the worst period of the Anglo-Saxon invasions in Britain and with the beginning of the Frankish power in France. From Ireland Christianity spread to Scotland; the Irish settlers, misleadingly termed Scoti, who inhabited the kingdom of Dalriada, which included most of modern Argyll, were already Christian in the sixth century, and St. Columba established himself on Iona in 563. He carried Christianity to Skye and to many of the Western Isles, and even penetrated into the Highlands to the Pictish stronghold at Inverness, where he converted the Pictish King. Meanwhile, in the south, the Romano-British Christians had been driven into Wales and the West Country. Thus when St. Augustine landed in Kent and converted Aethelberht in 597, Anglo-Saxon paganism was subjected to a double attack. The Celtic and the Roman Churches quarrelled over the date of Easter and over episcopal jurisdiction, but their contrasting traditions supplemented one another. The Celtic Church had developed monastic communities, independent of their bishops, on the Atlantic coast and in the Western Isles. Celtic and Iberian imagination has woven strange fancies round these missionaries and ascetics of the fifth and sixth centuries; the green of Atlantic seas, the curve of Atlantic breakers, are reflected in the colours and design of the manuscripts they copied and illuminated, giving to the original Byzantine patterns a new romantic quality.

Though it produced saints of originality and charm, and missionaries of dynamic zeal, the Celtic Church had never been strong in organization; many Welsh bishops in particular, whose authority had been vague, had become detached from their sees during the Anglo-Saxon invasion. The Roman mission, on the other hand, was well organized. Under Archbishop Theodore (669–90) the fruits of the Anglo-Saxon conversion began to be secured in the beginning of territorial dioceses and parochial organization; the Anglo-Saxon episcopate became rooted in the land, destined to play a great part in the life of England. These two supplementary strains, Celtic and Roman, united in the remarkable culture of Northumbria which produced the Venerable Bede, one of the most engaging characters of the Dark Ages, and the famous Alcuin, who carried Northumbrian learning to the Court of Charlemagne.

This Anglo-Celtic development was destined to bear fruit on the Continent. Merovingian Gaul had already been widely influenced by Irish missions; St. Columbanus of Luxeuil (*floruit* 585–615) had founded monasteries in Gaul as well as at Constance and in Italy. They did not possess the clear-cut organization of the Benedictine Order, but their cultural influence was valuable through some of the worst periods of Merovingian decadence. In 817 the Benedictine rule was imposed on them all.

The conversion of the Germans was initiated by an Englishman, Boniface of Crediton (680–754); he penetrated to Thuringia and Bavaria and founded numerous monasteries, his principal and favourite foundation being Fulda. He became Archbishop of Mainz and organized the dioceses in the newly converted territories; he met his death in Frisia at the hands of the local heathen near the North Sea. Thus both the French and the Germans owed a great deal to the missionary zeal and enterprise of English and Irish monks, and the Papacy found new allies in its task of conversion.

By the eighth century, then, out of the depressing welter of sub-Roman civilization and barbarian dynastic feuds, there had emerged two centres of initiative in Western Europe; the Latin Church and the Frankish power, originally centred on the Rhine and Meuse and also established on the Somme and at Paris by the end of the fifth century. The alliance of the Franks with the Papacy was consolidated in 800 by the coronation of Charlemagne at the hands of Pope Leo III and the creation of the Western Empire. The shift of political leadership from Italy to the north-west is the first landmark in the rise of mediaeval culture, of which the secular inspiration was predominantly French. The coronation of Charlemagne marks the creation of the political framework of Western Christendom.

Charlemagne (768–814) is still a famous figure in Western history and his empire extended over an immense area. It included the whole of France, part of Northern Spain, the Rhineland, and the Low Countries. In constant campaigns he extended his power to the east, for the first time including large tracts of Germany within the pale of Christendom. The great emperor is indeed a hero of German legend, the champion of an expanded Christendom. He beat back the Moors in Spain, he fought the Avars in the plains of Hungary, and he brought the Bavarians and Bohemians under his sway; at its greatest extent the Frankish empire included Croatia. Further, after a succession of gruelling campaigns, massacres, and deportations, he subdued and converted the heathen Saxons of the North German plain; a people who, under the Ottos, were destined a century and a half later to take the leadership of the Germanies with the revival of the Western Empire. Thus, in a political sense, Charlemagne added the Germans to Christendom; the sequel was a German drive to the east, beyond the Elbe into the northern plain; south-eastward from the Ostmark towards the Danube. The hitherto incoherent Germanic peoples were welded into a degree of unity by a common religion and began to absorb the cultural influences of civilization through their contacts west and south. The military might of Germany turned from westward expansion into campaigns south into Italy and eastward against the Slavs, the Poles, and the Magyars. A degree of order was imposed upon the Germanies which enabled the material resources of the area to be more fully exploited, and the trade routes from Venice through Bavaria to the Rhineland and the Low Countries to develop in relative security. Economically the Germanies thus came to be a power to be reckoned with; though the geographical incoherence of the area and the European preoccupations of the Emperor prevented the consolidation of a unified state, not only in the Middle Ages but in the sixteenth and seventeenth centuries.

Charlemagne, the initiator of these great developments, was a ruler of incessant energy and comprehensive interests. Huge, talkative, and polygamous, he was a formidable warrior and a great administrator. Contemporary coins do not represent him as the bearded figure of legend, but close shaven, save for a wide moustache; he was able to read, but never mastered the art of writing. The structure of his household formed the model for subsequent royal courts and administration; the Seneschal, the Constable, and the Chamberlain became the great officers of state; his secretariat, composed of clergy and supervised by a Chancellor, was the origin of the Chancellery common to the courts of Europe. For the administration of his vast empire, Charlemagne appointed counts responsible for the order, taxation, and military leadership of their districts; and he insisted on an oath of fealty from all his magnates. The secular authority of the courts was supplemented by joint commissioners, ecclesiastical and lay, termed *missi dominici*; throughout the vast territories of the Carolingian empire the parochial organization, supported by tithe, was further developed.

As well as setting about this reorganization, Charlemagne encouraged learning and attempted to extend it to the laity; Anglo-Saxon scholars from Northumbria settled at his court and in part inspired this revival. Its most important achievement was the development of a lucid writing, known as the Carolingian script, in which the manuscripts of classical authors were transcribed, for during the previous centuries even the habit of legible writing had fallen away. Without the Carolingian renaissance the texts of many ancient authors would have been lost. Further, the revival of education which Charlemagne and his administrators encouraged in the cathedral and monastic schools, preserved and spread the rudiments of Latin learning; the Carolingian revival was the foundation of the twelfth-century renaissance. This period saw also the widespread development of massive Romanesque architecture in France and the Rhineland; it derived from Roman and in part from Byzantine models, using the Roman vault and the rounded arch.

The enormous Carolingian empire gradually broke up after the death of Charlemagne, with adverse effects on the subsequent development of Europe. By the Treaty of Verdun (843), the outlines of the modern political map are first defined. Charles the Bald was given France, the Spanish March, and all Charlemagne's dominions west of the Rhone and Saône; to Lothaire were assigned the Low Countries, Alsace-Lorraine, the kingdom of Arles, Provence, Dauphiny, Savoy, Switzerland, and Northern Italy; the Rhineland and the Eastern dominions went to Ludwig the German. The political division between France and Germany was thus established, and Lotharingia, running from Switzerland to the Low Countries, emphasized the fateful partition. It would have been impracticable in such a barbarous age to have held together and administered the vast territories of the Carolingian empire, but it is tempting to speculate on the course of events had the Germanic and French peoples been accustomed to acknowledge a common ruler, and it is an ironical thought that this possibility was destroyed and the political future of Europe determined by the Frankish custom of equal division of a family inheritance, for as such the Carolingian brothers regarded the empire of their grandfather.

None the less, the Western Empire was now in being; the political expression of Latin Christendom. In the tenth century it became primarily a German institution, for it was in Germany there grew up the most vigorous military power of the day, the focus of a new political initiative. The power of the Carolingian

Ludwig had been based on the Frankish dominions in the Rhine-land and in the valley of the Main. Outside the Frankish area were the great tribal divisions of Germany; to the south-west the Swabians; to the south-east the Bavarians, now pushing eastward towards the Danube and south-east into the mountains; while the north-eastern coastal plain was occupied by the Frisians, and east of them were the Saxon tribes, now united under their dukes. It was from Saxony, so recently converted, that German leadership during the tenth century was to come; Henry the Fowler, Duke of Saxony, stopped the Magyars on the Unstrutt in 933, and saved Bavaria. In 955 his son, Otto, finally drove them out of Germany, when the heavy armed German knights caught and routed their mounted archers at the battle of Lech-feldt. The Saxon kings, in alliance with the principal German magnates and the great bishops, had rallied the military forces of Germany, and for the first time thrown their full weight against an invader. Saxon leadership was formally recognized when, in 962, Otto I entered Italy at the head of a great host, and following Carolingian precedent, added to the Iron Crown of Lombardy, assumed in 951, the European dignity of the Em-pire. The Western Empire, revived by Charlemagne, thus became predominantly German, and the first preoccupation of the German kings was to organize the Italian expedition, the prelimi-nary to their assumption of the imperial title. By the middle of the tenth century the German tribal duchies were united under at least the nominal supremacy of one authority, while in the West there was formed the nucleus of a national kingdom in France. Both these achievements were on a great scale and de-scend directly from the work of Charlemagne; but the main centre of European political power now seemed to be German.

II

Apart from these large-scale achievements, the other major barbarian contribution to the political life of Europe, the evolu-tion of self-governing institutions, was best realized in a smaller setting. Generally speaking, in the plains of Northern Europe, in face of the development of feudalism, the rudiments of self-government and local institutions common to most of the barbarian peoples failed to develop; such was the price of the establishment of great-scale power. It was in the smaller geographical compass of the British Islands and in Scandinavia, in the uplands of Northern Spain and in Switzerland, that the barbarian habit of primitive self-government principally developed; and in the former, in particular, Anglo-Saxon and Scandinavian influences combined to form a society destined to be the most powerful centre of democratic ideas.

The Anglo-Saxons, by the eighth century, had attained a relatively high culture, the result of a fusion of Celtic and Roman missionary influence. This combination of Celtic and Anglo-Saxon strains is the key to English history and one of the secrets of English success. When in the fifth century, Romano-British civilization subsided before the infiltration and the onslaughts of the heathen piratical peoples of the Frisian and Danish coasts, the eastern and southern parts of the island became predominantly Anglo-Saxon; but in Wessex, later to be the nucleus of the English state, the old influences were still powerful, and in Wiltshire, Dorset, Somerset, Devon, and the West the original population substantially survived. The theory derived from a misreading of contemporary chronicles that the native British were exterminated is long disproved, and the English are as much descended from Romano-British ancestors as from Germanic invaders.

For any continuity of culture there is less evidence. The invaders were barbarians who regarded the Romano-British towns with suspicion and fear; they were farmers who settled in villages and who brought to bear on the English countryside the methods they had practised on the Continent. Their axes and ploughs could tackle the forest and the richer soil of the valleys, while generally the superficial Celtic agriculture had been confined to the uplands. Though there is no conclusive evidence for the heavy plough before the ninth century, this systematic colonizing of the island was the basis of the subsequent wealth of Anglo-Saxon England.

The English in the fifth century had the reputation for peculiar savagery, but they rapidly became the staunch allies of Rome. The Anglo-Saxons practised from the earliest times the rudiments of local government; the tribesmen had some voice in the Folk Moot, and, later, after the settlement of the land, the Hundred and Shire Courts formed the foundation of local order; as law ceased to be tribal and became territorialized, the idea of the 'King's Peace' extended over an increasing area. To break this peace constituted an offence over and above the wrong done to the victim and his kindred; hence there arose the idea of a Law of the Land. Folk custom as declared by the Wise Men was the sanction of government, not divine right; men of any substance had a voice as a matter of course in public affairs and accepted in turn responsibility for keeping the peace of their neighbourhood. The ancient customs of Hue and Cry, of Burgh-bot and Brig-bot, of service in fyrd or militia, of compurgation, and, later, of jury service, assumed the co-operation of men of good will with government. This respect for custom and habit of working with the public authority to keep the peace is a foundation of democratic practice; it was destined to assimilate the old Roman conception of law overriding the authority of the ruler, and of the right of resistance to tyranny, as well as the feudal idea that the King was merely first among equals. Here is a development of cardinal importance for the future, not only of Western Europe, but of the world. A certain habit of responsibility seems to have been rooted in the small communities of the Northern peoples, who here display the same characteristics as their Indo-European relatives, the primitive Greeks and Romans. This development is profoundly different from the tradition of orientalized absolutism carried on by the Byzantine Empire, or the theocratic claims of the thirteenth-century Papacy. The northern races had thus created not only the great-scale political framework of Western and Central Europe, but had initiated, most lastingly in England, a new and powerful political influence.

None the less, the old English kingdom never achieved the unification of the island. The kingship retained the prestige of its tribal origins; English agriculture and local government were based on solid foundations, but no more than the Germans did the Anglo-Saxons solve the problem of national unity. The challenge of the first Danish invasions was successfully met by Alfred in the last quarter of the ninth century, and there followed a period of prosperity for the West Saxon Kingdom; but the power of Wessex never extended effectively over the North, and with the second large-scale Danish invasion and settlement, England became part of the Scandinavian Empire of Knut (1016–35). It was not until the Norman conquest that the destiny of England began to be apparent, but the vigorous Viking strain, with its sea-going traditions, individualism, and legal sagacity, its restless military and economic enterprise, brought a new and dynamic element into the English people. In Northern England and East Anglia this influence was particularly strong: it has since been reflected in maritime and colonial expansion.

By the eleventh century the Anglo-Saxons, though still on the fringe of Europe, and playing as yet a small part in the great political and economic movements of the Continent, had consolidated the settlement of their island, stabilized their racial inheritance, assimilated Celtic and Scandinavian qualities and displayed already some of the characteristics to be the foundation of their later influence. The Norman conquerors were a tiny minority, and the racial foundation of England existed before the Conquest, that final venture made by Latinised descendants of the Vikings.

III

The results of the Conquest will be examined in a later chapter; we must first observe the Scandinavian influence on Europe in general. It was not only in England and Normandy that this formidable people made their incursions and their settlements; Scandinavian war-bands harried the coast of Scotland and Ireland; they penetrated the Mediterranean and dominated Sicily; they founded Kiev-Russia. Despite their original ferocity, their influence on Europe was constructive, for their Norman descendants in particular were politically the ablest of all the mediaeval peoples, the moving force of the earlier Crusades and the greatest builders and lawgivers of their day.

The swarming of the Danish and Norwegian Vikings out of the Northern Fjords, out of Skania, Jutland, Funen, and Zealand, was the last of the Scandinavian invasions sustained by Europe and the most fruitful. To contemporaries it must have seemed a catastrophe; when the long war boats lay off the coasts of southern England and Northern France, the peasantry took themselves off to the interior, the local levies were hastily assembled and the priests gabbled prayers for deliverance 'from the fury of the Northmen.' Their first recorded appearance in the Channel is characteristic; a few ships, says the *Anglo-Saxon Chronicle,* put into Portland in Dorset: the local king's officer went down peaceably to ask their business, and was liquidated on the spot. They were, indeed, a ferocious people, with their clipped throaty speech, their horned helmets and painted shields. They loved colour and ornament and delighted in the looting of monasteries and the massacre of priests; they fought on foot in the traditional manner of the North, forming a shield wall and wielding the famous Viking axe. The use of this murderous weapon required skill and practice; it was five feet long, with the base of the haft curved to give a better grip, and the comparatively small axe head, razor sharp, with the full weight of the blow behind it, could take off a man's head at a cut; according to the Sagas it could shear through a horse's neck. The sweep of these axes required a wide space, and the *élite* household troops of the Anglo-Danish and Norwegian kings fought not huddled together, but spaced out before the standard. This order of battle was universal in the north, until, as at Hastings, the mounted knight proved too much for it.

These people were still in a prehistoric stage of development and formed a heathen society long after the rest of Europe had become officially Christian. Indeed, they represented a long and flourishing past, for the Bronze Age in Denmark had been prosperous. The early Viking incursions were simply plundering expeditions, undertaken in summer. The pirates would establish themselves in a river estuary; rounding up the horses, they would scour the countryside. They used all kinds of cunning tricks and outmanœuvred their opponents in diplomacy as well as in war. Later they came to settle in the conquered territories, as in East Anglia and Normandy, where they preserved habits of hardihood and independence.

These people possessed fine qualities; they were well organized, with a knowing business sense, traders as well as pirates; in the Hebrides a Viking tomb contained, among the armament of one of their chieftains, a pair of scales. The discipline of their war boats was severe; though quarrelsome and bloody-minded, they had a remarkable talent for law. It was the custom to hold Law Courts at the moots and assemblies, and to elect a Law speaker before whom suits were debated. Further, by their law, twelve of a man's neighbours would band together to guarantee his observance of an award. Throughout Scandinavian records this legal capacity is apparent; they were efficient and argumentative, shrewd judges of character, hard as the climate of the northern seas.

Scandinavian literature and mythology show affinities with Greek, but all is tinged with the gloom and mystery of the North. Their weird mythology, which owed some of its beliefs in trolls and demons to the aboriginal inhabitants they had enslaved, is pervaded with a sense of inexorable fate; gods as well as men are destined to perish in the final conflagration of Ragnarok, the Day of Doom. The legends of Thor and Odin, Loki and Frey, show ironical humour and descriptive power; they were born story-tellers and their poetry has an accuracy and realism different from the romanticism of French mediaeval writers. Its finest expression is found in the Icelandic Sagas, prose epics written down in the twelfth century, which display qualities unique in mediaeval literature, and their portrayal of character anticipates the insight of nineteenth-century writers. The self-reliance, dour common sense, and individualism of the Scandinavians is indeed most finely expressed in this isolated and original literature.

These peoples were difficult to govern; hence in part the settlement of Iceland and the successive marauders who came into Europe. But when disciplined by Latin method, which they quickly assimilated in areas geographically suited for centralized government, they displayed a ruthless efficiency which controlled a situation still fluctuating and insecure; for it would seem the Anglo-Saxon and Teutonic peoples often lacked politically the clear-cut, decisive qualities for which the Scandinavians were pre-eminent.

I V

By the close of the eleventh century Western Europe had thus survived the darkest period of its history, and was passing to the offensive signalized by the first Crusade. The remnant of Roman civilization had been saved, the barbarians of the North had been converted, and the new peoples had settled into the areas in which great national states were later to develop. The Papacy had secured its base in Italy, and had claimed the spiritual leadership of the Western Church; further, the Germans had achieved a measure of unity within a revived, Teutonized and nominally Holy Roman Empire, still a European institution. Checked in their westward migrations, they were driving east and south-east into lands of comparatively sparse population, where they were to meet the resistance of the Slavs. In England the Anglo-Saxons had achieved a high culture and were already showing some of their characteristic political qualities; finally, Scandinavia had sent her last wave of invaders into Europe, and contributed a new and forceful element to the common inheritance the Normans, in particular, displayed a genius for government which was to make them the leading political power in the West. This progress might well have been impossible had not the eastern gates of Europe held. The cultural development of the West owes an immeasurable debt to Byzantium, and before following out the rise of Western mediaeval civilization, we must turn eastward and trace the fortunes of the Byzantine Empire, which carried on for so many centuries the direct tradition of Rome and which played the part in relation to the Slavonic peoples that Rome played in the West.

CHAPTER VI

BYZANTIUM AND EASTERN EUROPE

WHILE the Western peoples were pulling out of the centuries which followed the decline of the Roman Empire and creating the framework of mediaeval society, developments of equal importance were going on in Eastern Europe. The Byzantine Empire maintained unbroken the tradition of Antiquity in an altered form, and the Slavonic peoples, racially indigenous to Europe, spread out from their homeland between Lithuania and the Carpathians and settled into Poland, Bohemia, the Balkans, and Russia. Meanwhile the Bulgarians and Magyars out of the Steppe drove a wedge into this predominantly Slavonic area, the former being largely absorbed in the Slav population and adopting the Orthodox Creed, the latter preserving their racial identity and following the Latin Church. While in the West the barbarian peoples settled their new lands, adopted Christianity, and in the fluctuating boundaries of their kingdoms foreshadowed future political developments, the Eastern European scene stabilized in essentials by the tenth century. And as southern civilization was handed down to the West by the Latin Church, a different version of the same inheritance was transmitted to the Balkan and Eastern Slavs by Byzantium.

The military power of the Germans had largely contributed to the destruction of the Western Roman Empire; now, with the better organization of the Western peoples, the main weight of the German drive turned east. The Slavs were none the less able to establish national cultures in Bohemia and in Poland, an essential part of Western Christendom; and in the distant future, after the establishment of the Russian Empire in the early eighteenth century, the Russians were able to alter the balance of European power. The expansion of the Slavs is culturally and politically an outstanding landmark in the history of the Continent.

While the civilization of the Czechs and Poles came from the West, the culture of the Southern and Eastern Slavs came from Byzantium, from the Eastern Mediterranean. The Serbs and the Bulgars realized extensive military hegemonies in the Balkans during the Middle Ages, and memories of mediaeval independence sustained their revived national consciousness through the centuries of Turkish domination. The structure of the early Russian state owes also much to Scandinavian leaders, who superimposed it on the agricultural and pioneering strength of their Slav subjects, with whom they became racially assimilated: Kiev-Russia, like the peoples of the West, particularly the English and the French, owed much to Scandinavian initiative.

The evolution of Russia, of all the European states the most continental and the most directly subject to Asiatic influence, thus conforms in its early history to the basic pattern of European development, reflecting the interaction of steppe and maritime influences, this time from the Baltic and the Black Sea. Spreading south and east across the neck of the great isthmus which joins the European peninsula to the Russian hinterland, along the Baltic-Black Sea trade route and only partially barred from the South by the steppe migration corridor, the Russians developed first along their great western rivers, later in the interior of Muscovy, an original and powerful state, largely an eastern expression of European civilization.

The history of South-Eastern Europe turns, then, on the political fortunes of Byzantium, and we must glance at the outlines of Byzantine history before tracing the development of the Slav peoples in the Balkans, Kiev-Russia, and Muscovy.

II

During the fifth and sixth centuries the empire was still Roman. The reign of Justinian (527–65) saw the climax of the Christian

Roman Empire; the foundation of Hagia Sophia, the Church of the Holy Wisdom; the codification of Roman law; the reorganization of the bureaucracy and the recovery of the Italian territories. The work of Justinian and his administrators ensured the weathering of the Arab attack in the seventh century, though the empire lost some of its richest provinces. The main assault on the capital lasted intermittently from 677 to the great siege of 717–18. The city was saved by Leo the Isaurian, whose dynasty continued until the reign of the Empress Irene, a Greek princess of evil reputation who blinded her own son, whose projected marriage in widowhood to Charlemagne proved impracticable, and who ended her days in Lesbos after a palace revolution (803).

In spite of internal struggles, notably the Iconoclastic movement, which aimed at the abolition of the pictures and images of Orthodox worship and increased the estrangement of the Eastern and Western Churches, Byzantine civilization reached the height of its power and brilliance during the ninth, tenth, and early eleventh centuries; a period which saw in the West the establishment of the Carolingian empire and its German sequel, the rise of the early Capets, and the full development of the Anglo-Saxon and Anglo-Danish kingdoms. During this period preceding the twelfth-century Renaissance, the cultural standard of Europe was set by Byzantium. With the loss to the Seljuq Turks of most of Anatolia, the principal granary and recruiting ground of the Empire, in the later eleventh century, the fortunes of Byzantium began to decline.

Meanwhile the Phrygian dynasty, which had seen growing prosperity and artistic achievement, was ousted by Basil I (867–86), who founded the Macedonian house and whose successors continued a military offensive east and west. The usurpers Nicephorus Phocas and John Tzimisces in the tenth century, carried on the work, which culminated in the reign of the restored Macedonian, Basil Bulgaroctonos, Slayer of Bulgars (976–1025). The second half of the eleventh century, the age of great Norman expansion in the West and South Italy, saw the cultural climax, but the political turn of the tide with the definite break with the Papacy in 1054, the increase of Genoese and Venetian competition and, in the doubly disastrous year 1071, the loss of Bari in Southern Italy to the Normans and the defeat of the Emperor

Romanus Diogenes by the Seljuq Turks at Manzikert. Alexius Comnenos (1081–1118) and his successor, John Comnenos (1118–43) saved the immediate situation, and by astute diplomacy staved off a new threat from the Crusading armies which appeared outside Constantinople in 1096. Though the Latins proved useful allies, there was another military disaster at Myriokephalon in 1176; friction between Greeks, Latins, and Venetians, and the dynastic feuds of the Comnenoi, culminated in the sack of Constantinople and the establishment of a short-lived Latin empire (1204–61). The Venetian Doge, Dandolo, had engineered the Latin attack on the city, the climax of years of Venetian scheming, and for Byzantium it marks the beginning of the end. Politically and economically it was a crippling blow; the structure of the Greek empire was broken, the trade on which its wealth depended disrupted.

While a Latin emperor was established in the capital, separate successor states at Trebizond, Salonika, and Nicaea carried on the ancient tradition; of these Nicaea was the strongest, and the reorganization carried through by Theodore Lascaris and John Vatatzes in the first half of the thirteenth century enabled Michael Palaeologos to retake Constantinople in 1261. For the Latin empire had proved ephemeral. The first emperor, Baldwin I, had been captured and strangled by the Bulgars within a year of his accession; his successors, handicapped by a preposterous feudal organization modelled on the Kingdom of Jerusalem and defined in the 'Assizes of Romania,' displayed the economic and political incompetence of their kind, and by the middle of the century were reduced to pawning their relics to Venetian creditors. The restored Palaeologoi thus regained a crippled inheritance, inadequate to meet the growing Ottoman threat, while in the Balkans there successively developed formidable Bulgarian and Serbian empires.

The Ottoman Turks, who during the thirteenth century had overrun the Seljuq Sultanate of Rum and the Emirates into whom the Seljuq power had disintegrated, first won a foothold in Europe in 1308. In 1329 they took Nicaea; in 1357 they took Adrianople, adding a Western to an Eastern threat. The rise of the Āsen Tsars of Bulgaria and of the Serbian Empire of Stephan Dushan (1331–55) marked the final waning of Byzantine influence in the Balkans. The enmity of Greeks, Serbs, and Bulgars played into Turkish hands: on the fatal field of Kossovo (1389), the Serbian empire was destroyed and the Ottomans won the domination of the Balkans; there was nothing left to Byzantium but Salonika, the Peloponnese, and the city itself. By 1397 occurred the first Turkish siege, but Byzantium was destined to hold for another five and a half decades. Successive emperors sought help from the West, but the Latin expedition of 1444 was destroyed by the Turks at Varna; in 1450 Salonika fell; finally in 1453, the capital itself, and the centre of the civilization of Eastern Europe became the seat of Muslim power. The European political scene had been transformed, with incalculable results for Europe and the world, not the least of them the voyage of Columbus westward in search of a new trade route to the Indies.

Such in bare outline were the political fortunes of Byzantium. For all these vicissitudes, the great empire realized a remarkable culture, the third great manifestation of Hellenic genius, following on the achievements of the classical and Hellenistic Greeks. Modern scholars have done better justice than Gibbon to this original, powerful, and widespread civilization, which not only held back the Asiatic menace from Europe for many centuries, but conserved the learning of the ancient world to contribute both to Muslim civilization and to the Italian Renaissance.

We have already remarked that under the menace of the disruption of the empire civilization withdrew eastward nearer to the lands of its origin; Byzantium was not only the direct heir to the old empire, known to the Arab world as Rum, with its citizens styling themselves Romans and speaking the Romaic tongue, but displays many characteristics of the ancient river valley civilizations of the Near East. The orientalized structure of the late empire was reflected in the absolutism of the Byzantine Autokrator, whose despotism extended over Church and state. The direct heir of the Caesars, he ruled through a bureaucracy of which the titles and organization descended from the days of Augustus. The parallel with the totalitarian structure of the Egyptian and Babylonian monarchy is plain; the emperor, hedged about with a ceremonial of Oriental complexity, being at once Supreme Law-Giver, Priest, and King.

The scale and sophistication of the great Byzantine state, its wealth, efficient bureaucratic and military organization, and illustrious name among the peoples of the East and West, its self-sufficiency and staying power, make it the dominant cultural influence in European history until the twelfth century. 'Tsari-grad' the Slavs called it; 'Micklegard' the men from the North; through the chronicles and poetry of the Middle Ages we can still discern the echoes of its immense prestige. And, indeed, Byzantium and the West make a startling contrast. When the illiterate Western barons appeared to Anna Comnena in the eleventh century as dangerous barbarians, incapable of discipline or foresight, the Byzantine armies were trained according to intelligent manuals of strategy and tactics, studied the psychology of their various opponents, possessed a complex organization of communication and supply, and were the only armies in the Middle Ages to possess a medical corps. When, in the West, learning was confined to the clergy, the Byzantine gentleman was educated in the full tradition of Hellenistic learning, could quote Homer and Pindar and dispute the finer points of Patristic theology. Certainly the ancient culture was distorted and overlaid with theology, and the Greek genius for disputation found there a fruitful field in religious controversy, often involved with politics; but this elegant, turbulent, and cosmopolitan society maintained a standard of civilization to which Europe could show no parallel.

The extent of Byzantine influence in the West and over the Arab world is reflected in the development of Italian and Muslim culture. Venice was a Byzantine, not a Western city; the Cathedral of St. Mark, the churches at Ravenna, and the domestic and ecclesiastical architecture of the Dalmatian coast are Byzantine. In the south, the mosaics of Monreale and Palermo are Greek, while over all Western Europe the massive structure of Romanesque architecture reflects the standards of Byzantium as well as Rome. The Carolingian and Ottonian courts of the ninth and tenth centuries looked to Constantinople for their artistic and cultural inspiration; the Muslim universities from Baghdad to Cordoba were profoundly influenced by Byzantine learning, and when Western Europe began to pick up the threads of its secular intellectual inheritance in the twelfth century, it was through the Arabic medium that much Hellenistic learning was revived.

The strength of the Byzantine state was due to a close centralization of structure and to the vigour of its provincial life. The various elements of the empire were included in a religious orthodoxy and a traditional and cosmopolitan culture. Though Greek was the language of the empire and Greek families played the dominant part in government, the army, the civil service, and the imperial throne itself were open to men of talent and initiative, whatever their origins. Macedonians, Armenians, Syrians, and Latins, Slavs and Scandinavians from Russian and the West, all carved out careers in the imperial service.

The life of Constantinople centred on the imperial household. Here, amid the pomp of a deliberately magnificent ceremonial, the Autokrator and the great imperial officers of state held the threads of a far-flung administration. There was nothing in the West like the complex and orientalized collection of palaces, pleasure houses, and churches, enlarged by successive emperors who brought Persian and Seljuq architects into their service. From landing stages on the Bosphorus and Golden Horn the imperial barges put out; within the compass of the palace walls were polo grounds where the emperor and his companions could take their exercise. In this close society was woven a web of constant intrigue; careers were made or broken by a turn of a phrase or an oblique disparagement; while behind the veneer of ceremonial and good manners lurked the menace of dagger and poison, of the hot iron which blinded the unsuccessful candidate for political power. In the arts of propaganda the Byzantine rulers were as *rusés* as in the use of apt violence; the changing costumes of the emperor and the great officials, the ceremonial prostration before the Imperial Person, the blazing mosaics and majestic chorales under the dome of Hagia Sophia were designed to impress and to overawe. Through the padded silence of carpet and tapestry, the rustle of the Imperial purple and the gracious words of the Autokrator would tell the outlandish ambassador he was in the presence of Divine Majesty Itself.

The great city, of which the imperial household was the heart, extended over a wide area, bounded by the sea to the south and east and north, westward by the triple ramparts built by Theodosius II in the fifth century. Great cisterns and reservoirs secured the water supply; immense fortifications, renewed and elaborated, defied generations of onslaught; only by the use of the new heavy artillery, betrayed by a Greek artificer, was a way blasted through the great western gateway by the Ottoman be- siegers in 1453. Today the traveller may still see in Istanbul the immense stone cannon balls, which, at a range of a few yards, gave the *coup de grâce* to the Byzantine defences in the final and fatal siege. Within these walls extended a city whose inhabitants numbered nearly a million, laid out into squares, arcades, and triumphal arches in the ancient Hellenistic tradition. The busi- ness quarter and bazaars housed a seething commercial life; in the poorer quarters the underworld of Constantinople was housed in a labyrinth of huddled and lively squalor.

The classical descent of Byzantium is shown in the cult of the Hippodrome; here the traditional chariot races and beast fighting of Antiquity continued. Like the Colosseum, it was the scene of public executions; here an emperor, crippled and blinded, might meet his end. The chariot racing provided not only for frenetic gambling; the factions of the Blues and Greens, organized under official Demarchs, played an influential part in politics. The circus was a perpetual sounding board and safety valve for a fickle public opinion, the Forum of New Rome. Like the Roman mob, many of the cosmopolitan and idle populace were fed by doles of corn and wine, and, generally speaking, the Byzantine government by lavish expenditure managed to keep subversive elements in hand.

This expenditure it could well afford, since the resources of the Byzantine state were fabulous. It is significant that in the mosaics of the eleventh century the emperors are represented holding not a sword but a money-bag. When Constantine founded the new city on the Bosphorus, he chose a site strategically and commercially of commanding importance; in the Greek phrase, 'like a diamond set between two sapphires and two emeralds,' the meeting place of two seas and two continents. Constantinople was the centre of a trade extending to Persia, China, and Ceylon; to Central Asia, Russia, and Scandinavia; westward to Venice, over the Brenner to the Germanies, the Low Countries, and the West. Greek merchant navies commanded the Levant, the Black Sea, the Adriatic, and, subject to the menace of Arab corsairs, the trade routes of the western Mediterranean, though later this supremacy was challenged and beaten by the Venetians and

Genoese. During the age of their greatest prosperity Byzantine merchant guilds held a practical monopoly of the brocade and silk industries, while the bankers extended their powerful ramification throughout the empire, developing methods of credit and exchange unknown in the West. Furs, honey, and slaves were imported from Russia; wheat from the Danubian lands; wine and oil from Italy and the Levant; the economic resources of the Middle East were tapped by Byzantine merchants; from the West came leather and wool, and from Africa and Hither Asia the spices so highly prized in the Middle Ages.

This complex civilization was governed by a great bureaucracy and protected by formidable fleets and armies. Under the supreme sway of the Autokrator of the Romans came a hierarchy of ministers of state; there were sixty great officials of the first rank, civilian and military heads of departments and commanders of the military divisions of the empire. From the Grand Logothete to the Katapans of the border provinces, their functions and precedence were carefully defined. The bureaucracy was carefully chosen, widely recruited, and thoroughly trained; it collected the immense revenues of the state with relatively little venality, and by careful handling of conquered peoples, diplomatic skill, and astute assimilation it proved the mainstay of the empire.

Byzantine revenues maintained the best army in Christendom; highly paid foreign mercenaries were the nucleus of Byzantine power. Adventurers from the ends of the earth, from Norway and the British Isles to the Armenian mountains, sought careers in the service; the famous Varangians, composed mainly of northerners, formed an important part of the imperial bodyguard; the most celebrated of them was Harald Hardrada, whose exploits are described in the Sagas. The professional Byzantine armies, like the Condottieri of the Italian Renaissance, practised an elaborate art of war, but, unlike the Condottieri, they had to face implacable enemies and would fight to the death. Their record against Seljuq and Ottoman, Bulgar, Persian, and Avar, shows fine fighting qualities both in victory and defeat, and their heavily armed cavalry, the famous Kataphracts, were the terror of the barbarians for centuries. There were also the provincial armies, led by local magnates, often a menace to the central power, as well as the garrisons of the Asiatic marches. Byzantine

fortifications were highly efficient; well-placed castles and extensive walls guarded the passes and danger points of the frontiers,
and over-awed rebellion inside the borders. The fleets were of
the first importance for the survival of the Byzantine state, whose
revenues and communications depended on the command of the
sea. The crews were drawn mainly from the maritime peoples of
the Levant and from Scandinavian mercenaries; though in the
closing centuries of its history the empire relied upon Venetians,
Pisans, and Genoese. The nucleus of the imperial fleet were the
great dromonds, heavy war galleys propelled by over two hundred
rowers and equipped for the projection of the famous Greek fire.

Within the security of these defences, Byzantine life was dominated by religion. Theological argument was a major interest to
all classes, and the churches were social as well as religious centres. The monasteries were numerous, rich, and influential, the
monks politically powerful; the populace was intensely superstitious, the merits of rival saints and the efficacy of the latest
miracle were hotly canvassed; the sacred relics formed the richest
treasure of the empire and one of the first acts of the victorious
Crusaders after the capture of Constantinople in 1204 was to
secure them. The ceremonial of the Orthodox Church, with its
complex and sonorous chants and litanies, the cadence of its
hymnody, and the thunder of its bells, formed the continuing
background to Byzantine life.

Apart from religious interests, intellectual life was highly
developed; the Byzantines spoke a modified version of classical
Greek and possessed texts of authors now lost. Their culture was
extremely conservative, expressed in a specialized literary language. As might be expected, they wrote good history; Procopius,
Constantine Porphyrogenitus, in particular Anna Comnena's
Alexiad, show an accuracy of observation and psychological insight worlds removed from the narratives of contemporary chron-
iclers in the West. The University of Constantinople produced
great scholars; the famous Psellos in particular, in the eleventh
century, was a notable philosopher and Platonist, and it was
mainly through Byzantine scholarship that the Platonic tradition
was transmitted to the Renaissance Italians. An intellectually less
reputable pursuit was the writing of voluminous hagiographies, a
favourite subject for Byzantine reading. Secular literature found

expression in popular tales of military exploits on the frontiers of the empire; of these the *Epic of Digenis Akritas* is the best known.

It was indeed from the great semi-feudal estates of Asia Minor and the frontier provinces that the empire drew its most able soldiers. This military background, both in Asia Minor and the Balkans, exercised a stringent and salutary influence; the emperors were constantly on campaigns which took them out of the hectic life of the capital and demanded high qualities of generalship and diplomacy. The great fighting emperors, a Nicephorus Phocas, a Basil Bulgaroctonos, were trained in a tough school of Balkan and Anatolian warfare. This military tradition runs through the chequered and brilliant history of Byzantium from the days of Justinian and Belisarius, to Leo the Isaurian's resistance to the Arab siege, through the zenith of power and civilization under the Macedonian dynasty in the tenth and eleventh centuries to the defensive exploits of the Comnenoi. Though the fourth crusade crippled and disrupted the empire, the Nicaean emperors carried on the tradition, and the restored Palaeologoi held out for nearly two centuries against the Bulgarian and Serbian power in the Balkans and against the Ottoman Turks who were finally to overwhelm the city. It was a remarkable achievement, lasting for over a thousand years, no mean sequel to the greatness of Rome.

III

Next to the long predominance of Byzantium, the outstanding fact of Eastern European history, from the fifth century onwards, was the steady outward colonization of the Slavonic peoples from their original territory in the forested and marshy area between the Carpathians and Lithuania, around the upper reaches of the Pripet, the Vistula, the Dniester, the Dnieper, and the Bug. They were a people of Indo-European origin who spread and multiplied among the great Russian waterways. They were impervious to the oppression of successive conquerors, intensely sociable, holding their clan property in common; they had been a principal source of replenishment of the slave markets of Antiquity.

While Goth and Visigoth fled before the menace of the Huns, the Slav peasantry remained in their villages and emerged unbroken after the Hunnish storm had blown itself out; their numbers and cohesion enabled them to outlast more mobile peoples.

The Germanic migrations had been their opportunity. They had pushed westward along the North German plain as far as the Elbe, and by the eighth century their most western outpost was established on the strategically important Bohemian plateau, thrust out into the heart of the Germanies and commanding the routes from the North European plain to the Danube.

The Western Slavs of Bohemia were fated to be closely involved in the affairs of the Germanies: racially alien to the Germans, the Czechs nevertheless drew their religion and culture from the West. Under the native Premyslid dynasty, they had achieved a degree of unity by the early tenth century; the ruler of the period best known to the West is the young Duke Wenceslas, the 'Good King' of popular carol, murdered at twenty-two by his brother Boleslav the Cruel (929). By the early eleventh century the Czech clergy had established an independent bishopric at Prague, and the Czech nation was set on the road to its mediaeval greatness. They were destined in the Middle Ages to exercise an increasing influence on Central Europe, and in the fourteenth century to give to the Holy Roman Empire one of the ablest of its rulers, Charles IV. In the fifteenth century the rise of a Protestant movement in Bohemia and Moravia added religious animosity to racial conflict, and in the religious wars of the seventeenth century Czech nationality became temporarily submerged in the surrounding Germanic tide.

The northern corridor of the Baltic-Black Sea isthmus, between the Pripet marshes and the sea, had been occupied since the ninth century by a Slavonic people known as the 'Poloni,' the men of the plains. In contrast to the Russian and south-western branches of the Slavonic stock, the Poles, like the Czechs, were converted to Christendom by the Latin Church. The first Christian ruler of Poland was Mieszko I, a contemporary of the Ottonian dynasty in Germany; in the early eleventh century Boleslas the Bold (992–1025) established an extensive suzerainty over Pomerania, Silesia, and Slovakia. Following the German colonizing drive to the east in the twelfth century, the conflict of Teuton and Slav intensified; but the history and the achievements of mediaeval Poland belong to that of Western Christendom, and will be followed out in the succeeding chapter.

The Southern Slavs, meanwhile, had steadily penetrated the Balkans during the seventh and eighth centuries: the Croats settled in the north-west, the Serbs and Montenegrins in the up-lands and plateaux of modern Jugoslavia. Along the Dalmatian coast there grew up flourishing cities, with a Roman inheritance and Venetian and Byzantine affinities; here the Slavs first made maritime contact with the Italian centres of Mediterranean cul-ture, and here in the Serbian uplands the first empire of the Southern Slavs was destined to develop.

In the Eastern Balkans there was also a steady infiltration; but here the Slav population was overrun by the Bulgars, a formi-dable people who moved down through Bessarabia from their distant settlements on the Volga in the seventh century. These conquerors intermarried with the indigenous population and established a powerful state, destined to be the most dangerous and constant western enemy of Byzantium.

The Magyars, moreover, racially alien to the Slavonic peoples, had entered Pannonia through the Carpathian passes by the close of the ninth century, drawn westward by the prospect of plunder and by the Pecheneg threat between the Dnieper and the Don. They were a nomadic people of Finno-Ugrian origin, who had lived on the steppe in summer and near the great rivers in win-ter, and they had thriven on the slave trade with Byzantium at the expense of their Slavonic subjects. They swept westward into Bavaria in the early tenth century, following in the track of the kindred Avar peoples, fought off, as we have seen, by Charle-magne. Then, as now, they were brilliant horsemen, and by their cunning in manoeuvre, feigned flights and deadly archery, they long proved a match for the German feudatories. But, like the other steppe peoples, they were unable to prosecute a siege, and by building strongholds and devising new cavalry tactics the Germans under the Saxon dukes were able to beat them back. So they turned south-eastward and harried the Balkans.

Centred on the plains of Pannonia, the Hungarians, after their conversion, became reconciled to German influence and, later, the most redoubtable of the champions of Catholic Christendom against the Turks. Their conversion at the close of the tenth century was due to German and Bohemian missionaries. Their ruler, Vajk, canonized as St. Stephen (985–1038) is an heroic figure in Hungarian history. He completed the conversion of the country and introduced Western methods of administration; in 1001 he received a crown and a cross from the Pope, and is commemorated in the great cathedral which dominates Budapest. The transition from tribal nomadism to settlement and conversion was far advanced by the middle eleventh century. Hungary developed its contacts with the West and proved a refuge for the descendants of Cerdic, driven out of Wessex by the Danes. Thus the Hungarian state was consolidated under Western influences, and formed a barrier between the Western Slavs in Bohemia and Moravia, the Southern Slavs in the Balkans, and the Eastern Slavs beyond the Carpathians.

The conversion of the Eastern and Southern Slavs and the Bulgars was due to two brothers, missionaries from Constantinople, St. Cyril (827–69) and St. Methodius (817–85). These apostles of the Slavs were born in Salonika. The former, whose original name was Constantine, had been librarian of Hagia Sophia and professor of philosophy at Constantinople; his brother, an able administrator, held high office in the Byzantine bureaucracy. From the monastery on Mount Olympus, Constantine undertook a mission to the Chazars in 860. Two years later he was invited west by the Czech ruler of Moravia, where he met opposition from the Latin Church. The allegiance of the Czechs was to be given to Rome, but the mission occasioned the creation of the Glagolitic script, composed mainly of Greek letters with Latin and Hebrew additions, and used for the translation of the Gospels and Liturgy.

Cyril died in a monastery near Rome; Methodius was imprisoned by the Germans in 881, though he died Archbishop of Moravia. Their followers, driven from Moravia, took the Gospel and the script to the Southern Slavs; in the end the chief legacy of the Glagolitic script and Liturgy fell to Russia, a country neither of the brothers had ever visited.

Orthodox Christianity was the strongest unifying force in the Byzantine empire; it was therefore of profound cultural and political significance that the great majority of the Slavonic peoples adopted the Orthodox Creed, that their literature was written in a script alien to that of the West, and that they looked not to Rome but to their own national churches and to the Oecumenical Patriarch for religious authority. The political significance of the division was fully realized by the Balkan rulers, who in the earlier stages of the conversion attempted to play off the Eastern against the Western Churches; with the crystallization of Balkan national feeling, political and religious hatreds combined.

The missionaries found a discouraging situation in the Balkans; the most powerful people in the area were the Bulgars, who, as we have noted, had penetrated the Eastern Balkans by the close of the seventh century. They were a formidable people, organized in clans led by Bagaturs, and ruled by a Sublime Khan. From their entrenched camp at Pliska they were attacking the Byzantines in Thrace in the days of Leo the Isaurian, and when they were not attacking Byzantium, they drove westward into Serbia, initiating the age-long struggle of Serb, Greek, and Bulgar for Macedonia. In the days of Charlemagne, their Khan, Krum (800–15), dominated Bulgaria and modern Wallachia; captured Sofia; trapped and killed the Emperor Nicephorus I and a great army in the Pass of Rasboyna (811). The skull of the emperor, polished and lined with silver, was used as a goblet by the conqueror, who practised human sacrifice and demanded from Byzantium an annual tribute of women and brocade.

By the middle ninth century the Byzantines had sufficiently organized their defences for the Bulgars to turn their attention to the Hungarians and Western Macedonia, and in 864 their ruler, Boris, was converted to Orthodox Christianity. He signalized the thoroughness of his conversion by changing his name to Michael and executing fifty-two of the leading Bagaturs and their families; during his reign the Slavonic Liturgy was adopted, and he died in the odour of sanctity in 907. His successor, Simeon the Great (893–927), established the first Bulgarian empire and struck out into Thrace and Serbia. He besieged Constantinople, took Nish and Belgrade and proclaimed himself Tsar; he entered into relations with the Holy See and obtained recognition from the Pope; during his reign the social and economic life of the country progressed.

The middle of the tenth century saw the waning of this empire; the Emperor Nicephorus Phocas, fresh from his victories in Asia Minor, refused the Bulgarian tribute. He suborned Svyatoslav, Grand Prince of Kiev, to invade the mouth of the Danube by sea; he captured and impaled the Bulgarian tsar, and though the Russians evacuated the country (971), the Bulgarians were hard put to it to resist the attack of John Tzimisces.

Meanwhile the Bogomil heresy had raised its head in Bulgaria, and was destined to spread in the Balkans, creating widespread schism and religious strife; it may indeed be said that the one unbroken theme of mediaeval Balkan history is the persecution of this misguided sect by all the contending parties. For, like many medieval heretics, they followed the Manichees, who believed in the natural wickedness of the creation and of human nature, 'mala in nobis natura existere.' They combined this belief with remnants of Neolithic fertility rites; they were, it was alleged, involved with witch cult and devil worship, and far from adoring the Cross they abominated it; 'veluti quae Dominum necavit.' These beliefs were combined with artistic sensibility and mysticism and won many adherents among the Balkan peasantry, whose credulity was exploited for political ends.

Weakened by internal schism and incessant war, the first Bulgarian empire fell before the onslaught of Basil II, Bulgaroctonos; after the defeat of Cleidion (1014) the emperor is said to have blinded fifteen thousand Bulgarian captives, leaving one man in a hundred with an eye to guide the rest; it is recorded that the sight of this macabre procession caused the Tsar Samuel to die of rage. By 1018 the remnant of Bulgarian power, driven westward as far as Okrida on the Albanian border, was extirpated by a Greek expedition from Salonika, and the first Bulgarian empire had come to an end.

During the eleventh and for most of the twelfth centuries the Bulgarians remained subdued, though rebellious, beneath the Byzantine power. But by 1180 the Greek influence over the Balkans was on the wane; with the decline of the Komnenoi, the Serbians, Bosnians, and Bulgars were able to assert their independence, and there arose a second empire under the House of Āsen, descendants of the former tsars. In the year of the crusaders' sack of Constantinople, Tsar Kalojan, 'Pretty John,' was crowned by the Papal Legate at Trnovo. So it came about that, in 1205, the first Latin emperor of Constantinople, Baldwin I, perished at the hands of the Bulgarians, and by the middle of the thirteenth century they again dominated the Balkans. John Āsen II ruled from Albania to Thrace; an autonomous Bulgarian church was established with an independent Patriarch, and a considerable prosperity attained. But by the close of the century, the dynasty, like most Balkan princely families, became enfeebled by dynastic feuds and its influence fell into decline. For the second Bulgarian empire was challenged by a new power; the Serbs were destined by the middle fourteenth century to establish their hegemony over most of the Balkans.

The beginnings of Serbian history are obscure. Since the eighth century the Southern Slavs had been established in Serbia; their ruler, the Veliki (Great) Zupan, exercised a precarious suzerainty over the tribal chiefs; urban development was backward and the Serbs waged constant war westward against the Hungarians, eastward against the Bulgars. In the middle of the twelfth century Veliki Zupan Nemanja established a dynasty which was to last over two centuries; he ended his life as a monk on Athos. He had laid the foundations of a widespread Serb domination, based on Montenegro and Western Serbia. It was in the thirteenth and fourteenth centuries, during the climax of Latin civilization in the West, that mediaeval Serbia came to her full stature; King Stephen Nemanjić, crowned 1217, and his brother, St. Sava (1196–1223), founder of the Serbian National Church, consolidated the royal power. His descendant, Stephen Uros II (1282–1321), was strong enough to invade Macedonia and threaten Salonika itself, and the Greek emperor sent him a Byzantine princess as his fourth wife. But in spite of the potential agricultural and mineral wealth of the country, and for all the vigour of this warlike people in their palisaded mountain strongholds, Serbian economy remained backward.

Serbian military power reached its climax in the fourteenth century; at the battle of Velbuzd the Serbs defeated the Bulgarians in the Struma Valley and killed their tsar. In 1331 Stephan Dushan (1331–55) seized the throne; he proved one of the greatest Serbian rulers. He subdued the Bulgarians by force and diplomacy, took Macedonia, and extended his dominion over

Moldavia and Wallachia, principalities founded by the Roumanian princes Rudolph the Black and Ivanko Basaraba. For
the Roumanians had descended out of Transylvania, the historic
refuge of the Romano-Dacian population, whither they had been
driven by the Tatars in the thirteenth century. They had re-
established the Roumanian hold on the Danubian lands, originating from the settlement of Roman legionaries in the time of
Trajan, in the area inhabited by the Dacians, where a flourishing province had developed, with Latin traditions, afterwards to
be the basis of Roumanian culture.

Stephan Dushan established his capital at Skoplje; he proclaimed himself Tsar and autocrat of the Serbs and Greeks, the
Bulgarians and Albanians; he drew up and did his best to enforce a famous code of laws. The scale and splendour of his empire surpassed that of the Bulgarian tsars, though it was destined
to be as ephemeral; an autocrat to his subject peoples and maintaining a guard of German mercenaries, he was none the less dependent on his magnates and on the Serbian Church.

Serbian society was aristocratic and military, based on a peasant foundation. The extent of this empire overstrained the resources and man-power of the rudimentary state, unequal to the
task of holding together such a mixture of races, religions and
language. Further, like other Balkan empires, all was liable to
collapse through feuds of the royal family, from which the nobles
were ready to profit. Yet the empire of Stephan Dushan marked a
period of Serbian glory which has been treasured and commemorated in chronicles and ballads; the memory of the lost empire
of the great Tsar has been reflected in subsequent Serbian ambitions.

Thus, throughout the Middle Ages, Bulgarians, Serbs, and
Greeks lived in traditional enmity, tempered by diplomatic ma-
noeuvres. All of them established in turn their domination over
the Balkans and none of them were able to consolidate it: in an
area naturally incoherent both by race and geography, disunity
was steadily increased.

The sequel was the conquest of the Balkan countries by the
Ottoman Turks. We have already traced the steps whereby the
Turks established themselves in Europe; already at the battle of
the Maritza (1371) they had defeated the Serbian tsar. On June

15th, 1389, on the Plain of Kossovo, the Field of the Black Crows, the Serbian empire was destroyed. To this day the Serbs commemorate this national disaster, and indeed it was a sinister and dramatic event. Before the battle, Miloš Obilić, a national hero of Serbian fable, obtained access to the Sultan Murad in his tent and there stabbed him to death. But, thanks to Turkish discipline, the generalship of Bajazet I, the Sultan's son, and to the treachery of elements of the Serbian army, the Turks obtained the victory. In one day Bajazet had broken the Serbian armies, taken and executed the tsar, strangled his own brother—a rival for the Turkish throne—and established Turkish domination over most of the Balkans.

The immediate results for the Balkan peoples were of the greatest importance. The political, cultural, and economic development of the Balkans, of Greece and the Danubian area, was swamped and diverted; during the sixteenth and seventeenth centuries, when great national states were consolidating, when the Renaissance and the beginnings of science were transforming the mentality of the West, the Balkan and Danubian peoples were still prostrate under a foreign power. In consequence, during this vital period, they had little share in Western progress and emerged into autonomy only in the nineteenth and twentieth centuries, without the political and cultural experience behind them which characterised many of the states of the West.

Such, in outline, were the political fortunes of the Southern Slavs who, after a fluctuating history of freedom and oppression, were to be subjected for many centuries to the Turkish yoke.

I V

While the Western and Southern Slavs were pushing south and westward into Central Europe and the Balkans, the Eastern Slavs were colonizing the waterways of Western Russia. They were forest dwellers and agriculturists whose hamlets and villages spread up and down the wooded and marshy areas along the upper reaches of the great rivers. The produce of their shifting settlements was supplemented by game and fur and fish; this surplus, together with the slave trade, formed the basis of the wealth of Kiev-Russia. The Black Sea-Baltic trade dates from prehistoric times; by the ninth century, when the Swedish Vikings established their domination over the Russian rivers, there had grown up considerable settlements at the key points of the trade routes. Kiev was founded in the seventh century; originally a trading post and place of refuge, it was to be the centre of the first Russian state. Northward from Kiev lay Smolensk and Novgorod, the latter destined to develop, in conjunction with the Hansa cities of the Baltic, into a formidable economic power.

Into this land of broad slow rivers and mixed forests came the Swedish Vikings to do for Kiev-Russia what their relatives were to do for England and Normandy. Gardarik they called the country, the Land of Castles. According to tradition, Rurik, the founder of the first Russian royal house, was invited to Novgorod in 862; his kinsman, Oleg, was ruler of Kiev by 882. These Scandinavians brought with them their native organization and law; their bodyguard *élite* troops, like the Danish huskarls, were known as the 'Rus,' possibly a corruption of the word 'Rothsmen,' the Men of the Sea, or of the Finnish word 'Ruotsi,' their name for Sweden. Like their western kinsmen, they were traders; they exploited the traffic down the Dnieper with Byzantium, cast covetous eyes to the South, entered into trading agreements with the Emperors, and launched piratical expeditions against Constantinople itself.

Meanwhile they established themselves securely in their new dominion. In winter they would proceed on sledges up the frozen rivers, halting to give judgement according to Viking law; to collect tribute in furs and slaves, honey, wax, and hides. At nightfall their camp fires glowed through the forest, the shouts of their feasting echoed over the ice. In the swift Russian spring, when the ice blocks jostled one another in the rivers, the Varangians prepared their convoys and their war-bands for the expedition to the south. Kiev was their point of assembly; down the Dnieper they went, by portages round the rapids, driving their slaves with them, and struck out across the steppes, infested by the nomads who preyed on the convoys. At Berezan, where a Swedish Runic stone remains, they reached the Black Sea, and so, coasting along its north-western shore, reached the mouth of the Danube, whence they pushed on to Constantinople. In the early tenth century, when the House of Wessex was ruling in England and the Ottos in the Germanies, they were already attacking Byzantium. In 907 Oleg, in 941 Igor, attacked the city, the latter suffering defeat at the hands of Theophanes, who employed Greek fire against his ships. The most devastating of these expeditions was conducted by the young Svyatoslav, Grand Prince of Kiev. We have seen already how he landed at the mouth of the Danube and defeated the Bulgars; he came again in 968 and pushed down into Thrace, where he took Philippopolis and threatened the capital. But he was defeated by John Zimisces, and in the following year caught by the Pechenegs, with the remnants of his host, making for Kiev up the Dnieper, and killed. He had schemed to remove his capital to the mouth of the Danube and there establish a great trading empire.

The next landmark in the histoy of Kiev-Russia was the conversion of Prince Vladimir I in 988. According to contemporary accounts, he had rejected Judaism owing to the plight and aspect of the Jews who had already percolated to Kiev, and Islam since it forbade drink, without which, he declared, life in Russia would be insupportable. As in other newly converted lands, Christianity was often imposed on the peasantry by force, and the peoples of Kiev and Novgorod were baptized wholesale. Vladimir, who had married a Byzantine princess, encouraged the settlement of Greek clergy, and the language of the Russian Liturgy, written in the Glagolitic script and derived from Bulgaria, became the written language of Russia. Church law books and monastic chronicles formed the nucleus of this literature and the Kiev-Russians inherited the Byzantine aptitude for historical writing, reflected in the Chronicles of Kiev, Novgorod, and Smolensk. The upper ranks of the clergy were appointed by the princes, and the rich monasteries and chuches of the eleventh century grew up under aristocratic patronage; the lower clergy were drawn from the peasantry and Russian popular Christianity remained tinged with pagan cults.

It was in architecture and painting that Byzantine influence produced its most immediate results; by the reign of Yaroslav I (1019–54), a contemporary of Knut and Edward the Confessor, great churches and monasteries were being built; Kiev became a Metropolitan See in 1037, and the famous Monastery of the

Caves, built into the western bank of the Dnieper, was already a refuge and a sanctuary. Russian architects reinterpreted Byzantine architectural fashions in the characteristic 'onion' domes which, coloured and gilded, are a peculiar glory of Russian building. Byzantine religious painters were to find brilliant and original pupils in Russian artists, whose icons were to be masterpieces of colour and design.

The reign of Yaroslav saw the climax of the political prestige of Kiev-Russia and contacts with the West increased. With the twelfth century, when Western Europe was entering on an intellectual and economic Renaissance, the fortunes of the grand princes began to decline. Vladimir Monomakh, one of the heroic figures of early Russian history, fought a losing battle against the encroaching Polovtsy, a Turanian tribe who had outsed the Pechenegs in the south. Here was the weakness of Kiev-Russia; it had never succeeded in dominating the Steppe. Further, the economic situation deteriorated; in face of the Turkish menace and the doubtful benefit of the First and Second Crusades, the Byzantine empire, too, was on the defensive. After Manzikert the days of Byzantine expansion were over; no more than the Russians could the Comnenoi hold open the trade routes to the North. In consequence both Byzantium and Kiev-Russia drew back into themselves, and the prosperity of Kiev diminished. The future was no longer with the Scandinavian-Slav commercial and military aristocracy which had enjoyed a period of prosperity in the tenth and eleventh centuries; the Varangian prelude to Russian history was ending. Yet the essential work had been achieved; the Eastern Slavs had been brought into the stream of civilization, the foundations of Russian law and culture secured, rooted at once in the native and the superimposed Scandinavian ways of life.

For long the Russians had been pushing north-eastward into the forests of the Oka and the upper waters of the Volga; it was into this area the population shifted with the economic decline of Kiev and the old water road. Turning away from the Steppe into the vast hinterland, sparsely inhabited by Finnish tribes, the Russian characteristically evaded the full weight of the Tatar invasions, which, in the thirteenth century, cut them off from the South and profoundly altered the development of Russian civilization. Deep in the zone of mixed forests to the north-east was the new city of Moscow, first mentioned in 1147.

The history of the thirteenth and fourteenth centuries, for Latin Christendom an age of such remarkable achievement, was for Russia a time of massive and brutal conflict, of isolation from the West. The Tatar invasions were a menace to Central Europe; for Russia they were a disaster, and they were combined with a threat from the West. Yet with Kiev-Russia overrun, first by the Tatars and later by the Lithuanians and Poles, the basis of Russian power remained unbroken in the North and East. On the northern waterway Novgorod maintained its independence and checked the Swedish and German drive from the Baltic. Meanwhile, backward and isolated in the great zone of Central Russia, the grand princes of Muscovy disposed of the resources and man-power to survive the Tatar incursions and to beat off the Lithu-anian-Polish attack.

In 1228 the Tatar peril first became acute. They routed the Russians at the Battle of the Kalka, feasting on a wooden plat-form which crushed the bodies of the wounded and the dead. They possessed crude siege artillery and in 1239 they sacked Kiev. Meanwhile the Swedes had overrun Finland; they were defeated on the Neva (1240) by the great warrior Alexander Nevski, whose epithet commemorates the victory. In 1242 he trapped and routed the Teutonic Knights of the Cross on the ice of Lake Peipus, a day famous in Russian annals. But this sinister brother-hood was still to play a major part in the history of Baltic lands. In 1245 Alexander defeated the heathen Lithuanians, and he was able to come to terms with the Tatars, who recognized him, in 1252, as Grand Prince of Vladimir.

Moscow met the Tatars by obstinate resistance and wily diplo-macy; but the supremacy of the Golden Horde was for long the dominant fact in Russian history. The struggle continued through the fourteenth century: Dimitri Donskoi, Grand Prince of Moscow, defeated the Tatars at Kulikovo (1380), but the Lithuanians had overrun the Ukraine and the Poles Galicia; in 1386 the dynastic union of the Poles and Lithuanians was achieved. In spite of this prolonged ordeal, the massive power of Muscovy continued to increase; it commanded the eastern trade route down the Moskva, the Oka and the upper Volga to Nizhny-

Novgorod; south-westward the route to Kiev; north-westward to Novgorod on the Volkhov. Slowly the grand princes spread their tentacles to the East and South; they reached out to colonize the Tatar lands and the interior to the north. Their policy was tenacious and consistent; their city destined to become the centre of Muscovy, the second great Russian state, ultimately the capital of all the Russias. Though with the decline of Byzantium and the Tatar invasions the focus of Russian culture was destroyed, thrown back on itself and deprived of Western influence, Muscovy maintained and augmented its inheritance. The spectacular mediaeval empires of Poland and Bohemia, of Hungary and the Balkans, never attained the solid concentration and racial unity of the relatively backward Muscovite state, and the steady increase of Russian man-power and economic resources was already a formidable fact by the close of the Middle Ages.

v

Such in broad outline was the course of events among the Slavonic inheritors of Byzantine civilization, who had been brought into Christendom by the Orthodox Church; a conversion and diffusion of culture which would have been impossible had not the Eastern Roman empire held.

With the expansion and settlement of the Slavs, the assimilation by the Poles and Bohemians of Latin Christianity, and the conversion of the Southern and Eastern Slavs to the Orthodox Church, the range of European civilization had been greatly extended. Great areas which under the Roman Empire had been mysterious and unexplored, the scene of fluctuating barbarian migrations outside the pale of civilized life, had become the centres of new and original cultures and of growing political power. The Hungarians and the Bulgars, moreover, had been assimilated, respectively, into Latin and Orthodox Christendom. Though the turbulent marches of Eastern Europe and the Danube never saw the concentration of centralized political power and the evolution of urban life which formed the basis of Western progress, traditions of nationality were created in Poland and in the Balkans; and indeed the modern history of the Balkans, save for the interlude of Turkish domination, is in some sense a continuation of mediaeval politics. But the most important Slavonic achievement was the settlement and eastward colonization of Russia. Based on the western waterways, Kiev-Russia had built the beginnings of a great civilization. After the decline of contact with Byzantium and the Tatar invasions, Muscovy carried on this inheritance which was modified by Asiatic influence. With all its handicaps, the scale of Muscovite power steadily increased; and with growing prosperity, the grand princes of Moscow, still the descendants of Rurik, the founder of Kiev-Russia, felt themselves the heirs to the Eastern empire. Here, in a vast area, hitherto unknown, civilization had reached out and created a state destined to combine the scale, the force, and the ruthlessness of Continental Asia with much of the initiative of Europe.

CHAPTER VII

MEDIAEVAL CHRISTENDOM

MEDIAEVAL Christendom was at once a sequel to Mediterranean Antiquity and the background of the modern world. Yet it was no mere broken imitation of the past, but an original and vigorous society which profoundly altered European development. We have observed how the Byzantine Empire, over so many centuries, transmitted to Eastern Europe the legacy of Greece and Rome; we will now turn to the achievement of the West, to the full assimilation by the Western and Northern peoples of the Christianised legacy of the South.

First it will be necessary to sketch the economic and social foundations of Western Christendom, and the major political evolution of the age, with its important consequences. Turning next to the mediaeval cultural achievement, to take account first of its ecclesiastical aspect, of clerical administrative development; of the twelfth-century intellectual Renaissance, of the original student life of the Middle Ages, and of the architectural and artistic achievements of this remarkable civilization. The secular aspect of mediaeval society was equally important; it is expressed in the customs of chivalry and in epic and romantic literature; in representative institutions which later, particularly in England, formed the instruments of responsible government, and in the rise of an increasingly independent bourgeoisie, based on a European economic revival.

Before mediaeval society declined in face of the conflict between Empire and Papacy, of a new kind of kingship in alliance with the towns, and of the revival of secular ideas inherited from Antiquity, it had created the tradition of the unity of Christendom, of respect for the rule of law and of vigorous community life, which contrasts with the individualism and ruthless power of Renaissance and seventeenth-century Europe, and from which the modern world has something to learn.

Western Christendom, like the Roman Empire, was a cosmopolitan society; it retained a sense of the unity of Western civilization, later in the surge of national and economic expansion after the Renaissance to be gravely diminished. The immemorial prestige of Rome had been reinforced by the Christian ideal of a Kingdom of God on earth, and the penury and ruin of the Dark Ages had driven home to all Christian men a sense of a common inheritance and a common danger. The Crusades were the answer Christian Europe gave to the African and Asiatic threat; by the end of the eleventh century Europe was no longer on the defensive. This sense of unity, of European order, dominates mediaeval thought, and although in practice it fell desperately short of the ideal, the assumption remained at the back of the minds of all thinking men.

Graeco-Roman society was organized by a cosmopolitan administration, superimposed on a world of city states; save in the Hellenistic kingdoms of the Levant, there is no development comparable to that of a national state. It was the same during the most characteristic phases of mediaeval society, though the co-ordinating machinery was less effective. Generally speaking, the economic basis of Christendom was the manor and the market town, self-sufficient within their locality and linked with the rest of Europe by an originally tenuous web of luxury trade. The social structure superimposed on this economic foundation was feudal; the national kings, who inherited the prestige of ancient tribal leadership, and were backed by the religious authority of the Church, were feudal magnates, 'first among equals' among their peers. After the economic revival of the eleventh century, a new class of burgesses came into being who did not belong to the feudal world; who increasingly bought themselves out of it; and who, finally, in alliance with centralized royal government, outsted the unpractical if picturesque descendants of the original fighting baronage, wrought the foundations of new national polities and created a new culture with its roots striking more deeply into national life.

The intellectual leaders of mediaeval society were the cosmopolitan Churchmen, spread out over all Europe, permeating all aspects of life with their influence, enjoying a prestige unknown to the priesthoods of the Graeco-Roman world, speaking a Latin lingua franca, and at the height of the mediaeval civilization, looking to Rome as their sovereign authority under God.

The basic economic theme of the earlier Middle Ages is the mastering of the land, already achieved in parts of Gaul and in the South, but still a formidable task in the North, particularly in Germany and in Eastern Europe. As the frontiersmen in nineteenth-century America and Siberia pushed into the wilderness, so there was a steady Germanic drive eastward, where it met the spreading colonization of the Slavs; in England, too, the Anglo-Saxon peasantry were steadily bringing a wider acreage under cultivation. During this period there is a multiplication of villages and new towns, Ville-neuves, Neuburgen, Neustadten. All this was made possible by peasant labour, fostered by seignorial and ecclesiastical leadership. Important as was this expansion, the static function of the manor was even more necessary; in the social disintegration of the Dark Ages it was the foundation never seriously shaken. The peasants weathered all storms; within the new framework of the manor they went on with their low-grade agriculture as they had gone on with it since Neolithic times. Through the black centuries they survived; illiterate, superstitious, their horizon bounded by the nearest market town, their diet in the main of coarse bread, vegetables, and cheese; 'adscripti glebae,' bound to the soil, they remained the patient and indestructible foundation of all the brilliance of mediaeval culture, the ancestors of the great majority of modern Europeans and of their descendants overseas.

With the collapse of the Roman world and the decline of Imperial and urban administration, the country districts had long reverted to a primitive and self-sufficient economy. In some areas the remnant of a Romanized estate remained the sole centre of order and protection; in others the stronghold of the local baron became, in default of anything better, the rallying point of these rudimentary communities. As we have seen, in more favourably situated districts, a bishopric often coinciding with the area of jurisdiction of an ancient city, or later, an abbey founded by one of the monastic orders, provided the leadership central authority was unable to give.

Such was the lasting foundation; imposed on it there grew up the clumsy structure of feudal society. Feudalism derives mainly from the barbarian custom of the 'following' gathered round him by the tribal king, common to all the Teutonic and Celtic peoples; less directly, from the private armies maintained by the magnates of the declining Empire. With the decay of monetary relations, the debasement and scarcity of coinage during the Dark Ages, and with the expansion of barbarian power following the consolidation of the Frankish, Anglo-Saxon, and Teutonic kingdoms, royal and ducal fighting men were rewarded and retained by grants of land; there grew up the institution which is the nucleus of feudalism, the fief. The upkeep of a castle and the furnishing of arms and equipment for the specialized fighting unit, the knight and his retainers, could only be met by considerable revenues. The fief might therefore consist of a number of manors scattered over a wide area, held by the personal tie of homage given by the vassal to his lord and carrying with it the obligation to put a specified number of knights into the field. The sum of these contributions was the feudal host, obliged to turn out and do service to the king, duke, or count for a specified and comparatively small number of days in a year. In this way there was mustered an array of highly specialized and relatively well-equipped fighting men, who could be assembled in emergency; who together with professional mercenaries, constituted the military power of the great kings; of Henry II of England, of Philip Augustus, of Barbarossa.

The strength of these kings varied according to their ability to control their magnates. In England, within a manageable area, the Normans and Angevins imposed their power over the whole land and won the direct support of the lesser feudatories; in the wider areas of the Continent, the French kings and the German emperors were hard put to it to control their feudatories and sometimes even to survive, for the great duke and princes, the provincial and Palatine counts and margraves, the Princes of the Blood Royal, asserted a dangerous and uncontrollable independence. In the end a new type of ruler, with an unfeudal mentality, practising Machiavellian tactics and business methods learnt from the urban Italian tyrants in the South, cut his way through the tangle of feudal arrangements and established a despotic and unbridled power, the price of a new order and a new 'state.'

The European political structure of the Middle Ages was ambitious and far flung. The comprehensive unity of Christendom, which in theory it expressed, was far beyond the limited resources of an agricultural society; yet in vision, and, indeed, in common sense, it surpassed the precarious balance of power maintained by the European Nation States of the eighteenth and ninetenth centuries and the growing international anarchy of recent times. The ideal of European order, expressed in the pronouncements of the great Popes and reflected in the philosophy of Thomism, and the conception of a secular European Empire set out in Dante's *Monarchia,* put to shame the fumbling Machiavellianism of later governments, who disposed of material resources far in excess of anything the mediaeval world ever knew.

Both the great European institutions, Papacy and Empire, were in direct descent from Antiquity. We have seen how Gregory the Great and his predecessors assumed the leadership and government of Rome and of wide areas of Italy; and how their successors, by their alliance with the Franks, won the backing of the greatest military power of their day. How Charlemagne, in imitation of the Eastern Basileus, assumed the regality and the insignia of the Holy Roman Empire; how that empire passed to Germany, to the Saxon emperors, and how close were their contacts both with Byzantium and with Rome.

During the tenth and early eleventh centuries, the fortunes of the Papacy had been fluctuating and often adverse; but with the Cluniac revival a new spirit had appeared. The pontificate of Gregory VII marks the beginning of the Papal attempt to assert a spiritual, and, later, a temporal authority over all Europe. By the beginning of the twelfth century, when mediaeval civilization was coming to its full strength, Papacy and Empire were already accepted as the universal political background of European society; Christendom, in theory, reflected a Divine Order of which the spiritual aspect was represented by the Papacy, the secular by the Empire. In spite of conflict and failure, the sense of Western and Central European unity was strong.

It was not, however, from these high theories that the political successes of the age were made. Only those rulers who concentrated on the possible built securely, and the majority attempted too much. This overriding theme unites the complex political history of Mediaeval Europe, and their successes and failures were to be fateful for the future.

II

With this background in mind, the main political evolution of the age will be sketched, starting from the nations of the western seaboard, turning next to the fortunes of Italy and Central Europe, and finally to the fluctuating history of the peoples of the Danubian and eastern plains.

By the close of the Middle Ages the pattern of subsequent European political development had been largely determined. In the West, relatively strong states had been consolidated, some sense of nationality achieved. In Germany and Italy there was no such development, but Hapsburg power dominated the Upper Danube, a focus of political influence comparable to that of the French monarchy in the west. Meanwhile, Poland, Bohemia, and Hungary had all achieved nationality, though through internal dissensions and Mongol and Turkish aggression, the political evolution of Eastern Europe remained relatively backward.

In the cosmopolitan world of fief and manor rudimentary national monarchies had emerged during the Dark Ages. The most efficient mediaeval government developed in England, following the Norman Conquest of 1066; the Norman kings, the rulers of the best organized state in Europe, imposed their authority on a richer and more civilized country. The Conqueror, and his two able sons, William Rufus and Henry I, brought order to this manageable area, without destroying the native institutions, which they adapted to their own ends. Following his marriage to Eleanor of Aquitaine, the Angevin Henry II (1154–89), whose empire extended over half France, showed a ferocious efficiency; his administrators, building on the work of Henry I, founded a state able to take the strain imposed by Richard I and John. A rudimentary bureaucracy developed; efficient judges built up a body of common law applicable to the whole land.

Richard I was a forceful and picturesque absentee, absorbed in far-flung adventures; John, in some respects an abler character, but cursed with the unstable temperament of his family, also nourished European ambitions. His coalition with the German Emperor, Otto IV, against the French, came to disaster on the field of Bouvines (1214), a landmark in English and French history. This failure put John at the mercy of his barons, who forced him to accede to the famous Magna Carta (1215), which came to be regarded as the foundation of the liberties of England. This very practical document secured the feudal rights of the baronage and the liberties of the burgesses and lesser gentry who had taken the baronial side. It represents the triumph of substantial elements of the realm against a feudal king who had broken the feudal conventions, and in that sense it is a national achievement. The interpretation put upon it by the lawyers of the seventeenth century was to make the Great Charter a cornerstone of political liberty.

The work of consolidation was carried further by the great legislator, Edward I (1272–1307), who invoked the co-operation of the gentry and burgesses in government. During the previous reign of Henry III, English parliamentary institutions, destined to have so great an influence on the political development of the world, had first been called into being. Their appearance reflects a movement common to most of Europe, and far advanced in Spain. The English Parliament lasted on in close alliance with the central government into the sixteenth and seventeenth centuries, and finally attained sovereign power. That it did so was due to the relatively close-knit texture of the English state, following the establishment of a strong monarchy in a limited area; to the habit of co-operation between the substantial elements of the English realm; and to the creation, by a series of great lawyers and administrators, of a body of law to which even kings had to defer. In England, the great mediaeval tradition of the Rule of Law, theoretically accepted all over Christendom, but so seldom realized, was implemented by a body representative of the whole realm. And there is a direct descent from the great jurist Bracton, who wrote in the middle of the thirteenth century, through Fortescue in the late fifteenth, to the political thought of Hooker and Locke, which inspired the evolution not only of the English state but of the spirit of the American constitution. In the limited area of their islands, the Lords and Commons of England, in a realm centralized by strong kings, worked out lasting institutions destined to influence the world; their co-operation is the best example of that concentration on the possible, rare in the Middle Ages, which alone could secure solid success.

Across the Channel, the French kings, though the rulers of a richer society, were faced with a less manageable problem; in the long run they, too, succeeded in creating a centralized but absolute state. Here areas were larger, the great magnates more formidable, provincial feelings stronger. The royal domain was confined to a small area round Paris and Orleans; but the French kings worked in steady alliance with the Church and they disposed of considerable religious prestige. Louis VI (1108–37), with the aid of the able clerical administrator, Suger, consolidated his power to the Seine basin and parts of the upper Loire; but his authority was negligible over the great fiefs of France; over Flanders and Burgundy, over Gascony, Guienne, Barcelona, and Toulouse. His successor, Louis VII, was to prove an ineffective rival to the able Henry II, who seized the opportunity of Louis's divorce to marry Eleanor of Aquitaine, for whose temperament he was a better match. Philip Augustus (1180–1223), one of the ablest of the French kings, extended his dominions steadily along the Channel coast, and south-west above the Loire. He watched the opportunities created by Angevin family dissensions; he was methodical, diplomatic, far-seeing; by the end of his reign he had secured practically the entire Angevin inheritance. His victory at Bouvines was due in no small part to the support of the levies of Paris and marks a real stirring of French national sentiment.

The middle thirteenth century saw the climax of mediaeval civilization; it was marked in French history by the reign of St. Louis (1226–70) a figure of European reputation. Like his predecessors, he based his power on Paris, and worked in close alliance with the clergy. While Henry III was rebuilding Edward the Confessor's foundation at Westminster, Notre Dame and the

Sainte Chapelle were rising in Paris; the King's Law was recognized according to the new Italian method; his reign marks a consolidation of royal power. His grandson, Philip the Fair (1285–1314), created a French government of European calibre, centralized, and with an increasingly lay administration, reflecting the economic expansion of the age, displaying a novel sense of business, strong enough to exploit the collapse of the Empire and the exhaustion of the Papacy and to thwart the ambitions of Boniface VIII. For the greater part of the fourteenth century, the Papacy, in exile of Avignon, was under the control of the kings of France.

Such in bare outline are the major landmarks of English and French history up to the end of the thirteenth century. Before turning to contemporary events in Scandinavia and Central Europe, we must glance at the evolution of Spain, the dominant theme of whose history was the struggle with the Moors.

The Reconquista begins in the second half of the eleventh century. The famous Roderigo de Bivar, known as the Cid from the Arab *Sidi,* Lord, was a contemporary of William the Conqueror. Based on the uplands of Leon and Castille, united under Ferdinando I in 1037, and on Catalonia, with its contacts eastward into Italy and Provence, the Spaniards recaptured Toledo, Saragossa, and Valencia in the eleventh century; Lisbon by the middle of the twelfth. In 1212 the Almohades' counter-attack was broken in the famous battle of Las Navas de Tolosa. Following the conquest of Cordova and Seville, the Moorish power had been extirpated from most of Spain save Grenada; the traditions of this long-drawn Crusade, in which knights from all over Europe participated, deeply affected Spanish development. The Castilian and Aragonese monarchies, the latter united with Catalonia and Valencia, combined centralized power with a settled constitution; by the close of the thirteenth century, Aragon was strong enough to take over the Sicilian kingdom from the House of Anjou and to dominate the Western Mediterranean.

Meanwhile, in the North-West, the Scandinavian peoples were building the foundations of a vigorous society. Denmark, the smallest but the most populous of the Scandinavian states, commanded the entry to the Baltic; Norway achieved the most far-flung expansion; Sweden, with essentially Baltic interests, was destined to become a great military power. All had stabilized into separate kingdoms by the middle eleventh century.

As already observed, the heathen Scandinavians displayed a sturdy economic individualism and an ingrained respect for law. Every free farmer and copyholder, whatever his economic status, could attend the Assembly or Thing. The Althing of Iceland, founded in 930 following the Norwegian settlement of the island. is the oldest national assembly in the world.

In Scandinavia, kingship, originally founded for plunder and glory, was superimposed on vigorous popular institutions. There followed a phase of consolidation and expansion. Already in the tenth century the Norwegians had colonized Iceland and were pushing north to Greenland; explorers are believed to have reached North America. We have already observed the extent of Knut's empire; in 1066 the Norwegian Harald Hardrada, the Varangian, fell before the axes of Harald Godwinsson's huskarls at Stamford Bridge, attempting the conquest of Northern England. Though the English conquests were lost, Denmark in the twelfth century remained the dominant power. Waldemar the Great and Waldemar the Victorious (1202–41) drove east along the Baltic and north into Estonia. Under Sverre of Norway (1177–1202) and Magnus Barnlock of Sweden (1275–90), national states were further consolidated.

The foundations of the three states was thus secured; but with the German drive eastward—the Teutonic Knights bought Esthonia from Denmark in the middle fourteenth century—and the rise of the Hansa cities, German political and economic influence increased. Since middle-class development was backward, in part through this competition, the kings had not the natural allies they found in the West. German princes exploited Scandinavian feuds; the Hansa had a vote in the election of the Danish kings. When a bid to unite the three kingdoms was made, it failed, for when the famous union of Kalmar (1397) was made between Denmark and Norway, Queen Margarethe ruled Sweden as well; but the Swedes soon broke away.

None the less, by the close of the Middle Ages, Denmark and Norway, together a formidable naval and military power, played an important part in the politics of North Germany; Sweden, united and independent, was already expanding along the north-eastern Baltic territories; all had a vigorous political, legal, and economic inheritance. Like the English, the French, and the Spaniards, and unlike the Germans, they had created the political basis of nationality.

While the peoples of the western seaboard had thus laid the foundations of national states, the history of the Germanies ran a different course. In the tenth century it had looked as if the main political initiative in Europe would be German; events now frustrated this prospect. The dominating fact of German and Italian politics from the tenth century was the existence of the Empire, with its Italian preoccupations. The Ottonian dynasty had been succeeded in the eleventh century by the Salian emperors; Conrad II and Henry III were already closely preoccupied with the affairs of the Papacy, and the death of Henry III (1056) was followed by a period of confusion. The geographical and political difficulties of government in the Germanies were even more formidable than in France; the great tribal dukedoms controlled only limited areas and were an obstacle to central administration; the situation paralleled on a larger and severer scale the disorganization of Anglo-Danish England. But the greatest handicap of the German rulers was their imperial inheritance; following the dream of universal domination and the lure of Italian ambitions, they were never able to consolidate a stable government. Henry IV (1056–1106) became involved in a prolonged conflict with the Papacy. Gregory VII, following the ambitious dream of universal Papal authority, struck at the ecclesiastical roots of Henry's power in Germany; in 1077, eleven years after Hastings, while William was riveting his power on England, Henry stood, a penitent, in the snow at Canossa.

The reign of Frederick Barbarossa (1152–90), coincident with the full twelfth-century renaissance, marks the climax of the Mediaeval Empire. Not since Charlemagne had an emperor enjoyed so spectacular a prestige; yet he never mastered both Germany and Italy. He found Germany devastated by war, the rising prosperity of the cities threatened by feudal disorder. He imposed a measure of stability, at first in alliance with the tribal dukes. To his cousin Henry the Lion, Duke of Saxony and Bavaria, he gave a free hand in the north-east; on the southeastern borders he created the Duchy of Austria; and he worked in alliance with the great bishoprics, Köln, Mainz, and Trier. But his Italian interests cut across his work in Germany; in 1154 he embarked on the first of six Italian campaigns. Regularly with the spring the motley feudal *cortèges* crawled over the Brenner; regularly they were decimated by Italian resistance and the Italian climate. Apart from the control of Rome, Frederick's principal objectives were the rich cities of Lombardy. After a gruelling struggle, in which the Germans razed Milan to the ground, the Lombard League, in alliance with the Papacy, routed his armies at Legnano (1176). Meanwhile, in the north, Henry the Lion, employing the latest siege technique learnt in Italy, had been waging unequal war with the Wends and Slavs of Mecklenburg, Schwerin, and the Baltic coast. In 1160 Lübeck had been founded; in 1163 Pomerania had been overrun; but by 1179 he was in rebellion, and Frederick had to break him and divide his inheritance. It was the end of the attempt at conciliation, and when, in 1189, Frederick set out on the third Crusade, and was drowned in the following year in a Cilician river, he left behind him an unstable inheritance.

Four years before his death, the Emperor had made a dynastic coup which was to set Germany and Italy by the ears for half a century, drive the Papacy into the clutches of the French kings and bring the Hohenstaufen power to destruction. He had married his son, afterwards Henry VI, to Constance, heiress of Norman Sicily, then one of the richest and best-organized states in Europe; the Papacy was to be caught between two fires and a Hohenstaufen dominion over both Germany and Italy realized.

The Sicilian kingdom, like the Norman state in England, had been founded in the eleventh century. From 1016 Norman adventurers had consolidated their grip on Sicily and South Italy; by 1071 Robert Guiscard had driven the Greeks from Bari. Soon they were masters of the whole of Sicily; Count Roger II was crowned king at Palermo in 1130. Here was established a government comparable in efficiency to that of Norman England. Henry VI, crowned King of Sicily in 1194, might have consolidated this inheritance, but he died young, and his son Frederick II was left an indigent ward of the most formidable of mediaeval popes.

In method, administration, and diplomatic skill, Innocent III (1198–1216) showed real greatness; if any man could have realized the ideal of a Papal theocracy controlling all Europe, Lothar of Segni would have succeeded. His pontificate marks the height of Papal prestige, of spiritual backed by temporal power. But he never healed the breach between Papacy and empire, and Frederick grew up with an intense hatred of the institution which had overshadowed his boyhood. He set himself to regain his inheritance in Germany; he, too, followed the dream of European domination. He attempted for decades the task of uniting Germany and Italy, and by the middle thirteenth century he was brought to defeat, humiliation, and death. The Papacy and its Italian allies brought him down, and with the empire in its old sense—at the price of calling in the French kings, to whom had now passed the main political initiative, earlier in the hands of the Germans.

The effort of breaking the empire had cost the Papacy much in popularity and prestige. The heavy Papal taxation; the spectacle of the Holy Father involved in power politics in an age which saw the foundation of the Dominican and Franciscan Orders and a brilliant intellectual revival; the increasing worldly commitments inseparable from the Papal attempt at European domination, all foreshadowed the sequel in the fourteenth and fifteenth centuries. That sequel began with Philip le Bel's deposition of Boniface VIII, who claimed all and more than his predecessors, and subsequent 'captivity' of the Popes at Avignon (1309–78). The great schism (1378–1417) further diminished Papal prestige; and with Nicholas V (1417–31) the Papacy became an Italian city state, srtuggling with success in the turbulent stream of Italian politics, and consolidated by the middle fifteenth century as a Renaissance principality.

The results of the struggle on the empire had also been disastrous; the faint prospects of German unity receded, the number of petty principalities multiplied. The empire passed first to the Czech kings of the House of Luxemburg, and finally to the Habsburgs; it could have no future save as part of a dynastic inheritance based on solid territorial possessions.

From the strategic key position of Bohemia, Charles IV (1346–78) attempted to stabilize the imperial constitution. The Golden Bull of 1356 defined the precedence of the Electors; disputed elections and Papal interference diminished. A realist of a new kind, the author of a candid autobiography, the Czech emperor exchanged his Italian rights for hard cash. But the competing claims of Bohemia and the empire made the Luxemburg power unstable; his son Wenceslas, a peasant type contrasting with his able father, was deposed from the empire in 1400. His successor, Sigismund (1410–37) attempted to stave off the disruption of Christendom by convening the Councils of Constance and Basle. But the emperor became involved in a conflict with his own people, occasioned by the Hussite wars; he bequeathed his dynastic claims on the empire; Bohemia and Hungary to the Habsburgs.

Back in the late thirteenth century, the first Habsburg Emperor, Rudolf, a relatively obscure prince from Switzerland, had begun a slow expansion, the foundation of Habsburg power. With the election of Albrecht II (1438) and his successor Frederick III, the empire became in practice hereditary in the Habsburg house. After the failure of the grandiose projects of the high Middle Ages, the imperial power revived in the hands of princes who had concentrated on the possible and developed a centralized dynasty able to compete with the new national monarchies of the West.

Italy, meanwhile, culturally, as will be seen, far in advance of the North, but politically disunited, remained a world of city states, a kaleidoscopic world of intrigue, a prelude to Renaissance politics. The predominant powers were Venice, Milan, Florence, and the Papacy, while French Angevin kings were established in Naples; their disputed inheritance was destined to cause a conflict between France and Spain which was to devastate Italy.

III

Thus the contest of Papacy and empire contributed to deprive both Germany and Italy of the prospect, always tenuous, of national consolidation, and Europe of the possibility of a united Christendom.

Though that ideal was fading by the thirteenth century, it had inspired an expansion to the south-east, outside Europe. By the eleventh century the Spaniards were beginning their long Western crusade in Spain: the first general Eastern crusade was launched in its last decade, a real counterattack. The course of the crusades and the history of the Latin States in the Levant is outside our present scope; though these European outposts were ephemeral, they were an expression of European unity, of a new vitality, and of the power of an idea.

Northwards, meanwhile, along the eastern borders, a dangerous threat had again materialized out of Asia. The Mongol hordes which appeared in South Russia in 1222, formed the western wave of a fantastic expansion. Its effects crippled the development of Eastern Europe for centuries. Jenghis Khan (1154–1227) had subdued Northern China, attempted to destroy the Sung Dynasty, devastated Bokhara and Samarkand, and crossed the mountains into India. His son, Ogdai Khan, overran Armenia, Georgia, and Mesopotamia; his subordinate, Batu, invaded Europe. As we have recorded, they dealt the *coup de grâce* to Kiev-Russia, cutting off Muscovy from Byzantium and the West. They advanced north-west into Silesia and Poland, through the Carpathian passes into Hungary. Europe stood helpless and demoralized, preoccupied with the struggle of Papacy and empire; but with the death of Ogdai in 1241 the Mongols withdrew; save for this happy event, the West might well have been overrun. Under Kublai Khan (1259–94) the Mongol aggression waned; but they continued in occupation of the South Russian steppe, terrorized Muscovy, and raided Poland. Though the West was saved, Eastern Europe had received a severe blow, which was to be followed by the Turkish invasion of the fifteenth and sixteenth centuries. Thus Christendom was successful in expelling the Moors from Spain and established short-lived crusading states in the Levant, but had suffered a severe setback on the eastern frontiers.

The early settlement of the Czechs, Poles, and Hungarians in Central and Eastern Europe has already been described. In the fourteenth century, Czech contacts with the West became closer. John of Luxemburg, famous in old age as the blind king of Bohemia, was a picturesque cosmopolitan figure, connected by marriage with the French dynasty. Guided by his pages, he charged into the mêlée at Crécy and there perished; though his crest, was adopted by the English Prince of Wales who inherited his plumes and motto from Philippa of Hainault. His son Charles

IV, was the ablest of the Bohemian kings; as we have seen, he attained the empire. Combining a Western and a Slav inheritance, he fostered the economic and cultural life of Bohemia; he invited French and Italian architects to rebuild Prague, the great Cathedral and the bridge over the Moldau. He encouraged industries in glass, pottery, and cloth. His reign coincided with the greatest period of mediaeval Czech painting; and in 1348 he founded the famous University of Prague, the leading centre of learning in Central Europe. The marriage of the emperor's daughter to Richard II of England may have occasioned the spread of Wycliffite ideas into Bohemia.

With the Hussite movement came the wars of religion, in which the Czechs defied the whole might of Catholic Germany. The burning of Huss at the Council of Constance in 1415, under circumstances of peculiar perfidy, gave rise to a national revolt led by the famous John Zizka. The Czechs beat off successive German attacks; though the revolt ended in 1434, it was on relatively favourable terms; a tough tradition had been created. With the election of George Podiebrad (1457), a Czech noble, the county achieved its greatest mediaeval phase of political independence and cultural development. But this period was short-lived; at the close of the century Bohemia passed by inheritance into the ephemeral empire of Vladislav of Poland and Hungary, to his successor Lewis; and finally, with the collapse of the Magyar power, to the Habsburgs.

North-east from Bohemia in the early eleventh century, the Polish Prince Boleslas the Great had extended his rule over Pomerania, Silesia, and parts of Slovakia, welding the Polish clans in a degree of unity and leaving traditions of Polish domination. But the Polish territories had little geographical unity. Boleslas the Bold, who made incursions into White Russia and Hungary, had been crowned King of Poland; but his successor divided his dominions among his sons, the senior principality of Cracow exercising a theoretical and intermittent suzerainty. These divisions, which long persisted, left the Poles hard put to it to meet the German and Tatar threat in the thirteenth century.

For by the twelfth century, the Germans were driving east along the Baltic. The settlement of the Teutonic Knights in Prussia was a new fact: in 1226 Conrad of Masovia had invited the aid of this Order—which had its headquarters at Venice and was experienced in the Palestinian crusades—against the heathen tribes of Prussia. By 1283 they had enslaved or extirpated the native Prussians and established themselves between Polish territory and the sea. Finally, the Mongol invasion devastated the country. In 1300 Poland came under Czech overlordship.

The Poles regained their independence under Kasimir the Great (1333–70), who consolidated his authority with method and foresight. He pushed south-east into Galicia and absorbed Lwow, initiating Polish ambitions towards the Black Sea, and he codified Polish law and encouraged urban settlement. In 1364 he founded the University of Cracow, the cultural rallying point of Poland for centuries; he also encouraged the large-scale settlement of Jews. Like his contemporary Charles IV, he was a builder and a founder of cities; his reign laid the foundation of Polish domination under the Jagellon kings. Kasimir was succeeded by his nephew, Lewis of Hungary, whose Polish dominions passed to his daughter Jadwiga. In 1386 she married Jagello, Grand Prince of Lithuania, who turned Catholic and ruled Poland as Ladislas IV.

The Lithuanians had long been pushing out from the Baltic hinterland over the Russian waterways to the southern Steppe; in 1251 the Grand Prince Mindamgas had belatedly abandoned pagan rites on his conversion to the Catholic Faith, and Olgurd, in the middle fourteenth century, had ruled from the Baltic to the Black Sea. The combined Polish-Lithuanian power could meet the Tatar and Teuton threat. In 1399 Vytantas of Lithuania and Ladislas Jagello checked the Tatars on the Vorskla; in 1410 he smashed the Teutonic Knights at Tannenberg, a turning point in the history of Eastern Europe, in the struggle of Teuton, Lithuanian, and Slav. Jagello fell fighting the Ottoman Turks.

The Jagellon kings supported the lesser nobility against the great feudatories, but the policy exacted its price; with Kasimir Jagellon IV (1447–92), the monarchy became elective and financially crippled. Along with widening political ambitions and responsibilities, went a diminution of royal power, and by the statute of Miezawa (1454) the privileges of the nobles were confirmed. Polish representative institutions, uncontrolled by central government, took a wrong turn. The external responsibilities of the Jagellon kings, their struggle with Turk and Muscovite, and their own dynastic dissensions, which rendered the maintenance of the Polish-Lithuanian union precarious, put them at the mercy of the nobility. After 1505 a single member of the assembly could defeat any measure by the 'liberum veto.' From this perversion of parliamentary institutions came many of the political misfortunes of Poland.

Meanwhile, south of the Carpathians, during the Middle Ages, the Magyars had increasingly absorbed Western influences. Following their conversion to Latin Christianity in the eleventh century, tribal society was giving place to feudalism. Under Bela III and Andrew II this westernizing process continued, and the famous Golden Bull of 1228 defined the privileges of the Hungarian nobility, jealously guarded into modern times. The Mongol invasions smashed and paganized much of the work of the thirteenth century; with Andrew III (1290–1301), the native Arpad dynasty came to an end. But under an Angevin family from Naples, Hungary became the main bastion of Christendom on the Danube: Lewis the Great (1342–82), a hard-hitting westernizer, subdued the great tribal Bans, encouraged urban development and western immigration, reformed the finances, exploited the gold mines of Transylvania. He extended his power into Croatia, Bosnia, and Dalmatia; he even attempted to control Naples. He ruled Poland and, as we have remarked, Jadwiga, his daughter, married Ladislas Jagello.

These spectacular achievements were followed by a long and gruelling struggle with the Turks. In the middle fifteenth century the famous Hunyadi family won control of the country. John Hunyadi defeated the Turks at Szeged (1442); four years later he became Regent of Hungary. He beat off Mehemet II from Belgrad, and his son, the renowned Mathias Corvinus, a contemporary of George Podiebrad of Bohemia, was elected king in 1458. Hungary again had a native ruler, and his reign marks the climax and foreshadows the decline of the Hungarian state. He was a humanist as well as a warrior and statesman, creating an administration and a standing army on the Western model; a real Renaissance prince, he founded the great library at Buda, and encouraged native architecture on Italian lines. He is the most splendid of the Hungarian rulers, but he died at fifty with no legitimate heir. Under his successor, Vladislav II, the Hungarian power declined, and on the field of Mohacs, in 1526, two-thirds of the country was lost to the Turks. It was the end of the greatness of mediaeval Hungary.

Such, in bare outline, were the fortunes of the Czech, Polish, and Hungarian kingdoms which bordered the Germanies to the east; all had created national traditions, all had passed through phases of spectacular political power and none had achieved the degree of centralized government which developed in the West.

Meanwhile in France, England, and Spain, strong national monarchies continued to consolidate. In England, the reign of Edward III saw a period of military expansion, and the development of France and England was set back by the disastrous Hundred Years War. The contest, starting in 1340, dragged on intermittently until 1453: its episodes are famous; Crécy (1346) and Agincourt (1415), the exploits of Joan of Arc, the relief of Orleans. The maintenance of the English hold on France was based on the alliance with Burgundy: the dependence of the Low Countries on the export of English wool cemented this common interest, but with the death of the English King Henry V (1422), and the reorganization of the French armies, the English domination collapsed.

The sequel was a remarkable French recovery. The famous *Chronicle* of Commines has recorded the force and cunning with which Louis XI (1461–83) outmanœuvred the great Duke of Burgundy, Charles the Bold, whose power extended from Switzerland to Flanders and the sea, and who met his death at the hands of the Swiss pikemen at Nancy (1477). Through successive dynastic chances and diplomatic manœuvres, Burgundy, Maine, Anjou, Provence, and Brittany reverted to the French crown; France by the end of the fifteenth century was the strongest power in the West. During the sequel in England, the Wars of the Roses, the great magnates massacred one another, and from it the Tudor monarchy emerged, destined to impose peace and a new political discipline.

Two factors were important in the French Burgundian struggle, the power of the Flemish cities and the efficiency of the Swiss pikemen. The commerce of Flanders had been fostered by the Burgundian dukes, for a practical bourgeoisie controlled this vital area of Europe. In Switzerland, in the late thirteenth century, the League of the Forest Cantons, Uri, Schwyz, and Unterwalden, had begun a long resistance of the Habsburgs, which ended in the recognition of Swiss independence, the independence of a non-feudal society.

Looking back, over the broad development of mediaeval history, we can observe that in the west—in France, England, and Spain—strong states are in being by the end of the Middle Ages, built on foundations laid in the twelfth and thirteenth centuries. Western governments had concentrated on the possible; in England, in particular, parliamentary institutions have been harnessed by a strong central power. In Germany and Italy, on the other hand, no national state has developed, for the rulers of the old empire had followed impracticable objectives, and the later empire had a future only as a Habsburg family concern. Here on the Danube, in the steady Habsburg expansion from small beginnings, is an equivalent to western development, and the dominant political fact in Central Europe.

Italy continued the prey of warring principalities and foreign adventurers; meanwhile the Papacy, now a Renaissance state, has been, like the Empire to the Germanies, the political curse of the country. In Bohemia and Eastern Europe, Czechs, Poles, and Hungarians have all achieved spectacular but ephemeral empires; but only in Bohemia has a solid tradition been built, and that is jeopardized by racial and religious strife. Meanwhile, Poland-Lithuania is attempting to rule from the Baltic to the Black Sea, and both Poles and Hungarians have long been involved in the struggle against Tatar and Turk.

By the end of the Middle Ages the main political future of Europe is largely determined; the rise of centralized states in the West and the development of Habsburg power contrasting with the unstable situation in the Germanies and Eastern Europe. The centres of political and economic power which emerge from the Middle Ages are the national monarchies in the West; the great cities of North Italy and Flanders, whose prosperity secured the foundations of the Italian and Flemish Renaissance; and the Habsburg family possessions; all are the result of a policy which has abandoned Mediaeval ideas of glory and universal dominion; all are the expression of forces which, at a price, looked to the future.

IV

Against this political background must be set the cultural achievements, ecclesiastical and secular, of the Middle Ages. Both were cosmopolitan, both the creation of men of diverse racial origins, drawn from all levels of society. The Church in particular provided opportunities for talent, and since its offices were not hereditary, continually recruited from the lay population; hence in part, perhaps, its vigour and relatively high level of administrative competence. The genius of Rome was indeed inherited by the Papal Curia, which in the time of Innocent III had become the centre of legal business from all over Christendom, and attained a bureaucratic efficiency in advance of any contemporary organization. To the Papal Court journeyed learned men from all countries; men of affairs, lay and secular, found in Rome a standard of systematic government and diplomatic subtlety from which they drew valuable experience. The splendour of the Papal ritual, the wealth and pomp which characterized the spiritual leader of Christendom, dazzled, overawed, and sometimes shocked the minds of innumerable pilgrims. These pilgrimages, not only to Rome but to the shrines of saints all over Christendom, led to a widespread habit of travel in a predominantly static society, among the poor clergy as well as among the fighting men and the rich. The pilgrim and student songs of the Middle Ages often attained a high dramatic and lyrical level.

The building of centralized government was primarily the work of clerical administrators; in the thirteenth century they were reinforced by laymen trained in the new Law Schools of Italy. Justinian's *Digest* was being studied in the middle-eleventh century in North Italy; by the twelfth century schools had grown up at Bologna for the study of Civil Law, expanded by glossators and commentators on the original text. This precise written Law, with its tendency to absolutism, became predominant in France, and by the early fifteenth century, in Germany; but in England and Scandinavia the native customary Law held its own, though modified by Southern influence. The English Customary Law, in particular, reflected the ancient decision of questions according to precedent, in consultation with the 'oldest men' who would 'declare' the Law. Supplemented by a body of Case Law, and systematized by southern method, this procedure was flexible but well defined.

This Customary Law proved a bulwark of English liberties; it sustained the tradition that custom and precedent, reflecting the sense of the whole community, was more powerful than the ruler's will; it was supplemented by the Roman idea of a universal justice, existing in its own right. This ideal justice reinforced barbarian conservatism, and in the Middle Ages over most of Europe the sanction both of custom and of universal law was constantly invoked against tyrannical rulers. This traditional hatred of arbitrary power proved one of the most important of the legacies of the time.

We have already noted the rise of representative institutions in the West; over most of the Continent, assemblies of notables, drawn not only from the nobility but from the smaller gentry and the towns, grew up from the thirteenth century onwards. In Spain the Cortes, in England the Parliament, in France the Assembly of the three Estates of the Realm, in the Germanies the Landtag, in Poland and Hungary the Diet—all reflect the same need. In Eastern Europe these assemblies remained aristocratic and representative only of upper class interest, since the central power was weak; in England, France, Scandinavia, and Spain, on the other hand, the minor gentry and the burgesses played an increasingly important part.

These assemblies met at irregular intervals according to the king's needs, not as a right but as a duty. They were convened to hear and discuss such business as the king's government put before them, to carry out such aspects of policy as came within their scope and to present petitions and grievances. Their primary function was to supply revenue; though the classes were separately represented, all met together at the same time. The pattern of these institutions varied; in England there were two Chambers, Lords and Commons; in France, as in Germany, three Estates— Nobility, Clergy, and the Third Estate; all reflected the mediaeval idea of a static social order in which all should co-operate and in which the various classes should receive their due according to custom and the divine order. These assemblies, most lasting, as we have seen, in England, proved the most important political legacy of the Middle Ages.

In the wider field, the development of mediaeval intellectual life was original and vigorous. The Carolingian period had preserved the basis of mediaeval knowledge; with the economic expansion of the eleventh century came the beginnings of a revival which reached a real brilliance in the twelfth and thirteenth centuries. The framework of this learning was rigid and alien to modern minds; in its full development it came to be known as 'scholasticism' and within its convention, achieved a wide range and acute analysis. It was purely logical, but its extreme rationalism had no roots in scientific experiment and proceeded from acts of faith. Its foundation was the routine study of Latin, of which the elements had to be mastered before the cosmopolitan world of mediaeval learning could be entered at all. In the monastic and cathedral schools there had survived the rudiments of teaching method, inherited from the decadent Empire. They taught grammar, 'rhetoric' or composition, and elementary logic, known collectively as the 'trivium': this was the foundation of scholastic learning and its inculcation was the main task of the teachers in the schools and later in the Universities. The more advanced subjects, the 'quadrivium,' consisted of music, arithmetic, geometry, and astronomy, all of an elementary kind. This rather restricted curriculum was, none the less, the gateway to a world of knowledge far beyond the range of an illiterate laity; for up to the thirteenth century few even of the kings could write. It gave access to a large number of Classical texts; the majority of Latin authors were already familiar by the twelfth century. All over Western Europe, and particularly in France, there was, indeed, a ravenous demand for knowledge among the younger generation at the beginning of the twelfth century, comparable to that shown by the fifth-century Greeks. The genius of modern France is now first apparent, logical, precise, direct; the Northern peoples were finding their feet and entering with crude vigour upon their ancient intellectual heritage. This new demand was met by institutions peculiar to the Middle Ages, which have proved one of their most original and valuable legacies. In Paris there grew up a University, an association of masters and pupils under the patronage of the bishop. Masters were licensed by the

Bishop's authority after examination. The preliminary course was known as the 'Faculty' of Arts and included Philosophy; there were also 'Faculties' of Theology, Canon Law, and, later, Medicine. The students were divided into 'nations' according to their origins, and the University governed by a Rector elected by the masters. From a jostling and penurious existence in inns and hostels, new 'colleges' grew up, often founded by lay benefactors. Here already in the twelfth century is a system which expanded over Western Christendom and on which Universities all over the world have been modelled.

The shortage of books resulted in great emphasis on disputation and oratory; students would flock to hear a popular master and his following would endure the discomforts and dangers of mediaeval travel. Controversy was passionate and often riotous; the sensation created in the early twelfth century by the brilliant mind of Abelard, whose doctrines were spiced with a flavour of heresy, is a famous example. With the coming of the Friars and of the Dominican and Franciscan Orders in particular, the intellectual life of the Universities became more strict and widespread. The German doctor, Albertus Magnus, at Cologne, and his pupil St. Thomas Aquinas, a southern Italian, were the greatest philosophical minds of the Middle Ages. St. Thomas set himself to reconcile the new Aristotelian learning, derived through the Arabs from Byzantium, with the dogmas of the Latin Church. His *Summae,* vast surveys of the whole field of mediaeval religion and morals, are the monumental expression of the scholastic outlook: cast in a rigid frame of systematic argument, they display within their convention an astonishing power of mind.

By the thirteenth century a solid structure of dogmatic learning had been built up; it served as an intellectual discipline at a critical phase of European development and produced not only philosophers and theologians but men of high administrative ability. The Latin, moreover, in which scholastic disputations were conducted and in which sermons were preached, developed into a flexible and powerful language which displayed distinctive qualities of its own. Derived in part from Patristic Latin, it became the instrument of a formidable eloquence.

And indeed, though there was much that was arid in mediaeval Christianity, there was much that was creative and picturesque.

During many centuries the Church had accumulated immense landed property and treasure; and it commanded the loyalty and the belief of the vast majority of laymen. In consequence the full resources of society were at its disposal, and buildings were erected of astonishing size; even when stripped of their ornament and glass, they are the admiration of posterity. The great cathedrals and abbeys up and down the length and breadth of Europe still testify to the spiritual unity of mediaeval Christendom and the skill of mediaeval architects. Out of the massive but relatively clumsy structure of Romanesque there developed the new and beautiful Gothic style of the twelfth and thirteenth centuries; built in the north particularly to display the blaze of stained glass, as at Chartres and Canterbury, the slender pillars supported a roof of a height unknown to Antiquity, balanced by flying buttresses of astonishing virtuosity. The exteriors were designed to display a wealth of sculpture which attained a superlative distinction in the twelfth century, particularly in Northern France and the Rhineland, the style of these figures combining a formidable spirituality and strength. The great Churches were the centres of civic life, the focus of their countryside. In the later Middle Ages a more elaborate style superseded the clean lines of the best period, but it displays magnificent craftsmanship and sound proportions. This later architecture was the expression of the wealth, the pride, and the piety of the new princes and merchants of the later Middle Ages. If a society is to be judged by the excellence of its art—very often a good standard of judgement—Mediaeval Christendom was a healthy civilization.

While the life of learning was carried on by the Church, the majority of Western Europeans remained illiterate, and military power was in the hands of a fighting aristocracy. They had their own tradition, which, in its full development, proved original and influential.

They were nothing new in Europe; the warriors of the Bronze and Early Iron Ages, a fighting class superimposed on the Neolithic peasantry, had anticipated this social pattern, and, indeed, the Celtic aristocracies, in particular, had shown strikingly similar characteristics. The Baronage of the early Middle Ages were brutal and savage, their interests confined to hunting and war, bounded by the horizon of their own countryside. The Crusades gave some of the worst elements a new outlet and increased the sense of European community, the contacts with new and civilizing influences. But Mediaeval secular society was military: it inherited and elaborated barbaric traditions, preserved in the later cult of genealogies, titles, and Coats of Arms, which was to dominate the upper ranks of European society until the French Revolution. The Northern ideal of a gentleman differed from that of Antiquity; the practice of duelling, for example, which persisted up to the nineteenth century, is a barbaric inheritance. The sentiment of honour and obligation, particularly when touched by Christian ethics, is a more constructive aspect of the same convention.

Feudal society, like the contemporary Church, was cosmopolitan, and the centre of feudal fashion and of feudal ideas was France. In their varying interpretations, the other European aristocracies imitated French customs; this influence long persisted in modified form and was later reinforced by French intellectual leadership. So a high degree of civilization grew up within the closed circle of the nobility and the richer gentry; exotic, interbred, and proud. In France, Germany, and Eastern Europe, this development was most typical, for, as we have noted, the most characteristic feudal society grew up in open country, along the Western Seaboard and in the Northern and Eastern Plains, rather than in mountainous areas or on the Mediterranean. In England rigid class distinctions did not persist, and in Scandinavia the tradition never took deep root, while in the South the nobility became urbanized and never developed the exclusiveness of France and Germany. But in the Eastern Marches of Europe the feudal class came to an exaggerated development; here huge tracts of country, originally granted to adventurers, had become more heavily populated, and vast estates had grown up. The racial divisions of Eastern Europe accentuated feudal arrogance.

Thus, with local variations, over much of Europe north of the Alps there grew up a similar social pattern, with similar standards of behaviour and mentality. This society grew up gradually; the crude baronage of the eleventh century, with their ringed mail sewn on leather, clumsy swords, and conical headpieces, contrast with their later descendants in elaborate and heraldic plate; while the lines of the twelfth-century civil dress are still Byzantine, very different from the spare, wasp-waisted figures of the fifteenth century. The barbarous wooden structures and the square-cut keep of Norman times are a world away from the huge and complex fortifications of the high Middle Ages.

This transformation was due, fundamentally, to economic causes, but the military class had become more civilized through the fashion of courtly chivalry which grew up during the twelfth century. The whole feudal upper class was bound together by the customs of chivalry; all, even the kings, were knights,—specialized fighting men trained in the use of expensive arms of which they held the monopoly. From the moment when the young noble received the 'accolade'—originally a clout on the back of the neck (col), later sophisticated into a sword-tap—he entered a world which observed a rigid code of behaviour within its own sphere. Protected by his armour, the knight was comparatively safe, and, if unhorsed, could reckon to be held for ransom and treated with courtesy. Chivalrous warfare was, indeed, a form of sport; it was only when Genoese cross-bowmen, Welsh archers, and Swiss pikemen—all of them outside the pale of knightly society—riddled the armour and crippled the horses, that the knightly game became deadly, and the preposterous feudatories tumbled into a ruin at Crécy, Morgarten, and Agincourt. Finally, at the close of the Middle Ages, the arquebus and the siege train superseded them.

Feudal class solidarity was affirmed in more peaceful ways; the nobles and gentry gathered round the households of the great magnates, where their sons learnt manners and the art of war. In this idle and picturesque society there grew up a cult of Romantic love, in which, for the first time in European history, the position of women was elaborately exalted. This Romantic convention, characteristically French, and the customs of gallantry it entailed, were imitated by bourgeois society. Here is one of the most original effects of the Middle Ages, differentiating subsequent European ideas from those of Antiquity or of most Oriental peoples.

The leisure of courtly society was beguiled by a literature which proved influential. We have seen that the barbarian peoples had a tradition of epic poetry, which, in England, Germany, and Scandinavia, produced a notable literature. French epic is more cosmopolitan and deals with events on a greater scale; its most famous early expression is the 'Chanson de Roland,' a panegyric on the glories of France. The hero is a champion of Christendom; the narrative is lucid, well designed, and memorable, easily intelligible and written in simple French. Its theme, a fight to the death against hopeless odds, has roots deep in popular imagination and the poem became widely known outside France. One of the great poems of Europe, it has the universality which was to be characteristic of later French literature. Other *Chansons de Geste* record the feuds and adventures of the baronage, depicting their life and mentality.

This epic poetry, the Christianized legacy of barbaric times, was superseded by the Romances of the twelfth century: the inspiration of this poetry came from the Midi, the lyrical poetry of the troubadours coming into Northern France with the Court of Eleanor of Aquitaine. It was composed by professional writers who worked up traditional themes drawn from Classical and Celtic legends—notably from the Arthurian cycle of Wales and Brittany, elaborated by Romantic digressions. Chrêtien de Troyes is the greatest master of this school, and created a convention which sometimes reached a notable level of prolixity and tedium in the later Middle Ages; a later and better example of this poetry is Malory's 'Morte d'Arthur,' a fresh and strong narrative. This romantic tradition is the background to Renaissance poetry: it greatly enriched subsequent literature.

French prose narrative early attained a high level in the chronicles of Joinville, Villehardouin, and Froissart; all are Romantic, high-principled, and naïve. In the late Middle Ages the *Chronicle* of Commines shows a much more realistic outlook. In England, Chaucer, at the close of the fourteenth century, had already fashioned the native speech into the precise and mellow narratives of the *Canterbury Tales*; while Langland, in 'Piers Plowman,' revived and developed the ancient alliterative English verse. In Germany a school of lyric poets grew up of whom the most famous is Walter von der Vogelweide; but the achievements of the Minnesingers gave place in the later Middle Ages to a prose literature which is often clumsy and banal. German mysticism is expressed in the writings of Eckhardt and Tauler.

In Scandinavia and Iceland there arose a remarkable literature; the *Danish History* of Saxo Grammaticus is paralleled by the work of the Norwegian, Snorri Sturlason (1179–1241), who wrote the *Heimskringla* or Circle of the World. The Icelandic Sagas, too, were written down in this age.

By the twelfth century, Europe north of the Alps was thus producing a new kind of literature in which barbarian and Celtic elements were fused with a Romantic interpretation of Classical legends, written in the vernacular languages and displaying qualities later to be developed in the great national literatures of the northern nations.

South of the Alps, where urban vitality had never been lost, a more direct classical tradition carried on. Dante, Petrarch, Boccaccio, are all forerunners of the Renaissance, for though Dante's theme and outlook are mediaeval, and he intended to write the *Divine Comedy* in Latin, his mastery of Italian is the first great landmark in the native literature. His poetry is the finest literary achievement of the Middle Ages; at once summing up the old outlook and ideals and giving promise for the future.

v

In the economic sphere, the rise of the merchant class is the dominant theme of fifteenth-century history. The bourgeoisie of the mediaeval cities were the forebears of the capitalist and professional classes of the seventeenth century, who were to create a civilization which differed profoundly from that of the Middle Ages. Yet they were long contained within the mediaeval framework, their activities limited and determined by the corporate ideas of the day.

In the elementary agricultural society of the early Middle Ages north of the Alps, a few of the Roman towns situated on key communications had survived; but the majority were simply small market towns, clustered for protection round the keep of a great lord, or, in Eastern Europe, centres of colonization and points of strategic advantage and refuge. But in Italy and Provence, the old civic life had persisted in a degraded form; the population had never fallen as in the north, and the ancient Mediterranean way of life had survived. It was from Italy that the economic revival of the twelfth century was to come, spreading north over the mountains.

The Italian cities had never lost contact with Byzantium; Venice, a trading republic founded amid the lagoons of the Adriatic, commanded the rich hinterland of North Italy; Amalfi and Naples in the South, later Genoa, Pisa, Marseilles, and Barcelona, maintained their contacts with the Levant. This Eastern trade in luxury goods and spices formed the nucleus of an economic revival, and it was in Italy that new business techniques of banking and accountancy were evolved. Money changers, particularly necessary owing to the debased condition of the coinage, began to accept deposits; they became rudimentary bankers. These Lombards, as they were called, spread into most of the important towns of Europe; but it was not until the fourteenth century that Arabic numerals were used and such elementary methods as bills of exchange or double book-keeping were invented.

The causes of the economic revival of the twelfth century, which led up to these developments, are obscure. It was in part due to the Crusades, which certainly increased the power and wealth of the Italian cities: to the opening up of the Baltic: to the imitation of Moorish methods in reconquered parts of Spain: to the rise of the wool trade in England, and to the working of the silver mines of Bohemia, Austria, and the Carpathians. By the thirteenth century Europe was richer and more heavily populated than in any time since the prosperous days of Classical antiquity.

To Venice and Amalfi came the trade of the Levant, the ships coasting along the shores of the Adriatic to Ragusa and the Dalmatian cities; round Southern Italy to Sicily, to Naples and Palermo. Luxury goods from Byzantium, spices and silks from the East, wine from Crete and the Peloponnese, textiles from Salonika—the emporium which tapped the resources of the Balkans—all contributed to the revival of Western and Central European trade. Venetian and Genoese merchants established themselves in Constantinople, where they learnt Greek craftsmanship and business methods. Increasingly they monopolized Byzantine economic life; with the establishment of the Latin Empire in 1204, Venice dominated the Eastern market, and a steady stream of commerce flowed back to the West.

Radiating from Italy, the great European trade routes struck northward over the Brenner and the western passes into Central Europe and France. The Brenner route, running through Innsbruck, carried the trade north-eastward to the Upper Danube and Bohemia and so into Poland, through Cracow and on into Germany, down the Elbe and Vistula, to the Northern Plain and the Baltic. North-westward, through Munich and Augsburg to Frankfurt and Mainz, into Thuringia and down the Rhine valley to Cologne, ran the trade route to the Low Countries, to the rich cities of Flanders, to Bruges, Ghent, and Antwerp, which in turn tapped the trade with England and North-Eastern France. The Baltic trade in timber, cordage, furs, and tar was the monopoly of the Hanseatic cities, Lübeck, Hamburg, and Danzig; eastward, of Novgorod, which commanded the interior of Muscovy. Westward the Italian trade routes ran through Switzerland, Savoy, and Burgundy to Champagne, where great annual fairs were held, attended by merchants from all over France and Germany. Meanwhile the wine trade from South-Western France to England developed through Rouen over the Channel and from Bordeaux round Brittany to the ports of Southern England. From Genoa and Pisa, through Marseilles, Avignon, and Lyons, ran the other western traffic from Italy with France; while from Barcelona came the produce of North-Eastern Spain, and already Lisbon carried on a flourishing trade with Bordeaux, Bristol, and Southampton.

As the tide of this revived commerce flowed over the European trade routes, it brought new life to the cities of the North. Gradually they began to emancipate themselves from their feudal overlords; the strongest earned freedom by rebellion and set up communes independent of the local prince or bishop. Others bought charters defining their rights against the overlord's representatives: others, particularly in Eastern Europe, were new cities with liberties secured by the terms of their foundation. Within their walls there grew up Craft Guilds regulating conditions of production and employment, catering for a very limited local market and maintaining a good standard of work. Later, with the development of a wider commerce and the handling of goods in bulk such as wool and timber, economic power shifted to the Guilds Merchant. In the later Middle Ages a mercantile oligarchy emerged, possessing some capital, often at odds with the smaller

producers, and farming out piece-work to journeymen and artisans. The Guilds developed mainly in the North; in Italy capitalist enterprise appeared earlier, the ruling families being closely
involved and the princes being often drawn from great mercantile and banking families.

So there grew up on the main trade routes powerful communities destined to be the centres of a flourishing civic life, not
only in Italy but in South Germany, the Rhineland, England,
France, Spain, Portugal, and in the Netherlands. The cities of
the Low Countries were to attain a civilization comparable to
that of North Italy; the great textile cities of Flanders, the ports
of London, Bristol, Paris, Rouen, and Bordeaux, the Baltic cities
—all shared in this growing prosperity.

The volume of trade was of course relatively small, and the
rudimentary capitalism of the later Middle Ages was on a limited
scale; there was little opening for enterprise and methods were
strictly conservative. Competition was fierce between towns, but
not in general between Masters of the same Guild; to attempt to
corner the market was contrary to mediaeval ethics and generally
to mediaeval practice, and the Church looked askance on the
lending of money on interest. Business enterprise was in the main
subordinated to a static and conservative society.

But the mentality of the bourgeois differed profoundly from
that either of the feudatories or the peasants; where the baronage
was feckless, proud, and insolvent, the townsman was often
methodical, prudent, and respectable. Crowded together in the
tortuous alleys of their little towns, they became sensitive to public opinion, observant and quick-witted; the French language and
idiom, in particular, was sharpened in this environment. Though
the great merchants of London and Paris might display a proper
civic pride, the majority of bourgeois accepted their humble station in the mediaeval world. All were united in a common
piety; each Guild had its patron Saint and all took pride in the
building and embellishment of churches and cathedrals. None
the less, the walled towns were small and insanitary, subject to
constant danger of fire and pestilence, without adequate police
or lighting, apprehensive of attack.

Yet the future was with the cities; it was on this reliable element that the new kings of the fifteenth century depended. Civic

wealth and civic method paid for and organized the standing armies which broke the power of the great feudatories and built the administration which gave continuity and efficiency to the new governments. Louis XI, Edward IV, Henry Tudor, all of them display bourgeois characteristics; they have little part in the old world of St. Louis, of the Plantagenets and the Hohenstaufen.

V I

Such were the broad characteristics and the contributions of the principal elements of mediaeval society; peasantry, clergy, nobility, and third estate. The great bishops and administrators, the scholastic philosophers, the students and the lawyers, were held together by a common solidarity and a common speech; the nobility and the gentry by their tradition as soldiers and land-owners and by the customs and manners of chivalry; the bour-geois by economic interest and an urban way of life; all con-tributed original and valuable legacies to modern Europe and all were sustained by peasant labour. These classes were included within the cosmopolitan political and ecclesiastical order of Christendom, conservative in outlook and limited in intellectual range: yet in spite of the credulity, the superstition, the practical incompetence of mediaeval Europeans, they preserved and to some extent realized the ideal of a united Christendom, of a social order reflecting Christian principles.

The weakness of the great European institutions, Empire, and Papacy, and the limitations of kingly power, made for inefficient government—but they made also for considerable freedom. The mediaeval realm was not and could not be totalitarian; spon-taneously, self-governing institutions grew up within it. The Church, the feudal aristocracy, the lawyers, the Universities, the towns, all evolved their own corporate life, and the vitality of the new Europe was expressed in diverse and original ways, to the lasting benefit of posterity. In these aspects mediaeval Christendom contrasts with the later Roman Empire.

Throughout this chequered period, moreover, the tradition of European order, inherited from Antiquity, was never lost; the classical respect for the rule of law persisted, and economic life was to some extent subordinated to a moral pattern of society. In all these aspects Christendom preserved and developed the inheritance of Antiquity, and compares favourably with many aspects of modern Europe. For, with all its limitations, mediaeval government and society reflected a common culture, and a common aim.

CHAPTER VIII

THE RENAISSANCE AND THE
DISCOVERIES

Two thousand years before the close of the Middle Ages there had appeared in the islands of Ionian Greece a new scientific outlook which was to be most fully developed in Europe, a spirit of dispassionate enquiry and methodical observation. Expressed in the writings of famous philosophers, expanded and systematized by Aristotle, developed with the rise of Hellenistic civilization, and surviving in part through the high Muslim civilization in Spain, it was to be reinterpreted in Europe in the sixteenth and seventeenth centuries to become the most powerful and original contribution of Europe to the world and to give to Europeans and their descendants overseas the domination of the planet. It was the formulation of that impersonal curiosity, that contriving genius, which through dark millennia had raised mankind out of the specialized routines of animal life, brought them into the dawn of history and created the Neolithic Revolution; yet among extra-European civilizations only China attained comparable advances in technology and applied science; and only in Europe would such enterprise be fully exploited.

Now although the Greek philosophers had made this extraordinary advance, the circumstances of their environment, both social and geographical, forbade the application of their ideas on a great scale. The aristocratic and literary bias of classical education, the existence of slavery, the contempt for banausic and mechanical pursuits expressed even by a writer so naturally scientific as Aristotle, would have prevented the application of scientific method to production on a great scale, even had the coal and iron resources of the Mediterranean world been less limited. The civilization of Antiquity was that of an urbanized minority, spread thinly over a huge area and without roots among the masses. It was indeed this failure to develop industrial and economic power which rendered the administration of the imperial government relatively amateurish, for all the force of Stoic morality and sense of mission. Further, the breakdown of the old social order, following on the loss of standards among the *élite,* and accelerated by the prevalence of emotional religion among the masses, hostile to the old culture, had struck a fresh blow at objectivity of mind. The great writers of Classical Greece had displayed realism and wisdom in their apprehension of life, if they had been uninterested in strictly scientific method; the analytic power of Plato and Thucydides is of the first order. But, for all the humanizing influence of the Christian Gospels, with the coming of an Orientalized religion, of a Judaized and apocalyptic cosmology and of fanatical doctrinal controversy, the rudiments of an objective outlook were overwhelmed. During the Dark Ages men lived haunted by fear and superstition and dominated by authority; what civilization came through survived through the prestige of the Church, the result of its emotional hold over both Romans and Barbarians. The Age of Faith contributed picturesque and valuable elements to modern society; morally and spiritually mediaeval civilization can compare well with any age, but practical incompetence and fear handicapped and haunted the mediaeval mind. In spite of the considerable technological advances of the Early Middle Ages, neither in Antiquity nor in mediaeval times was there any widespread idea of progress; the majority of Classical philosophers held that the world proceeded by a system of cyclic recurrence and to mediaeval thinkers life was overshadowed by the expectation of a Second Coming and a Judgement. The world was no place to be controlled and organized for the betterment of man's estate, and life was an ephemeral time of tribulation and temptation, the prelude to eternity.

So great was the vitality of the new Europe that this alien outlook, expressing the asceticism and fatalism of the East, failed to prevent the native development of European genius, and indeed served to tame and spiritualize the crude force of the Northern peoples, to preserve within a dogmatic framework the rudiments of the Classical inheritance. But already by the thirteenth century, the certainties of the twelfth had been shaken; the reception of Aristotle and the assimilation of Arabic ideas had undermined the foundation of ancient dogma. Heresies multiplied; the conflict of Papacy and Empire, the Avignon captivity, the political bankruptcy of the great institutions of Christendom, the spread of critical intelligence among clergy and laity and the rise of the urban middle classes, were demonstrating that the tide of power was flowing in a new direction, that the inheritance of the past, now beginning to be more fully known, could be contained no longer within the old boundaries.

By the close of the thirteenth century there had grown up in Italy a secular culture using the vernacular speech, destined to come to its zenith in Early Modern times. Already at the court of Frederick II this new outlook had appeared; Frederick himself, with the mentality of a Prince of the full Renaissance, sceptical, realistic, and many-sided—a portent indeed in the age of St. Thomas—gathered Greek, Arab, and Jewish scholars into his cosmopolitan entourage. When, with singular callousness, he investigated the origins of language by rearing children in isolation to discover a spontaneous speech, and when he caused a man to be battened into an air-tight barrel to observe the passing of his soul; though, both experiments proved negative since the children died and the soul proved invisible; but the Hohenstaufen Emperor was proceeding on the lines of rudimentary scientific method.

And, in truth, in the Mediterranean cities, the old Classical traditions had never wholly died; the same quick-witted Southern life which had characterized fifth-century Athens and Hellenistic Alexandria was to revive with a new and original vitality in Florence and Bologna, in Venice, and in Rome. This revival, like the economic expansion which preceded and sustained it, was to spread up over the mountains, and for the first time the main intellectual inheritance of Classical Greece was brought to bear on the practical genius and the natural resources of the North.

This inheritance had two aspects, scientific and humane. At first the humanistic influence was the more conspicuous, but, bound up with the new acceptance of life, the new interest in the world, and the new confidence and versatility, were the unobtrusive principles of scientific method, whose applications through the harnessing of power and the creation of wealth, backed by the natural resources and professionalized knowledge of the North, were later to endow Western Europe with an unheard-of mastery of nature.

The late mediaeval Renaissance was a gradual European movement pervading Early Modern times, the secular successor of the cosmopolitan Thomist thought of the Middle Ages, receiving a fresh interpretation in the different countries to which it penetrated and forming the foundation of the great creative achievements of European thought of the seventeenth century. Unlike the twelfth-century revival, which was more decisive, it was a conservative movement, interpreting old knowledge with new insight, but it prefaced the way for the scientific innovation which was its sequel. It worked itself out beyond the Alps long after its force had been spent in Italy, where it was side-tracked during the period of Spanish domination and by the influence of the Counter-Reformation. It came through the period of the wars of Religion; the individualism, the objectivity, the scepticism which were its outstanding qualities, emerged in their full power as the dominant intellectual influence of the late seventeenth and the eighteenth centuries. Together with the rise of great national states and the economic revolution following the discovery of America and the opening up of contacts with India and the Far East, these literary and scientific movements decided the future of Western civilization. In the following chapter the working out of these events will be traced; we are here concerned primarily with their prelude, with the Italian Renaissance and with the discoveries.

The social tendencies of the later Middle Ages, the establishment of centralized monarchies in the West, of flourishing city states in Italy, Flanders, and the Germanies, the rise of the merchant classes, dovetail closely into the history of this formative age. The Italians provided the ideas for which the rest of Europe was ready; the discoveries, new opportunities for economic expansion. We will therefore examine first the political and cultural aspects of the Renaissance, and, secondly, outline the major landmarks in the preliminary expansion of Europe, which was to transform the scale of civilization, and in its turn to expand and enrich the intellectual enterprise of Italy.

The political aspect of the Renaissance was expressed in a new secularized theory of politics. After the splendid but impracticable idealism of the high Middle Ages, perhaps most finely expressed in Dante's *Monarchia* in the early fourteenth century, which calls on the Emperor to reimpose on Christendom that universal peace in which alone the possibilities of the human spirit can be fully realized, a steady disillusionment had set in. It was the political practice of the Italian despots of the Renaissance that provided the theory of politics of the new age.

The life of the Italian cities centred on the courts of princes who competed with one another in a deliberate magnificence. In the ruthless struggle for power between families and factions within these city states, and in the diplomatic and military contests between them, qualities of cunning, system, and foresight were imperative. In this miniature world the prototype of modern government developed; the term 'State' means originally the household of the Prince. In Italy the political game reached a virtuosity unknown to the feudal world, and the most famous textbooks of this new statecraft were the *Principe* and *Discorsi* of Machiavelli. Their author had nothing to teach Aristotle or Thucydides, but he is a profoundly significant figure in the history of Europe; his writing marks the formulation of a new science of power, a nonmoral state theory, which aims at the attainment of security by any means. The evil motives of Machiavelli have been exaggerated; he did not make the romantic glorification of wickedness attributed to him by Marlowe and Shakespeare: he passionately admired the Roman Republic and praises the free institutions of the Germans and the Swiss; his ideal, indeed, by Renaissance standards, was strictly orthodox. But in the circumstances of his time and given the political behaviour of his contemporaries, he could see no way out except the use of force by a prince absolved from all moral restraint. Thus and thus alone could the twin objectives be obtained of the expulsion of the foreigners from Italy and the establishment of order. With these objects in view, he wrote his two treatises on the statesman's craft, which by their objectivity are so characteristic of the Renaissance and which served as a model for subsequent practitioners of power. The *Principe,* in particular, was immediately seized upon, for it formulated exactly the conduct which, in a piecemeal, empirical way, was being practised by the new rulers all over Europe, who, in alliance with the bourgeoisie and the more adaptable nobles, were building the foundations of the modern great State.

II

The political background to the Renaissance followed closely on the developments of the later Middle Ages. In England, France, and Spain, strong monarchies had consolidated their position; with the union of Aragon and Castile (1469) a powerful Spanish kingdom controlled the Aragonese possessions in the Balearics and South Italy. The economic life of Europe still centred on the cities of Flanders, the Rhineland, South Germany, and the North Italian plain; it was not until the full effect of the discoveries worked itself out, and the Ottoman stranglehold on the Levant had ruined Venetian trade, that commercial preponderance shifted to the countries of the Western seaboard. The most advanced areas of Europe, politically, were therefore the new monarchies of the West; culturally, the city states of Flanders and North Italy.

The prosperity of the German cities was impaired by the political disorder of the Holy Roman Empire. Although the Habsburg power was the only monarchy strong enough to face the military strength of the French kings, the Emperor Maximilian (1493–1519) failed to impose his authority on the great Electoral Princes. In spite, therefore, of the immense development of Habsburg dynastic power and the success of Charles V (1520–56) in the primary task of holding back the Turkish menace from the East, Germany itself failed to achieve the political unity of the Western States and her chronic internal disorders were accentuated by the Reformation. Bohemia had already suffered from the consequences of the Hussite movement and the religious rancour it invoked, while Poland-Lithuania, though superficially formidable, was increasingly paralysed by the perversion of representative institutions which hampered the authority of the Polish kings. Although in Poland the reign of Sigismund I (1506–48) saw the rise of a remarkable Renaissance culture, the internal state of the country was unsound. In Hungary, the exploits of Mathias Corvinus, whose reign had seen a climax of Hungarian culture and independence, had their sequel, as we have seen, in the crushing defeat of Mohacs (1526) and the loss of the bulk of Hungarian territory to the Ottoman Turks. The failure of the Czech, Polish, Lithuanian, and Hungarian kingdoms to achieve stable alliances was disastrous for Central Europe: while in the West great centralized states were developing, in Eastern Europe the political scene was increasingly confused, with power in the hands of a politically destructive nobility.

By the end of the fifteenth century, then, the two strongest powers in Europe were the French and Habsburg monarchies; their rivalry was destined to be the dominant theme of European politics for two and a half centuries. The Habsburg dynastic power was built up by judicious marriages; the marriage of Maximilian I to Mary of Burgundy, daughter of Charles the Bold, (1477) brought in the Low Countries, and by a second marriage he acquired Milan. His son, Philip, married Joanna, daughter of Ferdinand and Isabella of Spain, thus bringing in Spain, Sardinia, Naples and Sicily, and the Spanish-American dominions. His grandson, Charles V, dominated half Europe; he had at his disposal not only the Habsburg family possessions but the wealth and man-power of Spain, the economic resources of Flanders and Milan. The struggle of this laborious and often able ruler to hold together his vast inheritance, to defeat the French, to deal with the German Reformation, and to beat back the Turkish menace in the east, is the central fact of the period.

The Papacy and the King of England both manœuvred to weaken the Habsburg preponderance, though not to the extent of transferring it to the French. This struggle for power involved most of Europe and was fought out mainly in Italy; the Northern rulers, using Machiavellian methods and administration learnt from the Italian cities, now brought their greater resources to bear on Italian politics, and the relative peace and freedom which Italy had enjoyed during the earlier Renaissance was destroyed by these foreign conflicts. From the Peace of Lodi (1454) concluded between Florence, Milan, and Venice, to the first French invasion (1494) dates the most creative period of the Renaissance. In that year, Charles VIII, on the invitation of the Duke of Milan, entered Italy to win back the Angevin inheritance of Naples and Sicily. This disastrous initiative was followed up by Francis I (1515–47), who defeated an Imperial army at Marignano (1515) and conquered Lombardy. At the battle of Pavia (1525), he suffered defeat and capture at the hands of a predominantly Spanish army. Charles V was now able to settle accounts with the Pope; in 1527, to the horror of the emperor, an unpaid German army sacked Rome. Meanwhile, under Suleiman the Magnificent (1520–66) the Turks had overrun Hungary and two years later were at the gates of Vienna. At Cambrai (1529) Charles V concluded a statesmanlike peace with the French; in return for the surrender of his Burgundian inheritance, Francis abandoned his Italian claims. The Emperor was now able to make an expedition to North Africa where he captured Tunis and broke the Turkish Corsairs in the western Mediterranean. The conflict with France flared up again in 1536 over the Duchy of Milan, but, in the end, the Imperial power was victorious, and in 1559 the Treaty of Cateau-Cambrésis marked the final supremacy of Spanish and Imperial influence in Italy. The stage was set for the Counter-Reformation.

The worst aspect of these wars between France and the Habsburgs was the disunity they entailed in face of the Turkish peril; Francis I actually entered into alliance with the Grand Turk, and while with one hand the Habsburgs were attempting to impose the Counter-Reformation in Europe, with the other they were defending Christendom in the East; it is not the least of their achievements that in 1571 Don John of Austria destroyed the Ottoman naval power at Lepanto and saved the Central Mediterranean.

Such, in essentials, is the political background of Early Modern times, which, together with the religious conflicts following the Reformation, overshadowed but failed to prevent the diffusion of Italian culture into the North.

III

As already emphasized, the Italian Renaissance was no sudden event. Its origins go far back into the Middle Ages; the brilliance of Italian civilization of the Trecento and the Quattrocento, like the brilliance of fifth-century Greece, was an expression of the vitality of independent city states. The greatest contribution was made by Florence; already Dante (1265–1321), a contemporary of the English Edward II and the French Philip the Fair, had written Italian poetry which can compare with the masterpieces of any age. Petrarch in the fourteenth century is a forerunner of later Humanism: Boccaccio already commands a flexible narrative prose.

For over two hundred years Renaissance civilization was the dominant cultural influence in the West. The Italians have always respected intellect: unlike the northern baronage, who in general regarded learning with contempt, the Italian nobility had long been urbanized and intermarried with a commercial aristocracy. The Italian rulers—the Visconti, the Sforza, the D'Estes, the Medici—were highly civilized; they needed skilled diplomats and administrators; humanistic culture became the fashion and was indeed essential to political success. This sophisticated tradition forms the background of the High Renaissance, with its widening intellectual and artistic scope and omnivorous practical interests.

The achievements of the age present three main aspects, literary, artistic, scientific; in all of them the Italians altered the thought of Europe. The basis of Humanism was the critical study of the text of ancient writers, freed from the glosses and allegorical interpretations of the Middle Ages. The Humanists modelled their style and their thought on Roman and Greek originals; there was a passionate admiration for the past, a new understanding of pre-Christian Antiquity: the native realism of the Italian mind came once again into its ancient inheritance.

Contacts with Byzantium through Venice had long been close; but the most immediate stimulus came through the late Byzantine culture of Mistra in Sparta as well as through Byzantine refugees whose influence was gradual but cumulative, though their influence was never dominant. The spirit of the movement remained Italian.

A passionate interest in Antiquity captured the best minds; with instinctive sympathy the great Renaissance scholars wrote a flexible and idiomatic Latin prose and created a new art of letter writing. Politian described in felicitous Latin the seasons of the Tuscan year, and his vernacular poetry shows a new understanding of popular emotion. Already in the early fifteenth century the Florentine Poggio, investigating the ruins of Rome, can correlate archaeological and literary evidence; Pius II was the first to classify the antiquities of the environs of Rome, and Leo X was a passionate antiquarian.

Against this background of Classical study a new ideal of personality developed. At Mantua, under the patronage of the Gonzagas, Vittorino da Feltre (1396–1446) revived the Greek ideal of all-round cultivation of body and mind. His school became the most fashionable in Italy; here the sons of the nobility lived on equal terms with boys of talent from poorer families; da Feltre is one of the great pioneers of humanistic education. The abandonment of mediaeval class distinctions, the alliance between self-made rulers and men of ability, enabled individuals to stand on their own merits. The ideal Renaissance man of the world, competent, many-sided, a master of style in all aspects of life, is described in Castiglione's classic *Cortigiano* which won a European popularity; he wrote of the court circle of the Medici Pope Leo X. This ideal of the 'Universal Man' is finely expressed by Ariosto, the great epic poet of the high Renaissance; his *Orlando Furioso,* within the conventions of the age, is a brilliant portrayal of action, a masterpiece of living narrative.

We cannot here appreciate in any detail the cardinal artistic achievements of the Italians; here again Florence made the greatest contribution. Far back in the early fourteenth century, Giotto, the first great master of European painting, had broken away from the severe conventions of Byzantine design. Botticelli (1444–1510) developed a more secular painting, with a new sense of scenic background. In the art of sculpture, Donatello (1386–1466) was already creating masterpieces comparable to those of Antiquity. Leonardo da Vinci (1452–1519) and Michelangelo (1475–1564) are famous masters of European reputation. The powerful enigmatic genius of Leonardo ranged over the whole field of painting, sculpture, science, engineering, and the art of war; Michelangelo was not only a sculptor and painter of superlative achievement but a distinguished poet. Raphael, born at Urbino in 1483, appointed chief architect of St. Peter's, died in 1520 at thirty-seven; he brought a new perfection of line and colour to his serene masterpieces. With the later Renaissance, the greatest painting came from Venice; Titian born in Cadore in the Alpine foothills, the official painter to the Republic from 1516, achieved an unsurpassed splendour of colour and composition. The huge and dramatic canvases of Tintoretto, who attempted to combine the design of Michelangelo with the colour of Titian, the superlative compositions of Paolo Veronese, brought the Venetian school to its climax.

Apart from the great masters, the men of genius, Italy produced innumerable men of talent, who elaborated Renaissance culture and carried the movement beyond the Alps. The competition was intense, the struggle for patronage and a livelihood precarious; Italy was no paradise for the dilettante, but the scene of ferocious satire and mockery, of bitter personal feuds.

All these individualists displayed immense vitality. The best account of this competitive world is found in the Autobiography of Benvenuto Cellini (1500–1572), which depicts the background of the High Renaissance. He expresses the confidence, the versatility, and the ruthlessness of the age. This point of view is secular but not bourgeois, as far removed from middle-class respectability as from the conventional pride of the world of chivalry. The great Renaissance artists were a law unto themselves; where an Oriental potentate could order an architect to be impaled so that his masterpiece could remain unique, a Renaissance prince would never have dared or desired so to outrage public opinion. The artist enjoyed immense prestige; in no other civilization had he enjoyed the freedom he was accorded in Renaissance Europe, for he was no longer a monk illuminating manuscripts, at best designing a diptych, bound by convention and confined to religious subjects, but an individual, interpreting life according to his own genius and enjoying a personal fame. The long line of European artists, who, in affluence or in poverty, have defied through the centuries the conventions of their age, begins with the Renaissance, and how great has been the legacy of this cosmopolitan and unrepentant fraternity to the world!

In architecture Italian initiative created a revived classical tradition, destined to dominate Western civilization. Alberti read Vitruvius in the middle fifteenth century; Palladio fully applied the new principles in the early sixteenth. Space, proportion, and dignity were the notes of the new movement, expressing at once a return to the standards of Antiquity and the rationalistic outlook of the new age. If the conceptions of the great Renaissance architects were often too grandiose, in the second half of the sixteenth century the limits of the possible were recognized, and there appears a superb confidence and mastery. This architecture is the expression of a proud and expanding civilization, well at home in the world, with no room for romantic mystery; it belongs essentially to the South, but its principles of harmony and proportion were to be reinterpreted all over Europe.

The greatest advance made in Church music, was also Italian, for the oustanding master was Palestrina (1525–94), choir-master at the Basilica of St. John Lateran in Rome and later to Cardinal D'Este. More than any other man he created the idiom of modern music; his masses and liturgies show a clarity and sense of proportion which anticipate the genius of Bach. The Counter-Reformation, though its effects on painting were in the long run adverse, encouraged musical development. In the secular world music formed an essential background to social life; opera had not yet appeared, but numerous virtuosi and amateurs all over Italy achieved a new level of vocal and instrumental performance. The clavichord and the violin were already popular, the string quartette was already in being, and solo singing would later form a congenial medium for display of personality.

The insatiable curiosity of the Renaissance was expressed in scientific experiment, made possible by the designing of optical glasses and instruments of precision. For the first time there existed a public opinion favourable to scientific investigation. In the thirteenth century the lonely genius of Roger Bacon had to fight the opposition of his contemporaries; in the sixteenth there was an increasingly free field for experiment. It was natural for sixteenth-century Italians and their imitators to ask not why things happened but how things happened; a blind acceptance of Scriptural and Aristotelian authority was not enough. The study of the physical world had been encouraged by the diffusion of the ancient classics—Hippocrates, Ptolemy, Pliny. The Flemish Vesalius (1514–64) is the outstanding figure in Northern Renaissance medicine: he was the founder of modern anatomy, the greatest doctor since Antiquity. His vigorous and attractive personality swept aside the debris of mediaeval tradition; as court physician to Charles V, an exacting position, he commanded wide influence: his *De Fabrica Humani Corporis* is a landmark in medical science. Another medical man of the Northern Renaissance, characteristically named Auriolus Theophrastus Bombastus Von Hohenheim, more conveniently known as Paracelsus, came of Swiss origin. After a tumultuous career, he ended his days in a tavern brawl at Salzburg. He held to the methods of Hippocrates and is said to have prefaced his lectures by burning the text of Galen; his drastic experiments resulted in the use of a new range of drugs and in a widened knowledge of curative medicine.

But in cosmology occurred the greatest revolution, later destined to reach its full development in the century of Galileo and Newton. Copernicus (1473–1543), a conservative Polish mathematician, who had studied at Padua and who won little contemporary recognition, revived the ancient hypothesis of a heliocentric solar system; he conserved and adapted the mediaeval scheme and retained the doctrine of a finite and spherical universe. Such was the beginning: the new hypothesis was carried further by a Dane, Tycho Brahe, a systematic astronomer whose work of observation and classification laid the foundations of later knowledge.

But his contemporary, Giordano Bruno (1547–1600), made the greatest advance. This wayward and tragic philosopher, a renegade Neapolitan monk, burnt by the Inquisition after seven years' imprisonment, is one of the founders of the modern world. Bruno first broke the box-like traditional cosmology; his short tract, published in England in 1584, *On the Infinite Universe*

and its Worlds, shook the foundations of ancient belief. Basing
his hypothesis on the Copernican theory, he declared that the
Universe was boundless in space and time, informed with an immanent soul, containing worlds outside the solar system. His
hypothesis challenged the whole accepted order. Correctly, according to its dim lights, the Inquisition sensed the appalling
danger: Bruno was tracked down and perished, a martyr to his
own genius. In half a century his theory dominated the learned
world. The mediaeval cosmos shrivelled before the immensities
of his revelation; the background to the modern outlook had
been defined.

Such are some of the main landmarks, cultural and intellectual, of this brilliant epoch. The invention of printing was the
basis of this intellectual revolution; the use of paper, which originated in China, had been learnt by Europeans from the Egyptian Arabs by the fourteenth century; it did not become widespread before the latter half of the fifteenth. The printing of
whole pages by block impression was the first step; when transferable type was devised and paper became common, this cardinal
invention began to exercise its full influence. Here is a landmark in history comparable to the great inventions of the Neolithic and urban revolutions; the intellectual life of Europe was
broadened and deepened, the inheritance of civilization broadcast to a public which has no counterpart in Classical Antiquity
or the Middle Ages.

Printing was primarily a German invention; by the middle of
the fifteenth century presses had been set up at Mainz and Haarlem; in 1470 printing had spread to Paris. Aldo, an Italian
scholar, learned in Greek, was printing in Venice by 1490; by
1515 he had produced editions of the major Greek classics in
compendious form. Beyond the Alps, where theological interests
predominated, many editions of the Bible appeared in the last
quarter of the fifteenth century. Besides the vastly increased circulation of books and a widespread increase in the habit of reading, independent writers appeared, appealing to a wide audience,
pamphleteers, forerunners of the modern press; the intellectual
life of Europe had been secularized and vastly enriched. The
spread of the new knowledge made possible a novel juxtaposition
of ideas and facts, the development of a fresh standard of critical

judgement. With the spread of the new learning, scholasticism, which still retained its hold on ecclesiastical thought for centuries, was superseded by a lay culture with its roots deeper in national life. Though in a sense more parochial, this new literature remained cosmopolitan on its Classical Humanistic side; it was richer and more vital than mediaeval learning.

The sixteenth century saw the rise of great national vernacular literatures which expressed the genius of the new European nations. The movement, destined to create a new tie between the *élites* and the masses in each country, spread northward into Europe during the early sixteenth century in a broadening flood. Social conditions were favourable for its diffusion, both at the courts of the princes and among the new bourgeoisie. The most immediate effect was naturally in France, culturally the predominant influence in the West since the twelfth century. The French expeditions into Italy brought closer contacts with the Italian culture and fashion, while Provence and the Midi had always belonged to the South. In the *Song of Roland,* as we have seen, French had already attained the lucidity and universality which was to make it the successor of Latin as an international language; during the later Middle Ages it had been enriched and developed; the later Middle Ages had seen an improvement of prose and a widening of vocabulary, and the poetry of Villon had expressed the spirit and the pathos of the outcast and the poor.

The Court poets of the sixteenth century found a fine instrument to their hands; they introduced Italian classical forms, starting a new fashion which was to dominate French literature until the eighteenth century, more formal and more rigid than that of their predecessors. Ronsard and the writers of the Pléiade, at their best, combined the native melody of popular poetry with the disciplined measures of the South; at their worst they wrote a conventionalized esoteric verse. French humanists also created a great school of textual criticism and philology, more professionalized than the Italian; Scaliger and Casaubon are in the first rank of European scholars, and French industry and precision first compiled reliable dictionaries.

But it was the emancipated friar Rabelais who combined the new learning with the farce and fantasy of old French popular literature. This original and extraordinary genius, taking the world of Renaissance knowledge in his stride, rioting in a new wealth of idiom and idea, depicts with an Aristophanic gusto the panorama of his age. His immense vocabulary expressed all aspects of experience, a fine hatred of humbug and a boisterous self-sufficiency, characteristically and thoroughly French. In contrast to the 'Reverend Rabbles,' as he was known to his English admirers in the seventeenth century, Montaigne represents a mellower side of French genius; his *Essays,* serene discursive reflections upon life, mark a fresh literary form, destined to widespread and successful imitation, the expression of a new poise and introspection, more natural and more intimate than the set discourses of Antiquity.

In the field of painting, the Clouets, Jean and François, have left accurate representations of the French nobility, and Corneille de Lyon painted miniatures of remarkable grace, but it was not until the seventeenth century that French painting, following the liberating influence of the Flemish master Rubens, began its full development. In architecture Italian influence combined with the native Gothic to produce buildings of originality and charm. The flamboyant chateaux of this period combine fantasy with a more spacious and comfortable design; a great house was becoming no longer a fortress but a setting for civilized life. So France assimilated the Italian influence over all the cultural field and yet retained her native genius; her writers and artists were destined to refashion and expand the new forms.

Meanwhile, in the cities of Flanders and the Netherlands, a situation akin to the Italian had long been growing up. The wealth of the Low Countries had been reflected in painting and architecture since the later Middle Ages; the art of the Van Eycks and of Memlinc, of Mabuse and later of Pieter and Jan Breughel, can compare in its more limited field with that of Italy, while in domestic architecture and gardening the Netherlands were beginning a characteristic progress. Here was the beginning of a Northern Renaissance which was to bear full fruit in the seventeenth century, when, following emancipation from Spanish rule, in toleration and business enterprise the Dutch were to be the leaders of Europe.

The most famous Northern humanist was Erasmus, a Dutch writer, who displays a modern and trenchant realism. He was primarily a great Classical scholar who set himself to edit and translate the Greek text of the New Testament; he was also a brilliant letter writer and pamphleteer, a champion of toleration, of dispassionate analysis, a forerunner of the eighteenth century. His raillery and invective express a new independence and a range of interests; he had caught the spirit of the old Greek, and he commanded a European audience especially in Spain.

Closely bound up with the Low Countries and France was Tudor England. Henry VIII, a thoroughly Renaissance ruler, had succeeded his crafty and able father in 1509, and his court became the centre of a brilliant culture. Caxton had set up his printing press in London in 1477; already in the late Middle Ages Sir John Fortescue's famous *Governaunce of England* and the *Paston Letters* had shown the accuracy and force of written English, while in the mid-century, the poetry of Wyatt and Surrey, modelled on Italian originals, foreshadows the lyric genius of Elizabethan and Jacobean England.

The crisis of the English Reformation did not impair the influence of the Universities, but gave them a more assured and important place in the national life; the great minister Wolsey founded Cardinal College, later Christ Church, most splendid of Oxford foundations, and at the close of his reign Henry VIII re-endowed Trinity at Cambridge on a princely scale. Closely connected with the Universities, two great English schools were already in being; Winchester, in the heart of Wessex under the Hampshire downs, founded by William of Wykeham in the fourteenth century, and Eton, Henry VI's foundation, its towers rising from the meadows of the Thames valley. From all over England the parishes were sending their promising sons, no longer to con the learning of a cosmopolitan Church, but to create a new English contribution to the great European tradition, something more intimate and more homely, and to make for themselves careers, not at the ends of Christendom, but in their own island in the service of Church and State.

Tudor England was famous for its music; Tallis (1505–85) and Byrd (1543–1623), Queen Elizabeth's organist at the Chapel Royal, are the greatest English composers of the sixteenth century. But the most remarkable English interpretation of the Southern influence came in the drama, which through the Middle Ages, in England as in the rest of Europe, had led a pre-

carious and limited existence in mystery plays patronized by the
Church, and in elementary shows of buffoonery at fairs and fes-
tivals. In the late sixteenth century the genius of Marlowe expressed the pride, the enterprise, the curiosity of the Northern
Renaissance, touched with English romanticism. Though he died
young, Marlowe left plays of which the freshness, vitality, and
poetic power place him among the greatest writers of his age.

After the defeat of the Armada, England saw a period of literary brilliance which has justly been compared with that of
Athens after the Persian Wars. Shakespeare (1564–1616), the
most representative, the most profound and the greatest of all
English writers, wrote his plays under the patronage of the late
Elizabethan and early Jacobean court and nobility. Here was a
response worthy of the Italian initiative it reflected and absorbed.

The Renaissance in the Germanies, based on the wealth of the
South German and Rhineland cities, was expressed in a vigorous
development of architecture, wood-carving, and metal-work. But
German literary vitality was largely side-tracked into violent and
clumsy religious controversy; Luther's hymns are probably the
most valuable poetic legacy of the age. The curious genius of
Dürer (1477–1528), most characteristically expressed in engrav-
ings of notable power, met the widespread demand for religious
representation. Hans Holbein (1497–1543), after a short sojourn
in Basle, found the English Court a congenial environment for
his exact art.

Renaissance Poland achieved a vigorous intellectual life; in
1474 the first printing press was set up in Cracow; in 1491 Copernicus studied there. Polish Gothic came to its perfection and
gave place in the sixteenth century to a remarkable Renaissance
architecture. In the later sixteenth century in Spain the Counter-
Reformation produced magnificent painting; Flemish and Neapolitan influences combined to create a school of dramatic and
original power, specializing in a new contrast of light and shade.
El Greco, a painter of original and startling genius, born in
Crete, studied under Titian in Venice and settled in Toledo in
1575. No artist could have been more appropriate to portray the
mystical fervour and distinction of the Spain of Philip II.

The later sixteenth century saw a great age in Portuguese
painting, literature, and architecture. Nuno Gonçalves applied

Flemish techniques to portray character in a way that anticipates Goya. Camoẽs was a brilliant lyric and epic poet: *The Lusiads,* the epic of Portuguese expansion, built round the history of Vasco da Gama, express his personal experience, for Camoes himself voyaged east to Macao.

I V

It was natural that the literature of Portugal should be the first to reflect the influence of the new Discoveries. The Portuguese were the pioneers of a revolutionary expansion of Europe. This expansion, parallel with the Early Modern widening of intellectual horizons, is the greatest material achievement of the age. The geographical knowledge of Antiquity, though wider than that of the Middle Ages, had been extremely limited; when, therefore, Columbus inadvertently discovered the American continent, the outlook of Europeans was transformed. The mediaeval mind had been bounded by a cosmology inherited and garbled from Classical times; the knowledge that beyond the wastes of the Atlantic lay rich and inhabited lands came as a shock and a revelation.

The Portuguese had long been exploring the western fringes of Africa; they had already settled Madeira in 1420; Prince Henry the Navigator, the son of John, King of Portugal, and, through Philippa, daughter of John of Gaunt, descended from Edward III of England, was a sailor of technical proficiency and far-ranging imagination. He had improved the design of ocean-going ships and established an observatory and an arsenal on the Sagres promontory in 1418. It was known that the Barbary Arabs drew much of their wealth through the interior of Africa over the ancient trade routes of the Sahara from the Guinea Coast, and he conceived the project of a descent on the Senegal river. This was accomplished by the middle fifteenth century, but the progress he initiated in navigation and cartography was the most lasting achievement of this remarkable man, who combined the qualities of two seagoing peoples.

The Portuguese were to create a maritime empire in Southern India and the East Indies: in 1486 Diaz rounded the Cape;

twelve years later, Vasco da Gama's ships astonished the Mozambique Arabs by arriving from the South, and before the monsoon wind they crossed the Indian Ocean to Calicut. In 1502 the Portuguese destroyed a combined Arab fleet off the Malabar coast, for dhows were useless against their cannon; Albuquerque, during the next decade, broke the Arab monopoly of the trade routes from Southern India to the Red Sea and the Persian Gulf, and established a colony at Goa. He pushed eastward to Malacca, which commanded the entrance to the China Seas; by 1517 the Portuguese had reached 'Cathay' when they weighed anchor off Canton. The goal of contemporary exploration had been attained. Further, at the turn of the century, a Portuguese expedition, making for the Cape, had been carried westward and discovered Brazil. The foundation of a rich overseas Empire had been won for Portugal, and Lisbon became the centre of a great oceanic trade, linked with London and Bristol and the Flemish and Dutch ports; this prosperity was reflected during the sixteenth and seventeenth centuries in magnificent architecture.

But a more astonishing discovery had been made by a Genoese sea captain in the service of Spain. Christopher Columbus had studied the *Travels of Marco Polo,* the thirteenth-century traveller who had reached China and Southern India; his annotated copy of the book survives. He was also familiar with the charts and speculations of Prince Henry and had already voyaged to the Guinea Coast. Convinced of the curvature of the earth, but grossly miscalculating its size, he conceived the idea of reaching China by sailing west across the Atlantic. This dream he pursued with unbreakable tenacity, over years, in the face of every opposition and discouragement. He hawked his scheme round the courts and maritime cities of Europe. The Portuguese, technically too proficient to take the project seriously, were already on the track of the route to India round the Cape; the Genoese and Venetians would have none of it—it was the last thing they wanted, threatening ruin to their already diminished Levantine trade. So Columbus approached the King of England and the rulers of Spain. Isabella of Castile was less handicapped by the advice of maritime experts; her kingdom had a military, not a seagoing tradition; with incalculable results for the future, she decided to support the doubtful project. Too late, Henry VII invited Columbus to England; his idea was the property of Castile.

In the late summer of 1492 three little ships put out of the port of Palos on Cadiz Bay. Proceeding south to the Canaries, in the latitude of 'Cipangu,' they set course into the ocean, heading for 'India by the route of the Occident.' All through September they crawled westward over the long Atlantic rollers; never before had so great an ocean voyage been achieved. By October the crews were mutinous, but Columbus sailed on, set with invincible determination on the 'enterprise of the Indies.' On October 12th they sighted one of the Bahamas. They pushed on to Cuba and Haiti; they returned in triumph to Europe. The New World had been discovered.

Columbus made three other expeditions and reached the mainland of Central America; he termed the new lands the West Indies, convinced to his death that he had reached the Far East. A touch of comedy is added to the hazardous story by the circumstances of the naming of the new Continent. Amerigo Vespucci, a fraudulent character in the pay of the Medici, who had sailed with Hojeda in 1499, had written, and predated, an account of sensational discoveries. His *Novus Mundus* attained notoriety and success. Now it chanced that his writings had come to the hand of the Professor of Cosmography in the University of Lorraine, whose opinion was solicited on the naming of the new lands. In the mistaken conviction that Amerigo had discovered it, the learned man christened the new Continent 'America.'

So by the turn of fate, the Spanish monarchy, essentially a military land power, fresh from its struggle against the Moors, and inspired by Crusading zeal, mediaeval in outlook and profoundly conservative, attained an enormous empire in the New World.

The Papacy was at the time occupied by the notorious Roderigo Borgia, Alexander VI; he divided the New World between Portugal and Spain, assigning, by an expansive Donation (1493), all the lands west of a line midway between Portugal and Florida to Spain, all discoveries to the east of it to Portugal.

The story of the Spanish conquest of Mexico and Peru, of Cortes's storming and sack of the Aztec lake city of Mexico, of the dealings of Pizarro with Atahualpa, the Inca of Peru, form one of the most bizarre chapters in human annals. The Europeans had found a civilization, which for all its wealth lacked some of the most elementary inventions; it was still in many respects less advanced than that of the Bronze Age; the horse and the wheel were unknown. The influx of bullion from the plunder of these lands slowly transformed the economy of Europe; every year a great treasure fleet crossed the Atlantic bringing to Spain un-heard-of quantities of silver and gold. For more than a thousand years there had been a shortage of coin in Europe; now the money market was flooded with Spanish wealth. In consequence prices in the mid-sixteenth and seventeenth centuries tended to soar; governments were nonplussed by the new phenomenon, and Philip II's administration, incapable of dealing with the new situation, itself three times defaulted during the second half of the century which saw the establishment of Spanish rule in America.

On the politics of Europe the immediate effect of the creation of the Spanish Empire was an unexpected predominance of Spain. This power was thrown into the religious conflict which rent the Continent throughout the sixteenth century. The Counter-Reformation was backed by Spanish force, and the effort demanded from Spain exhausted her man-power and dissipated the new wealth. The Spanish government treated their new capital as income; they gutted the gold and silver mines of the New World in the interests of ideological warfare in Europe; but the Spaniards also created the civilization of Central and South America, and maintained peace over a vast area for centuries. The achievement of the Jesuit missionaries, of the Spanish scholars and architects who built the Universities and cities of this conservative and widespread culture, was indeed astonishing. At the same time Spanish civilization developed its peculiar and distinguished characteristics. Their painters have portrayed the sombre mag-nificence, the high dignity of the great Spanish hidalgos, who in war and diplomacy attempted the hegemony of Europe; Spanish pikemen dominated the battlefields of the Continent; and Span-ish war galleons controlled the Atlantic until Drake and the Elizabethan admirals challenged and broke their supremacy at Cadiz and in the Channel in 1588.

The Papal Donation of 1493 had long been defied by the

northern nations of the western seaboard. The Spanish monopoly was increasingly challenged by the English, the French, and the Dutch. Religious differences coincided with economic interest; Elizabethan adventurers plundered the Caribbean and returned to Plymouth and Bideford with tales of fantastic exploits. These half-mediaeval adventurers were astounded by an exotic world. As they pulled inshore over translucent water, strange fishes of unexampled brilliance darted beneath their prows, emerald parakeets rose screaming from the jungle. This strange experience, doubly odd to a northern people, was reflected in Elizabethan literature, and its echoes are still part of the English tradition, for the sixteenth century was the first age of English expansion.

It was not, however, in Central America that northern Europeans were destined to strike root, but in the huge mainland of the North. In 1496 Cabot had discovered Newfoundland and Nova Scotia; by the mid-century Hawkins was trading slaves from the Guinea coast to the Caribbean; by 1584 Raleigh had planted the first colony in Virginia. The trade with Muscovy, opened up after the turn of the century by Chancellor, had acclimatized English sailors to the navigation of northern waters and given them the idea of a north-west passage to Asia. In pursuit of it the eastern shores of Canada were opened up, with their promise of wealth in fish, timber, and fur, following the more widespread enterprise of the French, who, led by Jacques Cartier of St. Malo, had explored far up the St. Lawrence by 1541.

The combined results of the discovery of North and South America and of the Portuguese commercial supremacy in the Far East, together with the encroachment of the Ottoman Empire on the Danube and in the Balkans, transformed the economic situation of Europe. Commercial preponderance shifted from the Mediterranean to the Atlantic seaboard, and the balance of European power sustained an unprecedented alteration. Here is the prelude to the full expansion of Europe, to the political and economic domination of the peoples of the North, the foundation of the modern period of Western civilization. For the first time in their history the peoples of the Iberian Peninsula, the French, the British, the Dutch, and the Scandinavians, were in a better economic position than the cities of the Mediterranean.

The peoples of Central Europe did not profit by this new good fortune. The Germans had practically no participation in the new expansion; they had never been an ocean-going people, their North Sea ports were limited and their maritime enterprise satisfied with the Baltic trade. Their colonizing effort had been directed for centuries east and south-east, their economic life bound up with the transcontinental trade with Italy to the Low Countries and to the Baltic. Further, they were politically disunited; as we have emphasized, the existence of the Empire and the facts of geography prevented the consolidation of a national state as established in England, France, and Spain. This political handicap was worsened by the crisis of the Reformation, which kept Germany in confusion for more than a century and culminated in the prolonged agony of the Thirty Years War, a contest which devastated the economic and cultural life of the country. The Swedes, who had participated in the initial maritime expansion, became involved in this struggle and their energies also were diverted from more fruitful enterprise. When Western Europe was entering upon new prospects, the landbound peoples of the Germanies were unable to benefit; while the Poles and Lithuanians were in no better case, and had been long preoccupied with the struggle against the Turks, with expansionist ambitions eastward into Russia and over the Black Sea Steppe.

This contrast in European development was reflected in the social structure of Western and Eastern Europe. Where, in the West, the new expansion hastened and encouraged the rise of the merchants and professional men, resulting in an increase of capitalist and commercial enterprise, and while the creation of great states put increasing power into the hands of governments, in Eastern Europe social and political power remained the monopoly of the landowning aristocracy; a relatively insignificant commerce was the affair of the Jews, and a substantial native bourgeoisie did not make its appearance. Even the status of the peasantry, consistently ameliorated in the West since the later Middle Ages, became increasingly undermined.

In Russia, meanwhile, the Muscovite State was struggling successfully against immense difficulties, but had little participation in the Western Renaissance and no participation in the Western discoveries, though there was a rapid expansion across Northern Siberia in the late sixteenth and early seventeenth centuries, an epic of pioneering parallel to the opening up of the Americas. The dominant fact of Eastern European history was still the loss of Constantinople, the Balkans, and some of the best of the Danubian lands. In this respect Renaissance and seventeenth-century Europe, for all its expansion and growing wealth, was still crippled in areas which in Classical Antiquity had been profitable and important.

None the less the sixteenth century saw an enormous change: the new outlook, expressed in the beginnings of science and more immediately in the rise of Humanism, and, later, in the more original method of applied science, was destined to colour the mentality of Western civilization, and is still the dominant intellectual influence. It had combined a better understanding of Antiquity with that of the Middle Ages and given them a new interpretation. This expansion of intellectual horizons was paralleled and reinforced by geographical discoveries which revolutionized the economic and political life of Europe, presaged the establishment of great European nations overseas and the expansion of European culture and influence. The scale of events after the sixteenth century for the first time dwarfs the history of Mediaeval Christendom, of the Graeco-Roman world, and of the river-valley civilizations of the Near East. Henceforward, increasingly, our picture is on a world canvas; political and economic events become more complex and more incalculable, and with seventeenth-century scientific progress, the pace begins to quicken. All these things grew out of the intellectual and commercial initiative of Early Modern Europe, whose artists and scholars opened up new worlds of thought, and whose adventurers voyaged over unknown seas to unexplored continents to find their fortunes or their deaths. The intellectual and practical enterprise of Europe, the result of racial fusion and geographical circumstance, comes into its own with the sixteenth century.

CHAPTER IX

THE REFORMATION AND THE
NATION STATE

THE sixteenth and seventeenth centuries saw the making of the framework of the modern world. The disruption of Christendom in the conflict of Reformation and Counter-Reformation, the rise of great National States, the development of mercantile capitalism in terms of overseas expansion, and the rise of the new scientific outlook, made the age one of cardinal importance. In the complex web of events we will trace in turn the working out of these four fundamental changes, religious, political, economic, and intellectual.

The Reformation marks a far-reaching and incalculable revolution in the spiritual and political life of Europe. The doctrine which had held Christendom united over the worst period of social and economic decline and inspired the civilization of the Middle Ages ceased to command the allegiance of most of Northern Europe. The long domination of the Latin Church was broken, and the northern peoples reinterpreted Christianity according to their own temperament.

The later Middle Ages had seen an increasing criticism of the Catholic Church; ideas had been formulated which became dominant at the Reformation, the spiritual monopoly of the priesthood had been challenged. A mendicant Church, concerned solely with spiritual matters, was the ideal of many reformers.

As early as 1324, Marsiglio of Padua, the first medical man to write a book on politics, insists that the clergy have no business with political life, that the community of Christendom should be governed by a general Council of clergy and laity. This Conciliar solution, like the League of Nations in the twentieth century, was too academic, though it proved rich in constitutional ideas, later to be secularized. Its failure opened the way for the Reformation, the natural sequel to the circumstances of mediaeval development.

The critics of the Church commanded a wide popular following. Wycliffe in England, Huss in Bohemia, are famous; there were many others. The consistent theme is the attempt to return to the primitive simplicity of the Gospels, to strip the Church of the worldly commitments accumulated through the centuries. In this task the richer laity were ready to help the Reformers; by the sixteenth century political conditions were ripe for the success of Protestantism. It was destined to take two forms; Lutheranism, though it set the torch to the subsequent conflagration, was a spiritual secession, politically unconstructive, an inward-looking religion which stressed individual conscience but was prepared to submit to the rule of lay power. Calvinism, on the other hand, was a highly organized militant movement, claiming supreme spiritual authority.

Luther's revolt in Germany, the secession of England, the Calvinist movement in France, and the Protestant movements in Switzerland, Holland, and Scandinavia, decisively split the unity of Christendom, but they asserted ideas which would be vastly influential in Europe and even more so in North America. The Reformation was the result of a widening consciousness spreading among the dominant classes and increasingly permeating the masses. Where the Renaissance affirmed liberty of mind, the Reformation affirmed liberty of spirit. This development is new to mediaeval civilization: it stressed the worth and dignity of individual judgement and often resulted in an enrichment and variety of spiritual and intellectual life. It was a characteristic Northern European adventure, taking great risks, but in many respects creative and confident. The normal pattern of society had hitherto been authoritarian; the Roman Empire and the Catholic Church, like the priesthoods of the Near Eastern river-valleys, had attempted to impose a static and uniform religious and political order. Only in small city states had politically creative vitality appeared and that within a limited civic framework. Now the habit of liberty spread far more widely, at the cost of the disruption of political and religious authority. Two immensely powerful currents of opinion thus reinforced one another, and expanded and developed the ancient tradition of European intellectual and practical initiative, at the price of the destruction of the remnant of European order.

Only religious enthusiasm could have made so great a revolution. The Renaissance was at first the affair of a minority and it was very conservative; the new scientific outlook would emerge only after a conflict of the *Ancients* and *Moderns*. The Reformation was an affair of the masses. With the emergence of an educated laity, religious speculation increasingly broke the bounds of scholastic thought, and with the invention of printing, the habit of Biblical study became widespread. Meanwhile the old certainties disappeared; the palpable failure of the Papacy and the inadequacy of the Conciliar attempt at reform, left men without landmarks; while a growing prosperity and social change brought more minds to the threshold of religious and political consciousness. In such circumstances, doctrines which would have petered out in the wastes of scholastic controversy or been scotched as heresy were seized upon with avidity. Men's minds were still haunted by mediaeval terrors and obsessed by Jewish and Hellenistic ideas of sin and judgement, of Hell and redemption. Like St. Paul, they sought 'Salvation'; Luther offered Salvation by Faith, Calvin Salvation through Grace by Election. The obsession with sin, as in the Hellenistic religions, was countered by the guarantees of redemption. Doctrines and institutions which stood in the way must be ruthlessly destroyed, and, strong in the conviction of these ideas, men were willing to run into any extremity. The Calvinists in particular, like the Manichees, regarded human nature as intrinsically evil. 'Before we see the light of the sun we are polluted,' wrote Calvin. Unlike the Manichees, they retained their belief in the controlling power of God and held that by an 'immutable and incomprehensible decree' a minority were predestined by election to salvation. The conviction of election inspired the Calvinists to a spiritual pride congenial to the northern mind but reprobated by Calvin himself. Where Lutheranism was mainly introspective, voicing the emotional revolt of the German people against the discipline and authority of Rome, Calvinism had been inspired by a Frenchman who possessed the lucidity and organizing power of his people. Calvin's *Institutes*, translated into French in 1541, provided a clear trenchant doctrine; the Calvinist Church was strictly organized.

The Reformation originated in areas where the power of central authority was weak; in Saxony under the protection of the Elector and in the Swiss Republic of Geneva. Later it was reinforced by native movements of mediaeval origin, as in England where the Lollard movement had appeared in the fourteenth century but where it was imposed from above by Henry VIII, who always thought himself a strict Catholic. The Reformers were concerned not to create new Churches, but to reform the old one; they based their doctrines on the Scriptures and repudiated the authority of the Roman Catholic Church. All were convinced that their doctrine alone secured Salvation; all were determined to convert Christendom; all regarded their opponents as destined to eternal punishment. There was thus no increase in tolerance, though, since the educated laity had access to the translated Bible, there were greater opportunities for individual interpretation.

Lutheranism succeeded in Germany and Scandinavia; in Germany, in part through national feeling against the Italian clergy, who monopolized many of the best preferments, in part through the support of powerful princes and because it took root in the cities. The Lutheran Church abandoned the Mass and the Latin liturgy, conducted services in the vulgar tongue, laid a new emphasis on the sermon and substituted pastors for priests; but the price of the protection of the lay power was subjection to the authority of the lay rulers. Lutheranism spread over great areas of Germany, with varying success into Sweden and Denmark: as in England, the new movement was backed by the powerful elements among the ruling classes, covetous of the Church lands and impatient of the control of the Church Courts.

Calvin, who fled from France to Geneva, there created the model government of the Reformed Church. Authority was exercised by a consistory of lay elders and pastors who imposed a severe discipline upon their congregations. The movement was more extremely Puritan than Luther's, repudiating practically the whole Roman ritual and inculcating a dour and intolerant outlook. It succeeded among the urban bourgeoisie whose methodical and respectable habits it emphasized and reflected, though many successful capitalists were Catholic or Anglican; too much has been made of the influence of Calvinism on business, and Calvinist pastors were quick to denounce many capitalistic ways. It spread very widely into France, Scotland, England, and the Netherlands, and eastward into Hungary and Poland. Its international organization was efficient and far-flung; of all the Protestant Churches the Calvinist was the most powerful. But neither in France nor England did Calvinism become the established religion; Henry IV thought Paris worth a Mass, and the English devised a characteristic compromise in the Anglican Church. This compromise retained much of the old ritual and organization, but subjected the Church to the Crown and left the bulk of Church property and much preferment in lay hands.

The Roman Catholic Church, meanwhile, retained its influence over Spain, Portugal, and Italy; in France, in its Gallican form, the Church remained doctrinally Catholic, though politically independent of Rome. The Austrian Habsburgs continued the bulwark of Catholicism in Central Europe; Poland, about half Germany, and Southern Ireland continued within the fold. For, faced with this formidable attack, the Catholic Church reasserted its authority by every means. An intellectual and moral revival transformed the Papacy from a Renaissance principality into a European influence. The Jesuit Order, a closely disciplined *élite,* anticipating in some aspects the party organizations of the twentieth century, living in the world, highly educated in Humanistic learning and backed by the Inquisition, was the principal weapon of the Counter-Reformation. The Council of Trent, intermittently in session from 1545 to 1563, based its pronouncements on the Vulgate, the Latin translation of the Bible. The supreme authority of Rome was reaffirmed, and the Roman Church became more closely identified with the Mediterranean nations.

Both Protestant and Catholic movements became closely embroiled with the power politics of their day, which became embittered by sectarian hatred. Both parties violently attacked the princes who belonged to the opposite camp, defied their authority and appealed to religious and moral principles. Powerful religious minorities were found in many of the states of Western Europe, who refused to accept the authority of government: the united front of clerical and governmental power, which for all its internal dissensions had been widely maintained during the height of mediaeval civilization, was broken. Calvinists and Jesuits quoted Classical and mediaeval precedents, asserting the authority of law and the community in general against rulers they disliked. In consequence there got about in the political vocabulary of Europe ideas of law and even of popular sovereignty which would not otherwise have become current: in the furnace of religious controversy were forged the weapons of political revolution. Moreover, the intolerable cruelties and persecutions of the religious wars discredited rival extremists with a growing body of opinion, increasingly nurtured on the new Humanism and trained in more practical ways of thought. By the second half of the seventeenth century the climate of influential opinion had radically altered, and men were able to think in terms of religious and intellectual toleration.

So it was that the individualism of the Renaissance and seventeenth-century scientific method, with all the intellectual and spiritual enterprise and strength they entailed, were reinforced by the results of the Reformation, and ultimately enabled to expand in a new atmosphere of toleration unknown in Europe since Antiquity.

By the seventeenth century, in spite of all the violence of the religious wars, the tide was running towards the assertion of greater political, economic, spiritual, and intellectual freedom, though many people feared anarchy and, at the same time, political institutions were developing which cut across this process. The rise of great national states, claiming absolute authority, paying the merest lip-service to the idea of Christendom and conducted both in internal and external policy on Machiavellian lines, was the outstanding political fact of the sixteenth and seventeenth centuries. Within this framework, the new ideas and the new economic revolution worked themselves out. This development determined the political future and has today brought modern civilization into jeopardy, but in its beginnings the sovereign state was the largest viable contemporary unit of power, more extensive than anything achieved in the Middle Ages and a notable advance in security and organization.

The society of Antiquity and of mediaeval Europe had grown up in terms of civic communities on the one hand and of great cosmopolitan institutions on the other. The tradition of the unity of civilization had been maintained both under the Roman Empire and in Mediaeval Christendom. The sixteenth and seventeenth centuries saw a radical transformation of the political scene. The new national states were controlled by centralized governments wielding a power of unprecedented proportions, and recognizing no superior law. In its context this development, with all the vigour, richness, and diversity of culture it implied, marks a valuable stage in the evolution of European society. Given, also, the limited military power of pre-scientific and pre-industrial Europe, the existence of the sovereign State did not imply the disruption of the European civilization. Successive attempts were made, first to regulate the relations of these National States by the definition of a new International Law, by manœuvring for a 'Balance of Power,' so that no one State should be able to dominate the rest, and by a series of treaties and conferences of varying effectiveness. None of these expedients was permanently successful, and the history of Europe has become increasingly dominated by the struggles of these independent powers. As is well known, it is the supreme political problem of our own day to rid ourselves of this legacy of the sixteenth century, and to devise a supranational political order compatible with the scope of modern ideas and the range of modern inventions.

The origins of the Sovereign State are to be found in the economic and political situation of the later Middle Ages and in the courts of the tyrants of Renaissance Italy. As we have seen, in alliance with the mercantile interest and the more enterprizing nobility, and employing Italianate methods of diplomacy and administration, the Renaissance kings established governments of unprecedented efficiency and centralization. The new power found its theoretical definition in the writings of Bodin, who coined the term 'Majestas,' which has been translated 'Sovereignty.' 'The prince or people,' he writes, 'who possess sovereign power cannot be called to account for its actions by anyone but immortal God.'[1] Bodin justifies this doctrine as the alternative to anarchy. And indeed, by the context of his time, he was right. Since outside the Nation State, neither Papacy nor Empire commanded a European allegiance, and since, within it, government's authority was denied by powerful religious minorities, there remained as the ultimate sanction of authority nothing but naked force. Such was the origin of the theory of unbridled national sovereignty, a theory which sprang from the expedients of sixteenth-century politics, natural in its setting but morally disastrous, the theoretical consecration of the practices of power politics, writ large in terms of National States.

The background, then, of the immense intellectual, economic, and spiritual progress which began with the Renaissance and the Reformation, had been the power politics of the sovereign successor States to the cosmopolitan order of Mediaeval Christendom, itself the heir to the Roman Empire. It was a situation which paralleled on a great scale and with world repercussions the disastrous wars and manœuvrings of the Hellenistic successor States to the Empire of Alexander, states destined to be ground into a common subjection by the power of Rome.

Of course the rulers of the new nations invoked the authority of God, but claims to Divine favour could only be substantiated by the fortune of battle. In spite of the assertion in terms of national monarchy of the Divine sanction for government traditional since the dawn of civilization, Divine Right was wearing thin. In consequence a new and secularized theory of politics was defined in the seventeenth century, of which the most famous and trenchant expression is found in the *Leviathan* (1651) of Thomas Hobbes. The State is now sanctioned not by Divine Right or tradition but by its own efficiency.

Hobbes' argument is roughly as follows. The Law of Nature is self-preservation, but owing to the competitive pride and avarice of men, only by over-riding state power can security be established, and without security the law of self-preservation is void. The absolute State is, therefore, the expression of the law

[1] Jean Bodin, *Les Six Livres de la Republique* (1576), Bk. I, Chap. 8.

of Nature. Hobbes was a psychologist and a mathematician; in the fashion of his day he regarded the individual as a rational calculating unit, actuated by self-interest, greed, and fear; at the same time, following the current geometrical thought, he believed there existed a 'theorem' of politics, which consisted in 'certain rules.' These he believed he had discovered. The price of security was an absolute sovereign State, a 'mortal God' which saves man from himself. It is not a referee holding the balance between competing interests, but controls all aspects of life. The Church, the armed forces, finance, commerce, education, all are harnessed to this static and mechanical pattern. It originates with a social compact whereby men 'get themselves out of the miserable condition of war,' and its aim is strictly practical.

Such, very broadly, in Hobbes' view is the nature of the State; without it there can be no civilization: life is 'solitary, poor, nasty, brutish, and short.'[1] The conclusions of this cynical English philosopher, a student and translator of Thucydides, mark a radical departure in State theory and foreshadow in some aspects the doctrines of the modern totalitarian State. In the seventeenth century the price of order appeared to be despotism, and this theory became the practice of the great continental monarchies. Fortunately in England, Holland, Switzerland, and parts of Scandinavia, and in the new settlements in North America, the old traditions of self-government were preserved; they found their most influential expression in the writings of John Locke, but Locke, like Hobbes, gave the State a secular and practical justification, and wrote against Divine Right. The origins and the influence of this stream of thought will be examined in the succeeding chapter.

Given the circumstances of his day, Hobbes' remedy seemed obvious; the ablest administrators, Richelieu, Strafford, and Mazarin, proceeded on these lines, the logical outcome of the Machiavellian method on which the great European States were being built. Its weakness lay first in a static and mechanical outlook, which denied the organic relation between State and individual, taken for granted in earlier communities; in the suppression of free opinion, which in time was bound to destroy the vitality of the State, and in the failure to look beyond its fron-

1 Hobbes, *Leviathan*, c. 13.

tiers and envisage a European order. Hobbes compares princes to 'gladiators . . . in a posture of Warre' and takes this situation for granted.

The international position resulting from the rise of Sovereign States following Machiavellian policies, outraged not only the Christian but the Roman legal tradition. Academic men of good will cast about to mitigate the rigours of inter-state war, to devise an international law which, facing the realities of the day, would to some extent preserve the ancient order of Christendom. Of these lawyers the Dutchman, Grotius (1583–1645) was the most famous and the most influential; he is the father of modern doctrines of international law. After an academic and administrative career in Holland, he was forced into exile in France, where he set himself to investigate this new legal field. Like Hobbes and Locke, his approach to political theory is secular; the foundations of international law, he argues, rest on the natural sociability of human nature and on mutual benefit. Unless nations keep their contracts, civilization is impossible, 'the moment we recede from right we can depend on nothing.'[1] Christian nations are justified therefore in making war in the name of God and Humanity against those who violate their contracts. It must be made too dangerous for aggressors to prosecute their designs; 'their practices cannot possibly prosper for long, which render man unsociable to man and hateful to God.' Christians ought only to embark on just wars, humanely conducted. Grotius attempted to regulate the conduct of war and to define diplomatic procedure; following his initiative international lawyers have tried to mitigate the rigours of power politics, and to ameliorate the horrors of war. In modern total scientific war its conventions have been increasingly discarded. None the less, Grotius' fundamental argument remains valid: in a world of sovereign states only an alliance of predominant powers can enforce international law. Of this Grotius was himself aware, for he dedicated his book to the French King Louis XIII, who represented the growing might of France, destined to be the strongest nation for over a century after Grotius had written. To Grotius a European domination by the French Crown seemed the only practicable solution, the price worth paying for order.

[1] Grotius, *De Jure Belli ac Pacis. Prolegomina.*

II

Such in bare outline was the new secularized political theory
of the seventeenth century, justifying the naked power of the
dynastic sovereign state, and such the theory of international law
devised by Grotius. Against this background, European politics
were largely determined by the contest between the Protestant
movement and the Counter-Reformation, which cut across and
intensified the contest for political and economic power between
the rising national states. In these extensive, long, and sanguinary conflicts, economic, political, and religious interests are
closely intertwined, secular motives predominating in the seventeenth century.

We have seen how enormous was the Habsburg power during
the reign of Charles V, and how Spanish influence was increased
by the wealth of the New World. In the second half of the sixteenth century Spain put the drive of this new power behind the
Counter-Reformation in an attempt to reunite Christendom
under the Roman Church, for Philip II conceived this task as a
divine mission. In Germany also, the other branch of the Habsburg family set themselves to reimpose Catholicism: had this
Spanish and Imperial policy succeeded, Europe would have been
subjected to Habsburg domination. The French monarchy found
itself in a dilemma; its traditional policy was to weaken the Imperial power in Germany by alliance with the Protestant princes
and even with the Turks; on the other hand, the Catholic French
kings favoured the Counter-Reformation and needed Spanish
help against their Protestant subjects, even at the price of interference in French internal politics. The Guise family, the champions of the Counter-Reformation in France, were ready to work
with Spain; the French Calvinists attempted to gain English aid.
After a series of prolonged and indecisive campaigns and after
the notorious massacre of St. Bartholomew, the political realism
of Henry IV united Frenchmen in a national policy and built up
a monarchy destined, in the second half of the seventeenth century, to become the strongest power in Europe. At the time of his
assassination Henry IV was reverting to the traditional anti-

Habsburg policy in alliance with the German Protestants. Richelieu, the ruler of France from 1624 to 1642, the architect of the French absolute monarchy, pursued the same course. The cold genius of this artist in power largely created the framework of the French absolute state. Ruthlessly he put down the power of the nobility; he quelled the Huguenot resistance; he pursued a forward policy to secure the frontiers, to dominate Germany and the Western Alps. Under his successor, Mazarin, the French monarchy withstood the storms of aristocratic rebellion; by the peace of the Pyrenees (1659) an advantageous Spanish frontier was secured, and a dynastic marriage of Louis XIV (1643-1715) with the Spanish Infanta opened out dazzling possibilities of combined French and Spanish empire. By the second half of the seventeenth century France was the greatest power in Europe, united, centralized, and inspired with a new aggressive territorial ambition; the Continent was dominated by the rigid, bewigged, and arrogant figure of the Grand Monarque. But in the later sixteenth century Spain was still the most powerful state; and the Counter-Reformation brought Spain into conflict with the English and the Dutch, the two most vigorous maritime nations of the day. Here economic and religious rivalry coincided: there was a radical conflict in outlook and way of life. The English and Dutch Protestants were northern peoples, maritime and commercial, late comers to the colonial field, now expanding into a world horizon; Spain was traditional, still in part mediaeval, and the focus of the greatest land power in Europe. The conflict was inevitable; unless the Spanish and Portuguese monopoly of the New World and the Far East was broken, there could be no future for the English or the Dutch as world powers.

The traditional relations between Spain and England were friendly, following a mutual distrust of France; they had been consolidated by the marriage of Henry VIII with Catherine of Aragon. Philip II attempted to win back the heretical country by marriage with their daughter Mary, and even maintained at first good relations with Elizabeth I. Later James I, in the teeth of English opinion, was to revert to this ancient understanding with Spain; but as ideological warfare deepened after Elizabeth's excommunication, and as English and Spanish interests clashed in the New World, the conflict came to its crisis.

In the second half of the sixteenth century, Spain was faced with a revolt in the Netherlands (1568) of which Philip II was hereditary count. Alva, with his Spanish pikemen, trained in the new Swiss tactics, committed frightful atrocities in the Low Countries. Under William the 'Silent,'—the 'sluw,' better translated 'sly'—the Dutch put up an epic resistance. They flooded much of the country and took to the sea; obstinately they endured horrible sieges, Haarlem, Leyden, Alkmaar. Alva failed; Philip's mercenaries mutinied for lack of pay; they sacked Antwerp and Catholic and Protestant united against the 'Spanish Fury.' But Parma's diplomacy broke the union, and it was only the Dutch Calvinist provinces which formed, in 1579, the Union of Utrecht, the beginning of modern Holland. This new state was a federation of republics combined in a common religious and economic interest. The preponderant power was Holland, with its great cities, Amsterdam and Rotterdam; as elected Stadholders and Captains General, William and his successor, Maurice of Nassau, provided a common leadership. When William was murdered in 1584, the new state was secure; by 1609 the Spaniards were forced to a twelve years' truce. In the struggle Holland had become a great maritime power, sending her fleets to the East Indies and South America; when in 1621 the contest was renewed the Spanish Atlantic fleet was broken. There followed a period of commercial rivalry and intermittent conflict with England, of republican movements against the House of Orange; but the aggression of Louis XIV and the return of the Orange family in 1672, led to a gradual *rapprochement* in the face of common danger, which culminated in the accession of William of Orange to the English throne.

The consolidation of England under the Tudor monarchy, the tiding over of the Reformation without the disruption of the State, the alliance between the mercantile and landed interests and the Crown, had enabled the country to explore the new opportunities of expansion and to present a united front to the Spanish attack. The reign of Elizabeth (1558–1603) is generally regarded as the most brilliant in English history; it marked the triumphant weathering of a great storm, the emergence of England on to the threshold of world power. Elizabeth herself was a hard and versatile Renaissance personality, subtle in diplomacy, widely accomplished, far-seeing; in time of crisis of the quality of steel. 'Though I be but a weak woman,' she told her troops at Tilbury in 1588, 'I have the heart and stomach of a King, and a King of England too.' Her government was composed of able statesmen, representative of the new age—the great William Cecil, Lord Burleigh, his son Robert, Earl of Salisbury, a host of other remarkable men. All over the country the old aristocracy who had maintained their power at the Reformation, the new court nobility, the squires, and the owners of Church lands confiscated and sold by Henry VIII, worked in harmony with the central government which maintained its position with the minimum of force. After 1588 a new confidence and enterprise developed, and the union of the English and Scottish Crowns under James I deprived the Counter-Reformation of a potential base of attack in the North.

The conflict between the Stuarts and the classes which had been the mainstay of Tudor power came about through Charles I's (1625–49) attempt at absolute monarchy on the prevalent continental pattern; through the failure of the royal executive to reflect the will of the substantial elements in the nation represented by the House of Commons, and through the refusal of the Anglican Church to come to terms with the extremer Protestants. The victory of the Parliament was due in part to superior staying power, since it commanded London and the richest parts of the country, but immediately to the Cromwellian army. The uncompromising attitude of the King and the political incapacity of the Parliament led first to a military republic styled the Commonwealth, next to a Protectorate. Under this arbitrary regime, though it was bitterly unpopular at home, England became a major force in European politics. The Cromwellian navy commanded the seas, drove the Dutch out of the Channel and entered the Mediterranean; the Protestant cause in central Europe looked to Cromwell.

Meanwhile religious conflict and economic change in England had given rise to a chain of events of world importance. The Elizabethan projects of colonization in North American had been followed up; in 1607 a new colony was founded in Virginia; through desperate vicissitudes it survived. In New England, the Pilgrim Fathers made their famous settlement in 1620; by

1630 there were nearly seven thousand English settlers up and down the coast. Massachusetts, New Hampshire, Connecticut, Maryland, all saw the beginning of colonization in the thirties. A growing stream of emigrants crossed the Atlantic to these new colonies and to the West Indies. At first the latter were the more popular field of expansion; a rich West Indian area was won during the first half of the century and consolidated by Cromwell's seizure of Jamaica. But in spite of the preponderant economic position of the West Indies, the North American settlements were destined to become of far greater importance. Their existence decided that the political traditions of North America were to reflect the English practice of self-government and respect for Law; though through subsequent immigration, the racial stock of the United States was to be modified, their political inheritance was to remain English.

The Protectorate ended in 1660 with the Restoration of the Stuart dynasty. The fundamental question had long been decided, for the Parliament controlled finance, though not foreign policy. Charles II (1660–85), one of the shrewdest and certainly the most entertaining of the English kings, a notable patron of science, maintained a difficult position with negligent skill; but the Stuart cause was lost by the bigotry of his brother, James II— by what Charles termed 'la sottise de mon frère.' The sequel was the famous revolution of 1688, and the rise of England to economic preponderance in the West. The nature of this very English compromise will be examined in the next chapter.

In Scandinavia, meanwhile, following the Swedish revolt from the Union of Kalmar, a struggle had developed between Denmark and the native Vasa dynasty in Sweden for the control of the Baltic. By the middle seventeenth century predominance had passed to the Swedes, who under Gustavus Adolphus became the strongest power in the North. For Kristian II (1513–23), a brother-in-law of Charles V, had attempted to create a strong monarchy in Denmark; in 1520 his mercenaries overran Sweden and committed the notorious Stockholm massacre. In 1523 a revolt of the Danish nobility drove him from the throne: the revolt had been led by Frederick I, Duke of Holstein; his successor, Kristian III, turned Lutheran, and Frederic II, in the second half of the sixteenth century, revived the struggle with the Swedes.

The Swedes had found a national leader in Gustavus Vasa (1523–60), whose ability and prestige enabled him to bridle the nobility and organize a Protestant Church submissive to the state. He created a new Renaissance monarchy, and secured the hereditary succession of the Vasa House. His son, Eric XIV, was a homicidal neurotic, dethroned in 1568; his brother, John III, following a Polish marriage, reverted to a compromise with Rome. His successor, Sigismund, a Catholic and King of Poland, was deposed in 1599, and Charles IX turned again to the Protestant tradition of his family. The reign of Gustavus Adolphus (1611–32) saw the climax of Swedish expansion to the south, a meteoric and profitable intervention in the affairs of Germany.

While the maritime peoples of the West, consolidated in powerful states, were expanding into the New World and establishing increasing contacts with the East, and the Russians pushing across Siberia and south to the Caspian, the political disunity of the German peoples was worsened by an appalling conflict. The Thirty Years War was the fiercest of all the religious and political struggles of this turbulent age. It devastated the cultural and economic life of Germany; plague, pestilence, and famine followed in the wake of contending armies, though the population of the Germanies was not so much diminished as was formerly believed.

The immediate occasion of these wars (1618–48) was the deposition of Ferdinand of Habsburg from the Bohemian throne. The Czechs flung the Imperial envoys from a window in the Palace at Prague, and offered the crown to the Protestant Elector Palatine of the Rhine, son-in-law of James I of England. In 1619 Ferdinand succeeded to the Empire and proceeded to liquidate the Bohemian revolt. Religious conflict was reinforced by the perennial German and Czech animosity, and in the following year the Czechs were routed at the battle of the White Hill. An unsuccessful intervention of the Protestant King of Denmark, Kristian IV, one of the most formidable rulers of history, backed by English support, was disposed of by the Imperial army under Wallenstein; and in 1629 the Emperor extended the war into an attempt to resume possession of the Church lands, now in the hands of the Protestant princes. The Imperial mercenaries devastated the country; Richelieu, following the anti-Habsburg policy of Henry IV, encouraged Swedish intervention.

Gustavus Adolphus, profiting from the discomfiture of Denmark, was determined to win Swedish control of the Baltic and a voice in the affairs of the Empire. A soldier of genius, he had created a disciplined mobile army, using powerful artillery and new cavalry tactics. Seasoned in campaigns against the Russians and the Poles, he achieved spectacular success in Germany. He dominated Bohemia and captured Munich, but Wallenstein was a match for him, and he was killed at Lutzen in 1632. His Chancellor, Oxenstiern, continued to pursue the traditional Swedish objectives, obtaining at the end of the war the possession of Western Pomerania. In spite of the conflict, the Emperor's objectives were not attained; Wallenstein, scheming to create an independent authority based on Bohemia, had to be done away with in 1634, and although the Lutherans came to terms, the conflict dragged on. Richelieu subsidized the Swedes and the Dutch, attempting to create a Rhenish Confederation under French control: Spain, originally the mainstay of the Emperor, was crippled by bankruptcy and by Portuguese and Catalan revolts, by her long unsuccessful conflicts with the Dutch. When the war was concluded by the Treaty of Westphalia, the Habsburg Counter-Reformation had failed; effective Habsburg power in Central Europe was henceforward mainly confined to the Austrian territories, to Bohemia and Hungary.

Political power in Germany remained with the rulers of Bavaria, Saxony, and Brandenburg. Here the Hohenzollerns were now becoming formidable: the Grand Elector, Frederic William (1640–88) was to rule not only the Mark of Brandenburg but East Prussia, with a foothold in Western Germany in the Duchies of Regensburg and Cleves; the expansion of his influence is the first major landmark in the rise of the Prussian state. Over the rest of Germany the stage was set for a multiplication of petty principalities in the eighteenth century, while France gained control of Alsace.

Eastward, the sixteenth and early seventeenth centuries saw the greatest phase of Polish-Lithuanian expansion, followed by the disastrous collapse known in Polish history as 'The Deluge,' and by the short-lived revival under John Sobieski. The reign of Sigismund Jagellon I (1506–48) had been a time of relative peace and growing civilization; but he never secured the authority of the crown on a firm basis; in 1530 the monarchy became formally elective. Sigismund II fought the Russians, the Swedes, and the Danes, eastward and along the Baltic; the final union of Poland and Lithuania in 1561 secured an apparent consolidation, but the fatal weakness of the Polish crown continued. The rich Lithuanian barons of the Ukraine proved more unruly than the Polish magnates; urban and economic life was strangled. Further, the Hohenzollerns were already pushing into East Prussia and the Habsburg power increasing in the South. Protestantism, too, made considerable headway, but the Counter-Reformation triumphed in Poland; the end of the Jagellon House coincided with an expansion of Jesuit influence and a new militant Catholicism among the Polish upper class. Following an interval inadequately filled by Henry of Valois, afterwards Henry III of France, Stephan Bathory (1575–86), a Prince of Transylvania, secured the throne. He launched into further expansion; he took Danzig, fought the Russians over Latvia and captured Pskov, founded the University of Vilna, planned expansion to the Black Sea; his reign is a landmark in Polish military annals. He was succeeded by Swedish kings of the House of Vasa, who transferred the capital in 1596 from Cracow to Warsaw. Sigismund III (1587–1632) who supported the Counter-Reformation, had been expelled from Sweden by his brother, the Lutheran Charles IX. His ambitions were primarily Baltic, but his reign saw the deepest Polish penetration into Russia. His successor continued the eastern offensive and captured Smolensk; the reign of John Casimir Vasa (1648–68) saw the final flare-up of Polish military ambition.

By the 'sixties the tide was on the turn, for a Swedish-Russian coalition was formed which broke the Polish power. Kiev and most of the Ukraine were lost: large tracts of the country were overrun; in Poland and Lithuania there was civil war. In this desperate situation John Sobieski (1674–96) rose to power, and with French backing secured the throne. His brilliant relief of Vienna from the Turks was the last great military exploit of the old Poland. The second half of the seventeenth century, indeed, saw the waning of Polish-Lithuanian power, the reduction of Poland to a state largely dependent on Russia. The Polish constitution and Polish impatience of the discipline of a professional army left the country, in spite of French support, ill-equipped to face the centralized autocracies of Moscow, Vienna, and Berlin.

To the south-east, throughout the seventeenth century, the Turkish menace had remained severe: the Thirty Years War had crippled the German counter-offensive, and had not the Ottomans been preoccupied with wars in Asia, might well have proved the occasion of their overrunning Vienna and even penetrating into Southern Germany. The second half of the seventeenth century saw the final Turkish attempt to destroy the Habsburg base. In 1660 they invaded Transylvania and defeated the Hungarians; in 1683 they besieged Vienna. It was a major European crisis. The Emperor Leopold I fled; only the military genius of Sobieski rescued the city, an exploit ill required by the Habsburg House. In 1687 there followed a successful European counter-attack; the Turks were defeated, Transylvania cleared; in 1688 Belgrade was captured, and under the leadership of Prince Eugen, the collaborator in Marlborough's later campaigns, the struggle continued through the next decade until the Turkish defeat at Senta in 1697. By the Treaty of Karlovitz (1699) all Hungary and Transylvania were redeemed; it was the first landmark in the decline of the Turkish power in Europe, the ebb of a tide which had been encroaching since the fifteenth century. None the less, the Turkish Empire still sprawled over the Balkans and far up through Roumania, into Galicia and the southern steppe: the problems entailed by its slow decline were to poison the politics of Eastern Europe for two centuries.

In the depth of the mixed forest zone of Central Russia, the sixteenth century had witnessed the consolidation of Muscovy, still largely cut off from Western influences, but already disposing of great resources of man-power and seasoned in the long struggle against Tatar domination. By the close of the century the Tatar yoke had finally been broken, and the long contest westward against Poland-Lithuania had begun. The reign of Ivan the Great (1462–1505) marked an extension of territorial control and the assertion of the claim to the political inheritance of Byzantium. Ivan married Zoë, niece of Constantine Palaeologus, the last Byzantine Emperor; he proclaimed himself Tsar (Caesar); adopted the double-headed eagle, the Imperial device; refused the Tatar tribute.

He could afford to assert his independence, for the Tatars were at war in their own camp. Their domination, long wavering, received its death blow when, in 1502, the Crimean Tatars destroyed the Golden Horde. Meanwhile, Ivan, a ruler who showed affinities with his Renaissance contemporaries in the West, had subdued Novgorod, and extended his authority to the East. He imported Italian architects who rebuilt the Kremlin, he invited Western doctors to settle in Moscow, though under threat of execution should their remedies fail: his policy, after the manner of his time, was plodding and cautious. Under Vassily II, consolidation and expansion had continued; in 1514 Smolensk was won and the long reign of Ivan the Dread (1533–84) marks the final emancipation from the Tatars, the formal assertion that the Grand Prince of Muscovy, the White Tsar, is the autocrat of a new Rome, the third Divinely ordained Empire. With Ivan, the tsardom struck deeper roots. The first half of his reign saw important internal reforms; with ruthless ferocity he broke the power of the great landowning boyars; he established the beginning of a professional army, organized in part on the Turkish model; though his drive north-westward to the Baltic failed, he captured Kazan and Astrakan, giving Muscovy an outlet to the Caspian. In his later years he won an evil reputation, but he lives in Russian folk memory as a great tsar, unaccountable, terrible, absolute, even in his mania, a scourge of God. Ivan focused a new religious and national spirit; an Imperial autocrat, Orthodox and above the law, the heir also of Rurik and the traditions of Kiev-Russia. Yet with Feodor Ivanovitch, the house of Rurik came to an end, for though the great Tsar had outdone the English King Henry VIII by marrying seven times, he had murdered the tsarevitch with his own hands, and left only a weakling heir. The brief and disputed reign of Boris Godunov, Ivan's brother-in-law, merged into the 'Time of Troubles' (1604–13) when the full weight of the Polish-Lithuanian kingdom was thrown against the Muscovite state. The Poles captured the Kremlin, set up a puppet tsar and threatened Muscovy with extinction. The magnates engaged in civil war. Religious schism added to the confusion: the Poles were fanatically Catholic; their invasion coincided with the full tide of the Counter-Reformation; the Uniate Church, composed of Orthodox clergy ready to come to terms with Rome, had been founded under Polish auspices in 1596. Henceforward, in Muscovy Orthodoxy and patriotism became synonymous.

The challenge provoked a national reaction; all elements of the country, the middling gentry the townsfolk, and the peasantry, combined to drive out the foreigners. In 1613 the first Romanov tsar, Michael, was elected by the Assembly of the Land. The reign of Alexis Michaelovitch (1645–75) witnessed a successful counter-attack, the recapture of Smolensk and Kiev and with it most of the Ukraine. The conquest of this area meant not only the addition to Muscovy of the historic waterways, the cradle of Kiev-Russia, but the crippling of Poland-Lithuania which no longer reached from the Baltic to the Black Sea.

The acquisition of the Ukraine proved a cultural advantage to Muscovy; Kiev Academy, which taught not only the traditional Greek learning but Latin, began to provide Moscow with better trained administrators; together with the foreigners employed by the government, they introduced relatively modern ideas. Further, by the close of the century, the Russian armies, organized by German, Dutch, and Scottish experts, were becoming formidable, not only in numbers, but in the traditionally strong Russian arm, artillery. With the Polish menace ended, the Tsars turned their energies further afield, against Sweden and the Ottoman Empire. Swedish energies had been diverted into Germany during the Thirty Years War, but the opening decades of the eighteenth century were to see the final and decisive contest with Russia. Meanwhile Russian penetration of Northern Siberia had been going on since the late sixteenth century. Yermak had led his famous expeditions beyond the Urals during the years 1581–5; the Yenesei had been reached by 1607; the Pacific by 1640. In 1689 the Russians were coming to diplomatic terms with the Chinese over the Amur river.

Against this background Peter the Great, a tsar of extraordinary genius (1682–1725), carried through a fundamental revolution. Deliberately and violently the upper classes in Russia were westernized, the Government rebuilt on the prevalent Absolutist model. The story of this revolution belongs to the history of the eighteenth century, but with the advent of Peter, the semi-Asiatic Muscovite state becomes imperial Russia, and turning her face to Europe, swings for the first time into the full tide of European politics.

Such, in bare outline, were the hard facts of the European political scene in the sixteenth and seventeenth centuries, the result of the competition of great dynastic states for political and economic power.

In the West, the English and the Dutch emerged strengthened from the conflict, with expanding colonial empires. The Spanish and Habsburg attempts to reimpose Catholicism on Northern Europe fad failed; Spain, exhausted by the struggle, gave place to France as the dominant power in Europe, and it was against French hegemony that the wars and diplomacy of eighteenth-century power politics were to be directed. In the Germanies, in the heart of Europe, there persisted a mediaeval disunity, the Habsburg domination being confined to the south-east; but a new nucleus of power had appeared in Brandenburg-Prussia. The preoccupation of the Germanies with religious wars, and the failure to consolidate a national state, combined with their geographical situation to prevent their sharing the colonial expansion which was changing the balance of the world. Meanwhile, in the East, Poland-Lithuania, after a final phase of expansion, lapsed into a second-rate power, and in Muscovy the solid foundation of national unity was laid, later to be the basis of the work of Peter the Great.

III

Against this political background, with the rising dynastic states struggling in a mesh of 'real-politik,' with no motive save self-interest and little remnant of European order save a precarious balance of power, the sixteenth to seventeenth centuries saw a great economic expansion, reaped the full harvest of Renaissance and scientific ideas and determined the intellectual future.

We have seen that the new governments had emerged often in alliance with the bourgeoisie, in their turn borne up by the surge of economic expansion; how, with the discoveries, economic power and opportunity had shifted to the Atlantic seaboard; how the economic relations of Europe had become oceanic, and how the influx of gold and silver from the New World had gradually revolutionized prices. We have noted also that Protestantism took root particularly among the urban mercantile classes, and how the disruption of mediaeval ideas, with the close restraints they imposed on individual commercial enterprise and on the lending of money on interest, enabled the new chances to be seized. Both Renaissance and Puritan individualism seemed to emancipate the new men of the age from the traditional obligations of Guild and City and from the authority of the Church. The vigour, the constructive predatory enterprise of barbarian forbears was still in the blood of the merchants and adventurers of Northern Europe. Strong in their faith in Bible and counting house, respectable, confident, and masterful, this new commercial and mercantile oligarchy developed the small-scale capitalism of the later Middle Ages on a far more formidable scale. Here is a development of equal significance for the future with the Renaissance, the Reformation, and the rise of the great state. It implied the increasing control of improving means of production by individual capitalists, and later by capitalist companies; the rise of a class, living, not only by commerce and industry, but by investment; the supersession of the old economy of status by one of contract; the growing influence of the new business interest on government; the development of a great volume of overseas trade together with the creation of an unprecedented surplus of wealth and a general rise in the upper-and middle-class standard of living. All these things are characteristic of this formative period and provided the foundation of a great cultural and scientific progress. For good and ill, though the old establishment often adapted itself, the traditional social structure was altered; the long-term change was radical.

The price was heavy and borne immediately by the poorer classes, though in the long run they benefited by the rise of the standard of living. With a wage-earning economy came uncertainty and unemployment: during the later Middle Ages the condition of the peasantry in Western Europe had been ameliorated; with the rise of the new Capitalism the traditional social order was shaken, and in many parts of Western Europe the ancient routine of peasant life disrupted. There had been occasional but unconstructive peasant revolts during the Middle Ages; now they were reinforced by religious strife. In Germany there was a formidable Peasants' Revolt in 1525–6; in England, France, Spain, and Scandinavia there were parallel disturbances. None of these proletarian movements was successful, but they mark a new stirring of political consciousness.

In spite of the price paid in social unrest, the development of the new capitalism was highly successful; it was the basis of the transformation of society which occurred during the sixteenth and seventeenth centuries, and which resulted in an unprecedented wealth and security in the eighteenth. Though in political influence, population, and natural resources, France remained the dominant power, this prosperity made Holland, following her emancipation from Spain, economically the most modern nation in the West. In commercial method, in agriculture, in stock breeding, in the art of war, the Dutch led Europe. The close of the century saw economic predominance pass to England, where a business oligarchy combined with the great landowners to take over the reins of political power and conduct policy on modern lines. Following this evolution the discrepancy between the social progress of Western and Eastern Europe was emphasized.

I V

On the basis of this prosperity a great intellectual expansion took place; the seventeenth century in particular was an age of genius, scientific, philosophical, and literary. There had been three strains of thought developing in the Renaissance world, in part original and in part deriving from Classical and Mediaeval times, all tending to an accuracy unapproached in other civilizations. With its roots in the Law Schools of Padua and Bologna, and its precedents in revived Roman Law, there had grown up a tradition of secular law practised and administered by laymen; they displayed subtlety, system, and precision. Further, the discipline of scholastic philosophy had sharpened men's wits ever since the twelfth century, and the conflict of the Reformation had broadcast the habit of exact theological disputation. This tendency had been reinforced by the tradition of close observation of nature created by the artists of the Renaissance, by the questioning of ancient bookish authority. For centuries men had described the habits of the more outlandish animals by repeating the observations of mediaeval bestiaries; even illustrations purporting to portray more homely creatures followed not the lines of daily observation but mediaeval conventions. The Renaissance artists swept all this away. The third stream of thought, which reinforced and later dominated the other two, was mathematical. The use of Arabic numerals, and the assimilation of Arabic ideas had greatly increased the scope of applied mathematics; by the end of the sixteenth century logarithms had been devised by a Scots laird, Napier; the decimal system was invented by a Flemish mathematician. The manufacture of instruments of precision, of optical glasses and rudimentary telescopes in northern Italy, and the invention of microscopes in Holland, opened up a new range of observation. Leeuwenhoek, a draper of Delft who demonstrated the existence of bacteria, and Malpighi in Naples were pioneers in this latter field.

In the seventeenth century all these influences combined to produce an unprecedented progress. It was an international movement, like all the great movements of thought; making its way against stubborn opposition, sometimes against persecution. But since the religious enthusiasts were fighting themselves into a peace of exhaustion, the new thought came fully into its own by the close of the seventeenth century. However great the pressure of organized authority, and however massive the opposition of brute uninformed opinion, the genius of modern Europe followed the vision of scientific truth, and, in time, by unanswerable results following the accumulation of detailed knowledge won dominant authority.

The most famous scientific names of the seventeenth century are Galileo, Descartes, and Newton: all exercised a profound influence on the outlook of mankind.

The Italian Galileo Galilei (1564–1642) carried on the initiative of Copernicus and Bruno, and laid the foundations of the Newtonian cosmology. His principal achievement was first in the field of mechanics, later in astronomy: he demonstrated that the physical world was calculable and measurable, susceptible, therefore, to systematic exploitation and control. By his famous experiment at Pisa (1591), he destroyed an ancient fallacy of Aristotelian mechanics: in 1610 he published the pamphlet *The Messenger of the Heavens,* describing his lunar and stellar observations, experimentally supporting Bruno's theory of a plurality of worlds. By 1616 the Inquisition was on his track, but he published in 1630 his *Dialogue on the two chief systems of the world,* in which the Ptolemaic theory was ridiculed in favour of the Copernican. His researches were reinforced by the work of Kepler, Tycho Brahe's assistant, a German of deep intuitions and obscure expression, who discovered the principle of ellipses.

Such was the cosmic background of the new outlook by the early seventeenth century. It was the Frenchman, Descartes (1596–1650), who formulated the principles of the new scientific method. His *Discours sur la Méthode,* published in 1637, is the charter of modern applied science. Examining the problem of consciousness, he devised a revolutionary approach; 'never to accept anything for true which I did not clearly know to be such.' By systematic classification, ordered analysis of essentials, and marshalling of all ascertainable facts relevant to a problem, he reached conclusions of far-reaching importance. He set himself to 'arrive at knowledge highly useful for life . . . to discover a Practical, by means of which we might render ourselves the lords and possessors of Nature . . .'[1] His writings were widely influential and the fountain-head of scientific thought up to the nineteenth century.

Of less originality than Descartes, but an influential and commanding figure, a master of sententious and hard-hitting epigram, Francis Bacon (1561–1626), Lord Verulam, had carried on the work of secularizing knowledge, of destroying the conventions of scholasticism, still powerful in the early seventeenth century. His *Advancement of Learning* (1605) and *Novum Organum* (1620) are landmarks in the diffusion of the new ideas. Above all, Bacon understood that applied science could command nature and 'better man's estate;' the new concept of deliberate improvement spread.

Descartes was essentially a mathematician; it was along geometrical and mechanical lines that the great English genius,

[1] Descartes, *Discourse on Method,* Chap. VI.

Newton (1642–1727), following on the work of Galileo, formulated his explanation of the physical universe, a cardinal landmark in the history of thought. In 1687 he published the famous *Principia*, defining his theory of the cosmic order.

Newton displayed the humility of the greatest men of science: for all his knowledge he felt himself only on the edge of the mysteries of the universe. 'I do not know what I may appear to the world,' he wrote in the last year of his life, 'but to myself I seem only to have been like a boy playing on the sea shore, and diverting myself in now and then finding a smoother pebble or a prettier shell than ordinary, while the great Ocean of Truth lay all undiscovered before me.' This sense of strange horizons has since characterized modern scientific thought, in contrast with the close little world of classical and mediaeval cosmology.

The new spirit of toleration is expressed in the writings of the Jewish philosopher, Spinoza (1632–77). His application of scientific method to Biblical criticism earned him the hatred of his contemporaries, and though he found refuge from persecution in Holland, he had little influence in his day. His greatness has since been appreciated. He displays a new scientific detachment: he wished 'not to laugh at men, or weep over them or hate them, but to understand them.' 'The ultimate aim of government,' he writes, 'is not to rule by fear . . . but to free men from fear . . . to enable men to develop their minds and bodies in security and to employ their reason unshackled.'[1] The German philosopher, Leibnitz (1646–1716), made a new approach to the problem of knowledge and invented the differential calculus; unlike Spinoza, he won contemporary fame.

In medicine, though methods remained barbarous, the value of hygiene was not appreciated, and doctors were obsessed with ancient theories of 'humours' and blood-letting, the Englishman Harvey, in 1628, published his discovery of the circulation of the blood. He is the outstanding medical genius of his age, in stature comparable with Vesalius; with his discovery medicine became a dynamic science. With this great advance medical knowledge was beginning to pull out of the quagmire of superstition and quackery which dogged it into the nineteenth century; yet the rate of infant mortality remained high, the ravages

---

[1] Spinoza, *Tractatus Politicus*, Cap. 22.

of the plague and the smallpox continued, gout and ague were endemic until relatively recent times. But the new knowledge made its beginnings; it was fostered by intelligent opinion, and sometimes encouraged by governments.

Along with the dominating influence of the new sciences, based on habits of precise thought and on applied mathematics —in particular upon geometry—there went a brilliant literary, artistic, and musical progress, for this wonderful century saw a cultural achievement equal to that of the sciences. National cultures, striking deeper than mediaeval learning and chivalry, expressing the vitality of the new bourgeoisie and of intelligent elements among the nobility and gentry, with their roots deep in popular tradition, reflected at once the national genius of the several peoples and the cosmopolitan influence of the new Humanism. Painting, too, further developed, following on the Italian and Flemish initiative; architecture continued an expanding development, particularly in the North where Italian and Classical models were increasingly imitated; and music laid the foundations of its eighteenth-century achievements. In England, following on the brilliance of the Elizabethan and early Jacobean drama, the best English lyric poetry, written to be sung, appears in the first half of the seventeenth century; Herrick and Campion can compare with the poets of Ionian Greece. It was an age too of great prose. The Authorised Version of the Bible appeared in 1612, a translation of matchless felicity and power, which has done so much to mould the thought and language of the Anglo-Saxon peoples; the sermons of Donne and Andrewes and their contemporaries express a dramatic and sonorous eloquence, while the trenchant prose of Bacon and Hobbes shows a native force and good sense. Milton, next to Shakespeare the greatest English poet, again a genius of European calibre comparable to Virgil and Dante, wrote his *Paradise Lost* and *Paradise Regained* in the years after the interregnum, while his reverberating defence of the freedom of the Press is another landmark in the Anglo-Saxon outlook. After the Restoration, the splendid and complex language of the Elizabethan, Jacobean, and Cromwellian Age gives place to a more lucid but equally powerful style, following French models and best expressed in Dryden's prose. It was an age, too, of new and more intimate records, in which the traditions of Antiquity were blended with the observation of common life. The biographies of Walton and Aubrey, homely and shrewd, tolerant and racy, breathe the spirit of the country life in which this civilization was so deeply rooted, while Pepys's famous *Diary* shows an engaging humour and self-revelation. The old mediaeval tradition of lumbering satire was brought to a finer point by Samuel Butler, whose *Hudibras,* ridiculing the Puritans, developed the ribald vein of the Tudor poet, Skelton. This mastery of language was not confined to professional writers and preachers; it is found in the pithy speech of the people and in the utterances of statesmen; the seventeenth century was a great age of English language and literature.

In France also the period was one of great literature; as in England, it found expression in the drama. Molière, gathering up the inheritance of French urban wit and sly observation, created the first school of French comedy; this high-spirited, caustic ridicule portrays a social scene far more subtle than that depicted by the Roman dramatists, one which can compare with Greek comedy. The more formal conventions of high French tragedy were created by Corneille in the 'thirties, and by Racine in the closing decades of the seventeenth century; they brought the sonorous lucidity of spoken French to an unsurpassed perfection. In Pascal, who published his *Lettres Provinciales* in 1657, France produced one of the greatest of religious writers. On their smaller scale, the *Fables* of La Fontaine express in lucid and elegant verse the traditional folk tales of French countryside—'Maître Renard' and 'Maître Corbeau' have a direct mediaeval descent; the *Letters* of Madame de Sévigné depict the life of the Court and of Breton provincial society, and the cynical maxims of La Rochefoucauld show a shrewd insight.

In Holland, the great writer Vondel (1587–1679) set a new standard in drama and lyric poetry; in Spain, too, the seventeenth century saw the rise of a remarkable literature. Following on the earlier work of Lope da Vega, Calderon in the seventeenth century, priest, soldier, and dramatist, wrote plays which, within their convention, show an unsurpassed stage technique, while Cervantes, adapting the picaresque novel and the mediaeval Romance to his sardonic wisdom, had created one of the greatest masterpieces of European literature, the moving, disillusioned narrative of *Don Quixote.*

In Germany the literary achievement of the age was considerable. The mystic Boehme carried on the pietist tradition, but Opitz's mechanical imitations of French originals, collected in the *Book of German Poetry*, had stereotyped a clumsy convention, and the most characteristic expression of the times was Grimmelshausen's racy *Simplicissimus*, a disguised autobiography, set during the Thirty Years War. Pufendorf in the second half of the seventeenth century continued the solid inheritance of Teutonic legal erudition, but it was Leibnitz who initiated a more creative phase of thought. Czech scholarship found expression in the works of Comenius, 'that incomparable Moravian,' whose compendium of knowledge enjoyed a European reputation; much of his life was spent in exile following the disasters of the Thirty Years War; in 1641 he visited England where he became the friend of Milton and Pym.

In terms of art the seventeenth century was a great age. The Spanish school reached its culmination in Velasquez (1599–1660), Court painter to Charles IV; it saw the climax of Flemish painting and the creation of the French tradition. Following the emancipation of Holland, Flemish painters came into their own. Rubens (1577–1640) was the greatest master; he studied at Venice under Titian and became Court painter to the Stadtholders of Flanders; a successful diplomat and courtier, ennobled by the King of Spain, knighted by Charles I; the colour and sweep of his great canvases brought a new splendour to Northern painting. His pupil Van Dyck portrayed the high distinction of the royalties and courtiers of this formal age, while Franz Hals, a real 'bohemian,' caught the bravado and self-confidence of the Dutch Wars of Independence. Rembrandt (1607–69), the son of a miller at Leyden, was a deeper psychologist, a superb painter of mellow light and shade, a great landscape artist also; his harassed later life was a contrast with the careers of his prosperous contemporaries of lesser genius. After the ardours and perils of the War of Liberation, the Dutch painters of the middle seventeenth century turned to peaceful subjects. The calm interiors of Vermeer, and Peter de Hooch, with sunlight streaming through latticed panes; the landscapes of Ruysdael and Hobbema, with their wide perspectives, are all masterpieces of their kind; the canvases of Van der Velde, marine painter to Charles II, caught the greys and greens of the North Sea.

In France the liberating influence of Rubens was reinforced by the genius of Poussin (1594–1665). Versed in classical learning, Poussin spent most of his working life in Rome; he learnt much from the Renaissance masters, yet his pictures are profoundly French in the lyric quality of colour and line. The other great master of the period, Claude le Lorrain, was a pioneer in landscape composition. The balance, perspective, and solidity of his pictures is something new: there is a sense, too, of space and light which foreshadows the work of Corot and the impressionists. By the seventeenth century the great French tradition is fully established.

In music the Italian influence continued predominant. The early seventeenth century saw the rise of opera, 'lei nuova musiche', originally a Florentine invention. Monteverdi, director of music at St. Mark's in Venice, wrote his 'Orpheus' in 1607; Lully (1632–87) was the most famous composer of his age, with a European reputation. Brought from Florence as a guitar player at fourteen, he became Master of Music to Louis XIV, in charge of the Court ballet. He wrote music for Molière, creating a new and original Franco-Italian style of accompanied recitative. In England, Purcell (1658–95), organist at the Chapel Royal, who had studied under Lully in Paris, brought the new idiom into English music, combining the high foreign dignity of the Italian style with the native tradition. He wrote both religious and secular music, collaborating with Dryden in the setting of his plays; he is one of the greatest English composers. As the new opera became fashionable the cult of the individual singer developed in Italy, tending to swamp the formal unity of the performance, so attractive in the earlier work, but a new range of musical expression had been opened up.

The seventeenth century was a great age of architecture; the Renaissance influence was now fully assimilated in the North, where it was reinterpreted by native architects. French classical architecture achieved a superb style and dignity, formal, spacious, and hard. In Germany a more massive and heavily ornamented style developed, more attractive in Austria, where a natural elegance found expression. In England a more domestic and restrained tradition is apparent; Wren and his colleagues created not only the great masterpiece of St. Paul's, but the dignified proportions of the City churches, the calm seventeenth-century libraries at the Universities, the restrained and comfortable amenities of the English country house. In the Baltic the Hansa and Swedish cities adapted the vistas of Italian design to the pale shadows of the North, while under Peter the Great the Russians began to create a coloured and individual version of the Western and Southern style.

In all the arts the seventeenth century saw remarkable progress. Painting, music, and architecture developed and elaborated the fashion set by the Renaissance, the architects, in particular, discarding Renaissance bombast and achieving new clarity of design.

v

So it was that this formative age saw a profound change in the religious, political, economic, and cultural life of Europe. The period opens with the Reformation, with all its possibilities of intellectual and spiritual liberation; with ferocious religious controversy, culminating in the Wars of Religion, and subsiding into the beginnings of toleration by the second half of the seventeenth century. It marks the rise of great national states; the climax and the waning of the power of Spain; the assertion of English and Dutch maritime power; the beginnings of the European supremacy of France and the devastation of Germany by the Thirty Years War, which increased the political backwardness of the area and intensified and ingrained the Germany military tradition. The discovery and the settlement of North America and the opening up of trade with India and the Far East, transformed the economic life of Europe, encouraged the expanding capitalism of the age and ensured the commercial and political supremacy of the nations of the Western seaboard. In Central Europe, the Habsburg power, though it had failed in its bid to restore Catholicism in Germany, remained the guardian of the marches of the Danube against the Ottomans; though Hungary had been largely overrun and the Balkans remained lost to Christendom, the Turkish threat diminished by the close of the seventeenth century. The submergence of Czech nationality, following the Thirty Years War, is a tragic landmark in Central European history, while Poland-Lithuania, following her expansion in the sixteenth century, ceased by the close of the seventeenth to be a formidable power. The future of Eastern Europe was increasingly to be dominated by the rise of Muscovy, transformed under Peter the Great into Imperial Russia.

In the cultural field the promise of the sixteenth century was fulfilled in the seventeenth, which accumulated much of the intellectual capital of the modern world. Secularized empirical knowledge, systematized and expanded by men of genius drawn from many countries, began to bring in its immeasurable returns. In art and architecture, literature and music, it is a century of superlative achievement, in which the Northern peoples, in response to Italian influence, come into the accumulated wealth of humanistic Classical learning, into the full tide of the revived tradition of Antiquity and a new scientific method. Though it experienced undercurrents of fear as the old landmarks were lost, this great age displayed an unsurpassed tenacity and virility of thought; it had fought its way out of a background of persecution, confusion, and superstition; it had built systematically, realistically, permanently; it had realized the promise of Early Modern times. This hard, far-seeing, and creative epoch is one of the greatest in the history of Europe and of the world.

CHAPTER X

THE EIGHTEENTH CENTURY

THE eighteenth century saw the full working out of the effects of the great changes already described, the expansion of a secular and often bourgeois culture within a traditional and predominantly aristocratic social framework; it was a time of increasing civilization, of progressive amelioration of comfort and manners. In Western Europe, for the first time since the great days of the Roman Empire, the background of life became relatively secure; it was an age of confidence and leisure, of progressive, if often superficial, intellectual discovery. It was indeed, for Western Europe, a fortunate age, apparently so stable yet full of vitality and promise. Though the ancient structure of society exasperated the philosophers of the eighteenth century, they were confident in the power of 'reason,' of tolerance and 'enlightenment'; in this century the characteristic modern European idea of progress first became widespread; an idea later widely taken for granted, and which in the history of civilization is original and formidable.

The sixteenth century had marked a new confidence and a new acceptance of the world, a new alertness and curiosity. By the seventeenth, this outlook had been disciplined by mathematical analytic method; with prosperity and toleration, eighteenth-century thought achieved an attractiveness, an urbanity and an influence the seventeenth century had never known. Life was stable enough for independent men of goodwill to afford a benevolence and a sensibility paralleled only among a small minority in the Ancient World. There was a new public, ready to applaud writers who wrote with facility and elegance on the widest range of topics, cosmopolitan in outlook, and untrammelled by religious or nationalistic bias. The conclusions of Newtonian astronomy seemed to point to a mechanical and well-ordered universe, and although Christian dogma was scouted by the philosophers of the enlightenment, they held that the world was controlled by a benevolent power. The Great Architect of the universe had organized all things on an intelligible plan, and with education and opportunity, it was believed that humanity could organize itself in harmony with this reasonable order. Though the mass of the people were still poor, this same belief was inherited by the nineteenth century.

The writers of the period explored new fields of knowledge, apparently explicable by easy generalizations and elegant presentation; they were fortunate in the continued stimulus of geographical discovery and a deepening knowledge of new peoples. The manners and customs of the East, and of the indigenous Americans, are constantly quoted by eighteenth-century writers, while the importation of new luxuries, cultural and domestic, gave variety and novelty to the social scene.

The individualism and rationality of the eighteenth-century outlook was reinforced directly among the Protestant peoples and indirectly in the Catholic states by the long-term results of the Reformation. In the first place the movement had broken the united front of the Universal Church and destroyed the assumption that the state was the secular arm of a Divinely ordained society, controlling all aspects of life. In the modern countries, in intelligent circles in France, and particularly in England and Holland, which led Europe in cultural, economic, and social progress, the state was coming to be regarded as a convenience, holding the balance between social and commercial interests, and allowing, within limits, toleration of thought and religion. Increasingly a reasonable lay public found the confusion and cruelty of religious conflict intolerable in the tidy world they were trying to build. Men looked back with shame and horror upon the violence of the 'Gothick' centuries and upon the more recent atrocities of the wars of Religion. The rival exponents of salvation had indeed given a poor account of themselves during the sixteenth and seventeenth centuries, and 'enthusiasm' was at a discount. This indirect legacy of the Reformation was supplemented by the individualism the Reformed doctrines had encouraged, the hostility to established authority they had often implied, and by the self-reliance they had fostered, always native to the Northern peoples. The separation of powerful religious communities from the state, the conviction that a man ought to be let alone to 'work out his own salvation,' and the Protestant habit of self-government within the independent congregation, had important political results. In the West a tide of influential opinion was set steadily towards a more bourgeois form of government, in spite of the conservative and oligarchic structure of eighteenth-century society.

The most influential states of Western Europe during this period were England, Holland, and France. In both the former, commercial commonwealths had been established, controlled by modern-minded oligarchies and practising a measure of self-government and toleration. Together, through superior sea power, the statesmanship and tenacity of William III and the campaigns and diplomacy of Marlborough, in alliance with the Habsburgs, the traditional enemies of France, they had broken the attempt of Louis XIV to dominate the Continent. Both had won rich overseas empires and led the world in commercial and agricultural method. France retained her traditional intellectual brilliance, but was still organized according to the predominant seventeenth-century pattern of absolute monarchy. Yet the imposing structure of Bourbon absolutism was increasingly a façade; the wars of Louis XIV had overstrained the administrative and financial structure of the country and the eighteenth century, in spite of growing economic development, saw a period of increasing military, naval, and financial failure. The ablest minds of France no longer believed in the old order, attacked it with all the weapons of ridicule and invective, and looked with admiration at English institutions. When, with the Revolution, the crash came, the old order had long been undermined, it no longer believed in itself; the *ancien régime* was swept away, and France, not England or Holland, became the revolutionary state. In effect, therefore, in Western Europe, in spite of an apparent stability, the eighteenth century saw a steady drift towards ideas of self-government and intellectual freedom, first in the maritime commonwealths of England and Holland, and later in France. Further, the assertion of the independence of the American colonies under a relatively popular if still oligarchic regime not only carried with it the freedom of a continent, but strengthened the influence of radical ideas in Europe.

Meanwhile in Central and Eastern Europe, absolute monarchy, following the seventeenth-century French model, remained the dominant form of government; the Habsburgs remained entrenched in Vienna; Prussia became a great military power, and following on the work of Peter the Great, the Empress Catherine brought Russia into the full orbit of the politics of Europe. Though the political interests of East and West became more closely bound up together, the contrast in social development between Eastern and Western Europe, already apparent by the sixteenth century, was increased, with profound results.

Before following out the main evolution of the power politics of the eighteenth century, it will be well to examine the nature and origins of the ideas and institutions which found their fullest expression in England, which in a French interpretation, were broadcast to the world, and which formed the inspiration of the Revolution of 1789 and the democratic tradition of the nineteenth century.

The evolution of the English state had been fortunate. In a manageable area protected by the sea from invasion and well situated for the exploitation of the Atlantic discoveries, England had developed by compromise and common sense a form of government well suited to the opportunities of the age. It drew its vitality from four principal sources, with their roots deep in the past: from Anglo-Saxon traditions of local self-government; from the Mediaeval conception of a commonwealth, expressing the general interests of the diverse elements within it, ruled by law, and articulate through a Parliament; from the habit of centralized government and patriotism realized under the Tudors; and from the sense of common interest which united the aristocratic establishment, the landed gentry and the mercantile classes, who had together taken over the Church lands at the Reformation, and who had defeated the attempt at absolutism on the continental model made by Charles I. As already observed, by the Restoration of 1660 the Crown was left financially in the hands of a Parliament representing the propertied classes, and this revolution was completed in 1688 when the substantial elements in the country combined to oust the Stuarts, and to establish under William and Mary a monarchy more completely under Parliamentary control. Finally, following on the reigns of William and Mary and of Anne, with the advent of the Hanoverian dynasty (1714) and a more limited kingship, Parliament assumed a more complete power and the rudiments of cabinet government developed. Despite this power, however, through most of the eighteenth century the initiative remained with the Crown, and ministers were responsible to the monarch. Yet, the first two Georges, uninterested in British politics, easily became the instruments of the Whig oligarchy; power thus devolved upon the ruling factios which formed the executive. In the long run this form of government developed into the rule of the majority party in Parliament, sanctioned by the Sovereign as the expression of the national will.

Thus the problem of expressing the will of the propertied classes through an adaptation of a mediaeval institution had been met by a series of compromises; a modified form of monarchy retained, and flexible institutions devised, capable, without revolution, of adaptation to the later shift of power to the middle classes and later even to the mass of the people. This remarkable achievement was due to political good sense, to an insular position and a naval efficiency which made militarism unnecessary, and to a respect for the over-riding power of law, reflecting the sense of the whole commonwealth, superior even to the king.

Now this adaptation of mediaeval institutions and ideas had been combined with the new theory of the state as a necessary convenience defined by Hobbes, though Hobbes's absolutist conclusions had been discarded. The political thought of Hooker and Locke was the inspiration of this tradition. Both these writers, in characteristic English fashion, were concerned to justify an established fact; Hooker to defend the Elizabethan Church settlement; Locke the Revolution of 1688. Hooker's *Of the Laws of Ecclesiastical Polity* (1594–7) argued that the power of making law is derived from the entire society and laws are not valid unless they reflect 'public approbation.' This sense of the politically conscious community is reflected in his confidence that in this manner a 'convenient and practical' form of government will be devised. Hooker was asserting the doctrine of the supremacy of the whole commonwealth, one of the most valuable legacies of the Middle Ages. John Locke (1632–1704) reaffirmed and extended Hooker's principles. He argued that government is necessary to avoid the 'inconveniences of the State of Nature which follow from every man being a judge of his own case.' Deriving authority from the governed, its objects are security and the preservation of property. Government must rule by 'established standing laws . . . by indifferent and upright judges . . . and all this is to be directed to no other end than the peace, safety, and Public Good of the people.' No authority has the right of arbitrary taxation or imprisonment, and all government must reflect the will of the enfranchised and representative community; if the acts of government contravene the public good, men have the right to change it. Within the framework of such an ordered but flexible society, Locke advocates religious toleration. 'Toleration,' he writes, 'is agreeable to the Gospel of Jesus Christ, it is also dictated by the genuine reason of mankind. The care of each man's salvation belongs only to himself.' He insists also on freedom and variety in education.

Locke had laid down certain fundamental principles: sovereignty of the political community, freedom of property, and religious toleration. These principles were strictly limited by the social context of his thought, by the oligarchic structure of English society and by a strict limitation of franchise, but they were reinterpreted in a wider sense by American and French thinkers, and became the inspiration of a movement far more democratic than the Whig revolution. They were rightly so interpreted, for Locke assumed that man can be trusted; that human nature, left alone within the framework of ordered law, can develop a free intellectual and business enterprise which will assure the vitality and the prosperity of the state.

Such were the ideas which reflected the transference of political and economic power to the oligarchy of the English Revolution of 1688; they had been carried much further by the Puritan Radicals of the Civil Wars, who, in defiance of their leaders, had canvassed ideas of manhood suffrage and put conscience before the Law. The Leveller extremists of the Puritan Army demanded an equal voice for all in elections and repudiated property qualifications; they claimed a voice in the choosing of government as their 'Birthright,' and refused to obey a law of the land which they declared they had had no voice in making; they claimed an abstract Natural Right. These ideas commanded no wide following and were suppressed, but many substantial Puritans emigrated, adopting the only sensible course open to men who refused to obey their country's laws. In the New World, both oligarchic and radical ideas of Natural Right were worked out and modified into practical politics, and sturdy individualism was expressed in the political development of the United States. The influence of Locke and the English tradition, and the American example of drawing up written constitutions, together with these extremer Radical doctrines of a natural Birthright, contributed, along with the ideas of Rousseau and the Englightenment, to inspire the French Revolution.

While these developments were going on in the Anglo-Saxon world, the majority of European nations were still governed on absolutist lines. The model for this kind of government, and the centre of European fashion and culture, continued to be the French Court, which maintained the traditional and deliberate splendour inaugurated by Louis XIV. France was still the dominant military power in the West; the Habsburg Emperor on the Danube. The German princes imitated, according to their resources, the manners and organization of the French Court, while the Spanish monarchy added to its ancient ritual the pomp of eighteenth-century royalty. Frederick the Great, the predatory military leader of the new Prussia, assumed a veneer of French culture, and the Russian Court superimposed upon the Byzantine traditions of its Muscovite past the Western elegance of Versailles. All these Governments were conducted by the despotic authority of the monarch, ruling through favourites and ministers responsible to the Crown. Authority was enforced by a growing bureaucracy, by censorship and by standing armies. The nobility, as far as possible, were transformed into officials of the Court, dazzled and conciliated, but shorn of political power. Though scepticism and free thought were widespread in sophisticated court society, these absolute governments remained in close alliance with the Church, in a common attempt to prevent the spread of ideas likely to subvert the social order. Although increasingly dependent on bourgeois administrators and financiers, the outlook of the Courts and aristocracies remained conservative, arrogant, and military. The feudal inheritance of the Middle Ages was still in their blood; cosmopolitan and elegant, they regarded the bourgeois and the common people with contempt. The conduct of government depended on the personality of the monarch, and though many of the eighteenth-century autocrats were mediocrities, some were extremely able. Frederick the Great, Catherine of Russia, Joseph II of Austria, were all highly intelligent, and even the stupider Bourbons displayed a solidarity within their own caste, as well as astonishing skill in the ritual massacre of game. In spite of the power politics in which all these rulers engaged, they retained at least a dynastic sense of European unity and did not push their wars to extremities. All were anxious to retain the stability of their order and of the society dependent on it; Catherine and Joseph II, in particular, developed an 'Enlightened Despotism' which attempted to improve the condition of their subjects; all were united in repudiating the fundamental principles of democratic thought.

The prestige of this aristocratic social order, the last heirs to the ancient tradition of the European fighting aristocracies, remained immense, its influence deeply affected subsequent social development. In the first place, the new professional armies were largely officered by the nobility, the prestige of the calling of arms maintained. In the nineteenth century the officer class of the great national armies imitated the conventions and punctilio of the eighteenth century, and in Central and Eastern Europe the military profession retained the arrogance and often the exclusiveness of its eighteenth-century origins. Next, the incubus of eighteenth-century despotic government, its hostility to free thought and its police methods, alienated the middle-class writers and professional men, who in the more liberal countries readily put their services at the disposal of the state. Where Locke and Burke, both of middle-class origin, wrote in defence of the English Constitution, the best French writers were bitterly critical of the regime under which they lived, and this hostility to government gave their thought a more radical tinge and prepared a more sudden nemesis for the old order. Finally, the uncompromising attitude of the Catholic Church produced an anticlericalism of real virulence which has no parallel in Protestant countries. Even moderate Reformers became tarred with the extremist brush and the dreary discord of revolution and reaction, the curse of so many conservative European countries, began its course. In the more modern countries, on the other hand, the Protestant Churches were less successful in supressing new opinion.

II

Against this social background, absolutist, aristocratic, and conservative over most of the Continent; oligarchic, commercial, and increasingly liberal in England, Holland, and in North America, the political evolution of the eighteenth century must be set.

It was a period of Machiavellian diplomacy and incessant war, carried on between relatively small, expensive, long-service professional armies, elaborately drilled, uniformed and organized, playing a complex game of manœuvre and counter-manœuvre, of siege and envelopment, according to the tactical rules. Though the results of these wars were momentous, they were less exhausting than the religious conflicts of the seventeenth century, the massive contests of the Napoleonic era, or the total wars of the twentieth century; in spite of them the civilization of Europe maintained its resilience.

The power politics of the rival dynasts, indeed, who regarded their kingdoms as personal estates, and who fought and intrigued incessantly for territory and prestige, were cut across by their mutual interests in retaining the ancient social order. Though the Russian government encouraged Slav resistance in the Austrian Empire, it was also their interest to maintain the Habsburg power as a bulwark against social revolution.

These relatively limited wars had vital results for Europe and the world, and it is well to grasp their permanent effects. They fall into three main stages; first the successful resistance of an

Anglo-Dutch and Habsburg coalition to the ascendancy of France, embodied in the policy of Louis XIV. This struggle was ended by the Treaty of Utrecht (1713). The second phase was fought out in the War of the Austrian Succession (1740–8) and in the Seven Years War (1756–63), concluded by the Peace of Paris. Its consequences were of the utmost importance. It decided that Great Britain and not France should become the predominant power in North America and India, in the West Indies and the Mediterranean; that Prussia should survive as a great power, with all the long-term consequences for Europe; and it marked the first formidable intervention of Russian armies in a European conflict. The third stage saw a concerted attack against England by most of the great powers, and was occasioned by the revolt of the American Colonies from the Empire; in the East it saw the first partition of Poland (1772), finally completed (1793–5) during the French revolutionary wars. The struggle in the West was ended in 1783 by the Peace of Versailles, whereby the independence of the American Colonies was recognized. It will be apparent that the decisions reached by these wars were of the utmost importance, and we must follow their course in greater detail.

The first struggle opened when James II was driven from the English throne and the accession of William and Mary united the Dutch and English states; both were threatened by the French attempt to gain control of the Spanish Netherlands, which, if successful, would have ruined both Dutch and English commerce and jeopardized the hard-won Protestantism of both countries. It was to thwart Louis XIV that William III had gone to England, and his life-long purpose succeeded; although his land campaigns were indecisive, the first and essential round in the contest was won when, in 1692, the battle of La Hogue gave the combined British and Dutch fleets command of the Channel.

The second phase of the struggle is known as the War of the Spanish Succession. A Grand Alliance had been formed by the English, the Dutch, and the Habsburgs to prevent a dynastic union of the Spanish and French Empires. The traditional Habsburg-French feud, a constant factor in European politics since Early Modern times, had linked up with a permanent motive of British policy, constant since the Hundred Years War, the maintenance of the independence of the Low Countries. Superior sea power enabled the British to land well-found armies on the Continent; under the leadership of Marlborough, a combined Anglo-Dutch force with German and Danish contingents, acting in concert with the Austrian armies of Prince Eugen, struck across Europe into Bavaria, and brought the French, who were threatening Vienna, to defeat at Blenheim (1704). This victory was followed by a series of campaigns in the Netherlands which so broke the French power that France was threatened with invasion; it was the end of Louis XIV's attempt to dominate Europe. By the Treaty of Utrecht the Spanish Netherlands were transferred to Austria; Dutch independence was saved; England retained Gibraltar and Minorca, securing command of the western Mediterranean. Austria wrested predominance in Italy from Spain, while Newfoundland and Nova Scotia, together with limited access to Spanish-American markets, were confirmed to England.

While the British and Dutch had secured the basis of their prosperity and defeated the Franco-Spanish coalition, the Habsburgs had consolidated their grip not only on their Austrian inheritance but on Bohemia and Hungary. Leopold I (1657–1705), conservative and tenacious, was dominated by the Jesuits; even during the course of the desperate struggle against the Turks he was sending Bohemian and Hungarian Protestants to the galleys. The zealots of the Counter-Reformation, sacrificed in France to a policy of purely national aggrandisement and no longer able to count on Spain as a dominant power, found a new base in Vienna. After the relief of the city by Sobieski and the turning of the tide against the Turks, with the Emperor's son established as hereditary King of Hungary, and Bohemia well to heel, the Habsburg power became extremely formidable. The acquisition of a predominant voice in Italian affairs further strengthened the Habsburg hand; conservative, Catholic, and with a strong military tradition, the Austrian Empire sprawled over vast and polyglot territories, the strongest bulwark of the *ancien régime* in Central Europe.

This carefully built-up inheritance was jeopardized by the failure of the Habsburg male line. It was the constant preoccupation of the Emperor, Charles VI (1711–40), to ensure for his daughter, Maria Theresa, the succession to these vast dominions, and he devoted decades of diplomacy to this end. So anxious was the

Emperor to obtain a French guarantee, that in spite of the failure
of the French to put their candidate on the throne of Poland in
the War of the Polish Succession (1733–8), the Austrian government was willing to concede the reversion of the Duchy of Lorraine to France, after its occupation for life by the defeated
Stanislaus Lecszinski. Further, the Spanish Bourbons were allowed to keep the Neapolitan territories they had gained from
Austria: there they remained, in a state of increasing degeneracy
until their expulsion by Garibaldi. In return it was agreed that
Francis of Lorraine should marry Maria Theresa and that the
Austrian grip on North Italy should be consolidated by the reversion of Tuscany. In the event, none of these diplomatic ar-
rangements securied a peaceful succession. The death of Charles
VI was the signal for a European conflagration, known as the
War of the Austrian Succession (1740–8); to be followed, after an
uneasy peace, by the Seven Years War (1756–63).

It was Frederick II of Prussia who struck the first blow by a
sudden and characteristic pounce on Silesia; in this way Prussia
made her entry on the European stage as a great power.

We have seen how the Grand Elector Frederick William had
consolidated the Hohenzollern inheritance; he had laid the foundations of a formidable military power and of an efficient administration. His successor, Frederick I, had crowned himself
King of Prussia in 1701; his son, Frederick William I, was a ferocious autocrat who built up the military machine exploited by
the famous Frederick II (1740–86). The traditions of Brandenburg-Prussia were Baltic rather than German; the raw predatory
militarism, learnt in generations of warfare on the Marches of
Lithuania and Poland, harks back to the history of the Teutonic
and Baltic Knights of the Middle Ages. The East Prussian military caste, long intermarried with the Baltic Barons, serf-owning
and provincial, had never had anything but rudimentary contact
with the culture of Europe. Brandenburg itself, a relatively
barren country with a harsh climate and indefensible frontiers,
owed her survival to her military efficiency. The trade and *raison
d'être* of the rulers of Brandenburg had always been war. Moreover, her possessions in Western Germany and the political as-
tuteness of the Hohenzollerns enabled Prussia to emerge as the
most efficient state in Germany.

It is with Frederick William I that Prussian militarism was fully systematized, the whole country organized for war, a subservient and methodical middle class harnessed to the war industries and administration of the country. Heavy taxation was combined with economy on all expenditure other than that devoted to military ends. The king, like many of these dynasts, had a mania for soldiers and uniforms; he imposed conscription; he ransacked Europe for giants for the Prussian Guard; he discarded all amenities, militarizing his court and its fashions. The machine he had created was inherited by a neurotic, highly intelligent artist in war. Frederick II's intellectual leanings had been savagely repressed; his warped and extraordinary genius is a pathological study; as 'der Alte Fritz' he was to become a hero of Prussian tradition. Devoid of illusions, an admirer of Machiavelli, he regarded diplomacy as war by other means. The War of the Austrian Succession was his opportunity; the textile and industrial resources of Silesia were essential to supplement the limited resources of his kingdom; at an immense price he managed, after two decades of intermittent war, to retain the prize.

His incursion was the signal for the last round of the ancient Bourbon-Habsburg contest. France allied herself with the new upstart power; Bavaria and Saxony followed suit; the French occupied Bohemia, the Bavarians threatened Vienna. Maria Theresa was saved by the loyalty of the Hungarians and by the entry of England into the war, following her traditional policy of resistance to the European preponderance of France. Frederick, having won his spoils, drew out of the war, pocketing his Silesian conquests; the contest continued as a struggle between England and the Habsburgs against France. But in the autumn of 1744 Frederick struck again and occupied Prague; the next year, subsidized by France, the Stuart Pretender, Charles Edward, attempted and failed to re-establish his dynasty on the English throne. In the same year, by the Peace of Dresden, the Austrians formally conceded Silesia to Frederick. The war came to its conclusion in 1748 with the power of Prussia greatly enhanced and with the Hanoverian dynasty firmly consolidated in England.

In face of this failure, the French Government decided that its true interest lay in a sensational reversal of policy: aware of the danger from Prussia, they decided, in defiance of all precedent, to make a Habsburg alliance. Aware, too, of the Prussian danger, Maria Theresa entered into an offensive and defensive alliance with the French (1756).

Their assessment of Frederick's intentions was correct. In the autumn of that year Frederick struck at Saxony; the Seven Years War had begun. At once there was a renewal of the ancient feud between England and France, coincident with the struggle in Central Europe; a common Protestantism united Prussia with Hanover and Brunswick and with Hanoverian England.

The grand strategy conceived by the Elder Pitt was simple and for English imperial interests correct. The main effort of France was directed to a continental war; the main effort of the British to winning an overseas empire. British sea power was brought to bear; in 1759 the capture of Quebec won Canada, and Hawke's victory at Quiberon Bay reaffirmed British naval supremacy. Meanwhile, in 1757, Clive at Plassey had broken the French power in India. In 1760 the remnants of the French Indian Empire were destroyed by the capture of Madras. By these momentous events a decisive shift in the balance of world power had been produced; it had been decided that the civilization of North America should be predominantly Anglo-Saxon. This decision reflected the realities of not only British sea power but of American settlement, for the French dominion in America, though ambitious and far-flung, had never been consolidated as had been the British colonies between the Atlantic and the Appalachians, whose population far outnumbered the sparse settlers of the vast French territories in the interior and even on the St. Lawrence. Great Britain thus emerged from the Seven Years War in possession of an immense American Empire, with the foundations of her rule in India secured, and capable of playing a more decisive part in European politics.

Meanwhile Frederick, maintaining the Protestant interest on the Continent and aided by British subsidies, was facing a coalition of France, Austria, Sweden, and Russia. He displayed extraordinary virtuosity; forced to withdraw from Bohemia, he defeated the French at Rossbach in Saxony (1757); in December of the same year he routed an Austrian army at Leuthen in Silesia. But now a new factor intervened which, but for a stroke of chance, would have been his ruin; for the first time great Russian armies were advancing into Europe.

That this should be possible can only be explained by a retrospective glance at the situation in Russia since the accession of Peter the Great (1682–1725). We have noted that his westernizing policy had revolutionized the country, and brought it for the first time into the orbit of European politics. Peter was at once an autocrat in the Muscovite tradition and absolute monarch after the fashion of his day. Like Frederick William I, his predominant interest was war; his superficial westernizing of Russia was undertaken primarily to create an efficient army and fleet. Though his aims were Western, his methods were Russian; ruthless and dynamic, he built hastily, roughly but effectively, on an immense scale. His ambition was unbounded; to transform in a life-time the semi-Asiatic Muscovite state into Imperial Russia, with the whole resources of her vast territories and expanding man-power geared to war. Though he admired Western technique and pitchforked his country into a rough and ready imitation of Western methods, Peter remained profoundly Russian. With his great physical strength and stature, with enormous energy, he was the embodiment of the force, the vision, and the brutality of his people.

Peter's main objective had been the traditional Russian drive to the Baltic; in it he succeeded where generations of his predecessors had failed. Since the days of Alexander Nevsky, the struggle for the Baltic coast had been going on; in three years Peter had dominated the area. In 1703 he had founded St. Petersburg, the new capital which was to be a window on to Europe. These gains had been won in part at the expense of Sweden; they were retained during the long struggle known as the Great Northern War (1700–21), of which the climax coincided with the campaigns of Marlborough. The military traditions of the house of Vasa had flared up finally in Charles XII, who had embarked on a series of spectacular and desperate military adventures which culminated in an advance into the heart of Russia; on the field of Poltava (1709) his army had been annihilated and the Swedish Empire destroyed. By the Treaty of Rystadt Russia secured the Baltic Provinces, including Riga. Two years after Poltava, Peter had proclaimed himself Emperor; this, and the removal of the capital from Moscow, had marked the transformation of Muscovy into Imperial Russia and the orientation of Russian policy towards the West.

Peter's successors had generally worked in agreement with the Austrian Court; they had taken a hand in defeating the French candidate in the War of the Polish Succession. Under the Empress Elisabeth (1740–62), in alliance with the Austrians, they had launched their armies against Prussia. It was the man-power and fighting qualities of these armies, which, in spite of defective equipment and organization, nearly proved decisive in defeating Frederick II at Zorndorf (1758) and Kunersdorf (1759). In face of appalling losses, the Russians stood their ground; they occupied East Prussia and raided Berlin; by 1762 Frederick's position appeared desperate. England, after the fall of Chatham, was withdrawing from Continental commitments, and Frederick was reduced to negotiation with the Turks, his sole potential allies in Europe. He contemplated suicide, but a change of government in Russia saved him; for in that year the Empress Elisabeth died. She was succeeded by her son Peter III, an unstable character, crazed with admiration for Frederick. He immediately reversed Russian policy. In the same year he was murdered at the instigation of his wife, a Russianized German princess famous in Russian history as Catherine the Great (1762–96). Catherine, a realist like Frederick II, came to an understanding with Prussia, and from that time on, after the first taste of Russian military power, successive Prussian Governments were careful to avoid further conflicts. It was not until the twentieth century that the Emperor William II, flouting the advice of Bismarck and traditional Prussian policy, risked estrangement from Russia and a war on two fronts. Through this dynastic change in Russia, the Seven Years War came to an end with Prussia retaining Silesia and the dominant power in North Germany. Frederick's gamble had succeeded.

In the West, meanwhile, by the Peace of Paris, Britain was left in possession of an enormous overseas Empire. In the following decade much of it was lost. The new preponderance brought about a coalition against England, led by France and Spain, which took advantage of the conflict between George III and the American colonists. The attempt, pedantically enforced by the home government, to tax the colonists for purposes of imperial defence and to sacrifice their commerce to mercantile interests at home, provoked a resistance which led to the momentous secession of the colonists from the Empire. Conservative and radical elements in the Colonies were united by the policy of George III and his ministers; the colonists, who had kept alive the traditions of 1688 and the more radical principles of the seventeenth-century Puritans, appealed away from the absolute sovereign authority of the British Parliament to the earlier constitutional principles of Locke; they declared that the interests and the rights of the governed were paramount. They desired what was really a conservative settlement; the famous Declaration of Independence (1776) summed up the sense of earlier constitutions worked out in the separate States, all closely following the doctrines of Locke. This precedent of devising written constitutions was later followed by the French in 1789.

With the fall of Saratoga (1777) France and Spain intervened, while a coalition of Russia, Prussia, Holland, and the Scandinavian powers threatened Great Britain from the east. In 1781 the command of the Western Atlantic was lost, and the British army in America, cut off from reinforcement, surrendered at Yorktown. England was forced on to the defensive, but Gibraltar held; in 1782, at the battle of the Saints, Rodney regained command of the North Atlantic, and in India Warren Hastings had successfully defended British rule. The outstanding result of the war, concluded in 1783 by the Peace of Versailles, was the recognition of the independence of the American colonies, with all its far-reaching implications, and the war had also given the *coup de grâce* to the finances of France. The British, though they had lost so large a part of their first empire—the American colonies, Florida and Minorca—retained Canada, Gibraltar, most of the West Indian Islands, and their supremacy in India. In spite of the ineptitude of George III and his ministers, British sea power had been maintained and England retained vast overseas resources. These were to enable her to develop the commercial and industrial supremacy to outlast the ordeal of the Napoleonic Wars, and in combination with the resurgent peoples of Europe and the military might of Russia, prevent the domination of the Continent by Napoleon.

For while the continental despots were fighting for territory in Europe, nothing had been allowed to stand between the realization of the steady commercial ambition of the British oligarchy, which pursued, through all vicissitudes, the prizes of overseas empire which the expansion of the sixteenth and seventeenth centuries had made possible. In pursuit of this object the English fleets had repeatedly smashed obstinate opposition; from a position of mediocre political influence, England, by the close of the century, had become the greatest maritime and commercial power in Europe. France, on the other hand, at the beginning of the period the dominant power, by attempting at once a European and oceanic supremacy, had jeopardized the first and lost the second. Far from European battlefields, off the Atlantic coast, the slow ships of the line in the smoke of successive cannonades, with tattered sails and splintering timber, had decided the future not only of England as a power in Europe, but of overseas territories so vast that they dwarfed the entire expanse of the European peninsula.

While these great decisions were being made on the western seaboard and beyond the oceans, a notable international crime was being perpetrated in Eastern Europe. The partition of Poland, which brought into long eclipse the traditions and culture of an ancient people, was the result of a cynical compact between the three military autocracies which surrounded that distracted country. There were two areas which invited the expansionist ambitions of the Austrian and the Russian Empires; Poland, and the Ottoman territories of South-Eastern Europe. Habsburg diplomacy thought it wise to divert Russian ambitions from the Balkans; Frederick II was determined to hold East Prussia and for that benefit was willing to pay a price. In 1769 Austria occupied Slovakia; within the next three years the Russians had secured Eastern Poland, Frederick had occupied his objective, and the Austrians had absorbed most of Galicia. The remnant of Poland was left helpless, while Catherine devoted her energies to expansion over the Steppe to the Black Sea, her gains being recognized by the Treaty of Kuchuk-Kainardji in 1774. In 1783 the Crimea was absorbed, and by the Treaty of Jassy (1792), following on another war with Turkey, Russian dominance over the Steppe was finally secured. The final partition of Poland coincided with the outbreak of the wars of the French Revolution; by the close of the century Poland had been politically obliterated.

Such were the results for Europe and the world of the *Real-Politik* of the eighteenth century, the background to the remarkable cultural and intellectual achievement of the age. In spite, therefore, of the increased standard of living and the growth of humanitarian and rational sentiment among the privileged classes, and the prevalence of middle-class ideas of liberty and self-government in the West, the political realities of the age were hard. The military autocracies of Eastern Europe increased and expanded their power, realizing territorial ambitions of widening scope. It was not only the salons and the sensibility, the wit and the elegance of the dominant French culture, nor the comfort and good sense of the eighteenth-century English and Dutch ways of life which are characteristic of the period, but the mechanical and hard-bitten militarism, the disciplined carnage of highly organized professional warfare, the reek of blood and powder, the marching and counter-marching of the armies of military autocrats mad with ambition and obsessed, even in peace, by the glamour of military evolutions.

III

The successful resistance of the maritime powers to France and the toughness of Prussia were due in part to their superior commercial resources. It was in Holland and later in England that the new capitalism, already powerful in the seventeenth century, had fully developed, while the Prussian government had systematically encouraged commercial and industrial enterprise, all dovetailed to the purpose of war, regulated by the state and systematically taxed. The most significant feature of eighteenth-century society was the consolidation of the mercantile interests; the period saw a great expansion of private capitalist enterprise. The bankers of London and Amsterdam handled sums unheard-of in the sixteenth century; the period saw the rise of joint stock companies with transferable shares, often a risky development. The most lucrative trade was carried on with North America, the West Indies, India, and the Far East. West Indian sugar, tobacco from Virginia, tea from China, coffee and cocoa, were becoming not mere luxuries but necessities; Dutch and English shipowners became rich on the profits of this carrying trade, while bullion from Africa and India, precious stones, silks, Indian and Chinese luxury goods, poured into the markets of the West. At the same time, factories for the production of goods, hitherto made on a piecemeal basis by scattered local industries, came into being. With the growing circulation of newspapers, advertisements began to appear; there was a steadily expanding market and a rise in the standard of living. But the greatest profits came from the slave trade, with all its lamentable social results and its sequel in the Southern American states.

With the unprecedented accumulations of capital resulting from this capitalist expansion on the market, governments began to pull out of the state of insolvency chronic in the sixteenth and early seventeenth centuries; by means of State loans bearing interest, by transferable annuities, and the creation of a National Debt, they began to harness the new financial power to the prosecution of their policies. It was through superior financial resources that the English Parliament had worn down the King's Party in the Civil Wars, and it was through superior credit and administrative facilities that England was able to finance great war fleets, subsidize her allies, and emerge victorious in the prolonged struggle against France. The French Government, on the other hand, for all their great resources, were never able to apply the new financial methods to the conservative structure of French society, and it was a financial crisis which immediately brought about the collapse of the *ancien régime*.

Eighteenth-century governments conducted their economic policy on the 'Mercantilist' theory, inherited in part from the Middle Ages; they aimed at the concentration of maximum wealth and a maximum productive power within their own countries; at a trade balance in which exports greatly exceeded imports, and they enforced this policy by high tariffs. The economy of colonies and dependent states was sacrificed to the preponderant power, and this clash of interests was the main cause of the revolt of the American colonies and the prolonged embitterment of Anglo-Irish relations.

All this expansion and enterprise, the prelude to the Industrial Revolution, which had its roots far back in the eighteenth century, was superimposed on a traditional agricultural foundation. It was not until the last quarter of the century that fundamental industrial changes, originating in England, began to affect the habitual basis of society; this radical alteration, the most important material advance since the Neolithic Revolution, will be the subject of the succeeding chapter.

Meanwhile notable progress had been made in agricultural technique, first by the Dutch who introduced a new rotation of crops, including the use of roots and clover, with a resulting improvement in stock breeding. These methods were imitated in England by the landowners of great estates formed by 'enclosure' to the detriment of the yeoman and peasantry, particularly in the corn-growing areas of East Anglia and the South. Over most of Europe, however, although in the western lands the standard of living was going up, the traditional methods of cultivation persisted, and in Central and Eastern Europe the peasantry were in decline. The economic initiative was preponderantly in the hands of the capitalists of the West and the principal source of wealth an Oceanic trade.

IV

Against this economic background we must set the brilliant intellectual achievements of the eighteenth century, at once the elaboration of traditional Renaissance Humanism and the discovery and definition of the principal fields of modern knowledge, to be expanded and developed by the professionalized learning of the nineteenth century. For, in a sense, the pioneers of eighteenth-century thought were brilliant amateurs. Their optimistic and lucid thought was broadcast in a great cosmopolitan prose literature, which together with the traditional study of Classical writers, united the best minds of Europe. This literature found its most influential and characteristic expression in France and England.

The new secular knowledge was systematized in the great *Encyclopedia* edited by Diderot; to this work, the most brilliant writers of the day contributed and it became the means of spreading the new ideas to an audience of unprecedented extent. Though the Encyclopedists were hostile to orthodox Christian dogma, they believed in a benevolent Providence, in the capacity of reason, given free play, to ameliorate social injustice and mitigate the limitations of human nature. The most brilliant and the most influential of these French writers was Voltaire, whose voluminous, witty, and trenchant prose scarified the abuses of ancient custom, mocked at traditional dogma and expressed with verve and urbanity a passionate championship of the cause of reason. His famous novel, *Candide* (1759), which in a short compass describes with devastating wit the irresponsibility of government, the caprice of nature, and his view of average humanity, concludes with the epicurean aphorism that the wise man should 'cultivate his garden' and dismiss public affairs with a shrug. In his old age, by sheer brilliance of writing, Voltaire achieved a European influence; he expressed at once the realism and clarity of the French mind and the common sense of his age. Another great French prose writer, Montesquieu (1689–1755) in his *Esprit des Lois,* had anticipated to a remarkable degree the outlook of modern sociology. The manners and customs of mankind are relative, and reflect the varying environments of different peoples; all are the expression of Natural Reason ordained by a beneficent Creator, for human intelligence could not exist if the world were the product of 'Fatalité aveugle.' Ranging over a vast sociological field, from South America to India and the Far East, Montesquieu made his learning singularly attractive, and he won a wide audience. The dominant motive of his thought was the study of Man, the diversity and the perfectibility of human institutions.

Rousseau (1712–78) represents a reaction from the rational lucidity of his age. His brilliant flair for generalization, the deceptive vigour of his style, gave him an extraordinary influence. He defined ideas long current in intellectual circles in his time and won them a wide popular following. The basis of the State, he insisted, was not rational calculation but the general will of the whole people. Rousseau idealized the small democratic community of peasants, deciding their affairs 'under an oak tree' in the Cantons of Switzerland. Their 'general will,' the sense of their meetings, was 'always right.' This idea was to be less happily translated in terms of great national states, combined with the idea of popular sovereignty; Rousseau's influence upon the development of the modern world was to be immense.

In philosophy the eighteenth century was a great age; the British philosophers, Berkeley and Hume, carried to their devastating conclusions the implications of Cartesian analysis, the latter questioning the basis of causality itself. Kant, living in Prussia at the close of the century, founded a new and influential school of philosophy, attempting to find in the Will a certainty of which Hume's argument had deprived the processes of reason. In science, too, there were great advances, notably in chemistry; the English chemists Cavendish and Priestley, and the Frenchman Lavoisier, were both pioneers of the expanded professionalized research of the succeeding century. The success of the Scottish surgeons William and John Hunter raised the status of their profession, while Young revolutionized the science of optics. The Frenchman Buffon, and Linnaeus, the Swedish naturalist, began a new classification of species; the latter was the first to designate the human race by the hopeful term 'Homo Sapiens.' He prepared the ground for the great synthesis of Darwin, which was to revolutionize man's conception of his place in nature.

In England in the eighteenth century a great literature flourished; Dryden had created modern English prose, clear, flexible, and concise; and the dark genius of Swift infused the new style with a savage irony and a caustic wit. Defoe, too, was a master of sound prose and descriptive writing, while Richardson, Fielding, Smollett, and Sterne created the great tradition of the English novel. Pope, using a decasyllabic rhyming verse, wrote a hard-hitting trenchant style; in his *Essay on Man,* he expressed with fine dignity the eighteenth-century view of the cosmic order, while Gay created the first native English light opera. As the century matured, English writing became more elaborate; the rapier lucidity of Swift and Pope giving place to the splendid cadence of Johnson's argument and the rolling periods of Gibbon and Burke.

It was an age, like the seventeenth century, of superb and often melodramatic oratory; Chatham, Burke, and Pitt, all rose to the height of the political occasions their eloquence has commemorated.

In the theatre the Restoration comedy had portrayed the social scene with wit and realism; Congreve and Wycherley, following the footsteps of Molière, are masters in this essentially French art. Later, Goldsmith and Sheridan brought Irish genius to the

English theatre, and wrote a social comedy more congenial to a middle-class audience than the bawdiness and brilliant cynicism which had entertained the court of Charles II. In England, as in France, it was a great age for letters and memoirs; Hervey and Horace Walpole recorded the inner history of their times with a cosmopolitan sophistication, while the cynical pen of Lord Chesterfield summed up the conclusions to which half a century's experience of high politics and society had led a shrewd observer. These English writers were ballasted by experience of the realities of power, experience denied to their French counterparts.

In the Anglican Church it was an age at which enthusiasm was at a discount; the English universities, moreover, passed through a phase of relative torpor, but among the Non-Conformists, no longer persecuted but cold-shouldered from fashionable society, there grew up a fine tradition of education and philanthropy. Unostentatious but rich, these solid commercial families contributed much to the English tradition. They produced a famous scholar and poet in Isaac Watts (1674–1748), the author of hymns which are the inheritance of all the English-speaking peoples.

Outside the ranks of the propertied classes, the masses of the people remained in an elementary stage of civilization. It was to these mobs, as well as to the middle classes, that John Wesley's eloquence appealed. The Methodist movement his organizing genius created was destined to become a powerful social force in the nineteenth century, when the full task of civilizing the masses began to be undertaken, and a stabilizing influence during the worst crisis following the Industrial Revolution.

In art, French painters best express the spirit of the eighteenth century: Watteau (1684–1721) achieved a novel freshness of colour and line; he catches the elegance and gaiety of the French Regency Court. Boucher and Fragonard carried on the same tradition, while Chardin (1699–1779) developed the Dutch fashion of genre painting in a French idiom. As the century wore on, this brilliance was clouded by a false classicism and a cult of bourgeois sentimentality which often finds expression in the painting of Greuze, the forerunner of much inferior work in the nineteenth century.

In England, too, there were great artists; for the first time a truly native school of painters emerged; Reynolds, Gainsborough, and Romney express the security and freedom of English country life, at once homely and sophisticated. Gainsborough was the greatest artist, with a subtle mastery of colour and design, while Hogarth with biting observation depicts the harsher aspects of his age.

In music it was a great century; the climax of the old classical school, when German musical genius came first fully into its own. In the first half of the century, the Scarlattis, father and son, revived in Rome and Naples the traditions of earlier opera and brought chamber music to a new range, preparing the way for Haydn and Mozart. In Protestant Germany the outstanding composer was Bach (1685–1750), born in Thuringia and for thirty years Kapellmeister in Leipzig; a serene, domestic character, absorbed in his own genius. The past master of contrapuntal music, one of the greatest musicians so far produced by Europe, he set a new standard of harmony and proportion, the supreme musical expression of logical mind. Handel (1685–1759), who came from Halle in Saxony, benign and famous, the creator of great operas and oratorios, won his greatest popularity in England.

But by the middle of the century the musical capital of Europe was Vienna. Haydn (1732–1809), of Austrian and Croat descent, under the patronage of the Esterhazy family, developed the classical symphony and the string quartet; a real countryman, he incorporated Croat folk melodies in his genial, satisfying music. Gluck (1714–87) had a South German background, a strain of Czech ancestry. He grew up in Bohemia, the son of a gamekeeper, studied at Prague, in Italy, France, and Vienna: his peasant vigour and simplicity brought new life into Italian and French opera which he enriched and developed. But of all these musicians, Mozart (1756–91) is the most attractive, the supreme genius of the century. An Austrian from Salzburg, the son of a musician, a young prodigy, the great tradition was in his blood: no other composer has possessed the technical mastery, together with the feeling, the originality, of this brilliant, tragic figure. The great symphonies, the famous operas, 'Figaro,' 'Don Giovanni,' the 'Magic Flute'—an astonishing production in so short a life—have permanently enriched the human spirit.

In architecture the period saw a fuller elaboration of the great seventeenth-century tradition. Buildings became technically more perfect, sometimes developing a complexity akin to the later Gothic. In France, Germany, Italy, and the Iberian Peninsula there was an astonishing skill in rococo and baroque; in England and the North on the other hand, in the later years of the century, an increasing simplicity of design. Landscape gardening, still formal and artificial over most of the Continent, achieved a new harmony with nature in England, where, with the Gothic revival and the beginnings of the Romantic movement, there was a new cult of the natural and the picturesque.

In the widest sense of the term, therefore, the eighteenth century was an age of progress, of achievement and promise. A new broadmindedness and a new optimism were permeating the upper ranks of society. Although, like that of Classical Antiquity, eighteenth-century culture was confined to a minority, it was to an expanding minority; the bourgeoisie whose heyday was to be the nineteenth century, were assimilating the inheritance created by the patrons and writers of the old order. Hitherto, in all ages, except for certain exceptional interludes in Antiquity and during the Renaissance, the reign of custom, with all its injustice and inefficiency, had been taken for granted, and since the dark ages, the doctrine of original sin, of judgement and damnation, had overshadowed the Western mind. Now a new desire to shape and improve human institutions became widespread, a confidence in the universal benevolence of Providence, akin more closely to the original Christian teaching. The cult of sensibility brought a new pity into being; the callousness and resignation of previous ages gave way to a new humanitarianism. And indeed it was natural that these comfortable inhabitants of the salons and country houses of the high eighteenth century should regard the severity of their seventeenth-century ancestors with distaste, should contemplate with horror the relative barbarity of the Middle Ages, and with satisfaction the ripe achievements of their own century. Yet it was their tolerance, intelligence, and urbanity which made possible the subversion of their own order, the capture of political, economic, and intellectual leadership by the business and professional classes.

The eighteenth century, then, is memorable not only for political and economic decisions which determined the future of

Europe and of the European settlements overseas, not only for the realization of the full Renaissance inheritance, but as the greatest civilizing century in the history of Europe. The outlook of its intellectual leaders was secular and universal, transcending race and creed; they realized a cosmopolitan culture, and in spite of growing political conflicts reasserted the fundamental tradition of the unity of Western civilization.

CHAPTER XI

THE INDUSTRIAL AND LIBERAL
REVOLUTIONS

THERE are certain fundamental changes in technical method which have successively determined the material basis of society; in the dawn of history inventions were made and adopted which resulted first in the settlement of mankind in self-supporting agricultural communities, then in the foundation of cities. These long-term processes have been termed the Neolithic and Urban revolutions, for although their effect was gradual, so profound were the changes they inaugurated that the word revolution must be applied to them.

During the long ages of European development, during Antiquity, the Middle Ages, and the beginning of modern times, the material basis of life, though it had fluctuated and expanded, had remained fundamentally unchanged. The foundation of the whole social structure, of the political, economic, and cultural achievements of Europe, had been an agricultural routine in which the methods, though improved, had remained in principle the same. During these centuries, the pace of life had followed a similar tempo; the problem of the harnessing of power was little nearer solution in the seventeenth century than in the days of the Roman Empire. Land communications, indeed, were better under the Empire than at any time until the second half of the eighteenth century, and at sea there had been notable progress, since the peoples of the western seaboard had devised sailing ships of a size and manœverability surpassing anything known to Antiquity. But the East Indiamen and the men-of-war of the eighteenth century were still extremely slow; at Trafalgar the battle fleets approached one another at a speed of about four knots. On land, armies moved with incredible slowness; merchandise, proceeding by barge and wagon, could still be moved only in small bulk, and trade in perishable goods was still tenuous. In country districts, the resident gentry, though many of them cultivated and intelligent, were dependent for essential communications on a tardy and uncertain service of carriers and coaches; the bulk of the population had their horizon bounded by the nearest market town and remained rooted in their own neighbourhood. Dialects varied greatly over comparatively small areas; a picturesque variety of local custom and architecture persisted, and government remained the concern of a remote and intermittently effective minority. This static, provincial, and conservative way of life was the background of all the political and cultural changes we have hitherto recorded, and the impact of change was so gradual it must have been hardly perceptible.

The surplus wealth produced by such a slow-moving agricultural economy, though supplemented by an increasing volume of imports from outside Europe, remained relatively small and provided a limited prosperity only for a small upper class. The standard of living for the bulk of the population, though it had considerably improved by the eighteenth century in Western Europe, remained low; illiteracy was widespread, and cultural and political consciousness restricted. Waves of economic discontent and religious emotion, generally provoked by the threat of innovation, intermittently stirred the broad masses of the people; but such popular agitations were generally conservative, demanding a return to ancient ways. Under these circumstances, poverty and a strict limitation of opportunity was the lot of the masses of mankind; the surplus of wealth was insufficient to support anything but a small leisured class, with a conservative and relatively unpractical outlook; the latent resources of the world remained untapped and the creation of a large-scale economy was impossible. At the same time, society, set in its immemorial framework, remained stable within its limitations; the pattern of life well adapted to traditional psychological responses, and although the capacity of government for good was limited, its capacity for evil was also restrained. Traditional methods of political and economic organization sufficed, in conjunction with the inherited common sense of generations of agriculturists, to maintain a sound if unenterprising social order.

With the Industrial Revolution, a gradual event of shattering and far-reaching importance, man for the first time began to win a control over nature so great that an entirely different society and outlook became possible. Following on the harnessing of new sources of power and the application of new techniques to the production of wealth, society was radically transformed.

The application of scientific method to industry was first made on a great scale by English capitalists in the second half of the eighteenth century: the Industrial Revolution, with all its possibilities, was primarily the creation of British business enterprise and technical skill. It spread first into Belgium, France, and Germany, centering on the coal and iron fields which provided the basis of the new industries. It spread also into North America, where the immense resources of a new continent combined with an enterprising, businesslike and democratic society. The Mediterranean countries remained relatively backward in the race, in part because they did not command the coal and iron of the North; while the peasant countries of Eastern Europe and the Russian Empire, though rich in natural resources, were handicapped until the twentieth cenutry by a conservative social order, rudimentary organization and political unrest. The shift of power to the modern countries of the western seaboard and to the rising Prussian state, which commanded not only the North German plain but the industrial Rhineland and the Ruhr, was therefore emphasized in the nineteenth century, while the economic domination of Europe and America over the rest of the planet was confirmed.

This Industrial Revolution was paralleled in France by a political upheaval of the first importance. We have seen that the tide of social change, in spite of the conservative structure of eighteenth-century society, had long been set towards a more liberal outlook in the Western European countries. Increasingly middle-class influence had come to dominate the intellectual, administrative, and economic life of society. It remained for a political revolution to recognize this situation. But the French Revolution, beginning as a middle-class movement, soon escaped the control of the moderate liberals who had begun it, and proved the occasion for the spread of far more radical ideas. Hailed by liberal thinkers with acclamation, it proved the opportunity for a subversion not only of aristocratic but of bourgeois order. The excesses of the Revolution ended in the military dictatorship of Napoleon, the last of the enlightened despots, but a brilliant propagandist in a new way, who attempted, with the force of Republican Nationalism behind him, to win the domination of the Continent. Ultimately he united all Europe against him, so that a conservative settlement was imposed by the Treaty of Vienna.

In spite of Napoleon's failure, the European scene had been radically transformed. The changes his rule had effected in France were never swept away, and the ideas which the Revolutionary armies had carried over most of Europe continued to be influential. Further, the resistance the French invasions had provoked had given rise to a new sense of nationality among the peoples overrun, often to a degree of popular resistance unknown in the eighteenth century. The Revolution had, indeed, unleashed political ideas long familiar to eighteenth-century thought and won them a wide popular following. Here is the significance of the new movement; for the first time the common people became politically conscious and assimilated theories of government subversive of a social order hitherto taken for granted by the conservative masses of mankind.

The French Revolution had been provoked not only by the financial and administrative incompetence of the *ancien régime* but by the example of the American colonists, whose famous 'Declaration of Independence' defined ideas similar to those inspiring the revolutionaries.

'We hold these truths to be self-evident,' Jefferson had written, 'that all men are created equal; that they are endowed by their Creator with certain inalienable rights; that among these are life, liberty, and the pursuit of happiness. That to secure these rights, Governments are instituted among men, deriving their just powers from the consent of the governed; that whenever any form of Government becomes destructive of these ends, it is the right of the people to alter or abolish it.' Here is the essence of the liberal creed, deriving directly from the political thought of John Locke, but applicable outside the social and economic framework both Locke and Jefferson took for granted. These ideas were reinforced by the heady phrases of Rousseau's political writings. The doctrines of this inconsistent but brilliant writer were in fact relatively conservative; but their effect proved revolutionary. As we have noted, his doctrine of the General Will, actually derived from the practice of small-scale Republican communities, was applied to sanction the sovereignty of the people; later even of the dangerous theory of the infallibility of popular judgement and of the absolute authority of the Nation State.

The idea that the will of the people is the basis of all government was further linked with the theory of a natural Birthright, inherent in all individuals, irrespective of ability or property qualifications, whereby all men were regarded as politically equal. The logical outcome of such a theory is government by a majority vote, based on universal suffrage. This new democratic doctrine was of course incompatible in the long run with the monopoly of the means of production by private capitalists, but the application of democratic principles to economic problems did not bulk large in liberal thought. It remained for socialist thinkers to apply the new doctrines to economics.

In the intellectual sphere the Revolution had been reinforced by a new Romantic movement, for which it is difficult to find parallels in previous history. It was in part a middle-class reaction from the secure and conventional background of the eighteenth century, in part the result of wider opportunities for travel and the loss of religious certainty. It contributed an important and dynamic element to political ideas. Together with the romantic yearning for emancipation and action for its own sake, the whole revolutionary background was coloured by the facile optimism characteristic of certain aspects of eighteenth-century thought; this lack of realism explains many of the disasters of the nineteenth and twentieth centuries.

The Industrial Revolution and the spread of democratic ideas, both in the main originating in England, and the latter first becoming widely effective among the masses in France, were together destined to destroy the structure of society as it had hitherto been understood. Here was a radical break with the past which had rendered modern industrial and political society different from anything we have hitherto had occasion to study. The repercussions of these two outstanding events are still working out. It will be well, then, to study their nature and origins in some detail.

The Industrial Revolution was not merely a European but a world process; it merged in the nineteenth century into a Technical Revolution resulting from professionalized scientific research, which immensely accelerated the pace of social change. The impact of applied science on human institutions and the consequent need of a planned and flexible social order became the overriding theme of modern history. Staggering advances were made; the concurrent dangers have been underlined by a series of economic catastrophies and by two world wars; finally by the unleashing of nuclear power.

The beginnings of the Industrial Revolution date from the eighteenth century. We have observed that considerable accumulations of capital and the rudiments of modern financial organization had appeared in the maritime countries of the northwestern seaboard by the beginning of the period; that, acting on mercantilist economic theory, governments fostered and exploited the oceanic trade which provided most of this new wealth. In certain specialized trades, moreover, factory production was beginning to be organized.

It was in England that this new capital first financed great new textile industries and the exploitation of the immense latent coal and iron resources of the island by mechanical power. This enterprise in time gave rise to the creation of heavy industry.

The immediate occasion of the development of the English textile industry was the popularity of Indian cotton goods, leading to the importation into Lancashire of great quantities of raw cotton, a substance hitherto rare in Europe, there to be manufactured into textile goods for an expanding market. The Lancashire cotton mills were mainly driven by water power, and the first problem to be solved was the cutting of labour costs. With Crompton's invention of mechanized spinning, and Kay and Cartwright's invention of a mechanized loom, the method of cloth manufacture was revolutionized; techniques which had remained the same in principle since Neolithic times became suddenly obsolete, and factory production on a great scale first became possible. There remained the problem of a new source of power. Pumping contrivances, worked by coal, had been used for draining mines since the seventeenth century; now an improved steam engine, adapted by Watt, was applied to drive a steam mill, providing a cheap source of mechanical energy, superseding the use of water and horse power. By the close of the century, mechanized textile processes driven by steam had become general; an unprecedented revolution in the harnessing of power had come about.

In the sphere of heavy industry, meanwhile, coal was applied on a growing scale to the smelting of iron and to the working of other metals. In the areas of the Midlands and South Wales, where coal and iron seams were juxtaposed, great blast furnaces grew up which produced the molten 'pig-iron,'—so called from the fancied resemblance of the ingots to a pig's litter spread about the furnace mouth. The fortunes made out of the textile and heavy industries were invested in other entreprises; in Yorkshire woollen manufactures, the Potteries, and engineering firms of the Midlands; hardware, metallurgical and armament factories spread and multiplied. The resulting increase in capital led to further banking and financial enterprise. The foundation of the wealth of Victorian England was laid.

The social results of the Industrial Revolution were profound. Great manufacturing towns grew up; unplanned warrens under a pall of soot and smoke, in which an urban proletariat was housed in conditions of more than mediaeval squalor. These towns had only an economic reason for existence, and were devoid of civic and religious amenities. The motive force of the new industry was private profit, which drove to its objective, regardless of the interests of the 'hands' it employed, unrestrained by Government regulations or religious authority. Within a few decades there grew up in the new industrial slums a social problem so appalling that Government was forced to tackle it, and the 'thirties of the new century saw a concerted attempt to mitigate the worst evils of Industrialism, to extend the rudiments of civilization into the new towns.

By the 'thirties a revolution in communications was also well under way in Great Britain, which both encouraged the growth of the towns and increased the power of the central Government. The late eighteenth century had seen a network of canals linking up the principal centres of production; with the invention of macadamized roads, English coach communications had attained an unprecedented speed. All this was eclipsed by the coming of the railways. Rudimentary railroads had long been used to connect canals, for horses could draw heavier loads along the rails; it remained to apply the new steam power to the railroad. By 1814 Stephenson had invented the first practicable locomotive, and, following earlier development in the coal districts, in 1830 the first railway in the full modern sense of the term was opened between Liverpool and Manchester. It was the beginning of a revolution in transport which was to affect the whole planet. Within the next two decades, a network of railways, focusing on London, was flung over all England and an unheard-of velocity of transport attained. The new steam power was also applied to shipping; by the end of the 'thirties a steam vessel had crossed the Atlantic and a further revolution in transport had begun. It is difficult for us to realize the gulf between the age of coaches and sailing vessels and that of the railway and steamship; it can best be paralleled in contemporary experience by the relative speed of air and ground transport.

Such, then, in its essentials, was the Industrial Revolution, which originated in England, which spread rapidly to Western Europe and America, and gave to the white races during the nineteenth century the military and economic domination of the earth. It formed the basis of the Technical Revolution, which, beginning in the middle of the nineteenth century, has continued at an increasing pace into our own age. It was initiated and directed by private capitalists whose accumulated wealth soon gave them a preponderant voice in politics; these new fortunes, together with the capital acquired from eighteenth-century commerce, were invested in enterprises all over the world which cut across national boundaries. A great international network of investment grew up which further extended the power of Europe and North America; competition for raw materials and markets increased, but the full force of these developments, with all their international repercussions, was not apparent until the second half of the nineteenth century when British predominance was challenged by continental and American industry and enterprise.

It was the wealth created by the Industrial Revolution as much as that drawn from the colonial trade and the dependence of the Continent on British industries that enabled Great Britain to stand the strain of the Napoleonic Wars; this dependence forced Napoleon to embark upon a blockade, which by the economic and political results it entailed, resulted in the collapse of his European domination. From a self-supporting agricultural country, drawing its strength and traditions from the soil, with its wealth and population concentrated in the south and in East Anglia, England was to become the 'workship of the world,' a great industrial nation, drawing its main economic power from the Midlands and the North, immensely rich and powerful, but with an unbalanced economy, dependent on foreign markets and on imported food and raw materials. The price paid was heavy, the new opportunities immense.

The economic theory which reflected and encouraged the Industrial Revolution had its roots in the confident and rationalistic thought of the eighteenth century. In the sphere of politics it had been widely assumed that if the traditional restrictions and conventions of society were removed, the natural reasonableness of mankind would create an improved political system. In the economic field it was also believed that if the economic process was left to work itself out according to the laws of Providence, mutual benefit and prosperity would result. This optimism was reflected in the writings of Adam Smith, a Scotsman of genius who laid the foundations of economic science. The principle of the 'division of labour' he formulated laid down that if each man specialized in his particular skill and followed his own personal interest, the maximum benefit would result to all. Smith believed that the natural desire for betterment, irrespective of status, was the driving force of the economic process. Private and public interests were therefore coincident and the state should minimize interference with economic development. Yet Smith was not himself an advocate of the emancipation of economic life from Government control; he allowed for state control of roads and bridges, state education, public health services, even state limitation of interest, progressive taxation and control of investment. His followers, however, went further, advocating a much wider measure of *laissez faire*. Since administration and statistical knowledge were still rudimentary, their attitude to government was understandable, but it was extremely dangerous. Never before had a theory been formulated whereby economic activities, fundamental to the well being of society, had been emancipated from social and religious control. At a time when new forces were being released of unprecedented power, the theory got about that business was a law unto itself.

Smith's successors, notably Malthus and Ricardo in particular, carried further this theory of *laissez faire*, the former maintaining that a reservoir of poverty and unemployment was necessary to the healthy function of society, and that the misery of the poor was indeed a dispensation of Providence. Bentham, on the other hand, carried on the ancient English tradition of piecemeal reform. He was primarily a legal reformer. The object of government, he maintained, ought to be the 'greatest happiness of the greatest number,' and by this standard all laws must be judged. The artificiality of Bentham's psychology, with its precise calculations of pleasure and pain, did not prevent his exercising wide influence. The reform of the English criminal law, the modification in the nineteenth century of the Hogarthian atmosphere of the English prisons, can be traced to the diffuse influence of Benthamite ideas; a parallel systematization may be observed in the Code Napoléon. This sober reformism could not be equated with the heady enthusiasms of the French Revolution, or with socialist doctrines; it did much to mitigate the worst hardships of the new industrialism, and it had a great future before it.

The social impact of the Industrial Revolution was reflected in widespread and different lines of speculation; contemporary French and English writers anticipated many of the ideas of subsequent socialist movements.

Saint Simon (1760–1825) was one of the founders of French Socialism; he aimed at a managerial and peaceful economy which would supersede politics and in which the new industrialism could develop full productivity. His 'Nouveau Christianisme,' with its enthusiasm for Science and its emphasis on the social responsibility of the scientist, initiated a powerful trend of thought.

Sismondi (1773–1842), a Genoese historian, insisted that welfare rather than private profit must be the aim of the economic process and emphasized the importance of distribution. Intellectually less reputable, Fourier (1772–1837) advocated the establishment of 'Phalanstères,' self-supporting agricultural units, centred on large communal buildings; his eccentricities diminished his influence, but his attempt to transform the wage-earner into a co-operative worker and to supersede class antagonism by association, set a valuable precedent.

In contrast to these French forerunners of Socialism, all of them theoretical writers, Robert Owen (1771–1858), a self-made British cotton spinner, attempted a series of experiments in industrial organization which won notable fame. His attempt at New Lanark to create a better industrial environmental influenced factory legislation and he was consulted by foreign governments. The relative failure of his experiments and the economic crisis following the Napoleonic wars led him to advocate co-operative ideas which later attained realization. In spite of a strain of visionary Utopianism, his outlook was in the end reformist. A more radical criticism of society, reviving the extremist Puritan tradition of a natural Birthright and universal suffrage, was made by Tom Paine and Godwin in the last decade of the eighteenth century, while Cobbett championed the cause of the agricultural worker and criticized the evils of the new industrial society.

Already, even in its early stages, the thought provoked by the Industrial Revolution was both reformist and extreme. It was also beginning to encourage a new range of ideas, to render national boundaries obsolete, making continental peoples dependent on British industries; and, in turn, making British workers dependent on the fluctuations of foreign markets. Above all, it resulted, first in England and later in the industrialized areas of the Continent—notably in Belgium and parts of North Germany—in a vast increase of population, dependent for its livelihood on the successful functioning of the Industrial machine.

Meanwhile the crudity, ugliness, and brutality of the new civilization disfigured the social life of Western Europe. The new techniques were still rudimentary though very powerful: in the conspectus of world history the age must be regarded as in some sense barbaric. To borrow from the vocabulary of the archaeologists, it may well be termed the Palaeotechnic Age, the Age of the First Machines, destined to give place to the Neotechnic Age, in which more economical and less crude forms of power were utilized, and in which the benefits of the new wealth, organization, and professional skill began to counteract the brutal dislocations of the earlier time. Looking back through the haze of factory smoke which trails across the early industrial age, we may discern the relatively sunlit plateau of the eighteenth century, a world in miniature, relatively manageable for all its limitations, relatively secure. That world vanished for ever in the economic and social upheavals of the new times; but the traditions of European civilization it had maintained and developed are still decisive for the contemporary world and are still of great value.

II

Meanwhile in France, the second, political, revolution, which occurred at the close of the eighteenth century, had come into being. In 1789 the *ancient régime* was abolished. This upheaval had been brought about by bourgeois initiative, drawing its strength mainly from the middle classes backed by popular support, and its ideas from the writers of the Enlightenment. It was not due to the impoverishment of the peasants, whose standards of life had been going up, though it was strengthened by their discontent against their traditional obligations. The revolutionary objectives were originally moderate, aiming at a constitutional monarchy and a political organization modelled partly on British and partly on American institutions. The revolution aimed also at a large measure of local self-government and succeeded mainly in the great towns of France. Though in fact it brought greater centralization, and failed in many of its objectives, its negative achievements were of great importance, for by abolishing the ancient structure of convention and privilege, by the imposition of equality before the law and of improved legal and administrative methods, it made France a modern state.

Its immediate occasion was the bankruptcy of the French government and the failure to impose taxation on the privileged classes. The long-term result of the financial mismanagement of successive French governments, and the cost of the incessant wars of the eighteenth century, had forced Louis XVI's ministers to summon the Estates General, of which the Third Estate was elected on a new and relatively popular basis. The lawyers and minor clergy of this body proved strong enough to initiate radical change, and asserted their principles in the famous Declaration of the Rights of Man. They imposed on France a constitution based in the theory of the balance of powers; a structure of local government by departments, decentralized but cutting across the traditional boundaries of the great provinces of France; and they attempted to impose taxation graduated according to income. This constitutional phase of the revolution came to an end, first because the new government attempted to balance its budget by the confiscation of Church lands, provoking the opposition not only of the higher clergy, but of the more conservative bourgeois and peasantry; secondly because the nobility, many of whom had emigrated, attempted a counter-revolution with foreign support. Under these circumstances, the revolution naturally became more extreme; a ferocious republican dictatorship emerged, ruling increasingly by terror and drawing its strength mainly from ruthless elements in the capital. With the execution of the King, all the conservative interests in Europe were united against the revolutionaries, whose movement had taken the appearance of an international menace.

The invasion of France in 1793 by the combined armies of Austria and Prussia provoked a popular reaction of unprecedented violence; a new portent had appeared in Europe, a nation in arms. The long-term sequel to this development was the rise of similar popular movements in Germany, Spain, Portugal, and Russia and a general intensification of popular nationalism.

The Committee of Public Safety and its generals saved the Revolution; in spite of monetary inflation, internal treachery and popular discontent, they succeeded in imposing a modified conscription and in raising armies of unprecedented mobility and size. The French conscript armies, unencumbered by the conventions of eighteenth-century warfare, introduced new tactical methods and conducted mass invasions on a scale hitherto unknown. Promotion was by merit; they outnumbered their opponents and they lived on the country. To meet this international threat, the other European powers were forced to imitate French methods of administration, conscription and manœuvre; all of them emerged from the twenty years of struggle against France with a stronger grip on their subjects, if with diminished popular support. The casualties sustained in the revolutionary and Napoleonic wars were on a great scale; the life of Europe was convulsed in a manner foreshadowing the holocausts of the twentieth century, and the face of the Continent emerged transformed.

By 1795 the Revolution had become, in effect, a military dictatorship. Napoleon's Italian campaign, militarily the most brilliant of his career, had put immense plunder at the disposal of the French government; while their overrunning of the Netherlands brought command of the mouth of the Scheldt and of the Dutch fleet. It had involved them, also, in war with England. Reluctantly, the younger Pitt, faced by this threat to English trade and security, in 1793 accepted the challenge.

Napoleon always knew that here was the most deadly enemy; he and his advisers wished to settle accounts by immediate invasion. The sea battles of Cape St. Vincent and Camperdown put an end to that project. He was forced to the ambitious alternative of breaking the British Empire by an invasion of Egypt, and he contemplated the invasion of India. He conquered Egypt, but Nelson cut his communications at the battle of the Nile, and won control of the whole Mediterranean. Meanwhile, Austrian and Russsian armies, the latter led by the famous Suvaroff, were threatening the whole French position in Italy. Deserting his armies, Napoleon returned to France. He retrieved the military situation, in 1799 established the Consulate, in 1800 recovered Italy, and in 1802 became Consul for life. That year marked a breathing space in the monstrous struggle. France was left in control of four ephemeral satellite republics, two in Italy, the others in Switzerland and the Netherlands; but the Habsburg power remained unbroken, England unsubdued, Prussia still powerful, and the Russian armies a menace in the east.

During these years Napoleon reorganized France; government was centralized with modern efficiency, the law rationalized in the *Code Civile,* the Church conciliated by the Concordat; the Consulate marks the zenith of Napoleon's administrative achievement, the most lasting monument of his rule. The spectacular glories of the Empire were relatively ephemeral.

The main enemy remained unbeaten; in 1803 the war against England was renewed. For months the massed armies of France lay encamped at Boulogne; the whole force of Napoleonic land power menacing the existence of the country which stood between Napoleon and the domination of Europe and the world. Napoleon needed command of the Channel for a few weeks; like Alva and Hitler he failed to win it. In 1805, far to the south-west, off the coast of Spain, Nelson destroyed the combined French and Spanish battle fleets at Trafalgar; dying in the hour of triumph, he had saved England, and with England, Europe.

Napoleon cut his loss; he struck south-east into Central Europe and smashed the Austro-Russian armies at Austerlitz, commanding the Moravian corridor and the communications of Vienna with the North German Plain. In 1806 he abolished the Holy Roman Empire, for there could be only one Caesar in Europe. And such was his ambition; but only by consolidating a European dominion could he strangle the commercial life lines which sustained British power. In the same year he struck down Prussia; after the Battle of Jena he occupied Berlin and thence issued Decrees imposing the blockade. The British Government countered by forbidding neutral shipping to enter French harbours. So the deadlock continued. In 1807 Napoleon came to terms with Alexander of Russia; ironically, through Russian influence, Prussia in a truncated form was allowed to survive.

In 1808, to enforce the blockade, the French armies entered Spain; here at last was the British opportunity. A continental base, commanded by sea-power, was open for a counter-invasion. The traditions of a people of extraordinary tenacity and conservatism had been outraged; a large country with primitive communications, unsuited to support the invaders who had hitherto campaigned in the most productive areas of Europe, was brought into the struggle. Steadily English policy worked to renew the coalition; in 1809 the Habsburgs re-entered the war; again, at Wagram, outside Vienna, the Austrian armies were crushed. Napoleon following his project of European domination, became himself a dynast by his marriage to the daughter of the Austrian Emperor; and in 1811 an heir, the King of Rome, was born.

Meanwhile blockade and counter-blockade were dislocating the economic life of Europe. The vital Baltic export trade of Russia was particularly hard hit, and the Russian Alliance, long wearing thin, was finally disrupted by the Habsburg marriage. Napoleon was forced to his final gamble; in 1812 he invaded Russia with half a million men and it was the beginning of his downfall. Russian tactics of delay and evasion; the vast Russian spaces; the universal hatred of the Russian people for the impious invader; the Russian winter, combined to bring about catastrophe. Equally, all through that year of 1812–13 the Spanish situation had been deteriorating; the governments and to a great extent the peoples of Europe were conducting a war of attrition against the man-power of France. In the following year, at Leipzig, on the line of communication between South Germany and Berlin and from Western Europe into the Eastern Plain, the combined forces of Prussia, Russia, and Austria broke the armies of Napoleon. It was the end of his attempt to dominate the Continent; his ambition to unite all Europe under a military empire was reduced to the narrow confines of the Principality of Elba.

The great powers met in Vienna to rehabilitate the shattered Continent. There was one more upheaval, and the Hundred Days ended at Waterloo; but when the topsails of the *Northumberland* faded over the horizon of the South Atlantic, Napoleon's influence had not passed from Europe. This daemonic embodiment of eighteenth-century militarism and of the new forces of the Revolution, at once the last enlightened despot and the first of the popular Dictators who were to be the scourge of Europe, had swept from most of the Continent the foundations of the *ancien régime*. He had conducted wars of invasion involving whole peoples, imposed modern institutions over great areas of Europe, roused the masses in even the most conservative countries to some consciousness of nationality, and forced both Habsburgs and Hohenzollerns to a new standard of administrative and military organization. In the course of the struggle against Napoleon, Stein had reorganized the Prussian State; he built up the bureaucracy which was to be the most efficient in nineteenth-century Europe; he imposed universal short-term military service and made it obligatory for Prussian officers to take open competitive examinations. He aimed to 'forge a people armed with strength and will, a people that will wipe out a country's humiliation'; Stein's policy foreshadowed Bismarck's leadership of Germany. Further, by drastically reducing the number of the German states, Napoleon had paved the way for a German confederation, destined to be led either by Austria or Prussia, and so made possible the unification of Germany; and he had left England with the undisputed command of the sea and a consolidated and extended Empire. Russia, moreover, who had played so decisive a part of his overthrow, won a more powerful voice in the affairs of the West.

The Congress of Vienna and the sequel, the Grand Alliance, was the first attempt by all the great powers to impose peace on Europe. It is customary to criticize the Vienna settlement as a 'reactionary' effort to stifle the forces of progress; but the diplomats of Vienna were not without wisdom and the settlement they devised proved relatively lasting.

But the divergence of outlook and apparent interest between the Western Powers and the autocracies of Eastern and Central Europe broke the authority of the Concert of Europe. The turning point came over the attempt by the autocracies to restore the South American republics to the Spanish Crown; this impracticable project would have entailed the disruption of British trade with South America and the hostility of the United States. By 1823 England had drawn out of the Alliance and the Monroe Doctrine had been defined. It was the end of the indispensable coalition of sea and land power, of mercantile wealth and military force, which had brought down Napoleon and which alone might have been strong enough to stabilize the Continent. And indeed, the coalition had been disrupted not only by the clash of mercantile and oceanic with continental interests, but by a profound ideological and social contrast. The social and economic background of Eastern and Western Europe had been increasingly divergent for centuries, and in the West the Industrial and the French Revolutions marked the rise of the bourgeoisie to political power. The whole conception of liberal nationalism was incompatible with the continued existence of the polyglot military empires of the East, which still sought to rule vast territories on the dynastic principle; incompatible too, with the now modernized militarism of the Prussian State, cut back but not destroyed in the Napoleonic Wars, and now flourishing with a new nationalistic popular support and reorganized by administrative genius. The tragic situation had come about that the existence of a concerted European order was incompatible with the new forces of nationalism and democracy. The nineteenth-century was to witness a succession of liberal upheavals, some successful and some ineffective, and a new intensity of nationalistic hatreds, aggravated by economic competition and unredeemed by any effective institutions embodying and retaining the ancient influences for a common civilization.

For the French Revolution and its sequel had spread about Europe ideas not only of intellectual and economic freedom and of equality before the law, but also ideals of national autonomy. Just as individuals were regarded as by natural right free and equal, so also national communities, small as well as great, were regarded as possessing similar rights. Not only great and established national states, but submerged nationalities, the Czechs, the Hungarians, the Poles and with the disruption of the Turkish Empire, the Balkan peoples, all of them looking back to days of mediaeval greatness, claimed a similar right to autonomy. In the enthusiasm of liberation from the *ancien régime,* liberal thinkers, following the trend of eighteenth-century opinion, now tended, like their counterparts in the years 1918–39, to ignore the hard realities of government and the price of security. Similarly in the sphere of international politics, they assumed, that once freedom had been won, the problems of European order would solve themselves through mutual goodwill. In the event, the bourgeois electorate and politicians desired as spirited a foreign policy as their predecessors in the countries where they had attained power; and where they did not attain power, remained subservient to the expansionist policies of 'realist' leaders. Further, the middle classes were often devoid of political experience; inheriting the old tradition of power politics in its crudest interpretation, they played the old game with less sense of responsibility of European order than the dynastic and aristocratic governments. At the same time the influence of the Church had been greatly diminished; and the vague ideas of betterment which took the place of the ancient faith had less influence over the masses than the precise dogmas of the past.

But although the new liberalism had its dangers, it was full of promise. The prevalent optimism of the eighteenth century persisted into the nineteenth; the belief in progress, the confident individualism, all produced, particularly in the West, a dynamic and expanding society. The Romantic movement in literature and the arts reflects the break with the old conventions. The sedate, self-contained, and realistic outlook of the old society gave way to a cult of emotional self-expression, of the strange, the out-landish, and the original. This change is expressed in the dress of the period; the formal wigs, the stocks, the tight breeches and upright carriage of the eighteenth century gave place to easier fashions, sometimes deliberately extravagant. The Revolution and the Napoleonic Wars had imported neo-classical and orien-talized styles; the antics of the parvenu Napoleonic nobility are recorded in the memoirs and caricatures of the time. With the fall of Napoleon there came a reaction to a more civilian fashion, but it remained Romantic. The wind-swept hair, the open collar, of Lord Byron, were widely imitated. Even sedate statesmen pre-sented a tousled appearance above their uniforms, though the florid figure of George IV, 'the first gentleman in Europe,' com-bined an eighteenth-century richness with the new fashions.

The social influence of the Romantic movement was in part due to an increased habit of reading, particularly among women. Poets attained an unprecedented popularity; it was an age of great poetry, and which saw further development of the art of the novel, the one predominant literary form of the new age. The Romantic Movement, derived from far back in the eighteenth century, contributed new elements to the European literary tradi-tion. Increasing social security; the rise of a commercial and professional class which did not, after the manner of the leisured aristocracies, spend its main energies in hunting and war; the deliberate cult of sensibility and introspection; the humanitarian pity which coloured the finer minds of the age, combined with a new desire for strange scenes and places and a new preoccupation with the past. Scenery and history took on a fresh significance;

writers broke away from classical models drawn from Antiquity and from the portrayal of contemporary society; they revived and amplified the themes of mediaeval legend; the writings and the ballads of Scott in particular set the new fashion in historical romance.

The novel of introspection also became popular; Rousseau had set the fashion in his *Émile,* and in his intimate and unattractive *Confessions.* The German writer, Goethe, was not only master of the full range of contemporary classical and Renaissance knowledge, but won an extraordinary reputation in his short work *The Sorrows of Werther,* the record of the sufferings, the indecisions, and the melancholy of a young man who died by his own hand. His superb *Faust,* renewing an ancient theme, ranges over a vast field of thought and emotion. The culture of Germany, hitherto regarded as a provincial imitation of the West, now rose to a new influence in Europe; this unprecedented development, making for a more emotional outlook, was to produce decisive results in a critical period of the nineteenth century. The first manifestations of this movement were attractive; the writings of Lessing and Schiller's historical plays and romances, expressed the spirit of the new Germany, while in England the poets of the Lake School drew their inspiration from the philosophical contemplation of nature. Wordsworth, one of the greatest of English poets, adapted a colloquial style unfashionable in the eighteenth century which expressed the mystery of simple things; he was the master also like his friend Coleridge, of the full technique of traditional English verse, inherited from Shakespeare and Milton. He conceived it his mission to be a philosopher, a preacher, probing the mysteries of life, more than ever insistent with the decline of traditional religious belief. Shelley, brilliant and short-lived, wrote with an extraordinary freshness and originality; he extended the technical range of English verse and caught the rainbow light of the romantic morning. Keats, doomed like Shelley to early death, also widened the range of English poetry: a poet of youth, he expressed the yearning of a northern people for the south and the sun. Byron, the most famous of all the English Romantic poets, combines profound poetic insight with worldly cynicism in the spirited run of his reckless entertaining verse. His genius, his exile, and his death made him a figure of

European reputation, a symbol of the tendencies of his age. All these poets, except Wordsworth, found the conventions of English society insupportable; they contributed to a new conception of the poet as a rebel, increasingly fashionable as the century wore on, a view unfamiliar in the seventeenth and eighteenth centuries, which by patronage and preferment had generally included their poets in the normal pattern of society. This new conception of the poet and artist, characteristic of bourgeois society, was unfortunate and unusual; to some extent it persists, with adverse effect both for writer and public. In contrast to these tendencies, Jane Austen and Peacock showed a penetrating social observation; the lucid prose, subtle characterization and understatement of the former brought the English novel of the day to its perfection, while the latter's sly and comfortable humour is in an eighteenth-century tradition, touched with a new tolerance.

In France the Napoleonic era was relatively barren in literature; the writings of Madame de Staël show a new assimilation of German ideas; Chateaubriand expresses a sentimental introspection and a vivid sense of nature; both mark the transition to the Romantic movement. After 1815 the atmosphere changed; Lamartine first made his reputation in the twenties, and de Vigny and Hugo were beginning to be influential; but the full development of the French Romantic movement belongs to the middle years of the nineteenth century.

In Russia, meanwhile, the first-fruits of a great literary movement of European importance were coming in; Russian writers were absorbing and re-interpreting the inheritance of Western culture, and the great poet Pushkin (1799–1837) was in the full tide of his powers in the twenties and thirties of the new century. He was the precursor of a group of novelists and poets whose work can compare with the greatest writers of the West.

Aristically, too, it was a remarkable age. A new realism was expressed in the bitter canvases of the Spanish painter Goya (1746–1828), an Aragonese peasant, court painter to Charles IV; a sardonic and observant character, technically one of the greatest of artists, who portrayed the horrors of the Peninsular War; he was a portrait painter, too, of the highest distinction. In England, Constable (1776–1837), one of the greatest artists of his time, a Suffolk painter who gained a European reputation, depicted the landscape of East Anglia and Wiltshire with a mellow and loving skill. He was a painter of light who later influenced the French impressionists. His famous 'Hay Wain' created a sensation in the Paris Salon of 1824, though in his lifetime he won little reputation at home. His memoirs reveal a personality of singular charm. It was the greatest age, too, of the characteristic English art of water-colour painting; Cotman created the famous Norwich School, while Girtin, Peter de Wint and David Cox caught the play of light and shadow under the wind. The most spectacular and successful artist was Turner, at the height of his powers at the close of the Napoleonic wars; he achieved remarkable and original effects of colour, dramatizing a Romantic mode of experience. In France David had the most prestige; Ingres (1780–1867) was the greatest painter, a master of form and texture, whose best work dates from this period, though he lived beyond the mid-century. After 1815, the genius of Delacroix, following in part English influences, produced an artistic revolution, destined to open into the greatest age of French art.

In music, Beethoven (1770–1827), of all the great composers, the master of the widest range of technique, emotion, and instrumental colour, expressed the sense of form of the old century and the romantic imagination of the new. His tumultuous and superb genius, at once joyful and tormented, carried to its climax the tradition of Haydn and Mozart and opened the way for the music of the nineteenth century. He lived a great part of his life in Vienna, coming to the height of his musical powers in the years around and after the great Congress; it was fitting that this remarkable period should have produced so dynamic and far-ranging a figure. Schubert, a lesser genius but a master of original melody, died at thirty-one, a year after Beethoven.

IV

Such were the salient characteristics, economic, political, and intellectual, of this formative epoch, a turning-point in the history of Western civilization. With the Industrial Revolution and the rise of the commercial and professional classes to political power in the north-west, and the consolidation and modernizing of autocratic regimes, inherited from the eighteenth century, in Central and Eastern Europe, the stage is set for the massive developments of the nineteenth century. With the collapse of the old order, new classes and new ideas swept into the foreground; with the Napoleonic Wars most of Europe was flung into the furnace of a twenty-years conflict. It was an age of violence and confusion, of great movements of popular emotion, of careers open to talent, of far-flung and fateful military and social upheaval. In the smoke of Austerlitz and Waterloo, in the cannonades of the Nile and Trafalgar, the certainties of the eighteenth century had vanished. The future of whole peoples was decided in these conflicts; great conscript armies were flung into the field; peoples and cultures, hitherto cut off, were brought into a new and fateful contact. Economically and politically Europe was becoming interdependent; in spite of the failure to create a structure of European order, ideas of international significance were permeating the minds of widening strata of society. New talent and new enterprise were given their opportunity, and the thought and literature of the Continent was thereby enriched. The middle-class revolution, for all its failures, had brought with it, over a widening area new methods of administration and a new equality before the law. Ideas of self-government, hitherto in the main confined to the Anglo-Saxon, Dutch, Scandinavian, and Swiss peoples, had captured the minds of the leaders of French thought, and France still retained the cultural leadership of the Continent.

Beyond the ocean, meanwhile, the United States had come to greater power, exercising an important influence on Europe. And as the undertone to the surge of these political and social changes, a new motif had come into the history of mankind; the beat and thunder of machinery, of the harnessed power of the Industrial Revolution.

CHAPTER XII

THE NINETEENTH CENTURY

THE nineteenth century was an era of great cosmopolitan achievement within an international framework of increasing menace. The rise of the Western middle classes to political, economic, and intellectual predominance, the fulfillment of the social trend of the eighteenth century, implied an expansion of professionalized knowledge, an immense increase in wealth and power. The eighteenth century and the Napoleonic Wars had seen the disruption of the *ancien régime* in the West and North, though absolutist and aristocratic rule persisted over wide areas of Central, Eastern, and Southern Europe. Since the political and industrial initiative was with the West and North, liberal ideas became increasingly influential. Meanwhile, as the cumulative results to the Industrial Revolution and the new communications stepped up the tempo of social and economic change, though it did not reach the breakneck speed of the twentieth century, the advance of the Technical Revolution decisively outstripped social and political progress. It was an age of an immense increase of population, in the industrial West, in the peasant countries of Eastern Europe and in Russia: of steady emigration to the new countries overseas, of a widespread improvement in the standard of living. Apart from the period of crisis from 1848 to 1871, it was a time, too, of relative peace, but of a peace which after the Franco-Prussian War became increasingly tense, foreshadowing the catastrophes of the twentieth century. In an age in which the whole sense of European cultural development was international, in which the Continent became economically interdependent to an unprecedented degree, the evil legacy of eighteenth-century power politics, exacerbated by popular nationalism, framed the splendid achievements of knowledge and power in a cramped and dangerous convention that hypnotized even those who had most to lose by it.

The main achievements of the nineteenth century may be grouped under four headings, political, economic, scientific, and cultural. In all these fields immense advances were made, though there was a notable falling off in artistic and architectural standards, reflecting the vulgarization of bourgeois taste. This alarming symptom became more serious as the century proceeded; it expressed a corroding materialism, the result of disrupted social order no longer reflecting traditional values, though, in its emancipation, full of possibilities.

In North-Western Europe the prevalent political creed was liberalism; in Central, Eastern, and Southern Europe liberalism achieved superficial success, but, generally speaking, failed to win political power. A middle-class doctrine, deriving from the English and French sources already described, its prestige was greatly reinforced by the wealth of the Western bourgeoisie and by the growing power of the United States of America. And, indeed, it embodied some of the more valuable European ideals: freedom of thought, equality before an impartial and defined law, the right to a voice in government expressed through Parliamentary institutions. But the successful working of such ideas implied a high level of individual responsibility and judgement; they reflected a belief in the goodness and rationality of mankind; they were highly optimistic and had a better chance of success in countries with a long and stable political tradition, a relatively high level of education and standard of living. The attempt to impose liberal ideas on the more backward countries was to prove premature; and indeed they were in principle incompatible with the traditional organization of Europe in terms of armed sovereign states, exercising in the last resort ruthless internal and external power, and increasingly driven into maintaining conscript armies and expanding armaments. Further, the immense inequalities of wealth which orthodox liberal ideas sanctioned and the liberal tendency to allow the economic process free rein made the concession of political liberty to some extent unreal. Though doctrines of equality before the law and of a widening franchise conceded a degree of power to the masses, the majority of the people remained economically dependent. Hence, increasingly, socialist doctrines grew up, aiming at an economic revolution which would supplement the ideas of political self-government liberalism had brought to the horizon of the masses.

It was in England, Holland, Switzerland, and Scandinavia that Parliamentary institutions were most successful; in France the history of the rise of liberalism was much more chequered, though after 1871 the country reverted to republican institutions. In Italy the form of liberal institutions was accepted, though in a nation so newly constituted the road proved hard. In Germany and in the Austrian Empire, the ultimate failure of the liberal revolutions of 1848 left power in the hands of militaristic governments; while, in Russia, liberal institutions were long repressed and, when permitted, proved ineffective. In Spain, following dynastic strife, a regime of military *pronunciamentos* predominated, in spite of Parliamentary institutions.

The success of liberal ideas was difficult in countries where the Catholic Church retained the established religious influence. The Church in general long set its face against ideas emanating from the free thought of the eighteenth century, and this hostility often drove liberal movements underground and rendered them anticlerical. The aristocracies, moreover, tended to abandon the eighteenth-century fashion of free thinking and to support Catholicism as an ally against middle-class revolution. In the Protestant countries, on the other hand, where the Churches were less closely identified with the old order, compromise between the clergy and liberal ideas was possible; the Evangelical and Methodist movements in particular proved the allies of social reform. The toleration of racial minorities, an essential part of the liberal creed, became normal in liberal countries; but the emancipation of the Jews, which followed from the adoption of liberal and humanitarian ideas, gave rise to extreme bitterness in the conservative countries of Central and Eastern Europe. It was possible at the height of Victorian prosperity for Disraeli to become Prime Minister of Great Britain; Jewish economic power and intellectual influence increased in the West and in America; in Eastern and Central Europe, on the other hand, there remained a deep-seated racial prejudice.

The failures of liberalism were heavily outbalanced by its achievements. In England, Whig and Liberal governments, following the Reform Bill of 1832, which marked the assimilation of the bourgeoisie into the establishment, had set about a steady administrative reform. Their Conservative rivals also faced the problem of the condition of the masses. The Industrial Revolution had created appalling social conditions following the expansion of population and the mushroom growth of industrial towns; the situation demanded fundamental reforms, practicable only after a new statistical research. The social legislation of the middle decades of the century, the establishment of better local government, of essential municipal services, of an adequate police force, were achieved by successive English governments on a great scale. Further, as in Germany in the second half of the century, a new bureaucracy was built up, trained for the administration of a modern state. This initiative was paralleled during the middle and later years of the century to a varying extent, and with varying success, by all the states of Europe. It resulted in an increase in the power of governments; in a mitigation of the more flagrant social evils, hitherto accepted as a necessity of fate; and it surpassed the limited results achieved by 'enlightened despotism' in the eighteenth century. Parliamentary institutions, generally with bi-cameral legislatures and ministers responsible, at least in theory, to the will of popular representatives elected on a widening franchise, grew up over most of the Continent, except in Russia. In East and Central Europe these institutions were often a façade, power remaining in the hands of military autocracies. Liberal ideas, none the less, had penetrated into even the most conservative countries; increasingly and inevitably the power of middle-class wealth and the need for skilled administration had broadened and strengthened the basis of the state and familiarized a widening stratum of society with ideas of representation and self-government.

We have noted the development in England of a reformist movement which attacked the worst evils of the Industrial Revolution and the inefficient administration of the eighteenth century. The influence of the English writer Bentham, in particular, was reflected in the creation of institutions fitted to cope with the new age, both by voluntary and state effort. In 1824 trade unions were legalized; factory legislation regulating conditions and hours of employment, and a new drive to better the public health and education were initiated in the 'thirties and 'forties. This movement increased through the century, the economic distress of the middle decades provoking a new sense of responsibility among the ruling classes, driven home by the writings of Dickens, Disraeli, and Carlyle. Both the Tory and Liberal parties, led by new men often with a northern and industrial background, worked out a wider conception of the function of government, though still with a restricted franchise. In Germany a methodical and thorough system of administration grew up, in many aspects a model achievement. At the same time, administrative reforms on similar lines took place in France, where the authoritarian rule of Louis Napoleon, for all its political shortcomings, set in the forefront of its programme the betterment of social and economic conditions. In Holland, Switzerland, and Scandinavia, too, a steady and lasting advance in administrative method and social progress came about during the nineteenth century.

The purpose of the liberal-constitutional state was defined by many writers and political leaders: J.S. Mill's vindication of personal liberty admitted the need for a wider degree of state control: the two great English Prime Ministers, Gladstone and Disraeli, proclaimed in different fashion the trusteeship of government and sponsored reformist legislation on a great scale. But, significantly, the most eloquent definition of democratic principles came from across the Atlantic, when Abraham Lincoln, the famous President of a Commonwealth 'dedicated to the proposition that all men are created equal,' defined the principle of 'government of the people, for the people, by the people.'

The liberal movements were closely bound up with nationalism, which rightly asserted the freedom of national cultures. It expressed the emancipated middle-class consciousness of the great historical traditions of the European peoples, of which popularized history was making them aware, and in which they felt for the first time they fully participated. The assertion of this liberal nationalism, of which an eloquent prophet was Mazzini, was closely linked with the struggle against the old order and the fight for representative institutions. In Italy, for example, the achievement of national unity and the establishment of Parliamentary institutions had coincided. Further, the middle classes of the West, with memories of their own struggle fresh in their minds, naturally sympathized with the peoples of Central Europe who were attempting to assert similar liberties. Byron, who had given his life for the cause of Greek independence, had been a bitter rebel against the conservative government in his own country. It was believed that if the military and autocratic governments could be broken, or greatly modified by liberal influence, Europe might see a new international amity between nations, governed by middle-class parliaments and co-operating on a basis of free trade, humanitarianism, and respect for law. This dream was shattered by the failure of the liberal movements in Central and Eastern Europe, above all in Germany, the dominant political influence in the whole area. In the event, international liberal ideals were overridden by the more emotionally powerful sentiments of exclusive nationalism. The masses remained relatively impervious to the cosmopolitan and refined ideals of liberalism, but were readily moved by fear, aggressiveness, and hatred of foreigners. These feelings, together with the increased administrative and military power of governments, made popular nationalism a force disruptive of European order. Where the eighteenth-century aristocracy and men of letters, and indeed the feudal chivalry and the churchmen of the Middle Ages, had maintained the cosmopolitan traditions of Europe, the popular mind tended to revert to a more primitive and tribal outlook, untouched by liberal hopes of international co-operation. The course of nineteenth-century history and its sequel were to prove that, without the backing of the common people, liberal ideas of order and progress were destined to be ineffective. With the decline of traditional beliefs, the mythology of nationalism tended to attain the fervour of religion, so that its influence may be compared to that of the emotional cults which swept through the proletarian masses of the later Roman Empire.

The sentiment of nationalism was encouraged by the tendencies of early nineteenth-century speculation. In France and England, Rousseau and Burke, in reaction against the impersonal abstractions and individualism of eighteenth-century thought, had found in the will of the community rather than in the calculated rationality of individuals the principle of social cohesion. To them the state was no mere convenience; they had rehabilitated the community at the expense of the rationalistic individualism dominant since the seventeenth century. Burke had believed he had found in English history the evidence of a 'divine tactic' and appealed to the spirit of the English constitution as expressing the accumulated sense of the English tradition; here and not in the 'bloodless abstractions' of the French Revolution he found the essence of political wisdom. This conservative glorification of national tradition, expressed by Burke in a cautious and realistic policy, had been paralleled and caricatured during the Napoleonic wars in Germany by the less statesmanlike utterances of Fichte, expressive of resurgent German nationalism. But it was the German thinker Hegel who gave the glorification of the community the emotional and metaphysical form in which it became the background not only of nationalist and later of Fascist thought, but, in a distorted form, of the socialist doctrines of Karl Marx.

The contribution of Hegel (1770–1831) to philosophy was of importance and won a wide following, at first in Germany and later in Victorian England; but the pervasive political influence of this German thinker, whose doctrines coincided with the military predominance of Germany, was disastrous. Here, it seems, is one more aspect of the Romantic movement, which for the first time in European history gave Teutonic ideas a dominant influence. Hegel's worship of the state at the expense of the individual —so characteristic of German Romanticism which tends to require as its corrective the framework of absolute government—his insistence that only through conflict can progress come about, and his division of history into a preconceived pattern, with successive peoples predominating and the Teutonic phase as the climax, combined in its vulgarized interpretation to do incalculable harm. Just as Spengler in the twentieth century, intellectually far less reputable, won a wide popular following by an eloquent distortion of history, and contributed, by his false imputations of Western decadence, to the coming of the Second World War, so

Hegel's long-term influence encouraged popular ideas of national and class conflict. The reaction of the German governing classes against the French Revolution, their rejection of its whole basis, and their interpretation of politics exclusively in terms of power, were all reflected in the popularization of these doctrines.

For Hegel found in the pattern of world history the emergent will of God; the realization of the divine idea in time. This immanent will is realized in successive cultures. They emerge through struggle by a process of 'thesis and antithesis' which begets new achievement. This struggle was to be interpreted by Marx in terms of class conflict, reflecting successive stages of economic development; Hegel saw it as a conflict of nations and cultures. His view of the panorama of world history reflected the expansive and poetic genius of his age; but it led to strange political conclusions, to a state worship, contrary to liberal and constitutional ideas. 'The state,' he wrote, expresses the 'march of God in the world . . . the divine idea as it exists on earth.'[1] Like Burke, he regarded the State as an organism, reflecting the whole culture of a nation; unlike Burke, he swept into the obscurities of metaphysical abstraction. It was Hegel who popularized the term 'totality': 'the state,' he writes, 'its laws, its arrangements . . . constitute the rights of its members; its natural features, its mountains, air, and waters, are their country, the history of the State their deeds . . . a national *totality*.'[2] The rights of individuals, no longer based on a universal Natural Law, human brotherhood in God, or a natural birthright, exist only through participation in the State, 'on condition of . . . believing and willing that which is common to the whole.' Hegel thus endowed the nation state, a phenomenon relatively new to Europe, with a timeless and quasi-religious sanction. It was 'a living thing which manifests itself in attaining its ends in the world.' 'A nation is moral, virtuous, and vigorous when it is engaged in achieving its grand objects.' Once 'desire has been fulfilled,' the 'living substantial soul' has ceased to exist, for the spirit of a nation carries 'its own negation in it.' There is, of course, no evidence for these heady assertions; but such sentiments are easily

[1] Hegel, *Lectures on the Philosophy of History*, trans. Sibree, Bell, 1914, p. 41.
[2] *Ibid.*, p. 77.

popularized and they expressed the natural aspirations of many German patriots in the early nineteenth century.

Hegel had tried to reconcile personal freedom with social obligation in a creative way, but his ideas of national ascendancy and idolatry of the State were soon reinforced, particularly in Germany, by intellectually disreputable notions of racial purity and racial mission. The Germans, in particular, coming of some of the most mixed stock in Europe, evolved a myth of Nordic and 'Aryan' superiority. The term Aryan was originally one of linguistic classification, applied to the peoples of Central Asia speaking tongues ancestral to those of the Indo-Europeans who entered Europe out of the steppe. It was arbitrarily transposed to cover a non-existent Teutonic 'race' endowed with the qualities the Germans admired; the mixed ancestry of all the European peoples, interbred already by Neolithic times, was brushed aside by the prophets of this elementary heresy, which found a wide following.

The influence of Schopenhauer (1788–1860), a philosopher of bitter pessimism, an introspective romantic who questioned the fundamentals of ordinary life, contributed to the uncertainty and disillusionment of the German intellectuals in the middle century. But it was the brilliant Nietzsche (1844–1900)—who spent the last twelve years of his life as an imbecile—who in the seventies and eighties of the nineteenth century created the cult of the 'Superman,' of a pathological 'will to power,' which expressed the yearning of an exasperated invalid of genius. 'God is dead,' wrote this prophet, 'now we will that the Superman live.' He suffered, as well he might, from a 'great disgust'; he hated the 'ant-hill swarming of the mongrel populace'; he loathed women, whom he described as 'cows.' This philosophy, expressed with flashing originality and eloquence, was eagerly conned and absorbed in many quarters in Germany and beyond, for Nietzsche had faced the consequences of atheism. He advocated a ruthless neo-pagan cosmopolitan élite, but was misinterpreted as a nationalist. Earnestly German students set out to realize the doctrines of their master, and the just prestige of German scholarship helped to diffuse these explosive doctrines.

Such were some of the writers who expressed the ideas of a dominant school of German thought, and whose doctrines were paralleled in other idioms in other countries. Their theories are still worth attention, since after the unification of Germany the German Empire was to be the greatest land power in Europe.

I I

Against this background must be set the evolution of nine-teenth-century international politics. The political history of the Continent after the Congress of Vienna until the First World War saw the working out of certain overriding and interwoven themes: first, the disruption of the Vienna Settlement by the forces of liberalism and nationalism, increasingly backed by the fluctuating support of France and Great Britain; second, and arising from the first, the growing antagonism between the mainly liberal Western governments and the Central and Eastern powers, following the failures of liberal movements in Germany and the Austrian Empire, the persistence of autocratic govern-ment in Russia, and the development of Tsarist ambitions at the expense of the Turkish empire and in Central Asia; third, the shift of military predominance from France to Germany, follow-ing the unification of Germany under Prussia. This change en-tailed the tardy and reluctant abandonment of the British policy of withdrawal behind a screen of predominant sea power and concentration on imperial interests outside Europe. During the middle nineteenth century, the relative isolationism of Great Britain constituted the fourth major factor in nineteenth-century politics; it contributed directly to German preponderance and following on the development of imperial and maritime ambi-tions by Germany, it was gradually to be reversed. Yet, by with-drawing from continental commitments, while retaining com-mand of the seas during the nineteenth century, Great Britain attained unprecedented prosperity, and the undisturbed develop-ment not only of her own vast overseas empire, but of the colo-nial empires of other powers. British sea power and diplomacy were used consistently to maintain the peace: but British policy stopped short of entanglement in either the Danish War of 1864 or the war of 1870–1, and once only during the period were Brit-ish fleets or armies at war on the Continent, and that only because Russian ambitions appeared to be threatening extra-European interests. The revision of this policy and of the French attitude to Russia constitutes the fifth major event in European politics. In face of the growing might of Germany, Great Britain, France, and Russia drew together in the 'nineties, and in the first decade of the twentieth century, following the German challenge to her maritime supremacy, Great Britain entered the Triple Entente with Russia and France. Thus the ideological differences between the Western Nations and Tsarist Russia were gradually sunk in face of the common fear of Germany, now strengthened by the Triple Alliance with Austria and Italy. The Anglo-Russian Alliance of sea and land power, which had brought down Napoleon—the correct answer to the threat of European domination—was again brought into being. It was twice destined, in spite of the Russian Revolution, to prove too much for the ambitions of Imperial Germany once American power had weighed in.

Such, in bare outline, are the essentials of the changing European political scene during this period. We will first examine the successes and the failures of the liberal and national movements, prior to the Franco-Prussian War.

The Vienna settlement had too much ignored the divergence of outlook and organization between East and West: Metternich, who thought in terms of Central Europe, attempted to suppress the new forces of liberalism and nationality, both incomprehensible to the cosmopolitan rulers of the Austrian Empire. Bismarck was more realistic, he used the new movements for his own ends. The first half of the nineteenth century saw the rise of liberal ideas in the West and their superficial application to the Germanies and the Austrian Empire. After 1848, the Prussian and Austrian governments, taking the measure of the new movements, assessed their weakness among peoples unaccustomed to self-government: while conceding the form of Parliamentary institutions, they retained power in their own hands. In France meanwhile, Napoleon III employed the popular method of plebiscite to establish a dictatorship. So the attempt to establish constitutional government on the British and American model, though in form adopted in all the European States except Russia and European Turkey, succeeded only in countries accustomed to representative institutions; and nationalism, originally combined with liberal ideas of European fraternity, became side-tracked into power politics, adding popular support to the disguised dictatorship of Bismarck and Napoleon III. In Spain and Portugal the form of popular institutions was also adopted, but since the army was never brought under parliamentary control, power remained in the hands of rival military factions, while the wealth and influence of the Catholic Church remained the other dominant feature in Spanish politics.

The tide of liberalism in the West rose in two waves, the first in 1830, the second in 1848. In 1830 a revolution in Paris established the constitutional monarchy of Louis Philippe; in the same year the Belgians broke away from the House of Orange, thus destroying one of the major achievements of the Vienna Settlement, the short-lived unification of the Low Countries in a strong buffer state. To retrieve this setback, a joint guarantee in which Great Britian participated (1832) was given to the new Belgian state. It was to prove the immediate occasion of the British entry into the First World War in 1914.

The example of France and Belgium had set the torch to revolutionary nationalist movements in Poland and Italy, both ineffective. 'Congress' Poland, re-established after 1815 as a constitutional monarchy under the Romanovs, was incorporated into the sombre despotism of Nicholas I; in Italy the occasion served to advertise Mazzini's propaganda in favour of a united Italian republic.

In England, meanwhile, the internal crisis had been peacefully surmounted; the reformed Parliament of 1832 reflected the triumph of a cautious liberalism and the closer blending of the commercial and professional classes with a still aristocratic establishment. England remained the rallying point for liberal and nationalist movements. The 'forties of the nineteenth century saw much poverty and unemployment, the price of the spreading Industrial Revolution; popular discontent was reflected in England by the Chartist movement and in Paris by Socialist and Communist agitation. Again English political compromise weathered the storm; Peel's Conservative reformist legislation and the abandonment of the Corn Laws averted a popular outbreak, at the price of the disruption of the Tory party. In France a Radical Revolution broke out in Paris, ran to extremes and brought in Louis

Napoleon on the tide of a middle-class reaction. Meanwhile revolution had broken out in Vienna, coincident with revolts in Bohemia, Hungary, and Italy. Metternich was driven into exile, and the Emperor Ferdinand was forced to abdicate. But the Viennese liberals were no match for the Austrian general staff, and the organized power of the Austrian army soon turned the scale; revolts of the subject nationalities were ill co-ordinated, while the new railways allowed swift troop concentration. Schwarzenberg re-established the dynasty in the person of Franz-Joseph: Windischgratz broke the Czechs; Radetzky the Piedmontese at Custozza and Novara; with the help of the Russians, Kossuth's Hungarian revolt was crushed.

In Prussia the liberal movement was side-tracked rather than repressed. Though in 1848 Frederick William III had to conciliate the Berlin revolutionaries, neither Bismarck nor the Prussian military caste meant power to pass to a liberal bourgeoisie whom they regarded as social inferiors. But they were clever enough to exploit the new enthusiasms for German unity and the effects of the Industrial Revolution on Gemany. With the rise of modern industry the boundaries of the numerous German states had become obsolete; following economic realities, the Prussian government had formed a customs union of the states north of the Main. This forward-looking policy undercut Metternich's scheme of a Federal Germany under Austrian leadership with a Diet on traditional lines.

New political as well as economic tendencies were playing into Prussian hands. A Parliament representing all the German states assembled at Frankfurt in the spring of 1848, but clearly a liberal Germany could not include Austria. Forced to turn for leadership to Prussia, the liberals approached the Prussian King, who found himself unable to become a constitutional Emperor of Germany. After a year of ineffective debate, the Frankfurt Parliament was dissolved; it had failed to solve the problem of German unity by constitutional means. That unity was to be achieved by Bismarck by very different methods, behind a pretence of relatively liberal institutions. The cunning of this remarkable man, which turned to account the bourgeois ideology he despised, was more sinister and more successful than the arrogance of the Austrian Court which attempted to repress and ignore it.

For the Italians, in spite of the military failure of Charles Albert of Piedmont, who attempted alone to throw off the Austrian yoke, the prospects of unity were advanced by the events of 1848–9. The collapse of the projects of Federation, sponsored by the Liberal Pius IX, and of the short-lived Roman Republic—scotched in 1849 by a French expedition—proved that only through Piedmontese leadership and foreign aid could unity be achieved. These facts were recognized by Cavour, who set himself first to modernize the armaments, economy, and administration of Piedmont: secondly, to embroil the French in war with Austria.

By the mid-century the Vienna settlement had thus long been disrupted: the liberal movement had reached its culmination in 1848, but had failed both in Austria and Northern Germany, while, in France, a military adventurer of doubtful policy, and rather sinister antecedents, had revived the traditions of the Napoleonic Empire. After this turning-point in European history, the hope of a European peace under the leadership of liberal governments begins to fade; the European prospect darkens, and out of the plain of Northern Germany looms increased Prussian power.

Yet in the 'fifties France still dominated the politics of the Continent. Napoleon III needed spectacular successes. He made four initiatives; the Crimean War and the intervention in Italy, both successful; the Mexican expedition, which was a fiasco; and the War of 1870, which was disastrous.

The Crimean War was undertaken to check Russian expansion into the Balkans and over the Straits; it resulted in prolonging Turkish domination in Europe, the checking of Russia as a major factor in European politics for twenty years, and the alienation of Austria from Russia. During that period Italy became a nation, and Imperial Germany, under the leadership of Prussia, became the dominant power on the Continent.

The command of the Black Sea and the Straits had long been an objective of Russian policy; the seizure of Constantinople itself was a more doubtful project, since it implied disruption and partition of the Turkish Empire. The Russians considered it wiser to maintain a subservient Turkey than to risk the domination of the Straits by French and British fleets. Though, in 1829,

Russian armies had reached Adrianople, they had not attacked the capital, and when in 1833, the Turkish Government solicited Russian help to defend Constantinople against Mehemet Ali of Egypt, the Russians had obtained, by the Treaty of Unkiar-Skelessi, the closure of the Straits to the warships of foreign powers, and won their major objective. But by 1840 the Eastern Question had become international, a second attack by Mehemet Ali, backed by French support, had been thwarted by the joint intervention of Great Britain, Austria, and Russia. Again the disruption of the Turkish Empire was postponed. By the Convention of London a 'cordon sanitaire' was drawn round the Straits, the passage of foreign warships again banned. Russia, though denied access to the Aegean, remained in command of the Black Sea.

Again the major objective had been secured; the Black Sea ports, essential to the growing Russian export trade, were protected from the superior sea power of Great Britain and France. None the less, tension continued to increase. The repressive policy of Nicholas I (1825–55); his renewal of the censorship and revival of the secret police, his persecution of Russian liberals, won him a widespread unpopularity in the West. Further, the expansion of Russia east of the Caucasus to the borders of Afghanistan was held to threaten British interests in India, while the ancient Balkan question and the existence of Orthodox minorities in the Turkish Empire led finally to the outbreak of the Crimean War (1854–6).

The struggle proved disastrous to Russian ambitions; by the Treaty of Paris (1856), Russia lost command of the Black Sea, renounced her claims on Moldavia and Wallachia, and relinquished Southern Bessarabia. The war had shown the rottenness of Nicholas I's regime, and Alexander II (1855–81), following on the emancipation of the serfs (1861), embarked in the 'sixties upon a policy of internal reform. For the next critical decade he had his hands full.

Bismarck had watched the Franco-British adventures in Eastern Europe with satisfaction; neither the British nor the French commanders had shown notable military skill, though their administrative inefficiency had been surpassed by that of the Russians and the Turks. Cavour moreover, in return for his token expeditionary force, had enhanced the international prestige of Piedmont.

The year 1860 was to see the next initiative of Napoleon III. By a secret agreement, concluded at Plombières (1858), he had arranged to support Piedmont against Austria in return for the valuable concession of Nice and Savoy. In the following year Cavour succeeded in provoking the Austrians into war. The French entered Lombardy; at the bloody battles of Magenta and Solferino the Austrians sustained defeats which broke their power in North Italy. Victor Emmanuel emerged as the ruler of a state including all the North Italian plain except Venetia; Tuscany and the Romagna joined the new kingdom, and Napoleon III took his reward—Nice and Savoy, useful and picturesque additions to French territory.

It remained to add Southern Italy to the new Italian state. This objective was achieved in fine romantic style, with less expense of blood and treasure than the unification of the North. In August 1860 Garibaldi sailed from Genoa with the Thousand. The military incompetence of the Neapolitan Bourbons and the gallantry of the expedition quickly resulted in the capture of Sicily and Naples. This relatively bloodless exploit of inspired brigandage stands in sharp contrast to the orthodox and sanguinary blunders of the Crimean War. Garibaldi became the hero not only of United Italy, but of liberals all over Europe, endowing the new Italy with romantic glamour. Following Garibaldi's success, Victor Emmanuel's government acted swiftly; to forestall an advance on Rome, the northern armies advanced to the Volturno. There the King met Garibaldi, who acknowledged him as the Sovereign of United Italy. The new nation was established with its capital at Florence, under a liberal constitutional government, though Venetia remained Austrian, and Rome, under Papal control.

But again the shift of European politics threw opportunities into the hands of Italian diplomacy; in 1866 as the price of an unsuccessful attack on Austria, synchronized with the Prussian attack in the north, the Italians acquired Venice; in 1870 the withdrawal of French troops from Rome enabled the Italians to command the city. In a decade the dream of generations of patriots had been realized—the creation of an Italian National State, uniting the entire peninsula, with its capital in Rome.

Napoleon III had made a fatal error; he had allowed Prussia to destroy the Austrian power in Germany. For it he was to pay with his throne. In 1862 he had embarked upon his third foreign adventure, engineered by clerical and financial interests. The attempt to impose a conservative Catholic government on Republican Mexico was undertaken without knowledge of the country and in the mistaken calculation that the Monroe doctrine could be ignored, since North America was engaged in the War Between the States (1861–5). The resounding failure of the project diminished the waning popularity of the Second Empire, but more important had been the diversion of French armies to Mexico at a critical juncture in European politics.

For Bismarck had long decided to settle accounts with Austria, and his objectives were achieved one by one. He had always been convinced that only through 'blood and iron' could German unity under Prussia be achieved, and he was determined never to subject Prussia to the will of an elected German Parliament—to prevent the establishment of liberal democratic institutions in Germany. The desired conflict with Austria was brought about by diplomacy and force at the expense of Prussia's nearest defenceless neighbour. Jurisdiction over the Danish-speaking Duchy of Schleswig and German-speaking Holstein was in dispute between Denmark and the German Federal Diet; already hostilities had broken out. By the Treaty of London the Powers had decided that Christian of Glucksburg should rule both Denmark and the Duchies, in succession to the reigning Frederick VII. On the death of Frederick VII in 1863, Prussia and Austria, both signatories of the Treaty, intervened to impose the agreed solution. But Bismarck coveted the Duchies for Prussia; he therefore recognized Christian—over the head of a candidate put forward by the Federal Diet—but at the price of impossible demands. When King Christian resisted, Prussian and Austrian armies overwhelmed the Danes. Palmerston threatened British intervention, but public opinion was not behind him, and Bismarck called his bluff. In October 1864 both Duchies were handed over jointly to Prussia and Austria. The first objective had been achieved.

Bismarck thereupon provoked a war with Austria over the disposition of the Duchies, having, as already observed, squared the Italians by the hope of obtaining Venetia.

For the first time nineteenth-century Europe had its taste of a modern *Blitz-Krieg*; on July 3rd, 1866, at Königgrätz (Sadowa) in Bohemia, the Austrians were routed by the modernized Prussian armies, mobilized and massed by the new strategic railways. The fruit of long foresight and careful planning, of co-ordinated diplomacy and the latest armaments, was there for the taking; on August 23rd, by the Treaty of Prague, the Austrian Government conceded all the Prussian demands. So swiftly had Bismarck moved that Europe was confronted with an accomplished fact.

He was careful not to impose a vindictive peace. Austrian influence was eliminated from Germany, but, apart from the loss of Venetia, the Habsburg dominions were left intact. Prussia absorbed Schleswig-Holstein, Hanover, and Hesse-Cassel, thus linking up with her Rhenish provinces, dominating the entire North German plain and Central Germany north of the Main. A North German Confederation was established, whereby, behind a show of constitutional government, power was vested in the hands of a Reichskanzler responsible in fact to the King of Prussia, and working through a Bundesrat of State representatives who met in secret. A Reichstag elected by universal suffrage from all over the Union was a sounding board and safety valve for popular opinion; it possessed no jurisdiction over the armed forces, finance, or foreign policy.

Bismarck could now count on the enthusiastic support of the majority of German liberals and of the growing business community. There remained the final objective, the inclusion of the Southern German states in a German Empire. Events played into Prussian hands. Bismarck and the Prussian General Staff knew they possessed an instrument of war different in quality from the French armies, and they were set on the creation of a German Empire through the conquest of the traditional enemy. When, therefore, the Spanish throne fell vacant, a Prussian candidate was put forward. As had been foreseen, the French at once reacted to this threat to their security; a stiff demand was sent to the Prussian King to withdraw the candidature. The elderly William I fumbled the catch; he agreed in principle to the French demands; but when the French Ambassador asked verbally for guarantees that the candidature should not be renewed, he received a courteous but firm refusal.

The famous Ems telegram, in which the King gave Bismarck

an account of the incident, needed only a little doctoring. Bismarck was a skilful journalist: his published version set in train the fatal series of events which were to lead not only to his immediate war, but to the world conflicts of 1914–18 and of 1939–45. The French, construing the affair as a national insult, declared war amid scenes of enthusiasm; England, suspicious of French designs on Belgium, held aloof. It was believed among the military experts and the general public that the French armies would destroy the Germans in a few months. Another *Blitz-Krieg* disillusioned them. The war had opened in July; by September the French armies, out-manœuvred and encircled, had surrendered at Sedan; the Emperor was a prisoner; the remaining forces shut up in Metz; Paris besieged. On January 18th, 1871, the German Empire, including the South German states, was proclaimed at Versailles. French military prestige had been humbled to the dust; the Second Empire had been destroyed, and Germany had become the dominant power in Europe.

This domination was the cardinal fact of European politics during the armed peace which followed the Franco-Prussian War. It was Bismarck, who, in 1878, together with Disraeli, devised the Treaty of Berlin which deprived Russia of the settlement of the Eastern Question her victories in a renewed offensive against Turkey had put within her grasp (1877–8).

But although Germany called the tune of European politics after 1871, it was the sea power of Great Britain which had confined armed conflict to Europe and continued to limit German ambition. The European political conflicts of the 'fifties and 'sixties had coincided with events of far-reaching importance overseas. The American War Between the States had brought victory for the North and big business; the British attempt to modernize the army of India had resulted in the Mutiny and the revision of the entire basis of Indian administration; in the Far East the exploitation of China and the awakening of Japan had begun; significantly the full modernization of Japan in 1871 coincided with the establishment of German unity. In Africa, Livingstone, Speke, and Stanley were exploring the interior of the continent: in 1869 the Suez Canal was opened and with it the entire strategic picture of the Middle East was changed; while Canada, Australia, and New Zealand were being increasingly opened to European settlement. Meanwhile, in South America new republics, the successors of the great Spanish and Portuguese empires, had grown up, often at war among themselves, but independent of European interference. All these great events took place against the background of the Pax Britannica, ensured by the British sea power, and the development of the new territories was heavily financed by British capital. Increasingly British interests seemed bound up with these overseas territories and with the development of an empire whose value increased with the working out of the Industrial and Technical Revolutions. With these world-wide pre-occupations in mind and with this gathering wealth and power behind them, British statesmen came to the conferences of Europe; naturally, in view of their vast trading interests, their influence, apart from the blunder of the Crimean War, was for peace and compromise, so long as their sea power remained unchallenged.

With the expansion of German ambitions into the colonial field, however, and the competition of German industry, Anglo-German rivalry loomed on the horizon, and gradually the French and Russian governments, in common fear of German military power, veered towards a policy of mutual assistance. The path of this development and of the British abandonment of comparative isolation was slow and difficult. Accommodation was repeatedly sought with Germany; considerable colonial concessions were made both by Great Britain and by France. Bismarck, indeed, who realized the danger of a war on two fronts, attempted to limit German expansionist ambition, and prevent a Russian *rapprochement* with the Western powers. But after the accession of William II and Bismarck's dismissal, Germany entered upon a naval armaments race which made her intentions clear. As we have seen, the Franco-Russian Alliance of 1893 was followed, after the demonstration of Russian weakness against the Japanese and German hostility to Great Britain during the Boer War, by the Franco-British Entente. Thus by the early twentieth century Great Britain had again entered into heavy commitments in Europe, and Russia, whose hostility to Austria had increased, following the Austrian attitude during the Crimean War and the growing clash of Austrian and Russian interests in the Balkans, had aligned herself with France.

Such in simplified outline were the major events of European politics during the nineteenth century. After a long period of peace, the intellectual progress and social amelioration of the age had been overlaid with a web of diplomatic and military manœuvring which resulted, between 1848 and 1871, in four considerable wars, numerous minor conflicts and a series of international crises in which war was narrowly averted. The expansion of wealth and the improvement of administration resulted in larger armaments and more widespread conscription. After 1870, compulsory military service was common to all the great powers except Great Britain, while a growing proportion of revenue was devoted to armaments.

A novel aspect of the international tension of the age was the inflammatory influence of the press on public opinion. The British press bawled for war against Russia in 1854; a wave of nationalistic fury swept over Germany over the question of Schleswig-Holstein; the frenzy of the Parisian mob to some extent forced the hand of Napoleon III's government in 1870. All over Europe not only the bourgeoisie but the masses acquiesced in war in the name of national prestige. Far from the spread of literacy diminishing the will to war, as liberal thinkers had anticipated, popular sensationalism often inflamed the occasions of conflict. The clash of national armies involved, too, the economic future of the various nationalities, the standard of living as well as national prestige; while the development of expanding capitalism was beginning in the second half of the century to drive governments into imperialistic adventure.

III

Yet the political realities of the age were masked after the 'forties by a feverish prosperity, for the economic background was one of increasing expansion and power. The Industrial Revolution had spread by the mid-century into Belgium, Northern France, and the Rhineland, and in all the advanced states of the West there was a great increase of mechanical production. Factories supplying an expanding market employed an increasing labour power, and the profits they realized vastly augmented the amount of available capital. This, in turn, was reinvested in new enterprises, and increased the wealth of the propertied classes. By the second half of the century, the wealth of the owners of invested capital was beginning to preponderate over that of the landowners, though many of them had developed their urban and mineral wealth. In England, the repeal of the Corn Laws, which had hitherto protected the landowning interest from foreign competition, marks a significant turning point, while in France the influence of bankers and financiers and of big business generally was reflected in the policy of the Second Empire. The middle of the century saw, indeed, the transference of economic and political power to the moneyed men: it was the heyday of plutocratic enterprise. There grew up a *rentier* class, living on invested capital, which finds no parallel in numbers or extent in previous history. With the discovery of gold in California and Australia, bullion became more plentiful; until the 'seventies prices rose steadily, while in the 'fifties the full effect of the revolution in transport became apparent. The Bessemer process of manufacturing steel altered the scale of railway, shipping, factory, and building enterprise. A huge network of rail communications rapidly developed over the Continent, transforming the tempo of commercial life, and bringing new markets to the factories. In their turn the agricultural producers benefited, since rail transport brought perishable goods to the urban market. The coming of the railways, as already observed, revolutionized war, enabling governments to concentrate masses of men and material far more rapidly and increasing the hold of the military empires over their subject peoples.

And already on the oceans, steam, after the turn of the century, had ousted sail. Huge overseas markets were now at the disposal of European industries; the emancipation of Latin America, assisted by the policy of the British minister Canning, greatly benefited the commerce of Western Europe. In the United States a tremendous business activity captured the North in the middle years of the century; the resources of the continent were exploited on a great scale; and the spate of immigrants from the poorer European countries was easily absorbed in new industries, where they were ready to work in conditions uncongenial to Americans. This immigration, and the tempo of American business profoundly altered the racial and mental characteristics of the

United States. It also made North America a formidable competitor with European industry.

The development of intercontinental trade was accelerated by the invention of the electric telegraph and the cable. During the eighteenth century research had been going on on the nature of electric currents; in the early nineteenth, Volta and Ampère had devised batteries to supply current for railway telegraphs; in 1831 Faraday (1791–1867) had invented the dynamo, which in the 'sixties developed into a source of electric power. Later, the researchers of Clerk-Maxwell and Hertz on electro-magnetism opened up the whole field of wireless telegraphy and ultimately of radio transmission. The use of oil fuel was beginning in the 'fifties and 'sixties, later to increase on a vast scale with the invention of the internal combustion engine into its full revolutionary exploitation in the twentieth century. In addition to steam power based on coal, two new sources of power had thus been discovered by the middle nineteenth century.

The result of the expansion of capitalist industry and commerce was the creation not only of a large plutocracy, but of a great industrial proletariat over most of Western Europe; except in France, the growth of population was unprecedented. A massive urban society had been suddenly called into being, increasingly dependent on an international economy. This new population was often exploited, but its level of political consciousness and education was higher than that of the illiterate peasantries which had hitherto formed the bulk of the population of Europe. The organization of the factory, the routine of industrial life, the technical efficiency demanded by the new processes, were reflected in spontaneous working-class organizations. Social reform was increasingly demanded. The demand was expressed in two ways, first, by reformist movements, secondly, in extremist agitation which aimed at the violent overthrow of bourgeois society. These streams of thought were reflected in the subsequent development of Socialism: their interaction will be examined in a later chapter. This spread of socialist doctrines marks the emergence of the masses to political consciousness; an international landmark comparable in importance to the rise of mercantile capitalism in the sixteenth and seventeenth centuries, and a dominant political fact of the modern world.

So, after the mid-century, a great international network of commerce and industry, of finance and credit, was expanding over the whole planet, bringing peoples and territories hitherto remote into close relations with Europe and America. This expansion was international, cutting across the old boundaries; the policy of governments was increasingly influenced by the interests of big business, by the competition for markets and raw materials, which in the later years of the century was to become acute, and to increase the political tension between the European states. The scale and destructiveness of war was also increased by the new inventions. The Crimean War was conducted with armaments not essentially different from those employed by the Napoleonic armies; but with the invention of steel cannon, firing explosive shell, and of the breech-loading rifle, a new era had begun. The Napoleonic Wars had seen the appearance of great conscript armies and the drive of national democracy had been put behind war; now the power of machinery was harnessed to the time-honoured custom of international slaughter.

IV

The rise of professionalized science had other effects, more permanent and more profound. The nineteenth century saw a revolution in man's conception of his place in nature. The appearance of Darwin's *Origin of Species* (1859) and *Descent of Man* (1871) are landmarks of cardinal importance in the history of thought: the broad conclusion of Darwin's life work, though modified by the researches of Mendel, have never been fundamentally challenged, and their implications have not yet been fully assimilated.

According to the theory of natural selection, the higher animals, of which man is one, have evolved through the interaction of species and environment, a process extending over millions of years. The perspective of thought, hitherto confined within the Biblical chronology, was radically altered. The millennial vistas of biological and geological time, the slow evolution of species, the apparent wastefulness, impersonality, and power of Life, revolutionized and disconcerted the outlook of the nineteenth century.

Darwin found in T. H. Huxley a colleague of tenacity, eloquence, and lucidity of mind. Huxley, who admired Descartes before all other philosophers, championed the cause of 'organized common sense,' his definition of science. He possessed the polemical qualities Darwin lacked, and he was determined that science should face its social responsibilities. His attacks on obscurantist opinion and stoical acceptance of the implications of the new knowledge, made him, like Darwin, a figure of European stature. Although the conclusions of the new biology were received with horror by conservative opinion, so formidable was the authority of professional research and so remarkable the technical achievements of other branches of contemporary science that it was impossible to circumvent them. Nor was there need; the Darwinian hypothesis was never materialistic but reflected the power of living organisms over environment and implied the creative drive of emergent mind. Unfortunately Darwin's conclusions were widely misinterpreted. According to the hypothesis of natural selection, the species best adapted to its environment had survived; this process was popularly described as the 'survival of the fittest.' The phrase was coined by Herbert Spencer, a writer who popularized doctrines of progress, individualism, and evolution, and enjoyed an undeserved but European influence. To the popular mind the fittest meant the toughest, not merely the best adapted to surrounding conditions. In fact, as biologists are well aware, animals highly specialized for violence are far less numerous and therefore biologically less successful than the majority of pacific species; further, animals of the same kind do not normally prey on one another, and man has won his supremacy not by superior brute strength but by intelligence and adaptability. None the less the picture of a nature 'red in tooth and claw,' dominated by the more spectacular carnivores, though hardly borne out by the facts of evolution, coloured the nineteenth-century vision of life. The idea of strength through struggle, already, as we have noted, popularized by romantic metaphysicians, was reinforced in the 'sixties and 'seventies by a dramatized distortion of the conclusions of the biologists, and conflict between classes and nations was held to reflect the law of life. In face of the neutral biological facts, it was thought realistic to maintain that an unchanging human nature, individualistic and ferocious, reflected the struggle for existence; that motives of aggression and cupidity were stronger than the motives on which the biological success of humanity had been based. Such were the vagaries of popular belief, reflecting the social context of the time and characteristic of the transition from a dogmatic to a more fully scientific outlook.

Apart from biological discoveries, the expansion of scientific knowledge continued: in chemistry, Dalton had already (1808) put forward an atomic theory which went far to explain the nature of matter, though it pointed to a materialistic explanation which has been superseded by modern theories of atomic structure. The vital concept of cellular organism was put forward by Muller in the 'thirties; in geology, Lyell's *Principles* had appeared in 1830, creating the modern classifications of the science; his work was carried further by von Humboldt. For the first time the immense antiquity of the earth had been scientifically demonstrated. In medicine, also, remarkable advances were being made: Pasteur (1822–95), who came of peasant stock from the Jura, made a revolution in the study of bacteria and of infectious disease; his researches brought cholera, hitherto an accepted scourge, under relative control. Lord Lister (1827–1912), the son of an Essex Quaker, and professor in the University of Glasgow, was the greatest surgeon of his time. In face of steady opposition, he introduced antiseptics into the operating theatre (1867). The close of the century saw two other advances of the first order; Röntgen, a Rhinelander of genius, discovered the use of X-rays; Ross, the diffusion of malaria by the mosquito, a discovery of obvious importance for colonial development.

While these fundamental discoveries were being made, new literary movements developed. The dominant prose form was the novel, often published by instalments in periodicals, a staple form of popular reading. In England, Dickens, Thackeray, and Trollope are the most famous names of the mid-nineteenth century. Dickens, who himself had emerged from poverty, wrote of the common people and the middle classes; his humour, his technical ingenuity, his delineation of personality verging on caricature, his intensity of moral purpose, won him a wide reputation not only in England but abroad. Thackeray depicted the foibles of upper-class society with caustic wit; George Eliot analyzed the problems of the age, and Trollope, a profoundly

English writer of placid and amiable genius, portrayed with shrewd humour the quiet stream of Victorian ecclesiastical and rural life. Later, in the closing decades of the century, Hardy, a Dorset writer with a painter's eye, described the characters, the humour and the tragedies of the Wessex countryside; he was the last of the great Victorian novelists, inspired with a stoic pity in an age of waning faith. He was a poet, too, of a high order; in *The Dynasts,* the tragic drama of the Napoleonic Wars, he took all Europe for his background, depicting on an immense canvas the blind arbitraments of fate. He has been well described as a belated Elizabethan in the grandeur, the breadth, and the sympathy of his mind. In English drama, in the 'nineties, Wilde produced comedies of remarkable virtuosity, and Shaw, with a more violent wit, used the resources of his dramatic skill for a startling and influential unmasking of conventional illusions. But of all these writers Wells, the prophet and the popularizer of the conception of science as he learnt it from T. H. Huxley, exercised perhaps the strongest and most lasting influence on the minds of the younger generation.

In France Balzac combined the romantic tradition with a new realism. Regarding himself as a naturalist of society, he undertook to describe all aspects of French social life; like Dickens, he painted the portrait of the *petit-bourgeois,* though he loved, too, the glitter of the metropolitan society he romanticized. His gift of narrative, his torrential descriptive power, make him one of the greatest of French novelists. But by the 'seventies the romantic convention was on the wane. Stendhal, whose writing was distinguished by a superlative elegance and lucidity in the old French tradition, first represents the new disillusionment, while Zola brought a detailed and conscious realism to the study of society. Flaubert (1821–80), the son of a surgeon at Rouen, anatomized with hatred the banality of bourgeois life, and evoked in a lapidary style the colour and cruelty of Carthaginian antiquity. The Scandinavian dramatist, Ibsen, also brought a profound analytical power and a strange imagination to the problems of society.

In Germany the poetry of Eichendorf and Mörike developed the romantic tradition of Heine, a romanticism expressed in prose by Hoffmann and Jean Paul Richter, by Novalis and the plays of Kleist. But the most important German contribution was in Classical and historical scholarship; in the latter field Ranke and Mommsen won European celebrity.

The nineteenth century saw, too, a great enrichment of European literature by Russian writers, of which the promise, as we have seen, had already been apparent in the writing of Pushkin. Tolstoi is one of the greatest novelists in any age; his capacity to create living characters, his understanding of all ranks of society, and his intense feeling for nature, are expressed with the force of a great personality. Dostoevsky, who was technically influenced by Dickens, brings the discursive speculative Slav genius to a fine intensity; his originality, genius, and insight, give his novels disconcerting power. Gogol, too, shows a formidable power of description and analysis. Turgeniev describes the life of the Russian countryside, and implies the complex and heart-breaking social problems of his day; while in the second half of the century Chekhov portrays in miniature the indecisions, the introspection, the boredom and the charm of Russian middle-class life before the Revolution.

The age saw also great poetic achievements. In England Tennyson, the admired master of Victorian poetry, was a craftsman of superlative skill; he could touch deep chords of beauty and insight, and voice, too, the optimism of his day. Browning, a robust philosopher, expressed many aspects of contemporary thought; Matthew Arnold evoked a new introspective melancholy, while Swinburne, in flaming revolt against contemporary convention, wrote an exotic and original poetry which swept like a hot wind through the lush garden of late Victorian England. Of the French poets, Victor Hugo (1802–85) was the most famous and the most prolific of the romantics; essentially a great lyric writer, he combined epic and narrative gifts. Lamartine, following the tradition of Chateaubriand, expressed a romantic religious sensibility and love of nature: the genius de Vigny was more pessimistic. By the second half of the century the realist reaction was reflected in poetry. Baudelaire, whose poems *Les Fleurs du mal* appeared in 1857, expressed a powerful, elaborate, and morbid sensibility. Later, the symbolists, Verlaine, Rimbaud, and Mallarmé, wrote an allusive, subjective, and complicated verse, further developed in the twentieth century.

The nineteenth century was the greatest age of French painting. Corot's earlier work shows a purity of colour and soundness
of design in the best French tradition, though he later fell into a
certain sentimentality. The liberating influence of Constable and
Delacroix was reflected in the work of Courbet and Manet, who
went straight to nature to transfigure subjects, hitherto thought
commonplace, into new beauty. The great impressionists, Monet,
Pisarro, Renoir, and the supreme master of them all, Cézanne,
revealed new worlds of colour and construction. This brilliance,
strange in the drab background of so much of nineteenth-century
society, can compare with the greatest painting of the past. Later
the post-impressionist, Gauguin, who found his finest inspiration
in the South Seas, and the extraordinary genius, Van Gogh,
achieved an equal splendour of colour and original form.

In England, the fine artistic traditions of the earlier part of the
century were not fulfilled in the Victorian age; there were excep-
tions—illustrators of genius—but, in general, painting reached a
depressing level of banality. The Pre-Raphaelites, though their
experiments are technically of interest, were an exotic clique,
who often identified art with a feeble self-consciousness; William
Morris exercised a more vigorous influence on decoration and
book production, but the Victorian bourgeoisie got the art they
deserved in the canvases of Watts and Alma Tadema.

The architecture of the middle and later nineteenth century
also displays a falling off from the traditional level, hitherto, except in the later Roman Empire and the Dark Ages, extremely
high through most of European history. Before the Industrial
Revolution, architecture had been consistently well suited to its
environment and expressive of the function for which it was designed. By the middle of the nineteenth century this admirable
tradition had been broken. The combined vulgarity and incon-
venience of most nineteenth-century building is unsurpassed;
this decline was due in part to the hasty and unplanned expansion of the new towns, in part to the bad taste of a philistine but
affluent middle class; but considering the excellence of the
models which confronted architects on all sides, and the growing
technical skill and variety of materials, this aspect of bourgeois
civilization is difficult to explain. It was due perhaps mainly to
an ill-considered romanticism, which sought to acclimatize a

medley of styles in an inappropriate setting, so that a railway station was built to represent a Gothic town hall, and a hotel the stronghold of a mediaeval brigand. Buildings consistently masqueraded as something other than what they were; the rapid transport of church building materials struck at the ancient local traditions of building, and a soulless uniformity grew up in the grimy wilderness of the industrial towns. Apart from certain odd felicities of an antiquarian kind, it was indeed a lamentable age for building, which has left an inheritance of formidable ugliness. The activities of nineteenth-century architects were not confined to their own buildings; they destroyed, under the guise of restoration, the achievements of their predecessors. The commercialized romantic movement in architecture has indeed much to answer for; yet the essentials of good design were at their disposal and by the close of the century a more functional architecture was beginning to develop, appropriate to an age of expanding comfort and scientific power.

Music, following on the great classical tradition reinterpreted by Beethoven, developed along predominantly romantic lines. Chopin combined French elegance with Polish fire; the brilliant virtuosity of Liszt expressed the vigour and the spaciousness of the Hungarian tradition; Mendelssohn, Verdi and Weber displayed a melodious technical brilliance, while Rossini and Offenbach caught the lighter sentiment of the age and Russia gave Europe two great composers in Moussorgsky and Tchaikovsky.

The superlative technical skill of Brahms was combined with an august distinction, while Wagner's genius marks a new departure in orchestration and in 'Music drama'; the force and size of his achievement is characteristic of the later nineteenth century. All these musicians belonged to a cosmopolitan world; they enjoyed prestige and reputation in the major capitals of Europe, and indeed the growing popularity of this musical inheritance marks a new and attractive aspect of civilization. Even more directly than literature, music could cut across national boundaries and unite an increasing audience—an aspect of the cultural assertion of a common European civilization which was developing along with its political denial.

The nineteenth century thus saw remarkable achievements in literature and the arts, the full expansion of middle-class culture based on professionalized knowledge, and the economic exploitation of a new technology. By the closing decades of the age this economy had become world-wide; it had from the beginning been always on a European rather than a national scale. Europe was on the threshold of an economy of plenty unprecedented in history, hitherto strictly conditioned by scarcity based on a conservative agriculture. The most original intellectual achievement of the age was a new understanding of nature; both in biology and physics a radical expansion had come about, comparable to the seventeenth-century advance in mathematics and astronomy. This advance was paralleled in the social sphere by a remarkable progress in administration, most fully developed in the West, in a steady and detailed attack on the causes of social maladjustment. Together with this reformist movement, inspired by the belief in progress inherited from the eighteenth century and armed with a new statistical knowledge, there had grown up a great literature which analysed in the novel the whole panorama of society. The eighteenth-century novelists had been concerned primarily with character; the romantic writers had paid a new attention to background; in the mid-nineteenth-century these two streams combined with a new sociological approach and descriptive realism, and the writers of the period made an original and powerful contribution to European literature.

Not only was man winning unprecedented control over nature, and an unprecedented knowledge of his own society, but also a deeper understanding of the past. Historical method applied to Law and the social sciences linked up with the biological outlook which saw all life as one. It gave to history and sociology a new depth and a new power. Both in the scientific, technological, and sociological fields, therefore, in spite of political crises and their sequel, the nineteenth century saw a new hope of man's mastering his environment and a new expansion of the horizons of knowledge.

v

Such are the most original aspects of the nineteenth century; together with the fuller realization of the promise of the eighteenth, they make the epoch a great age. All this achievement, though rooted in national culture, was cosmopolitan; fresh knowledge had reinforced economic expansion; the new learning, scientific and historical, legal and literary, musical and artistic, cut across the political divisions of the Continent. Not since the days of the Roman Empire had so cosmopolitan a civilization been known in Europe, and the cultural interdependence of the Continent been more strongly affirmed.

In contrast with the rich variety of this progress, there remained the brutal fact of national and military sovereign power. In an age of unprecedented cultural achievement, the European national states showed growing antagonism, greed, and hysteria; nineteenth-century civilization was increasingly at the mercy of political intrigue and military force. On the canvas of world history the outstanding men of the age are the scientists, the engineers, the administrators; the great writers, artists, and musicians; in the ugly political perspective of their own time their influence was negligible.

Yet to the majority of law-abiding Europeans the facts of the international situation remained unrealized. Governments and dynasties still retained sufficient prestige to inspire belief that statesmen could in the last resort control the situation; the traditional trappings of military and royal power still retained their glamour and provided a picturesque spectacle in a world which had lost much of its traditional colour. Far other was the outlook of those responsible for foreign policy. They knew the precariousness of the international balance, the gulf which was threatening to swallow the achievements of the age. For, as the century drew to its close, Europe was not only riven by traditional antagonisms, but became the focus of a clash of empires extending to the ends of the earth. With every expansion of colonizing enterprise, with every increase in wealth, as the new inventions succeeded each other with bewildering rapidity, the European peoples advanced a step nearer the catastrophe their political and economic disorganization implied. The nineteenth century contained unprecedented possibilities both for progress and catastrophe; it saw the climax of middle-class civilization and the prelude to world conflict.

PART II

THE CONTEMPORARY CONFLICT

CHAPTER I

WORLD WAR AND THE ECLIPSE
OF EUROPE

By the close of the nineteenth century, in spite of immense prosperity and expansion, Europe, following the clash of interests already described, was set for political disaster, moving with inexorable momentum towards the First World War. The fundamental causes of this development were the unbridled sovereignty of national states, now rendered more dangerous by popular nationalism; the profound maladjustment of European economic life, and the ambition of united Germany. The peace which still precariously held between the Great Powers was bought only at the price of expanding armaments; international and economic catastrophe were the fated sequel to a period of optimism.

Meanwhile, ironically, applied science confronted the world with opportunities of unprecedented scope; nothing less than the extension of the full inheritance of civilization to all mankind. Never had a society so far-flung, so powerful, or so rich been seen upon the face of the earth; as the great liners cut their course over the oceans, the sleek expresses tore through the Simplon and the Gotthard, and the new cosmopolitan hotels rose in every capital, the more prosperous heirs of the nineteenth century enjoyed a well-being which seemed superficially secure. To this affluent generation in the West there opened new vistas of enterprise and prosperity, while in Central and Eastern Europe the military and landed aristocracies enjoyed the Indian summer of their power. Yet, beneath the veneer of progress, there lurked the forces of violence and disruption, of popular nationalism and social revolution, problems urgent for solution; the voice of the masses demanding a new deal.

During the nineteenth century the common people of Europe were becoming literate and articulate; by the twentieth, governments were challenged to organize and control the beginnings of a new popular civilization. The increase in population, the intricate world-wide structure of modern industry, the revolution in transport, called for a coherent international and economic order. The alternative before the ruling minorities was increasingly plain; to organize a cosmopolitan society for civilized ends, adapting ancient institutions and including the common people in the inheritance of the old culture, or to risk international conflict and social revolution, followed by the seizure of power by extremists. Yet, closely immersed in the immediate task of fending off the successive crises, few men in positions of power could appreciate the situation; and if they did, they could command no widespread support.

It has been the fashion to decry the statesmanship of governments during the years leading to the First World War; yet numerous international crises were surmounted; successive threats of conflict postponed. But the liberal statesmen of the West were caught in the network of an international system they were powerless to control, rendered doubly unworkable by the historic discrepancy between the political and social development of Western and Eastern Europe, and the obsession of the most powerful nations on the Continent with power politics.

From 1914, when the old order committed political suicide, to 1945, Europe, save for a twenty years' armistice, lost her world domination and became a plague spot of global conflict. Following Prussian military ambitions and convinced of 'encirclement,' the Germans twice tried to break out of Europe in a belated bid for 'Weltmacht,' to be overwhelmed in a war of attrition by powers that dwarfed Europe. After an illusory phase of imperial power in the 'twenties, France and Great Britain, exhausted in the second bout of conflict, went into relative eclipse, and Germany, ruined in the First World War, was partitioned after the Second. Save for American power, Western Europe itself might have been overrun. Yet the stark threat in 1945 was the instrument of recovery, for it led Europe to sink its differences and within twenty years to achieve a degree of unity which, though still limited, had been unthinkable for centuries.

With this background in mind, one can appreciate the major events which marked the climax of the German phase of European domination, and have led to the shift of power to the mainly extra-European unions which have brought that domination to its close.

The chequered and disputed course of early twentieth-century history and the assessment of contemporary cultural achievement is outside the scope of the present survey, which can only outline the major consequences of the First World War and the evolution of the dictatorships of the Left and the Right which were its sequel and which led up to the second bout of conflict, the eclipse of Europe, the collapse of its colonial empires, and to Europe's current and still partial rehabilitation.

II

The First World War was a struggle to attrition between two incompatible conceptions of government, unreconciled by international control, the result of tendencies developing since the Middle Ages. That the war was decided in favour of the liberal Western powers is the cardinal fact of the early twentieth century, too often obscured by the failure of the peace. The first German attempt at world conquest had been stopped; an opportunity made to face the problems of international and economic disorder.

The political structure of Europe emerged transformed from the struggle. To all appearance the phase of German domination was past. For the first time in history a permanent international organization was created to maintain the peace. The commitments to which the Covenant of the League of Nations bound its participants were specific. They undertook to boycott any state committing an act of war; to impose economic sanctions; to support one another against aggression, and to afford passage through their territories to force co-operating to protect the

Covenant.[1] Indeed, the League came to ruin, not altogether through defective structure, but through the failure of the signatories to carry out their obligations, and through 'factors beyond the control of the statesmen of the time—the immaturity of American policy and the social upheaval in Russia.'[2] For all its failure, the Covenant is a landmark in the history of international order; the first attempt at the permanent organization of world security.

The emergence of the successor states of the Austrian Empire —Czechoslovakia, Poland, Yugoslavia, and Greater Roumania— was the second consequence of the war. The political scene in the Danube area and in Eastern Europe was revolutionized in terms of sovereign nationality. There now existed no nucleus for federation in the area; no centre of political order other than this principle. Yet the multiplication of sovereignties, though it reflected overwhelming popular sentiment, gave rise to acute minority problems and political and economic friction.

The third outstanding fact of European politics in 1919 was the existence of the Bolshevik dictatorship in Russia, pledged in this phase of development, to world revolution. The downfall of the tsar had its sequel in the establishment of a proletarian dictatorship. The emergence of this new society marked a radical departure in history; sociologically the most significant result of the First World War.

In Southern Europe, meanwhile, social and economic unrest had brought about the collapse of Italian democracy; but where in Russia, following the liberal failure, power fell to the Bolsheviks, in Italy, in 1922, emerged the first Fascist dictatorship, vowed to opportunist expansion. Here was the fourth political landmark of the 'twenties, the lapse of the majority of Italians into a regime of personal tyranny, in part traditional and in part an attempt to reorganize an ineffective democracy. And Fascism was destined, in its German interpretation, to a future transcending its Italian origins.

The background to these European developments was the renewed isolationism of the United States. Wilson, the principal

---

[1] *Vide* Article 16 of the Covenant.
[2] Marston, *The Peace Conference of 1919,* p. 229, Royal Institute of International Affairs, 1944.

architect of the Covenant, had gone down in political ruin, and the Americans, having helped to save the liberties of Europe, understandably withdrew from the commitments victory implied.

Such were the realities of the post-war world in Europe—the establishment of a new machinery of international order, backed at first by the combined power of the British and French empires, but never underwritten by the United States; unable, also, to count on the combined sea and land power an understanding with Russia could guarantee; and the creation in Central and Eastern Europe of new states, collectively powerful, but with little political experience or economic stability. Meanwhile the failure of liberal democracy in Russia and Italy had given rise to dictatorships of the Left and of the Right; the former destined to subscribe to the Covenant of the League, but in the 'twenties isolated by the Western powers and its own policy; the latter, for all its brilliant cultural traditions, under Fascist domination.

In spite of these dangers there was a decade of uneasy equilibrium. Germany was prostrate; even without the backing of the United States and the U.S.S.R., the League disposed of sufficient power to counter any threat of German revenge. The Geneva Protocol of 1924 might have ensured the League's effectiveness. Had it been adopted, and public opinion created to implement it, the Covenant might yet have been a reality.[1] The rejection of the protocol may well be regarded as the first disastrous turning-point in the fortunes of Europe and the League; within a decade the victorious powers were to throw away the achievements of the hard-fought war. This disaster was due in part to the overriding causes already enumerated; in part to bad leadership which failed to drive home to the peoples the consequences of international anarchy, in part to ineffective League propaganda; but primarily to the increasing habit of popular nationalism, disrupting the natural unity of European civilization. For in spite of the lessons of the war, public opinion was slow to apprehend the realities of the contemporary world, unable to adapt itself to the facts of scientific power. The Covenant was thought to be a visionary project,[2] where its enforcement was the way of realism.

[1] For text see Protocol for the Pacific Settlement of International Disputes, International Conciliation (Carnegie Endowment), Dec. 1924, No. 205.

[2] *Vide* McCallum, *Public Opinion and the Last Peace*, O.U.P., 1944, for an illuminating analysis of English public opinion.

Accustomed to the unbridled sovereignty of national governments, unable to assimilate the idea of international security,
forgetful of the common inheritance of Europe, the masses, as
well as the majority of their leaders, connived at their own destruction. Though with better excuse, the people as well as the
statesmen were directly to blame for the consequent disaster.

The failure of the Versailles settlement to face the economic
problems which had contributed to the war, and which were destined most immediately to wreck the peace, was another shattering cause of the collapse of security. Fantastic war expenditure
had left Europe heavily in debt; many overseas markets, on
which the international capitalist economy depended, had been
lost. The war and its consequences had undermined the traditional basis of credit and exchange, imposed habitual budget
deficiencies, ruinous taxation. It had long been apparent that the
economy of the world was interdependent, yet political tendencies ran clean contrary to economic facts. 'Indeed,' writes a contemporary observer, 'when economic integration was becoming
irresistible, political fragmentation was still continuing. . . . At
the moment when nationalism was becoming out of date and
unworkable in the economic field, it was flourishing with unprecedented luxuriance in the political field. This deep-seated con-
tradiction in society was a source of confusion and unrest in
many parts of the world, but nowhere so acutely as in Europe.'[1]
National economies, moreover, were at the mercy of an international trade cycle demanding combined action for its control.
Finally, the feverish prosperity of the post-war years in America
broke in the world financial crisis of 1929. Faced with economic
disaster, governments reverted to 'autarky', reviving mercantilist
ideas of the eighteenth century, attempting to build self-sufficient
national economies in a world naturally organized in terms of
international trade. By the middle 'thirties economic disaster ran
level with political collapse.

The third cause of the renewed catastrophe was the disarmament of the victorious powers. It was undertaken in part for
economy, in part in deference to popular hatred of war. Anxious
to avoid a recurrence of conflict, unmindful of the obligations of
the Covenant, which, if enforced, might have secured peace,

[1] Harold Butler, *The Lost Peace*, Faber & Faber, 1941, p. 171.

British governments in particular followed the parochial course of 'setting a good example' to a world increasingly dominated by gangster Fascist dictatorships.

The fourth cause of the collapse of security, with its opportunity for renewed German attack, was the threat of class war. It produced widespread fear of world revolution, of the violent subversion of capitalist society. In politically backward countries this fear contributed to a collapse of democracy before military dictatorships following the model of Italian Fascism. These dictatorships were tolerated by democratic opinion, hypnotized by the fear of Bolshevism. Regimes incompatible with freedom or security grew up over wide areas of Europe.

In less than fifteen years, the victorious democracies had thrown away the military power and political unity which could have maintained peace, while no sufficient public opinion or adequate political machinery had taken root in Europe to enforce the authority of the League, vitiated from the beginning by the obsession of national sovereignty. The international disorder and economic dislocation which had contributed to the First World War had greatly increased, and only in European countries with a solid tradition of self-government had unimpaired democratic institutions survived—in Great Britain, Scandinavia, Holland, Belgium, and Switzerland, while in France, for all her great traditions, social and political conflict divided a nation over-strained by two German wars, and by the long sustained effort to maintain the military leadership of Europe. Of the new countries, the Czech republic alone at that time seemed to possess the political maturity to maintain democratic institutions successfully.

These four factors—the failure of the League, the depression, democratic disarmament, and the threat of class war—obscured the fundamental danger the Versailles Treaty had been designed to prevent—a German war of revenge. By the early 'thirties, the brief lull in the phase of German domination was past. For while liberal democratic governments pursued contradictory piecemeal policies, initiative was passing to the totalitarian states.

These dictatorships marked a formidable attempt to direct the political and economic drive of whole peoples towards a set goal. They marked, indeed, an attempt to tackle the overriding problem of the twentieth century, the organization of a new mass society. This radical departure was made constructively by Marxist socialism, destructively by Fascism. The former, at a heavy price, and in an industrially backward country, initiated a new society, powerful, centralized; for all its crudity and intolerance directed to the 'betterment of man's estate,' and at least an attempt to deal with the problems of nationalism and unbridled capitalism which were the overwhelming legacy of the nineteenth century. The latter, an expression of disintegrating democracy in areas where democratic ideas had no long pedigree, exploited popular nationalist frenzy, and the destructive impulses of men caught in a mechanized civilization they were unable to control.

I I I

Democratic institutions were still taken for granted in the politically and economically advanced Western states and in America, but the totalitarian dictatorships set the pace of the post-war world, and the ideas which inspired them must be examined. It will be necessary first to take account of the ideology of Marxism, to trace the rise of the U.S.S.R., the modification of Marxist ideas by the stress of events and by the historic tendencies of Russian evolution.

We have already touched on the socialist writers of the early nineteenth century; their influence had created two streams of thought, one reformist, the other revolutionary. Reformist movements, aiming at 'welfare,' in alliance with the administrative advance which transformed Western society in the nineteenth century, still worked within the existing social framework. The heir to the liberal tradition of gradual improvement, achieved without the wasteful extremities of political violence, it offered, and would seem still to offer, a way of adjusting civilization to contemporary reality. In politically advanced countries, with traditions of responsibility and compromise, the painful transformation of the power state into the welfare state may be achieved. This possibility will be discussed later.

We must now turn to the more drastic remedy inspired by Communism, and to the Fascist reaction, for which the violence of international Communism was in part responsible. It was not until Karl Marx (1818–83) and his collaborator, Engels, formulated the fighting creed of Communism that the movement became formidable. Its success has been phenomenal. The *Communist Manifesto* was published in 1848; the first volume of *Das Kapital* in 1867; by 1918 the Bolsheviks were ruling Russia. Though this revolution had been achieved not according to the Marxist pattern, but through the collapse of the Tsarist government and through circumstances peculiar to Russian society, and although the period of War Communism was short-lived, many of the fundamental doctrines of Marxism were to be realized in the U.S.S.R.

What, then, were the ideas which in less than a century inspired this revolution? They have been clearly set out by Marx in the middle nineteenth century. Popular revolts have been sporadic throughout European history; but they were unconstructive; in politics, homely peasant wisdom got nobody very far. Marx for the first time provided the militant industrial proletariat with a clear-cut political programme. He claimed to have discovered the laws of society as Darwin had discovered the laws of evolution. 'The final purpose of my book,' he wrote in 1859, 'is to discover the economic law of motion of modern society.' He wished to dedicate *Das Kapital* to Darwin, who declined the offer. At that time, both in physics and biology, ideas of automatic process were dominant; Marx's generalizations reflect this outlook. 'The economic structure of society,' he says, 'is the real foundation on which rise the political and legal superstructure, and to which correspond definite forms of social consciousness':[1] successive economic stages create their appropriate ideology. Where Hegel saw in history a spiritual evolution, Marx adapted the Hegelian historical process to a materialistic interpretation. 'With Hegel,' he wrote, 'Dialectic is standing on its head . . . it must be turned right side up again;'[2] and he took from Hegel the idea of evolution through struggle which he interpreted in terms of class conflict.

Marx reinforced the historical generalizations of German thought by statistical data collected by English economists. *Das Kapital* is largely founded on the reports of English social work-

---

[1] Preface to the *Critique to Political Economy*.
[2] Preface to *Das Kapital*.

ers, doctors, and government officials, contained in the Blue
Books to which Marx had access in the British Museum. He
swept these data into a great framework of generalization, welding their cautious statement of fact into a vast and bitter indict-
ment of bourgeois society. He argued that the rise of bourgeois
capitalism meant the destruction of the relationships of feudal
society, the reduction of the small property owner to a wage
earner, dependent on the great-scale capitalist, who exploited the
labour force of the proletariat. This process inevitably created a
reservoir of unemployment and was dictated purely by the interests of private profit; it resulted in a vast extension of industrial
power, but the surplus wealth created brought no benefit to the
masses. Yet by the concentration of wealth into fewer and fewer
hands the great capitalists would bring about their own ruin;
they would become a minority in a sea of poverty and hate. In
due course the proletariat would unite, expropriate their property, and take over the means of production capitalist enterprise
had made. 'The development of modern industry cuts from
under its feet the very foundations on which it lives. It produces
its own grave diggers; its fall and the victory of the proletariat
are equally inevitable.'[1] Marx believed the revolution would
come about in the countries economically most advanced—an
international movement, uniting the workers regardless of national sentiment—and the *Communist Manifesto* concludes, 'The
communists . . . openly declare that their ends can be obtained
only by the forcible overthrow of existing social conditions. Let
the ruling classes tremble at the communist revolution; the pro-
letarians have nothing to lose but their chains. They have a
world to win. Working men of all countries, unite!'[2] This tough
appeal to force cuts across the hard-won principles of political
compromise by majority decision within the framework of a constitution, which have been worked out in prosperous social democratic societies. But its very extremity made it formidable.

The dictatorship of the proletariat, established on the ruins of
capitalism, would imply the common ownership of all natural
resources, of the factories, mines, railways, and banks; the state
planned exploitation of these resources for the benefit of all and

[1] *Communist Manifesto*, 1848.
[2] Ibid.

the distribution of wealth according to the principles of social-ism. 'All have the right and the obligation to work,' wrote Marx. 'From each according to his ability, to each according to the work performed.' All children would have a right to free education; ability wasted under the old capitalist economy would be put at the disposal of society. Marx apparently believed that, following the establishment of this social order, the power of the state, nec-essary to impose the will of the proletariat during the initial stages, would gradually become superfluous. Far from the masses being at the mercy of a bureaucracy, the full communist regime would be realized.

Such, in bare outline, was the doctrine of Communism; its predictions have not been realized but, in various altered forms, its success has been immense. The inevitability claimed for the theory made it a formidable fighting creed. Marxism has inspired a movement already a dominating factor in the modern world, the dogma and faith of a formidable contemporary politico-reli-gious doctrine. Jewish writers in the past had seen the cosmic process as an inevitable working out of a divine plan for the re-demption of Israel, and their ideas were reflected both in the doctrines of the Roman Church and of Calvinism; Marx, too, provided a clear-cut but now godless dogma, intelligible to the masses, appealing to strong motives of self-interest, and offering compensation for the injustices of the social order. Here is a movement comparable to an emotional and dogmatic religion, capable of stirring the masses to action, and aiming at plain material objectives. But the extreme rancour of Marx's writings, a reflection of the circumstances of his life and temperament, of the perennial extremism of dogmatic minds, has naturally caused a bitterness of reaction as well as of attack.

The principles of Marxism as interpreted by Lenin and Stalin were to be realized in Russia and the following were the stages of this achievement. The first, War Communism, comprising the October revolution, the defeat of the conservative counter-attack, the liquidation of the old regime, lasted from 1918 to 1921. The second, covering the period of the New Economic Policy, from 1921 to 1928; the third, marking the new revolution, was ini-tiated by Stalin, and included the three Five-Year Plans, of which the last was interrupted by the German invasion of 1941.

The first period was one of atrocious and prolonged crisis, when the iron will of Lenin built the framework of the new state. In the chaos following the collapse of the Tsarist government, the close-knit Bolshevik party was alone equal to the situation: Lenin, a Russian from the Volga with a shrewd understanding of his countrymen, had a realist's instinct for the possible. He coined the slogan 'All power to the Soviets' and these spontaneously created committees of workers and peasants—reflecting already characteristically Russian institutions—were made the basis of his new order. By ending the war at a terrible price and handing over the land to the peasants, he won the support of the most powerful elements in Russia. The vanguard of the 'class conscious proletariat,' the Bolshevik party, seized all key positions. The counter-revolution was defeated. In spite of appalling suffering, of ferocious civil war, of the famine of 1921, the regime emerged secure. By the constitution of 1923, sovereign authority was vested in the Supreme Congress of Soviets, divided into the Soviets of the Union and the Soviets of the Nationalities. And the party retained dominant political power.

By now it was clear to Lenin that the full attainment of Communism was immediately impossible. The 'New Economic Policy' was designed to stabilize a desperate situation. It reflected the need for temporary compromise, since only through the peasants could the revolution be saved. Though the fundamentals of Marxism were retained, small-scale individual enterprise and property were permitted. After the death of Lenin (1924), a conflict of principle and temperament developed between Stalin and Trotsky, both collaborators with Lenin from the beginning. Stalin, with his systematic realism, believed in the firm establishment of a practicable form of state-socialism in Russia before all other aims; Trotsky, in the priority of a Communist world revolution. By 1927 Stalin had won. With this victory it may be said that an increasingly nationalist policy triumphed over internationalist doctrine.

By the late 'twenties the political scene was already darkening in Europe. In spite of the industrial backwardness of Russia, Stalin was determined to create a state invulnerable to attack. In face of this gigantic task, he set about a second revolution, nothing less than the imposition of total planning, agricultural and industrial, on the vast resources of the Union. In the five year plans of 1928–33 and 1933–7 he carried through a staggering transformation. He brooked no compromise with the small-holding peasantry; he avoided large foreign loans which would put the country in the hands of Western creditors; through the communist party, the commissariats, and the Polit-Bureau, a ruthless policy was carried out. The problem of illiteracy was faced and diminished; in 1914 only one-fifth of the population was urban; by 1939 the proportion was one in three. It was an unprecedented revolution, made, even by Russian standards, at formidable cost.

Under the New Economic Policy, hostility between the town proletariat and the 'Kulak' peasantry had become acute. The five-year plans implied the 'liquidation' of the Kulaks, the collectivizing and mechanization of agriculture. Production was diverted to buy imported machinery for the heavy industries to make Russia more self-sufficient. There grew up nearly half a million consolidated collective farms, a modernized version of the native Russian 'artel,' all of them state property, mechanized and following centralized direction. Meanwhile, industrial construction was pushed on by foreign experts and a new generation of Russian engineers; a great proportion of the national income was reinvested in expanding enterprise which has spread far across Siberia and into Central Asia. Great armament factories were built; in spite of inefficiency and setbacks, the plan was carried through. Its relative success, despite the sacrifices it exacted and the suffering imposed by an extraordinary single-mindedness, was to be proved by the crushing reaction of the Soviet Union to the Fascist attack.

The government was determined ultimately to overtake and surpass Western capitalism. According to the Constitution of 1936, 'The economic life of the U.S.S.R. is determined and directed by the state plan of national economy for the purpose of increasing the public wealth, of steadily raising the material and cultural level of the toilers and strengthening the independence of the U.S.S.R. and its power of defence.'[1] Considerable rights of citizens to personal property in their work, income, domestic property, and inheritance were now permitted. The Union was

[1] Chapter 1, Article 11, of the Constitution of the U.S.S.R.

organized as a federal state, on the basis of the association of the Soviet Socialist Republics. Citizenship of the Union extended to all the nationalities, and for all the federal status of the constituent states, questions of war and peace, organization of defence and direction of the armed forces were in effect decided in Moscow. The central government determined the plans of the national economy, the administration of credit, of transport and communications and the basic principles of educational and health policy. Compulsory military service was universal.

Such, in essentials, was the transformation wrought, in spite of immense difficulties and suffering, over some of the most backward areas of Europe and Asia. The principles of Marxism have been modified and reinterpreted according to Russian conditions, but never abandoned. Thus the Communist revolution, scheduled by Marx to take place in the most advanced industrial societies, came about through the overthrow of a tyrannous and incapable government in a relatively primitive country by the spontaneous effort of the Russian people and through the use of the opportunity by the Communist minority. The phase of War Communism was brief; the opportunist realism of Lenin, the cold ruthlessness of his successor, at least adapted the revolution to the hard facts of the internal and external situation. The qualities of the Russian temperament, generally less individualistic than the peoples of the West, reinforced the most fundamental principles of Marxism. The public ownership of land and factories; the direction of the full power of the State, equipped with modern technology, in a centralized pervasive heavy-handed attack on poverty, illiteracy, and ill health; the revived might of the Russian armies, all owed their success to increasing popular support of what was now a typically Russian regime.

This revolution had been brought about with a brutality and at a price and pace comparable, on its vaster scale, to the revolution in Russia made by Peter the Great, and with greater effectiveness. In centralization of power, bureaucracy, and military tradition, it has come increasingly to reflect the native development of Russia. It retains a suspicious dogmatism extremely dangerous in a politically and economically interdependent world; its success presents a challenge to the basic economic and social systems of the rest of the world. In the age of the hydrogen bomb, its future, as much as that of the rest of mankind, is dependent on the establishment of world order, a fact that the showdown with the United States over Cuba underlined.

The original Communist regime had been established by force in an area unaccustomed to free parliamentary institutions, following the breakdown of the Tsarist government, and the political incapacity of the Russian liberals. Following the success of the Bolsheviks, the movement gained power in other countries, provoking fierce resistance. The challenge of Communism contributed to the rise of the Fascist dictatorships.

Over wide areas of Europe, where democratic institutions were weak, there grew up movements also employing unconstitutional force, ostensibly designed to combat international Bolshevism. Extremists of both sides were thus ready to resort to violence and disrupt the traditional fabric of the state. They scouted democratic ideas of peaceful evolution. But where the Communists were proceeding, albeit with violence and extremity, on coherent principles, the Fascist movements were irrational, glorifying war for its own sake and appealing to the baser passions. Where the aims of Communism were ultimately world-wide, Fascism drew much of its strength from a virulent nationalism; it signalized a real social collapse.

The ideas of Fascism, though still to be reckoned with, belong to a period of political nightmare, part, it is to be hoped, of a decadence best forgotten. They have demonstrated how near a great civilization may come to ruin, following the failure of constructive leadership. Nor have the economic conditions provoking the movement yet been abolished. It is necessary to analyse the causes of its power.

Italian and German Fascism and their imitators reflected national characteristics, but their fundamental ideas were similar: both Mussolini and Hitler were in some ways comparable to the proletarian despots of the full decadence of the late Roman Empire. Like the emperors, they made their way by treachery and murder. Both were the declared enemies of Christian and humane ideas, with a contempt for free institutions.

The causes of Fascism were political, economic, and psychological. The movement originated in Italy, its roots in a society long accustomed, in spite of high sophistication or perhaps because of it, to political gangsters. It spread into the Balkans and Spain and found its most virulent expression in Germany. Italian Fascism, for all its revolutionary trappings, descended directly from the tyrannies of the Renaissance, centering on the personal authority of the prince—nothing new in the South, but with a new cultural barbarity. Mussolini, a familiar Condottiere type, imposed a personal domination; the party hierarchy, the organs of state, the administrative structure of Fascism, served the will of one man; the modern apparatus of propaganda, education, economic planning, sustained an opportunist absolutism. Fascist principles and ideology were always subordinate to the exigencies of the moment. The justification of the regime was power.

It would seem Mussolini regarded the chaotic Fascist mythology as a means of political warfare; with success came a demand to systematize the myth. In 1932 Mussolini himself botched together a sequence of ideas derived in part from a misinterpretation of Nietzsche and from Sorel, a founder of syndicalism, who aimed at the forcible overthrow of bourgeois society; in part from Pareto, that crabbed and able hater of democracy. All these writers were destructive, fundamentally lacking in common sense, politically immature; but they rationalized Mussolini's lust for personal power. From the farrago of humbug with which the dictator justified a movement whose leaders were too astute for the bombast that inflamed their followers, there emerged one key idea—the glorification of the state. 'For the Fascists,' wrote Mussolini in 1932, 'all is in the state and nothing human or spiritual exists, much less has any value outside the state.'[1] The state creates its own will, its own law; it recks nothing of the sacredness of life or the worth of personality. 'Fascism is a way of life in which the individual, by abnegation of himself . . . and even by his death, realizes the entire spiritual existence which makes his value as a man.' Here is a poisonous idolatry in which thought is lost in action; it implies a deliberate and imbecile cult of violence. The Fascist 'disdains the comfortable life . . . Fascism believes neither in the possibility nor the utility of perpetual peace. . . . War alone brings to its highest tension all human energy and puts the stamp of nobility upon the people who have the courage to meet it.'[2] 'War,' proclaimed Mussolini,

[1] Article by Mussolini in the *Encyclopedia Italiana,* 1932.
[2] *Essay on Fascism,* Part II.

'is to man as maternity to a woman. . . . Imperialism is the eternal, immutable law of life.' Nothing could have been more dangerous than this nonsense, in a world of increasing scientific power.

This militant cult provided an excuse for popular destructiveness and for the imposition of 'discipline.' All societies are in practice largely controlled by a changing *élite;* Fascism sought to systematize such a domination in a party state. Freedom of thought was, naturally, destroyed; corruption sapped the sense of public responsibility; the inspiration of the movement, apart from the personal ambition of Mussolini, was the greed of his followers, the lust for destruction of a minority.

While such ideas were inflaming Italy, in spite of her ancient civilization, and spreading about Southern Europe, Germany was ripe for a revolt against the Weimar Republic. The Fascist glorification of the state at the expense of the individual, the cult of violence and herd discipline, appealed to the worst instincts of many of the German people: Hitler was destined to reinterpret the ideas of Mussolini on a more formidable and systematic scale, reinforced by the fear of encirclement and the urge for expansion, still unassuaged.

The decline of the Weimar Republic (1919–33) may be summarized as follows, for its history falls naturally into three phases. The first saw the era of confusion following the Armistice; the second, apparent recovery under Stresemann; the third, economic and political collapse—following the world crisis of 1929 and the dismissal of Brüning—the rise of Hitler and the foundation of the Third Reich. The republic, in the absence of politically responsible public opinion, was devoid of prestige and inexperienced in government, the scapegoat of humiliation and defeat; it never controlled the general staff or the great industrialists. Faced with Communist agitation and civil war, the German government tolerated independent Freikorps, paramilitary formations schooled in conflict in Bavaria and along the Baltic. The Weimar Republic thus never asserted the fundamental principle of the subordination of the armed forces to civilian control.

It was in those days Hitler emerged from obscurity and discovered the baleful gifts of leadership which were to hypnotize the German folk and lead the world to a new catastrophe. In

1923 his Munich *Putsch* failed, but in the winter of that year he employed a forced detention in the composition of *Mein Kampf*. Meanwhile, Stresemann, a cool negotiator whose frankness concealed an iron determination to redeem the fortunes of Germany, set himself a policy of apparent co-operation with the West: but it was not an accident that the renewal of German diplomatic influence in Europe was marked by an increase of tension between the Western powers. The apparent triumph of Locarno (1925) and the German entry into the League (1926) meant less than the establishment of Hindenburg as Reichspresident.

The reward of Stresemann's diplomacy was a spate of foreign investment and a lightening of reparations. A false prosperity masked the German economic position, the weakness of the republican government. But in 1929 the third period of the Weimar regime opened with the world slump. After the death of Stresemann, Brüning balanced between the foreign policy demanded by the general staff and the industrialists' desire to maintain credit abroad. Faced with growing unemployment and political violence, he could find no sure ground; dismissed in 1933 by Hindenburg, he had served his turn. For by now the external and internal situation seemed ripe for a strong hand; the manœuvres of the industrialists, the generals, and the Nazis produced the alliance of Hitler and von Papen which marked the end of the current democratic experiment in Germany. In January 1933, Hitler became Reichskanzler. The prologue to another European tragedy had begun.

The causes of the Nazi revolution are plain. The collapse of Hohenzollern leadership, which had symbolized the recent unity of the Germans; the desire for revenge; the ingrained old-fashioned militarism; the wiping out of upper-class and bourgeois security by a roaring inflation which made their capital nominal; the apparent incapacity for democratic self-government, all had left the masses looking for a political Messiah. It appears there was then in Germany no hard core of professional upper-middle-class solidarity, and the social democratic government had none of the military glamour without which the majority of Germans seemed unable to recognize leadership. We have already described the philosophical theories which had contributed in the nineteenth century to German instability, the frequent lack of political sense, the emotional escapism, which made them easy victims and abettors of Fascism. Further, following the slump of 1929, despairing men were thrown into the labour market without prospect of security or employment; criminals saw the opportunity of a career; frustrated intellectuals the possibilities of power. A rancorous if understandable envy was directed against the relatively prosperous victors of the war, and there was little sense of the degree of German responsibility for the catastrophe. The inflation, which had wiped out the fortunes of many substantial families, had shaken the confidence of the more solid elements in Germany. The younger generation could see few openings; the traditional military career was largely closed; the universities overcrowded and relatively expensive; the prospects of employment overseas negligible. Under these circumstances, the sense of collective insecurity made for hysteria; for a desire among a minority for destruction for its own sake. The majority probably believed that somehow German greatness might be reasserted by bluff without another conflict.

Here was the opportunity for the Nazi revolution. Great war industries were built up, the whole nation reorganized; the Party gave immediate remedy for unemployment, an outlet for traditional military ambition. Fantasies of racial superiority and world rule clouded the mind of German youth. Through Nazi propaganda they were living not in the twentieth century, but in a dismal world of their own; their loyalty and efficiency sacrificed to a stupid and old-fashioned lust for military domination, regardless of the older German traditions of Christianity and intelligence. Thus the Nazi movement, though originally influenced by the Italian example, was profoundly national, expressing with a bestial iteration that same theme which had menaced Europe since the rise of Prussia in the eighteenth century. That such a fate should have overtaken the land of Kant and Leibnitz, of Goethe, Bach, and Beethoven, is the measure of the aberration of the German spirit in the nineteenth and early twentieth centuries—an aberration a new generation in Western Germany have largely sloughed off by developing a sense of European and even Atlantic community.

For the rest, the landmarks in the fatal drama are familiar. In 1933 Germany withdrew from the League; in 1934 Dollfuss was butchered, and the Rohm purge showed the quality of the new rulers of Germany. In 1935 general conscription was imposed; the creation of a great air force and a mechanized army set in train. In the next year followed in swift succession the re-occupation of the Rhineland, the creation of the Berlin-Rome Axis, the pact with Japan. In 1937 the Anglo-German agreement sanctioned the building of a U-boat fleet. The rest of the story is well known; the tragedy of Austria, of Czecho-Slovakia, of Munich, of Poland. It was a natural sequence of events, following with pitiless logic from the premises of Prussian thought and practice for over two hundred years; above all from the weakness, the disunity, the lack of vision of recent Western statesmanship. So it was that the old militarism, banished only for a decade and a half, once more threw its shadow across Europe, to lift only after a Second World War.

I V

So the old problems of nationalism and economic maladjustment, inherited from the nineteenth century, and aggravated by the new proletarian Fascist and Nazi movements led by gutter élites, returned to haunt a civilization still intellectually and technologically brilliant. For throughout the post-war years the tempo of material progress surpassed even that of the nineteenth century, and with every invention the complexity and interdependence of the world's economy increased. First, the automobile had revolutionized transport; then followed the conquest of the air. Radio transformed the possibilities of the diffusion of knowledge, and, for good and ill, the possibilities of propaganda. Finally, the scientific outlook was profoundly altered by the discovery of the structure of the atom, destined to give rise to the shattering revolution implied by the harnessing of nuclear energy in 1945. Against a background of increasing social instability, a new range of historical appreciation and humanistic scholarship was achieved; a brilliant if disillusioned and introspective literature continued to flourish in the West.

For in the perspective of world history the second German bid for world domination was destined to prove belated. World history had, indeed, passed beyond the stage of European power politics. The extra-European resources that had defeated Napoleon and Wilhelm II defeated Hitler. Political and economic power, indeed, was already shifting beyond the oceans, beyond Europe, and the new structure of the United Nations Organization was at least to reflect this reality.

Yet, in the 'thirties, the prospect had appeared black. Democratic institutions had failed over most of Southern, Central, and Eastern Europe; there was profound distrust between the liberal democracies and the Soviet Union; in the Far East imperialist Japan was a formidable ally to the Fascist tyrannies in Europe; the United States was still unwilling to face the commitments demanded by her own security.

Yet, when the challenge came, the forces reflecting the predominant social and economic drift of the twentieth century combined in overwhelming power. The might of America and the British Commonwealth, of the Soviet Union and the European resistance, proved to outweigh the German advantage of position on interior lines. In alliance with the U.S.S.R., the manpower, the wealth, the technical ability of the Western Democracies swung slowly into line; leaders, born and bred in the tradition of constitutional government, took over control of the democratic commonwealths and again the initiative passed to the peoples whose civilization embodied the more humane traditions of the Continent.

It has already been observed that the three great problems inherited from the nineteenth century were nationalism, economic dislocation, and the race in armaments. The recurrent crises of the third problem contributed to the solution of the first and second; and it is profoundly significant that the three great powers whose combined land, sea, and air power crushed Hitler's attempt at world domination, had in their different ways gone farthest to solve the problem of nationalism, the main problem from the nineteenth century. All, after their fashion, were supranational commonwealths, including immense and diverse populations on a world-wide scale.

Further, the second outstanding problem inherited from the nineteenth century, the problem of economic maladjustment, had been faced radically in the Soviet Union; in the United States by

Roosevelt's New Deal; and, characteristically, in Great Britain by unadvertised but fundamental change. The demands of the Second World War gave rise to a new standard of planning and execution in the complexity and scale of great combined operations: the range of high strategy was reflected in the world organization of U.N.O. Unlike the League, this organization was underwritten by the United States and, after a fashion, by the Soviet Union, now the only power of comparable influence. But their failure to cooperate has hitherto limited its effectiveness.

So the crisis of the Second World War brought about a new attempt at world leadership, backed by new technical power. The rulers of the U.S.S.R. had never lacked realism; the Western democracies, forced again into a native efficiency, recovered the spirit defective leadership had obscured. And, indeed, for all its imperfections, their way of life embodies, as has been apparent, some sense of that broadening civilization to which the nineteenth century was tending, but of which the realization was cut short by economic and popular nationalism, now finding its most dangerous expression in Germany. That way of life had, moreover, long been expanding into a world influence, and had won an extra-European backing at a time of great need, so that Europe was given, as it were, another chance. How far that chance has been taken, and the circumstances under which the choice can be made, will now be considered.

CHAPTER 11

POST-WAR EUROPE AND THE DISMANTLING OF EMPIRE

In the Great War of 1914–18 the international anarchy which had cut across the increasing economic and cultural interdependence of Europe had brought the continent to catastrophe. The liberal experiment had been jeopardized, for it had failed to extend the rule of law into international affairs, and its social progress had been shown to be precarious. The barbaric reality of total and mechanized war had thrust itself into this high civilization.

Anyone unversed in politics might have expected that the horror of war apparent in 1919 would have inspired a creative reconstruction, recognizing the fundamental common interests of Europe. On the contrary, the momentum of old mentality and institutions carried on, and nationalist hatreds were reinforced by fear and the desire for revenge. The enfranchised masses, far from promoting international understanding, often proved more rabidly nationalistic than their former masters; and where parliamentary institutions broke down and the old establishments were wiped out by inflation, gutter élites took charge, riding tigers of nationalism and social revolt. With singular prescience, Foch had termed the Versailles settlement a 'twenty years armistice', and the record of 1919–39 has already been described. We are here concerned with the sequel after the Second World War.

The second conflict had mobilized resources and spread devastation even more widely than the first, and on both sides of the
world. Air power had wiped out whole cities and massacred non-
combatants by the thousands; by 1944 many of the greatest German cities had been reduced to rubble; the devastation in Russia
had been colossal; rockets had fallen on London, and in the following year, the first atomic bomb defeated Japan. When the
Soviet Union, too, acquired nuclear weapons, a new era, with its
'balance of terror' between super-powers had begun.

Europe had thus become the battleground where gigantic
extra-European powers based in North America and Eurasia had
combined to crush Germany but, in spite of Roosevelt's illusions,
were united over little else. With victory, a 'cold war' developed,
cutting across the 'liberated' but prostrate continent, and the
Soviet Union was left predominant over all Poland, over Eastern Germany, Czechoslovakia, Rumania, Bulgaria and Albania,
as well as over the Baltic states, already occupied before the second conflict. Of these, only Greece, after a civil war, remained in
the Western orbit. Austria was later neutralized by agreement,
and Jugoslavia, at odds with what was left of the Eastern bloc,
gradually resumed a wary relationship with the Atlantic powers.
Meanwhile most of Europe, including Great Britain, was now
economically crippled and the exhausted belligerents were only
saved from bankruptcy and social collapse by the generous im-
provisation of Marshall Aid. And but for American military
power, the Soviet Union might even had tried to overrun the
West. Sweden, heavily armed, had preserved her neutrality, but
Denmark and Norway were vulnerable and Finland, defeated by
the Russians in 1940, maintained only a precarious independence. The dictatorships in Spain and Portugal, the former established in 1939, with the nationalist victory in the civil war, were
in a more favourable strategic position, though all the West was
in fact dependent on the power of the United States.

No such situation had occurred in all the centuries of Western European history. The Mongol invasions had been ephemeral and the Turkish threat contained; though the rulers of Prussia and the Austro-Hungarian empire had been no friends of the
Western maritime states, they had recognized a common interest
in keeping the Eurasian Russia power out of Central Europe,

and the French and British had combined in backing the moribund Turkish regime against it.

Now all the barriers in Eastern Europe were down. Such were the conditions on the continent, already summed up in 1946 by Churchill's phrase that an 'Iron Curtain' had been drawn across it. Further, the British Empire was being swiftly dismantled into a politically amorphous Commonwealth which even its members found hard to define, and the French Empire was disintegrating, while colonial wars in Indo-China and Algeria would blight French internal politics until the 1960's. The Dutch Empire, too, was all but lost, and the Belgian regime in the Congo, much more precarious than it looked, was destined by 1960 to go down in massacre and confusion. So rapid was the collapse of nineteenth century European world domination following the political suicide of the great European nation states.

The reaction in Western Europe was naturally profound. Haunted by memories of mechanized carnage and by the ruins of devastated cities, many of the younger generation, who had known only war and occupation, demanded a new deal. The old political parties seemed discredited either because, as in Italy they succumbed to Fascism, or as in France became tainted with collaboration. The resistance groups of the Left were working for a more radical international solidarity. The Catholic groups of the Right tried to promote their own version of better international or supranational order, and evoked the ancient tradition of a united Christendom. The European universities, liberated from Nazi domination, reaffirmed their old fraternity, and politicians, many of them with genuinely idealistic motives, were trying to promote various forms of European integration. The American saviours and masters of the Western continent, often unable to fathom the depth of the historical prejudices of the old world, also encouraged the idea of European union, even of federation, as something they had achieved themselves in a very different context. And of course the most steady and effective backing for the new policy came from big business, for it was obvious that only in markets comparable to those of the United States could European industry provide the employment and growing productivity that alone would make the existing order viable. The obsolescence of national tariff barriers, customs and exchange

controls in an age of jet aircraft, super highways, and the modernized railroads, which on the Continent were replacing those
destroyed in the war and were making European nations interdependent in reconstruction, was increasingly apparent. Thus, many
different, even incongruous elements combined to demand a political and economic structure or infra-structure that was larger
than the nation state. With this backing, the idea of Western
European union won surprisingly rapid success. Though it soon
ran into political difficulties and even became temporarily bogged
down, its acceptance and partial realization in little more than
two decades has been remarkable, considering that twice in this
century the greatest European powers have been at each other's
throats.

If this process continues, it seems likely that the nineteenth- and
early twentieth-century phase of European centralized sovereign
nation states, piling up great armaments and imposing conscription on their subjects and manœuvring without regard to any
superior authority, will have proved relatively short, and that the
Continent will return to historically more normal conditions.
Graeco-Roman civilization had been cosmopolitan, and, for all its
practical limitations, mediaeval Christendom had been culturally
and socially on a continental scale. Even the sovereign monarchies which had emerged in the sixteenth and seventeenth centuries and reached their climax in the eighteenth, had tempered
their conflicts in a common dynastic interest, and the culture of
the Renaissance and the Enlightenment had been as cosmopolitan as that of the Middle Ages. Now, before the consequences of
the unbridled nationalism and belligerence of the nineteenth-
and early twentieth-century nation states and empires, Western
Europe was being forced by the realities of modern political and
economic power to unite itself for survival in terms of an Atlantic community, while Eastern Europe, cut off from the West in a
new way, was being forced into a new integration of its own.

The landmarks of this process will now be considered, first
during its early phase of success in the West when the fear of
Russian attack promoted close collaboration, then in its phases
of political set-back and economic advance through the Common
Market. The entire project, in any realistic view, was always dependent on the United States, and it grew up within the frame-

work of the North Atlantic Treaty Organization, called into being by the continuing division of Europe and the threat from the East. Stalin was long the principal architect of the unification of Western Europe and the logic of modern industrial production its main force, though an authentic European feeling had emerged from the years of resistance and liberation.

II

Anyone coming from Atlantic Europe or America who in the late 'forties entered the still devastated Ruhr, formerly the heart of industrial Germany, or observed the stark ruins of Münster, Köln or Hamburg, famous European cities, saw a devastation as great as that committed by Hitler's armies in Russia. The area was pervaded with the stench of death; and scraps of greenery, struggling to maintain themselves on what appeared to be slag heaps made the picture more macabre. And still, as these words are written, the blocks and entanglements of the Berlin wall mark the division of Western and Eastern Germany, and steel helmetted sentries are still vigilant to kill.

Such, against a landscape of utter devastation, was the fate of Hitlerite Germany. Indeed the horror that Hitler inspired had been so great that the victors seriously considered whether German heavy industry should be permanently abolished and the country deliberately reduced to a predominantly agricultural economy.

In the event following the partition which reflected the mutual distrust of the two super powers, the Western Germans achieved an extraordinary and rapid comeback; and the policy of the Soviet Union led to the opposite result from that intended —a surprisingly swift alliance between the West Germans and their former enemies in the West. It was considered that only with German manpower could the West present a credible front in 'conventional' warfare, and that only in the context of a United Western Europe and an Atlantic alliance would the Germans remain 'good' Germans. Even the French, whose experiences in three great wars, 1870–71, 1914–18 and 1939–45, had given them ample cause for fear and distrust, were ready to pay that price for reinsurance, and the British in their insular way were ready to forget old enmities and return to civilian concerns. The Italians, whose part in the Axis alliance had hardly been disinterested, were ready, with their usual realism, to turn the occasion to account, to 'work their passage home', as the phrase then went; and the Dutch and Belgians were anxious to promote a reconciliation that would prevent their countries from again becoming a battleground, and to provide their economies with wider scope. Thus, in Western Europe, with the Iberian dictatorships concerned with their own affairs but hostile to communism, the former continental belligerents came together in a common fear of attack from the East, synchronized, perhaps with internal revolt. And this reconciliation was fostered by the United States.

The British public, on the other hand, remained largely indifferent, while their Foreign Office maintained its traditional view that the interests of Great Britain demanded that no one power should so dominate the continent that it could become a threat, and that this threat could be as real from a Europe led by Germany and France as from one dominated by Napoleon or Hitler. The alternative to this traditional policy, which was to enter a European union, economic and political, then appeared so radical that it was discarded; and in any case public opinion would then have rejected the novel commitment with all its implications for the Commonwealth. Thus in the opinion of advocates of European Union, Great Britain, then at a height of prestige, threw away the leadership she might then have had for the taking. To the historian, the British behaved according to type, for they had long been insular towards the continent, and if not insular, had their eyes on extra-European oceanic economic and political horizons. Only with the final dismantling of the empire would the continental commitment seem more realistic, and then only in the context of an Atlantic alliance or even union. The British had emerged triumphantly from a war, in which they had been involved through continental entanglements, only through their oceanic power and their special relationship with the other Anglo-Saxon states. The lesson seemed clear: no wonder they played for time.

III

Meanwhile, radical changes had taken place in Eastern Europe, where a much more rapid integration was going on. Following decisions made at Teheran and Yalta, when Stalin's objectives had been little understood and the war with Japan seemed to make Soviet collaboration in the Far East important, the Soviet Union had swamped the ramshackle buffer states created by the Treaty of Versailles both to contain Germany and to insulate the West from Eurasia. Here, even more than in the West, the nations state had long been becoming unviable; and, in spite of militant popular nationalism, the regimes constructed out of the ruins of the Ottoman and Austro-Hungarian empires were less deeply rooted than the great maritime nations. Poland, Czechoslovakia, Hungary, Roumania, Bulgaria and Albania all became 'people's republics' under Soviet power, and only Jugoslavia reasserted its independence. Most important of all, the partition of Germany was stereotyped when the Soviet-occupied area became the East German republic, cut off from the Western Germans and linked with the West only by jointly occupied Berlin and the corridor that led into it.

The facts of eastern Central European history already described will alert the reader to the profound significance of these decisions. The maritime areas of the European peninsula, with their access to the ocean and their widespread prosperity, had long been sheltered from Eurasian attack by the military autocracies of the Eastern marches. In an area which, save for the Bohemian massif and the Carpathians, is devoid of natural frontiers, the mediaeval regimes fluctuated in a way that has been recorded. It will be recalled that the Polish-Lithuanian state had dominated a vast area, far into Eastern Russia; the Hungarians and the Czechs had created flourishing mediaeval kingdoms, and in the Balkans, the Bulgar empires of the Āsen tsars and the Serb Empire of Stephen Dushan had flourished before being overwhelmed by the Ottoman Turks. The attempt of the Treaty of Versailles to revive the political power of these peoples had been historically intelligible; but in the twentieth century their independence could only be sustained by Western power. Further, if to the Western states these peoples had appeared allies—in particular since the Poles, Lithuanians and Hungarians had been militant Catholics against the Orthodox Christians of the East— to the Russians they had long appeared as aggressors, while the Bulgars and Southern Slavs of the Balkans had sometimes appeared potential allies in a pan-Slav expansion.

The division of Europe was not, therefore, due mainly to the doctrine of world revolution which it was the mission of the Soviet Union to realize, but more to the reversion of the Soviet rulers to the fears and ambitions of the tsars. From the Russian point of view, their Western neighbours, Teutonic Knights, Lithuanians, Poles and Swedes, had long been dangerous enemies; and the memories of the Napoleonic invasion, and now of two devastating German assaults, made them play for what they thought would be safety, since it was inconceivable to their rulers that the genuine offers of compromise made by the Americans could be sincere. Against this historical background, the Soviet Union, which had already mopped up the Baltic states, moved heavily into Central Europe.

Their attempt to integrate this notoriously unmanageable area into a Eurasian super-state was ruthless; and, though it provoked mounting resistance, it was successful at least in terms of military power. While Western European integration was mainly economic, tentative and relatively slow, often the work of cosmopolitan pressure groups influencing national governments, in Eastern Central Europe it was politically imposed. Soviet-orientated governments controlled by the local Communist parties were installed; the Soviet armies continued to occupy all the ground gained. But during the year 1947–48, as their side of the bargain with the West, the Russians restrained the Communist parties in France under Thorez and in Italy under Togliatti from further subversion. Within this political framework, to be formalized by 1954 in the Warsaw Pact, economic integration proved difficult, though it was driven hard. The Stalin regime tried to unite the area in a vast economic bloc subject to planning on the Soviet pattern, with the usual emphasis on heavy industry at the expense of agriculture. Though the East Germans and the Czechs had advanced industries, Poland, Hungary, Roumania, Bulgaria and Albania were all peasant countries, recalcitrant to an urban and mechanized society. And it was fear of economic exploitation that, as early as 1949, led Jugoslavia's Tito to break with the Kremlin.

Indeed, that year marked the turn of the tide of Stalinist expansion. The Americans had at last been alerted; Truman adopted a more realistic policy than Roosevelt, and in 1948–49 the Russian bluff over the blockade of Berlin was called. After the death of Stalin in 1953 the Kremlin turned to more flexible tactics, though its long-term strategy remained consistent. But although in 1956 after the Twentieth Party Congress of that year Krushchev, now on better terms with the Jugoslavs and following a de-Stalinization policy, was admitting that different economic roads might lead to the same objective, in the same year an Hungarian nationalist rising had to be crushed by the Red Army.

By 1958 Khrushchev set new objectives for a seven-year plan (1959–65), which would so integrate Eastern Europe that it would be irreversible. In the following year currencies were made convertible within the Eastern bloc; and within the limits of overall policy, the governments, to fulfill their objective, were given a freer hand. But still, in 1968, the Czech resistance, like the Hungarian twelve years earlier, was occasioned in part by the sacrifice of the advanced Czech economy to the rest of the enormous area. Again, and at an even heavier price in external reputation, the Kremlin was driven to military repression.

So, with the break up of the Habsburg Empire and a brief phase of national independence, underwritten by the West as an insurance against both Russia and Germany, the successor states in Poland, Czechoslovakia and Hungary, along with the East German people's Republic, Roumania and Bulgaria, were incorporated into a Russian-dominated Eurasian regime, including territories even larger than those of the North American continent, with global objectives far beyond those of the peoples concerned. In the long conflict, predominantly between Teuton and Slav, the Russians had tried to protect themselves in the traditional way against further attack and were reaching out for traditional objectives in the Balkans and the Levant. They were also now more directly aware of the wealth and industrial power of the maritime West as possible objectives. Further following mounting concern with the potential super-power of China, since 1949 dominated by Mao Tse-tung, the rulers of the Soviet Union were even more determined to keep control of their frontiers in the West. And among these heavy commitments, the division of Germany, with West Berlin deep in Eastern controlled territory, presented the worst problem created by the collapse of the wartime coalition.

Liberated from Nazi Germany, the European continent had thus been sharply divided into spheres of influence between non-European super-powers; the West indirectly dependent on the United States; the East under direct domination. So little had the lessons of the Second World War been assimilated, and so ineffective had been the attempt at world order made through the United Nations, that all that had emerged was an old style balance of power, now changing with the advent of nuclear weapons into a balance of terror.

I V

The Western process of integration now demands more detailed attention. By 1948 the Soviet attempt to blockade Berlin and gain ground in the Levant through Greece and Turkey had made it plain that the old collaboration had been replaced by a cold war. The reaction in Western Europe, as already observed, took two forms, political and economic, and in contrast to the situation in Eastern Europe the latter proved more successful. The development of both these aspects of integration will now be surveyed.

By 1948 the Treaty of Dunkirk between France and Great Britain, made the year before, had been expanded into the Brussels Treaty including the Low Countries and directed against aggression from any quarter. By 1949 a more comprehensive deterrent was devised. The United States and Canada were now formally included in the defence of Western Europe in an Atlantic Pact; exactly the commitment refused by the United States after the First World War. American isolationism was now officially abandoned, for it was obvious that if Western Europe were overrun the United States itself would be endangered. By 1950 a North Atlantic Treaty Organization included the United States, Canada, Great Britain, France, Italy, Denmark, Norway, Holland, Belgium and Luxemburg, and strategically important Iceland and Portugal, as well as Greece and Turkey. By 1954, by an extension of the Brussels Treaty, even the West German Federal republic would be included. Sweden and Switzerland remained neutral, relying on their own defences; Finland and Austria, by international agreement. Only Spain was thought too reactionary to be countenanced, though in fact American bases were established there.

This alliance, which created a whole infra-structure of political and military consultation, looked stronger than it might have been in practice; but it served its turn as part of the supreme deterrent of the nuclear bomb, then the monopoly of the United States. It was an aspect of the global commitment now accepted by the Truman government to contain what they believed to be a concerted communist threat in Europe and, by 1950, in the Far East in Korea.

The West Europeans were also economically rehabilitated. The concurrent American commitment of Marshall Aid, also offered to but rejected by the Soviet bloc, now financed a European Recovery Programme (E.R.P.) There was a swift economic revival, most marked in Western Germany, and reflected in the rise to power of governments further to the Right. Christian Democrat parties, led by Adenauer in West Germany and by de Gasperi in Italy, with powerful Catholic influence behind them, promoted closer European union: the existing social order was to be saved by a reaffirmation of Christian values in social welfare and rationalized by cosmopolitan big business. And convinced 'Europeans' now began to develop institutions which would foster the habit of collaboration and promote a European outlook. In 1948, at a Congress of Europe at the Hague, Churchill had given the European Movement his backing, though the insular Attlee government that had ousted his administration in 1945 had not been interested. In 1949–51 a Council of Europe was set up, with a Council of Ministers and a European Assembly elected by the existing parliaments. So the tide of events, political and economic, carried the European idea a surprisingly long way.

Such was the political framework improvised in the West within ten years of the end of the war in Europe. It had been brought about by the logic of events, since the European idea fitted the facts. It had followed on the polarization of power between the United States and the Soviet Union which had divided the Continent into rival spheres of influence and which had, in effect, superseded European freedom of action not only in the East, but in the West. A global power struggle had made the old national sovereignties and the old rivalries obsolete.

They were also made obsolete by economic facts. The turning point in the recovery of Western Europe had been Marshall Aid, and, parallel with the formation of political institutions, the Schuman plan had devised a functional rather than a directly political approach. In 1951–2, mainly on the initiative of the Christian Democrat governments, a European Coal and Steel Community (E.C.S.C.) was set up. It was directed by a High Authority with direct powers over the industries in all the countries concerned. It was joined by France, West Germany, Italy and Benelux, who agreed that over a five year period barriers in these basic commodities were to be abolished.

Following a phase of political frustration when, in 1954, the French refused to ratify the agreement made to join the European Defence Community, the next decisive step was also economic. It was made in 1957, again by the Six: France, Western Germany, Italy, Holland, Belgium and Luxemburg. The Treaty of Rome now created a European Economic Community (E.E.C.) and a European Atomic Energy Community (Euratom). In the following year a European Parliamentary Assembly met at Strasbourg with Robert Schuman as its president. The objective was nothing less than to create a European Common Market, as barriers to the movement of goods, capital and labour were abolished, communications were rapidly improved and an economy emerged of modern and continental scope. Thus a functional economic integration proved more constructive than political moves. Though in theory national sovereignty was still paramount, the Council and the Commission now set up had important powers; all the more so because they were designed to harmonize general policy with the essential interests of the states concerned, within the common structure.

So, by 1957, the most constructive move towards uniting Western Europe had been taken. But it had exacted its price. The British, as already recorded, were suspicious of moves to unite continental Europe which might create precisely the situation which they had for generations been accustomed to fear—a power stronger than themselves with the resources of the whole area behind it. Nor could they bring themselves to give up the amount of economic independence demanded by the Treaty of Rome. By 1959 they had formed a European Free Trade Association (E.F.T.A.) which included the Scandinavian states, Austria, Portugal and Switzerland, and known, in contrast to the Six, as the outer Seven. France meanwhile, since de Gaulle's advent to power in 1958, had been showing a different attitude towards the Common Market. Her European policies were no longer dictated by her economic interests or by a general commitment to the building of United Europe, but rather by de Gaulle's archaic interpretation of France's national interests. In the agricultural crisis in the Common Market in 1962, France's farming lobby, long accustomed to holding their government to ransom, seemed, with de Gaulle's support, to want to do the same to the whole Community.

Indeed, when in 1966, the French even formally withdrew from N.A.T.O. itself, intent on asserting their freedom of action, they were apparently hankering to lead a Europe strong enough to be a third force, independent of the 'Anglo-Saxons'. This ambition also inspired the French veto, when the English, belatedly convinced that the Six would succeed, abandoned their centuries-old policy towards the Continent and applied for membership of the Common Market. In 1969, after the fall of de Gaulle, the French appear more realistic.

Such at the end of the 'sixties, has been the chequered but substantial progress in Western Europe towards transcending its ancient rivalries and resisting subversion from the East. During the two decades since the Iron Curtain had descended over Central and Eastern Europe, the progress towards Western integration seemed slow to those who lived through it and, in particular, to Americans, accustomed to their own Federal Union which covers an even larger and more diverse area; but to an historian, the progress has been surprisingly swift, considering the deep-rooted conflict of interests in Europe and beyond, so long taken for granted between the greatest states, and the memories of mutual slaughter and occupation common to most of them. So strong already have proved the technological and economic facts of the mid-twentieth century, facts which are making nonsense of the divisions of national sovereign states. The problem today looks not so much how to prevent the Western European nations destroying each other, but how to reconcile a new cosmopolitan order with the internal liberties and variety of culture and way of life which they have achieved. It would be a heavy price for peace and prosperity if Western Europe were to be dominated by a cosmopolitan technocracy, who would be unlikely to live up to the visions that Saint-Simon had of them in the early nineteenth century. And these dangers are most likely to be avoided if Western Europe can be organized not as an inward looking 'little Europe', but as part of an Atlantic community with much wider horizons and, on balance, more successful political experience and traditions.

V

The division of Europe by an 'Iron Curtain' and the economic and political dependence of the former colonial powers on the United States went along with a dismantling of the Western European empires. This abdication, voluntary or forced, changed the face of world politics; but it did not undo the permanent transformation of the outer world made by West Europeans since the sixteenth century. In the Americas and Australasia, nations of European descent have now been long established, and even if the political mark left by Europeans in Asia and Africa was more superficial, their economic and cultural influences have been decisive. The withdrawal or eviction of the colonial powers could not undo this lasting influence, and even resistance to it had been carried on in terms of the European political slogans of socialism, nationalism, and democracy.

Far the greatest of the West European empires had been the British. But Canada, Australia, New Zealand and South Africa were all now sovereign states; and India, for a long time far the most important dependency and the strategic base of British power in the East, also became independent.

Acting according to their political principles, and discarding political ties that had become unworkable to preserve economic interests, the post-war Labour government had decided on an immediate transfer of power. In 1947 it was made, at the price of the partition of the sub-continent between Hindu India and Muslim Pakistan and of the mutual massacres that followed. By 1950 India was a republic, though, like Pakistan, it remained within the British Commonwealth. Ceylon and later Malaya, followed this example, though Burma chose a different course.

In the Middle East British interests had long been compromised by the mounting conflict between Jews and Arabs following the establishment of a national home for the Jews, when, in 1922, Great Britain had been the Mandatory power under the League of Nations in Palestine. Following the British withdrawal in 1949, a full-scale war had resulted in the establishment of the embattled state of Israel. And although during the Second World War Egypt had been held and used as the springboard for the decisive counter-attack in North Africa, by 1954 the British had agreed to evacuate even the base at Suez guarding the Canal, which had, in fact, lost its strategic importance. Then, in 1956, the Anglo-French expedition designed to bring down Nasser's government proved a fiasco, a last gesture of the old imperialism. Discountenanced by the United States and threatened by the Soviet Union, the British and French withdrew, leaving Egypt a focus of Arab nationalism and another area in which the super powers could prosecute the cold war.

The British also swiftly disembarrassed themselves of their other commitments in Africa. In 1956 the Sudan became independent of the Anglo-Egyptian condominium, in 1957 the Gold Coast colony was transformed into the state of Ghana, and by 1960 Nigeria, the most successful of the West African administrations, gained independence, to lapse by the end of the decade into tribal warfare. In East Africa, Uganda and Kenya became independent, and Tanganyka became the republic of Tanzania. The Rhodesian Federation having broken down, Northern Rhodesia became independent as Zambia, and Nyasaland as Malawi. But after the British government had refused to allow Southern

Rhodesia to become independent without some guarantee of eventual majority rule, the government of Southern Rhodesia declared unilateral independence of the British. For the Southern Rhodesians, followed the South African policy of maintaining white supremacy rather than admitting a black African majority to the franchise and coming to equal terms with the new states of black Africa, if necessary, at the sacrifice of the interests of the Europeans concerned. So, by the end of the 'sixties, the British Empire had been dismantled. But the Commonwealth survived, linked formally by the Crown and informally by economic and social interests.

The dismantling of the other great European empire was less realistic. The French had always pursued a centralizing policy, where the British had practised devolution, and disasters in Europe had made them the more determined to assert their waning power. In 1945 they had sent troops to repress revolt in Algeria and, two years later, in Madagascar; and although Tunisia gained independence in 1956, and Morocco soon after, by 1954 the French soon had a full scale war in Algeria on their hands. Here a large indigenous European population had long been settled, and passions were unloosed in French home politics which could have led to civil war. It took de Gaulle, with his control of the army, to make a settlement and to formulate the idea of a French Community to which those areas who wished do so could adhere.

Since 1946 the French had also become involved in a gruelling war in the Far East. Indo-China had escaped the full rigours of Japanese occupation since the French authorities had adhered to the Vichy regime, and Laos and Cambodia had gained independence without war; but in what would become Vietnam, a militant nationalist movement had emerged, and in the north under Ho Chi Minh it had Communist backing. Though the metropolitan French government tried to come to terms with Ho Chi Minh, the French army in Indo-China would have none of him. A jungle war developed. By 1950, after the advent of the Communists to power in Peking, the Korean war had forced the Americans to intervene in the Far East, and the French briefly obtained American aid. But by 1954 they came to spectacular disaster at Dien Bien Phu, and, in the following year, the area was divided into North Vietnam, controlled by the Communists, and South Vietnam controlled by a government more amenable to the West. Thus, like Korea, this part of French colonial Indo-China became a battle ground in which the 'cold war' hotted up, and in which, during the 'sixties the United States became heavily involved to prevent a Communist take-over deeper into South-east Asia. Such was the legacy of French colonialism in the Far East.

The Dutch Far Eastern empire, too, ended in conflict. Following the withdrawal of the Japanese, the Indonesian nationalists demanded complete independence, and by 1949, after four years of intermittent war, they got it, though the Dutch still retained New Guinea. The Belgian colonial empire in Africa also disintegrated. In 1960 the Belgians, who had made no attempt to raise an African elite to whom to hand over control, threw in their hand, in the hope, perhaps, of retaining the rich mining area of Katanga at the price of letting the rest go. International Communism started to fish in these troubled waters and only the intervention of the United Nations restored a precarious order. So, by the end of the 'sixties only the Portuguese, the most archaic and undeveloped of the African colonial empires, remained apparently intact in Angola and Mozambique; since, said their rulers these areas were constitutionally an integral part of Portugal, no colonialism was involved. Spain also retained minor territories. Thus, in a swift debacle, the European colonial empires were largely abandoned. The British felt they had best keep the good will of their former dependents; their ties with Canada and Australasia and, economically, with South Africa, remained close, and for the emancipated territories, the Commonwealth still offered economic and cultural advantages. But in Africa the legacy of bitterness was perpetuated by the social problem of South Africa, economically far the most advanced area on the continent. Here white settlement was so old that those of European descent had as much standing as Africans as anyone else; but this white minority to whom the main development of the country was due, held to a precarious policy, directly contrary to the political trend in the rest of Africa, and which, in their own eyes, appeared justified by the political and economic conditions in the states under black African control.

The dismantling of empire had its effects on Europe, but they were less adverse than might have been supposed. Following the massive emigrations of the nineteenth century, the more enterprising or the more desperate people had long looked to the Americas more than to the empires, while the administrative and military careers now closed only concerned a minority. In Great Britain, in particular, in spite of the racial ties with Canada and Australasia, the insular mass of the people had never set much store by the empire, which had been much more the concern of the upper classes, the City, the professional army and the navy. The majority were now preoccupied with their own affairs; anxious to obtain social security and the benefits of a welfare state established in an adverse economic climate, and concerned with dismantling the British system of class, if only to substitute other forms of inequality. But the more enterprising élites were still looking to America, Canada, and Australasia, or advocating the entry of Great Britain into the Common Market. The dismantling of empire had gone far to achieve its economic objective, the maintenance of trade and cultural contacts within the Commonwealth.

Thus, in the perspective of world history, the political disruption of the Western European colonial empires did not diminish their most important legacy. English and French are world languages, and will continue to be so; as Classical Antiquity set standards for the peoples who succeeded it, so European civilization has profoundly influenced the former colonial peoples, in particular those in South America and Africa. And the revolutionary and world-wide influence of an originally Western European science and technology is ineradicable.

VI

Since the Second World War, this scientific knowledge has further transformed the prospects of mankind. The archaic power politics which still threaten destruction, are a legacy of nineteenth-century political theories of anarchic nationalism, 'inevitable' class war, and age-old habits of violence in the use of public power. Yet so frightful are the consequences of the hydrogen bomb that, during the Cuban crisis, both sides recoiled from the encounter, and in the cold war the balance of terror has been held. Europe, unlike Vietnam, has not been the scene of open warfare, though it still contains a dangerous frontier. With the rise of the gigantic Chinese power in the Far East, the eyes of both America and Russia are bound to turn in its direction, and it would appear in the interests of both super-powers to maintain at least the *status quo* in Europe. The discrepancy between the high standard of living in the economically advanced areas of the world, in which North America and Western Europe take the first place, and the poverty of teeming millions in the under-developed countries outside the North Atlantic areas will also lead to other joint preoccupations. But Western Europeans, at least, would seem to have learnt the lesson that internecine conflict is impracticable; and, if they can set their own house in better order, they may well have a major contribution to make to the global problems that lie ahead; for in spite of twentieth-century catastrophes their civilization has been the most dynamic and influential in the world.

CHAPTER III

EUROPE IN WORLD HISTORY

Such, in broad outline, has been the political and economic sequel to the Second World War. The climax of conflict and disruption, and even the division of Europe, led in the West to a reaffirmation of the ancient and historically predominant tradition of a common civilization, distinctive in relation to the rest of the world. And this swift rehabilitation, if at first based on external aid, has demonstrated great resilience and vitality. Indeed, the conflict itself called out singular powers of organization, ingenuity, and endurance, and often showed the effectiveness of a 'planned' economy in a new way. It also occasioned revolutionary discoveries that, paralleled and developed by American inventiveness, technology, and resourcefulness, first led to the epoch-making release of nuclear power. This achievement, like the development of jet-propulsion and the exploitation of penicillin, derive mainly from European research occasioned by the war. And though it would be premature here to assess current developments, political and economic disasters have obviously not inhibited the creativeness of the many-sided European culture described in these pages. Whatever its political record in the first half of the twentieth century, Western Europe remains dynamic.

II

In the light of this survey, it is now time to consider just what are the qualities that have combined to make this civilization so decisive in science, politics, economic enterprise, intellect, and the arts.

The most original aspect of modern European civilization is at once apparent. It has been the practical grasp and drive that have distinguished the West since the sixteenth century, and which, with the industrial revolution, created the first possibility of a world civilization. This initiative, so characteristically European, may reflect the prevalent family structure. In contrast to societies organized into extended kinship groups or even castes, the European family structure places responsibility for its well-being and advancement on one individual who may thus be impelled to enterprise and innovation. The mediaeval Chinese were technologically more advanced than the Europeans, and the Hindu and Muslim civilizations were long more advanced in mathematics and medicine, but the early modern Europeans could not only invent, they could follow up. They formulated and professionalized a new scientific method and technology and applied them to the deliberate exploitation of the world. The method foreshadowed by Copernicus and Galileo, by Bacon and Descartes, and followed up by Newton and Darwin, has since led to the increasing control of environment by a revolutionary understanding of physics, chemistry, biology and medicine, an understanding which has now transcended all frontiers and created a world-wide scientific community going far beyond Europe, which began it. In contrast to the conservatism of all previous civilizations, Europeans had deliberately set out to change the world. Here is the most original and the most decisive influence, which has altered the whole material aspect of the human condition, enabling mankind increasingly to shape the world and even get outside it. And if political ideas and institutions have so far lagged behind this inventiveness that it now threatens destruction, we now at least have the prospect of dealing with the poverty that still enslaves half mankind. That this prospect even exists is due originally to European initiative.

Europeans, moreover, had been the first people to explore the whole world. The Phoenicians had traded beyond Gibraltar and to the Indian Ocean; the Indians of Maurya and Gupta times had voyaged to Indo-China and Indonesia, the Chinese had navigated their own seas and penetrated to Southern Arabia and the Philippines, and the Arabs had exploited the monsoons of the Indian ocean and established a far flung trade in mediaeval times; but it was not until the Portuguese had rounded the Cape and outflanked the massive land powers of Asia, Columbus had discovered Central America, Magellan and Drake had circumnavigated the Globe, and Cook had explored the Pacific and Australasia, that any civilization had apprehended the world as a whole.

And this mastery of environment, scientific, technological and geographical, has been reflected in a realistic philosophy, in the light of which a salutary re-examination of metaphysical and political mythology is being made. This modern tendency has, indeed, been paralleled in the nineteenth century by Hegelian and Marxist systems of thought, as abstract as the wilder myths created outside Europe, and which in their claims to total explanation and prediction have been second to none in popular appeal; but, the most characteristic and original Anglo-Saxon and French contribution has been to purge philosophy of abstractions and to chart the limitations of mind; a much needed influence in a world made increasingly dangerous by scientific power misused. This objectivity, which bore its first fruits in the sciences, is now bringing in its returns as it is extended to other disciplines, not least to that of the sociology of knowledge. Seeing through the pretensions of myth in whatever field, it may even lead to more rational treatment of the affairs of mankind. Though one of its first lessons is the limitations of reason in public affairs, it may even help reason to circumvent them, if pragmatic methods backed by enough political and economic power become more widely employed. And this kind of pragmatism is likely to become intelligible everywhere, just as scientific method became increasingly accepted over the world.

III

The political legacy of Europe has also been decisive, though often more superficial than generally understood. Though Europe has produced some of the most frightful tyrannies known to history, reaching their climax in the twentieth century, Western

Europeans have also managed to create the forms of constitutional self-government and the rule of law, which have long protected fundamental liberties and proved the best way of adapting societies to peaceful change by consent. Further, this sophisticated political achievement has been paralleled by an attempt to redistribute wealth among the mass of the people in a way never previously attempted in other continents. This has been done both by constitutional means through a welfare state, and by more primitive and revolutionary methods, following the originally European ideology of Marxism and its later European and extra-European interpretations. Thus, both in terms of liberal democracy and of the various forms of socialism, Europe's political influence has been decisive for the whole world.

The fashion for liberal democracy which spread about the world during the phase of European domination has often been superficial and transient, even in its native continent; but it has proved deep-rooted in the countries of its origin and in the nations which have developed from European colonies of settlement overseas.

In the United States, the richest and most powerful state in the world, constitutional self-government has been adapted to a continent which dwarfs Europe, and a federal constitution devised which has united the whole area. In Canada and Australasia federalism and social democracy have also been successful, and in India parliamentary institutions and Western forms of administration have survived the withdrawal of British rule. Thus, in addition to the states of Western Europe, in which constitutional government has long been established, huge extra-European countries have developed Western European political ideas and institutions and the area controlled by them is still collectively the most powerful in the world, if no longer commanding unchallenged supremacy. Moreover, the moves towards Western integration here described have been designed on constitutional lines, and both the League of Nations and the United Nations Organization were devised in terms of responsible self-government and aimed at the rule of law on a world scale. Both these rudimentary instruments of world order have thus aspired to promote the originally European concept of the rule of law in international affairs, without which world politics must continue to be conducted under the precarious sanction of a balance of terror between super-powers.

Naturally the idea of the rule of law and government by consent is not peculiar to Western Europe and the European nations overseas. But it has been far better realized both in theory and practice in Europe and North America than anywhere else. It derives from habits of election, and the consultation of the elders who 'declare' what tribal custom decrees, habits common to most primitive societies; but it was in Europe that these were best defined, organised, and followed up. When Plato and Aristotle insisted that public power ought to have a moral aim and promote the 'good life', it was a good life only for a privileged minority; but the basic principles were defined, that power should be directed to a moral and humane end. Similarly, Aristotle formulated the classic and unanswerable case for the rule of law, since he pointed out no man or group of men can be trusted with absolute power. The principle that people are more important than abstraction, and that the purpose of the state is not the glorification of a God, king or a military despot or even a political party beyond the law, had already been stated for all time in Hellas. It has already been demonstrated how this principle was worked out in terms of Christianity; of barbarian and feudal custom; of the surviving mediaeval institution of parliaments, and of the democratic ideas which by the English promoted the American and the French revolutions. How, though often defeated by arbitrary power, it was realized in institutions and ways of life in the politically mature states of the West and by their descendants outside Europe, has been demonstrated in this survey. The art of combining liberty and order is hard to learn, and it has always been very imperfectly practised; but Western Europeans and the overseas peoples of European origin have come nearer to solving the problem than any others. Moreover they have possessed the means of protecting a relatively civilized way of political life, morally and practically superior to the cult of tyranny, the practice of arbitrary power, censorship of literature and the arts, and the distortion of scientific research by political dogmas. All these achievements derive from the political legacy of Western Europe.

In the social and economic sphere, also, Europeans have formulated doctrines of more ambiguous but immensely powerful influence. They have devised, for example, the current dogmas of nationalism which identify national culture and way of life with the sovereign nation state; they have also formulated the various doctrines of socialism, both constitutional and revolutionary, of which the basic objective is to abolish the poverty of the mass of the people by the use of state power in the redistribution or confiscation of wealth. The dangers which go along with this erosion or destruction of private wealth and enterprise have been amply demonstrated in the growing power of the state bureaucracy and in the undermining of personal initiative; but in any modern society the grosser inequalities of wealth are bound to be resolved slowly as the price of avoiding revolution, and so maintaining the economic growth which alone can raise the standards of living throughout the whole society. The alternative, often adopted in politically more primitive societies, has been revolutionary dictatorship, through a party regarding itself as above the law. Class war, confiscation of property, political murder and deportation are desperate remedies. They have been evoked by desperate situations. But the welfare state and the 'people's democracy' are also attempts at something without precedent; they endeavour to abolish the poverty of the vast majority of mankind. That such an idea has ever been accepted is due to European initiative, for in other civilizations, including pre-industrial Europe, a static social order has been taken for granted, and it has been assumed that, inevitably, civilization has been the concern only of élites. A genuine popular culture including the mass of the people has only recently been made possible, and it stems from the novel command of environment won by Europeans following the principles of scientific method already described, and first implemented by the Industrial Revolution, and by the successive technological revolutions which have followed it up.

IV

For the other, and in recent times overwhelming, achievement of Europe has been economic. Here the first modern capitalist society grew up and the Industrial Revolution was first launched, to be followed by cumulative technological advances that affected the whole world and dragged political and social institution behind them into new dimensions.

The original European capitalism was mercantile: in principle no different from the accumulations in other cultures by maritime and caravan commerce, mainly in luxuries traded to the rich. The *nouveau riche* who has cornered the market is familiar in Roman history, and avarice was a constant theme of denunciation by the mediaeval church. Indeed, in the early middle ages usury was so frowned upon by the Church that finance was largely in the hands of the Jews, who went wherever opportunity beckoned in Christendom and elsewhere, themselves impervious to religious prejudice, if not to periodic attack. Gradually these inhibitions were abandoned, and by the mid-thirteenth century Italian bankers were taking over even in the North. But all these ventures were precarious; sustained by interest at fantastic rates and apt to end in the bankruptcy of the lavish and warlike monarchs who had pledged their revenues for cash. It was not until the later middle ages, when a more regular and substantial volume of trade had been established in staple commodities—wool, cloth textiles, timber, cordage, salt fish and furs, cereals and wine, as well as in costly spices, silks, hunting dogs, weapons and armour—that really substantial commercial capital could be built up. And it was not until the fifteenth and sixteenth centuries that the Medici in Florence could translate great wealth into political power, and the Fuggers of Augsburg could finance the new factory-made cannon and mass-produced weapons that made the armoured knights obsolete, when rudimentary factory production had been applied to heavy industry as it had already been to cloth manufacture.

Further, when great ocean-going fleets were built for commerce and war, and first the Portuguese and Spaniards, then the Dutch, French and English, traded with other continents, the scale of mercantile enterprise was transformed. This development was something new. In Antiquity there had been mass production, but mainly by slave labour. As already observed, the mentality of the ruling classes in Classical and Mediaeval Europe was similar to that in other great conservative civilizations in which the craftsman and the mechanic were accorded only a humble place, and where the warrior and the priest, as in the earliest times, had far the most prestige. Since labour was cheap and power won and held by the sword and by awe inspired by religion, mechanical work, like the toil of peasant agriculture, was thought degrading; there was little incentive to exploit inventions and only a few unrepresentative minds had any vision of the technological possibilities of applied science, itself subordinate in mediaeval Europe to the conventions of scholastic thought. It is, indeed, extraordinary how rare the notion of punctuality and regular routine appear to have been until Europeans began to set store by them in the later middle ages; and even sixteenth century Europe would appear strangely casual to a modern observer. Roman methods of recording time and calculating transactions cannot have been promoted by their clumsy calendar and numerals; the latter not superseded until centuries after originally Indian symbols had been adopted from the Arabs. Further, the pressure of craft and merchant guilds long limited enterprise; for they tried to maintain standards of traditional craftsmanship and ensure monopoly rather than push out into expanding mass markets. It was the destiny of Europe, in contrast to the other great civilizations, to change this mentality and change it rapidly.

This transformation reflects the practical bias of Western Europeans, predominant since the times of Descartes and Newton; that flair for the 'rational manipulation of the human and material environment'[1] already observed; the successful and unusual capacity to draw 'the boundary line between fantasy and reality.'[2]

The Western European nation states had now shouldered themselves forward into a new standard of power and administration, and were exploiting their position on the trade routes of the oceanic world. This extrovert self confidence had first grown up in autonomous city states, and depended on a security of life, property and contracts seldom found in other civilizations, where the caprice of a crazy tyrant or the corruption of an effete bureaucracy could dislocate commercial enterprise and capital accumulation. In Western Europe, indeed, the commercial classes

[1] David S. Landes *The Unbound Prometheus*. Cambridge University Press. 1969 p. 16 q.v. for the best general account.
[2] Ibid. p. 25.

were now obtaining a greater say in government, and in Holland and England, the pioneers of the new sort of economic enterprise, they were combining with the landowning establishment to control public power. The modern entrepreneur was coming forward, and 'private enterprise in the West possessed a social and political vitality without precedent or counterpart.[1] This enterprise, backed by the mercantilist policies of governments, reached out for raw materials and markets into the new world and into the ancient civilizations of Asia and came to dominate them. Along with the considerable improvements in agriculture and technology achieved since the late middle ages, this sort of enterprise had already made Western European civilization more prosperous than any other; 'already rich before the Industrial Revolution—rich by comparison with other parts of the world of that day or with the pre-industrial world of today.'[2] Moreover, Western Europe had the advantage of a small area with a high population density which provided a ready and accessible market for commerce and industry such as, given the communications of the time, could not have existed in larger areas whose population was more diffused. It was with this wealth that Western Europeans created the Industrial Revolution; the take off into a new dimension of self-sustained productivity which has since cumulatively transformed the environment of mankind.

As already recorded, it began in Great Britain, where massive resources in coal and iron combined with comparatively good communications by road and canal; relatively good standards of banking; and with a social order in which wealth could bring advancement, whatever its origins; and where the rigid hierarchies, still prevalent over much of the Continent, had long been adapted to the facts of social and economic power.

The sequel is familiar, and has already been indicated: the spread of great industry and cosmopolitan communications over the whole world, confirming the impact of European ideas and exploiting the discoveries of the European explorers, who first, as already emphasised, enabled humanity to apprehend the planet as a whole and brought at least the idea of a universal civilization to the horizon. Such, along with the scientific and political

1 Ibid. p. 12.
2 Ibid. p. 12.

originality of Western Europe, has been the economic revolution that Europe has made—materially the most obvious of all its achievements, and one in which, in spite of two world wars, Europeans have since made a formidable contribution in inventiveness and expertize.

V

In science, politics, economics and technology, the achievement and influence of Europe has thus been immense. Its culture has also been outstandingly many-sided and dynamic; reflecting both Christian and Humanist influences, the great variety of environment and languages within a relatively limited area, and the contrast of North and South, of continental and maritime climate and mentality. Europe, indeed, has been the most creative of all the great civilizations; both the United States and the Eurasian Soviet Union have mainly derived their culture from it. Further, the impact of Europeans on South America, the East and Africa has been decisive.

Apart from the uniquely developed scientific method already described, European culture has been unusual in its range and versatility; being long-established, it has also, like the Chinese, Islamic and Indian civilizations, attained singular depth, maturity, and sophistication. Yet perhaps the quality which most distinguishes European culture from any other is the combination of a strict sense of form with romantic imagination in architecture, music, art, and literature. It has also shown great powers of assimilation and innovation.

Consider, for example, the variety and contrasts in European architecture recorded in this survey. Originally adapted to a Mediterranean climate, with a stress on form, proportion, and balance, as in the elegant simplicity of the Parthenon or the massive structure of Roman basilicas, the Classical tradition evolved into the splendours of the Baroque, and was reinterpreted in the more austere style of the early nineteenth century, both in Northern Europe and the United States. On the other hand, the Gothic mediaeval architecture, though just as functional, is intricate and romantic, its high-pitched roofs and spires appropriate to Northern winters; the great windows of Chartres,

never since equalled, glowing like jewels against the austere and
lofty interior. Where, as already remarked, the late Roman and
Byzantine mosaics reflected light, mediaeval stained glass lets it
through and transforms it. Moreover there is much variety within
the mediaeval as within the Classical styles; as where the Portuguese late mediaeval Gothic was elaborated into a quasi-tropical
profusion, or where the peoples of the Low Countries and the
Baltic, lacking stone, built Gothic cathedrals—as they built Renaissance palaces—in brick, and put roofs over them, as at Roskilde
in Denmark, which weathered grey-green. The Russians, also,
adding oriental motifs to Byzantine Romanesque, created the
distinctive 'onion' dome, and in Leningrad adapted Southern
Classical buildings to the North by painting them in vivid
colours.

Add to this the fact that Northern Europeans cast far the
finest bells in the world, their sound rolling out majestically
over the Rhine and the Isle de France—the solemn voice of the
North; or, with more sentiment, sounding over the English
countryside or chiming through the mists of Amsterdam and
Copenhagen. Nor is the legacy confined to cities, but rooted in
the countryside in all its variety from the Mediterranean to the
North, so that even modern industry and technology cannot
pulverise it or reduce the Continent to the uniformity of less
ancient civilizations.

The European bells are only a minor aspect of an immense
musical inheritance, far surpassing that of other civilizations, so
that European conductors and orchestras tour the world. This
musical creativeness became fully apparent in the sixteenth and
seventeenth centuries, and, as already recorded, reached its climax in the eighteenth. And here, again, what is remarkable is
variety and many-sidedness. The great composers speak for their
own people, their own climate and environment—Handel for
Protestant Germany; Mozart for the lake-country of Austria as
well as for metropolitan Vienna—for he based some of his
greatest works on folk melodies; Beethoven for the surge and
force of the German romantic movement. Later, Berlioz wrote
in a predominantly French idiom; Dvořák was a Czech, Liszt an
Hungarian, Chopin, a Pole; Wagner, also, typically expressed
the wilder romanticism of Imperial Germany, and Verdi evokes

the ambience of nineteenth century Italy. And here, as in literature, the Russians made their contribution. Moussorgsky and
Tchaikovsky, as already emphasised, were both in the first rank,
bringing melodies from the Steppe with suggestions of limitless
horizons into the romantic idiom.

The artistic legacy of Europe as here surveyed, is also astonishing in variety and range. The early Greek sculpture, as in the
Acropolis museum at Athens, like that of French twelfth and
thirteenth century at Chartres, can compare with the Chinese
and Indonesian masterpieces; while the more elaborate virtuosity
of the age of Hadrian and Antonines, as now displayed in the
Vatican galleries at Rome, is reinterpreted and surpassed by the
masters of the Renaissance and the Age of the Baroque. In painting, the best work of Antiquity has been lost; but by the thirteenth century, the Italian masters, reinterpreting the formal
Byzantine religious style that had survived, were creating new
dimensions of form and light, comparable already to the contemporary Chinese painting on silk or the art of the Ajanta caves in
India. There followed, as is well known, five centuries of unparalleled creative brilliance, of which the landmarks have been already described. To recall only the representative masters, there
were Leonardo, Michaelangelo, Raphael and Titian in Italy; in
Flanders, the late mediaeval painters Memlinc and the van Eyks,
then the great liberating geniuses, Rubens and Rembrandt; Velasquez in seventeenth-century Spain was followed by Goya in the
late eighteenth and early nineteenth centuries; nor were the English painters negligible; there were Turner, and John Constable,
the first English painters to influence the Continent. There were
French masters, Poussin and Claude and Chardin who were
surpassed in the nineteenth century by the most original and
creative of all the French painters, the impressionists and
Cezanne, the greatest modern master of form.

The pictures of these European artists, and of a host of others
of singular originality and distinction, line the galleries of Europe and America; the Prado in Madrid, the Uffizi in Florence,
the Vatican galleries in Rome, the Louvre, the Rijksmuseum in
Amsterdam, the National Gallery in London, as well as the galleries in New York and Washington. Great as have been the
contributions of the Chinese and of India and of Islamic art,

the European achievement has surpassed them all in its world-wide influence and its variety.

It would be superfluous to dwell further on the variety of drama and literature already described in the preceding pages: suffice it that although the other great civilizations were creating great art, poetry, fiction and drama when most Europeans had sunk into illiteracy after the decline of the Graeco-Roman civilization, the European Classical tradition revived, and was reinterpreted by the nations of Northern and Central Europe and also in Russia. For the influence of Antiquity through Rome and Byzantium has provided the basic cultural unity of European civilization. As has been well written, 'other influences have made us what we are; but the Graeco-Roman strain was one of the strongest and richest. Without it, our civilization would not merely be different. It would be thinner, more fragmentary, less thoughtful, more materialistic—in fact, whatever wealth it might have accumulated, whatever wars it might have fought, whatever inventions it might have made, it would be less worthy to be called a civilization, because its spiritual achievements would be less great'.[1] On this foundation in drama, prose and poetry, the genius and talent of European literature have been deployed. And, here, as in music, the great writers have been drawn from the whole area; Tolstoy, the greatest of all novelists, Puskin, Turgeniev and Dostoevsky from Russia, while England, often a peripheral culture in the arts, produced the greatest of dramatists, William Shakespeare. The famous names are familiar: without them world civilization would be immeasurably impoverished, and it is likely that, even with the passing of the relatively brief colonial empires, the artistic and literary legacy of Europe may become almost as important to this world as that of Classical Antiquity has been to Europeans and their descendants overseas.

V I

Such, in brief and restrospective outline, are the main qualities which have emerged in this survey of European history, and

[1] Gilbert Highet. *The Classical Tradition*. Greek and Roman influences on Western Literature. A Galaxy Book (reprint) 1957, p.l. q.v. for the best general account.

which have distinguished European civilization from any other. As already emphasised, the most distinctive common features is forcefulness and versatility. And that is to be expected if the geographical environment of the Continent and the British Isles be considered. Within an area of predominantly temperate climate which, in comparison to the extent of the Americas or Asia, of Africa or even the Indian sub-continent, is relatively small, there is intricate variety and striking contrast. The Mediterranean countries, with their sunshine and olive groves, vines and cypresses, their glittering sea and strong light, extend from the Greek peninsula to Southern Spain, and have been the original basis of European civilization—a singularly favourable environment, in touch with the ancient cultures of the Near East. But beyond the Alps, very different country lay open for settlement, and considerable populations were already in being when the Romans extended their empire to the North-West. And beyond the Pyrenees, lay the great Spanish plateau, different from anything else in Europe, with the pastures and vines of Andalusia to the south of it, a country with African affinities. And to the West of it, Portugal, which combines an Atlantic and Mediterranean environment.

North of the Alps and the Pyrenees lies France, the most favoured of all the European countries, extending from Mediterranean Provence to the North Atlantic and the Channel. It includes the best wine growing areas in the world, Burgundy and the hinterland of Bordeaux, the vineyards of the Loire and around Rheims; it contains the Savoyard mountains and the Western Jura and the meadows and orchards leading up to them, the broad cornlands of the Beauce and the fisheries of Normandy and Brittany, as well as the great industrial areas of the North East, their grim towns contrasting with the mellow and historic cities of the Loire and the Yonne.

North-East lie the Netherlands; the Dutch towns as clean as a well found ship, redolent, even inland of the sea. The tang of fish and tar and timber pervade all the North-East up to Scandinavia —the Baltic lands of schnapps and beer and broad-sounding speech. Here are square brick houses and snug interiors fending off the cold; the churches, bare of ornament for preaching and psalm singing, in contrast to the Southern buildings, which are designed to display the incense-laden mystery of the mass.

Very different again, the German environment is massive and more continental; the civilization more military. The ancient fortresses still stand along the Rhine, their turrets angular as helmets above ruined keeps, the majestic bulk of great cathedrals still dominating their cities. And here, as in France, is much variety; the Baltic coasts and the Northern European plain contrasting with the forests of Thuringia, the vineyards of the Rhine, Moselle and Wurtemberg, and with the rich uplands of Bavaria and the Alps beyond.

Eastwards, Vienna dominates the great valley of the Danube, which sweeps through the Hungarian plain, an offshoot of the Steppe, and proceeds through the Iron Gates to Roumania and the Black Sea. The city was long the bastion of Central Europe against the East, and the natural focus of whatever political and economic coherence was there achieved; for its rulers controlled Bohemia and the Carpathians, the main strategic bastions of the area. Beyond these mountains, North and East of them, lay the Northern forests, the Ukrainian black earth with its rich agriculture, and the grass and desert of the Steppe, providing an environment which is as much Asian as European, and giving rise to a civilization that has been affected as much by Asian as by Scandinavian, Byzantine and German influences; in Europe and yet not altogether of it.

Similarly, though much more intimately part of the West, Great Britain has been at once European and part of a wider and, by contrast, oceanic world. Here again, is great variety in a miniature setting. Here Scots, Welsh and Irish have all maintained their traditions, and contributed to European settlement overseas; while the insular English civilization itself grew up in the agricultural and maritime south, and has only rather recently been transformed into a great industrial power, out of all proportion to its native resources and now viable only in a wider Continental and oceanic context. Immune for nine centuries to serious invasion, the British have created a rich civilization which combines Celtic, Latin and Germanic traditions in an extraordinary way; one with a self sufficiency and, hitherto, a self confidence comparable to that of the French,[1] and a natural link between Europe and the English-speaking world overseas.

[1] See my *England, a Portrait*. Praeger, New York, 1966.

VII

Such has been the environment—a racial melting pot at the end of a land mass—in which many vigorous peoples, speaking dissimilar but related languages, have achieved the most creative civilization in world history in all its many facets and interpretations. The racial fusion of the Continent, already far advanced in prehistoric times, has blended the varieties of a fundamentally similar stock, different from the Semitic, African or Asian peoples, and yet sufficiently inter-related from the Mediterranean to the North, to make nonsense of the nineteenth century racial and nationalistic mythologies.

Nor has the geographical variety of the continent prevented successful attempts at uniting much of it. With colossal effort the Romans created an empire which included all the West, save Ireland, and most of South Eastern Europe. Their legions slogged through Swiss foothills and passes and along the twisting and precipitous roads of the Maritime Alps, and their roads spanned relatively vast distances from the Levant to Northern France. Even in the relatively rudimentary conditions of the Middle Ages, Empire and Papacy kept up their European ambitions, and Charles V, ruling an equally extensive area with worse communications, made a final valiant attempt to retain the old solidarity of Christendom. As already remarked, 'the period of competing nation states, of the naked power of unbridled sovereignty, has extended only over five centuries, and during that time the cultual, if not the political, life of Europe has continued in an expanding tide. The cosmopolitan culture of Antiquity and of the Middle Ages extended for a greater duration, and probably the stabilized order of the future will dwarf the phase of confusion which has come to its tragic climax in the twentieth century'.[1]

Since the main text was written, soon after the Second World War, the course of events has vindicated a qualified optimism. For the scale of modern civilization has become increasingly Continental and, after the political catastrophes of the first half of the

[1] vide supra. p. 9.

twentieth century, it has made nonsense of parochial and nationalistic divisions. These facts, both political and economic, are hard for the mass of the people, aware of their own national way of life and naturally defending it, to apprehend; given intelligent leadership, the situation will probably in time be understood. For the economic and technological as well as the political and cultural facts seem set to reaffirm the ancient solidarity of most of Europe, for which this survey has provided objective historical evidence. In a global context this unity of European civilization is its most significant aspect and explains the formidable impact of Europeans on the world; their vitality, originality and resilience.

SELECTED SHORT BIBLIOGRAPHY

The books here listed may be found useful for following up some of the main themes of this volume. For the most accessible and comprehensive bibliographies the reader is referred to the Cambridge Ancient, Mediaeval, and New Modern Histories.

I

CHAPTER I.   THE DAWN OF CIVILIZATION

Smith, C. T. An Historical Geography of Western Europe Before 1800. London, 1967.

Church, R. I. Harrison. An Advanced Geography of Northern and Western Europe. London, 1967.

Houston, J. M. The Western Mediterranean World. London, 1964.

Osborne, R. H. East-Central Europe. London, 1967.

Coon, C. S. The Races of Europe. New York, 1939.

Clark, G. World Prehistory. Cambridge, 1969.

Clark, S. and Piggott, S. Prehistoric Societies. London, 1965.

Piggott, S. Ancient Europe. Edinburgh, 1965.

Frere, S. Britannia. London, 1970.

Daniel, G. Ancient People and Places, Series. 1950 ff.

CHAPTER II.   THE GENIUS OF HELLAS

Bowle, J. Western Political Thought. London, 1947.

Barker, Sir E. The Politics of Aristotle. Oxford, 1948.

The European Inheritance. (Ed. Sir E. Barker, Sir G. Clark, and P. Vaucher.) 3 vols. Oxford, 1954.

Andrewes, A. The Greeks. London, 1967.

Bowra, C. M. Greek Lyric Poetry. Oxford, 1936.

Bowra, C. M. The Greek Experience. London, 1957.

Higham, T. F., and Bowra, C. M. The Oxford Book of Greek Verse in Translation. Oxford, 1938.

Tarn, W. W. Hellenistic Civilization. London, 1927.

Jones, A. H. M. The Greek City. Oxford, 1940.

Glover, T. R. The Ancient World. Cambridge, 1935.

Swindler, M. H. Ancient Painting. Yale, 1929.

Beazley, J. D., and Ashmole, B. Greek Sculpture and Painting. Cambridge, 1932.

CHAPTER III. THE ROMAN PEACE

Grant, M. The Roman World. London, 1962.

Highet, G. The Classical Tradition: Greek and Roman Influences on Western Civilization. Oxford, 1949.

Ferrero, G. The Life of Caesar. London, 1933.

The Oxford Book of Latin Verse. (Ed. H. W. Garrod.) 1912.

Syme, Sir R. The Roman Revolution. Oxford, 1939.

Gibbon, E. The History of the Decline and Fall of the Roman Empire, 1776-81. Edited in 7 vols. by J. B. Bury. London, 1896-1909.

Rostovtzeff, M. Social and Economic History of the Roman Empire. 2 vols. Oxford, 1926.

Rostovtzeff, M. Iranians and Greeks in South Russia. Oxford, 1922.

Cambridge Ancient History, vols. X-XII.

CHAPTER IV. THE CHRISTIAN REVOLUTION

Moffatt, R. The New Testament (revised edition). London, 1934.

Montefiore, C. G. The Synoptic Gospels. 2 vols. London, 1927.

Montefiore, C. G. Rabbinic Literature and the Gospel Teaching. London, 1930.

Streeter, B. H. The Four Gospels. London, 1936.

Streeter, B. H. The Primitive Church. London, 1929.

Cumont, F. Les réligions orientales dans le paganisme romain. Paris, 1929.

Cochrane, C. N. Christianity and Classical Culture. Oxford, 1940.

Cambridge Ancient History, vol. XI, ch. vii.

Cambridge Mediaeval History, vol. I.

Brown, P. St. Augustine of Hippo. London, 1967.

CHAPTER V. THE NORTHERN PEOPLES AND THE LATIN CHURCH

Seignobos, C. A History of the French People. (Trans. C. A. Phillips.) London, 1933.

Halphen, L. Les Barbares, des grands invasions aux conquêtes turques du XIe siècle. Paris, 1926.

Wallace-Hadrill, J. M. The Long Haired Kings, and Other Studies in Frankish History. London, 1962.

Halphen, L. Charlemagne et l'empire carolingien. Paris, 1947.

Pirenne, J. H. Mohammed and Charlemagne. (Trans. B. Miall.) London, 1937.

Stenton, F. M. Anglo Saxon England. Oxford, 1943.

Southern, R. W. The Making of the Middle Ages. London, 1953.

Loyn, H. R. Anglo-Saxon England and the Norman Conquest. London, 1962.

Ker, W. P. The Dark Ages. Reprinted London, 1955.

Anderson, I. A History of Sweden. London, 1955.

Brøndsted, J. The Vikings. (Trans. E. Bannister-Good.) Harmondsworth, 1960.

Kendrick, T. D. A History of the Vikings. London, 1930.

Kendrick, T. D. Anglo-Saxon Art to A. D. 900. London, 1938.

Clapham, A. W. Romanesque Architecture in Western Europe. Oxford, 1936.

CHAPTER VI. BYZANTIUM AND EASTERN EUROPE

Jones, A. H. M. The Later Roman Empire, 284-602. (3 vols.) Oxford, 1964.

Vasiliev, A. A. History of the Byzantine Empire, 324-1453. Oxford, 1952.

Buckler, G. Anna Commena. Oxford, 1929.

Brehier, L. Le Monde byzantin, vie et mort de Byzance. Paris, 1947.

Dalton, O. M. East Christian Art. Oxford, 1925.

Schlumberger, G. L. L'Epopée byzantine à la fin du 10e siècle. Paris, 1925.

The Balkans. A History, by various authors. Oxford, 1915.

Runciman, S. Byzantine Civilization. London, 1933.

Runciman, S. The Mediaeval Manichee. Cambridge, 1947.

Parker, W. H. An Historical Geography of Russia. London, 1968.

Vernadsky, S., and Karpovitch, M. A History of Russia. 5 vols. New Haven, 1944-60.

CHAPTER VII. MEDIAEVAL CHRISTENDOM

Lavisse, E. (ed.) Histoire de France Illustré, Tom. II-III, par A. Luchaire. Paris, 1900-11.

Powicke, Sir F. M. Henry III and the Lord Edward. (2 vols.) Oxford, 1947.

Petit Dutaillis, C. La Monarchie féodale en France et en Angleterre. Paris, 1933.

Keen, M. A History of Medieval Europe. London, 1968.

Barraclough, G. The Origins of Modern Germany. Oxford, 1946.

Pirenne, H. Economic and Social History of Mediaeval Europe. London, 1936.

Davis, R. H. C. A History of Mediaeval Europe. London, 1957.

Bloch, M. La Société féodale. 2 vols. Paris, 1939.

Gregorovius, F. History of Rome in the Middle Ages. (Trans. A. Hamilton.) 13 vols. 1894-1902.

Ker, W. P. Epic and Romance. London, 1934.

Taylor, O. The Mediaeval Mind. 2 vols. (4th edition.) 1925.

Grousset, R. L'Empire des steppes. Paris, 1939.

Trend, J. B. The Civilization of Spain. Oxford, 1944.

The Legacy of the Middle Ages. C. G. Crump and E. F. Jacob. Oxford, 1926.

The Legacy of Israel. E. R. Bevan and C. Singer. Oxford, 1927.

CHAPTER VIII.   THE RENAISSANCE AND THE DISCOVERIES

Parry, J. H. The Age of Reconnaissance. London, 1963.

Boxer, C. R. The Dutch Sea-borne Empire. London, 1965.

Burckhardt, J. The Civilization of the Renaissance in Italy. London, 1937.

Vasari, G. Lives of the Painters, Sculptors, and Architects. (Trans. A. B. Hinds.) 4 vols. Everyman. London, 1927.

Machiavelli, N. The Chief Works and Others. (Trans. A. Gilbert.) 3 vols. Durham, 1965.

Brandi, K. Charles V. (Trans. C. V. Wedgwood.) London, 1939.

Trevelyan, G. M. English Social History. London, 1944.

Elliot, J. H. Imperial Spain. London, 1963.

Singer, C. J. A Short History of Science to the 19th Century. Oxford, 1941.

Singer, C. J. A Short History of Medicine. Oxford, 1928.

Baker, J. N. L. A History of Geographical Discovery and Exploration (revised edition). London, 1937.

Brebner, J. B. The Explorers of North America, 1492-1806. London, 1933.

Prescott, W. H. The Conquest of Peru. London, 1908.

Williamson, J. A. The Ocean in English History. Oxford, 1941.

Beer, J. L. The Origins of the British Colonial System, 1578-1600. New York, 1908.

Merriman, R. B. The Rise of the Spanish Empire in the old World and the New. 2 vols. New York, 1919.

Scholes, P. The Oxford Companion to Music. Oxford, 1938.

Bell, Clive. An Account of French Painting. London, 1931.

CHAPTER IX.   THE REFORMATION AND THE NATION STATE

Clark, G. N. The Seventeenth Century. Oxford, 1929.

Hazard, P. La Crise de la conscience européenne. 2 vols. (Second edition.) Paris, 1946.

Bowle, J. Henry VIII. Boston, 1964.

Neale, J. E. Queen Elizabeth. London, 1934.

Neale, J. E. The Age of Catherine de Melici. London, 1943.

Dickens, A. G. The English Reformation. (revised). London, 1967.

Febvre, L. Un Destin, Martin Luther. Paris, 1936.

Roberts, M. Gustavus Adolphus. 2 vols. London, 1953-8.

Geyl, P. The Revolt of the Netherlands. London, 1932.

Wedgwood, C. V. William the Silent. London, 1944.

Wedgwood, C. V. The Thirty Years War. London, 1938.

Ehrenberg, R. Capital and Finance in the Age of the Renaissance. (Trans. H. M. Lucas.) London, 1928.

Willey, B. The Seventeenth Century Background. London, 1934.

Whitehead, A. N. Science and the Modern World. Cambridge, 1926.

Abbot, W. C. The Writings and Speeches of Oliver Cromwell. 4 vols. Harvard, 1937-44.

Rowse, A. L. The England of Elizabeth. London, 1950.

Rowse, A. L. The Expansion of Elizabethan England. London, 1955.

Dick, O. Lawson. (ed.) Aubrey's Brief Lives. London, 1950.

The Oxford Book of English Verse. Sir A. Quiller-Couch. Oxford, 1900.

The Oxford Book of French Verse. St. J. Lucas. Oxford, 1923.

CHAPTER X.   THE EIGHTEENTH CENTURY

Lough, J. An Introduction to Eighteenth-Century France. London, 1960.

Williams, B. William Pitt. Earl of Chatham. 2 vols. London, 1915.

Namier, Sir L. B. England in the Age of the American Revolution. London, 1930.

Namier, Sir L. B. The Structure of Politics at the Accession of George III. 2 vols. London, 1929.

Plumb, J. H. Sir Robert Walpole, 2 vols. London, 1956-60.

Miller, J. C. The Origins of the American Revolution. London, 1945.

McIlwain, C. H. The American Revolution. New York, 1923.

Padover, S. K. The Revolutionary Emperor. (Joseph II.) London, 1934.

Sumner, B. H. Peter the Great. London, 1950.

Nussbaum, F. L. A History of Economic Institutions in Modern Europe. New York, 1933.

Mowat, R. B. The Age of Reason. London, 1934.

Becker, C. The Heavenly City of the Eighteenth Century Philosophers. New Haven, 1933.

Bury, J. B. The Idea of Progress. London, 1920.

Thompson, E. P. The Making of the English Working Class. New York, 1966.

CHAPTER XI.   THE INDUSTRIAL AND LIBERAL REVOLUTION

Mantoux, E. The Eighteenth Century Background to the Industrial Revolution. London, 1947.

Halévy, E. A History of the English People. (4 vols.) London, 1924.

Halévy, E. The Growth of Philosophic Radicalism. (Trans. M. Morris.) London, 1928.

Knowles, L. C. A. The Industrial and Commercial Revolution in Great Britain in the Nineteenth Century. London, 1922.

Thompson, J. M. The French Revolution. Oxford, 1944.

Mathiez, A. La Revolution française. Paris, 1928.

Woodward, Sir E. L. French Revolutions. Oxford, 1934.

Lord Rosebery. Pitt. London, 1891.

Landes, D. The Unbound Prometheus. Cambridge, 1969.

Sorel, A. L'Europe et la revolution française. (8 vol.) Paris, 1896-1911.

Mowat, R. B. The Romantic Age. London, 1937.

Brinton, C. Crane. The Political Ideas of the English Romanticists. London, 1926.

Gray, A. The Socialists Tradition. London, 1946.

Markham, F. M. H. Napoleon. London, 1963.

Longford, E. Wellington. The Years of the Sword. London, 1969.

Hobsbawn, E. J. The Age of Revolution: Europe 1789-1848. London, 1962.

Carr, R. Spain, 1808-1939. Oxford, 1966.

CHAPTER XII.   THE NINETEENTH CENTURY

Briggs, A. The Age of Improvement. London, 1959.

Blake, R. Disraeli. London, 1966.

Magnus, Sir Philip. Gladstone: A Biography. London, 1954.

Woodward, Sir E. L. The Age of Reform. Oxford, 1938.

Ensor, R. C. K. England, 1870-1914. Oxford, 1936.

Morris, J. Pax Britannica: The Climax of Empire. London, 1968.

Brogan, D. W. The Development of Modern France, 1870-1939. London, 1940.

Thomson, D. Europe Since Napoleon. London, 1957.

Thompson, J. M. Louis Napoleon and the Second Empire. Oxford, 1954.

Taylor, A. J. P. The Course of German History. London, 1945.

Taylor, A. J. P. The Habsburg Monarchy, 1815-1918. London, 1941.

Miller, W. The Ottoman Empire and its Successors. Cambridge, 1923.

Morison, S. E. The Oxford History of the United States. (2 vols.) London, 1927.

Russell, B. Freedom and Organization. London, 1934.

Baumont, M. L'Essor industriel et l'imperialisme colonial. Paris, 1937.

Berlin, Sir I. Karl Marx. London, 1939.

Bowle, J. Politics and Opinion in the Nineteenth Century. New York, 1964.

Young, G. M. Portrait of an Age. Oxford, 1960.

Woodruff, P. The Men Who Ruled India. (2 vols.) London, 1953-4.

II

CHAPTER I.   WORLD WAR AND THE ECLIPSE OF EUROPE

Seton-Watson, H. Eastern Europe Between the Wars. London, 1945.

Dehio, L. The Precarious Balance: The Politics of Power in Europe, 1494-1945. London, 1963.

Wilmot, C. The Struggle for Europe. London, 1952.

Churchill, Sir Winston. The Second World War. (abridged ed.) With new epilogue. London, 1959.

Bullock A. Hitler: A Study in Tyranny. (revised.) London, 1959.

Deutscher, I. Trotsky. 3 vols. Oxford, 1959-63.

Deutscher, I. Stalin: A Political Biography. Oxford, 1949.

Ulam, A. B. Lenin and the Bolsheviks. London, 1966.

Woodward, Sir E. L. British Foreign Policy in the Second World War London, 1962.

Thomas, H. The Spanish Civil War. London, 1961.

Churchill, Sir Winston. The World Crisis. (6 vols.) London, 1923.

Cruttwell, C. R. M. F. A History of the Great War. Oxford, 1936.

Keynes, J. M. The Economic Consequences of the Peace. London, 1919

Butler, H. The Lost Peace. Oxford, 1941.

McCallum, R. B. Public Opinion and the Lost Peace. Oxford, 1944.

Butler, R. D'O. The Roots of National Socialism. London, 1941.

Trevor-Roper, R. The Last Days of Hitler. London, 1947.

CHAPTER II.   POST WAR EUROPE AND THE DISMANTLING OF EMPIRE
and CHAPTER III.   EUROPE IN WORLD HISTORY

Ortega y Gasset. The Revolt of the Masses. London, 1932.

Carr, E. H. Nationalism and After. London, 1946.

Sabine, G. H. A History of Political Theory. New York, 1959.

Lasswell, H. D. The Analysis of Political Behaviour. London, 1947.

Mannheim, K. Man and Society. London, 1940.

Mason, P. Patterns of Dominance. London, 1970.

Plamenatz, J. On Alien Rule and Self-Government. London, 1960.

INDEX